Crossing boundaries

An analysis of Roman coins in Danish contexts

Crossing boundaries

An analysis of Roman coins in Danish contexts

Vol. 2: Finds from Bornholm

Helle W. Horsnæs

PNM
Publications of the National Museum
Studies in Archaeology and History Vol. 18

Copenhagen 2013

Publications from the National Museum, Studies in Archaeology and History Vol. 18
Crossing Boundaries
An analysis of Roman coins in Danish contexts
Vol. 2: Finds from Bornholm
Helle W. Horsnæs

Copyright © The National Museum and the author
All rights reserved

PNM editorial committee: Lene Floris (chairman), Michael Andersen, Mikkel Venborg Pedersen, Morten Ryhl-Svendsen, Ingrid Wass

Cover design by Christine Clemmensen
Typesetting by Pia Brejnholt
Printed by Narayana

Published by The National Museum of Denmark
Royal Collection of Coins and Medals
12 Frederiksholms Kanal, DK-1220 Copenhagen K

On commission at University Press of Southern Denmark

ISBN: 978-87-7602-188-7

Funded by:
Farumgaard-Fonden
Dr. Margrethe II's Arkæologiske Fond
Letterstedtska Föreningen
Landsdommer V. Gieses Legat
Lillian og Dan Finks Fond
G.E.C. Gads Fond
Den Hielmstierne-Rosencroneske Stiftelse
P.L. Jørgensens Mindefond

Cover: Roman denarius struck during the reign of Antoninus Pius. This coin type (RIC type 137, 145-161 AD), is known from 14 specimens in Bornholm. The specimen comes from the Biskopenge 5 site in the Ibsker settlement complex, inv.no. FP 7049.1, BMR 1760x15. Photo: John Lee/The National Museum.

Contents

Acknowledgements	13
Foreword	17
1. Introduction	21
Archaeology of Iron Age Bornholm	21
From antiquarians to archaeology	21
Iron Age Bornholm	25
Roman coins on Bornholm	27
The first reports	27
Changing find patterns, detector archaeology 1980-2010	28
Approaching the finds	34
Coin registration	34
Site registration	37
The geographical distribution of Roman coins	39
Chronology	40
Hoards and single finds – problems of interpretation	43
Terminus post quem and deposition date – a difficult relationship	45
2. Coins	49
Denarii	49
Chronological composition of denarii from sites with several finds	52
Subærati	52
Implications	54
Denarius imitations	55
Reworked denarii	56
Denarii in graves	60
Denarii from other dated contexts	61
Siliquae	62
Solidi	62

Reworked solidi	64
Antoniniani	65
Base metal coins	66
Reworked base metal coins	67
Ancient coins in Viking Age contexts	67

3. Bornholm in a wider context — 71
Chronological composition of denarius finds from Barbaricum — 73
Regional differences within the 'late' or 'eastern' denarius group — 80
Solidi in the West Baltic area — 81
Bornholm – a stepping stone or a final destination? — 85

4. Coin usage on Bornholm — 89
Find density — 89
Contexts — 90
Coin finds within the settlements — 91
Hoards — 92
Isolated finds? — 93
Coin influx to Bornholm c. 500 AD, an alternative suggestion — 94
  Time — 94
  Source — 95
'Hortfundhorizont' — 95
Why hoarding? — 96
Ritual depositions — 96
The 6th century — 97
Raw material — 97

5. Conclusions — 101
Lack of impact? — 101
An assessment of detector archaeology — 102

6. The sites with Roman coin finds — 105
A Field of Gold - the central place in Ibsker parish — 105
  Sorte Muld — 114
  The gold hoards from Fuglesangsageren — 114
  Brændesgård — 115
  Brændesgård area II — 115
  Engegård — 115
  Dalshøj — 115
  Baunehøj and Kanonhøj/Sønderhøj — 119

Højemark	121
Sylten	122
Frennegård/Hallebrøndshøj area	124
Biskopenge	125
The Iron Age settlement complex – summary	127
Viking Age finds from the Ibsker complex	128
The Saltholmgård Hoard – marking a boundary?	128
Outside the Ibsker complex	129
Other sites in Øster herred	129
Denarius sites around Østerlars	130
Between Østerlars and Gudhjem	132
North-western Bornholm	135
Egesløkkegård	135
Between Teglkås and Vang	135
Between Hasle and Klemensker	137
South-western Bornholm, between Rønne and Åkirkeby	139
Smørenge – settlement, hoard and cult site	140
Other inland sites	144
Almindingen forest	145
Lilleborg Castle mound	145
Borresø	149
Ravnebrohus	149
The coastal area	149
South-eastern Bornholm between Åkirkeby and Nexø	152
Sandegård	152
Other sites in southeastern Bornholm	154
Rævekulebakke, Smedegård and Hundshalegård	154
Slusegård	155
Between Læsø and Øle Å	155
Coin lists	**161**
Denarii from individual sites (in numerical order)	161
060101 sb 217: Denarii from Egesløkkegård, BMR 3140	161
060104 sb 190 and 235: Denarii from Nygård/Skovgård, BMR 1640 and 2001	161
060104 sb 196: Denarii from Kistehøj/Simblegård, BMR 888	162
060104 sb 201: Denarii from Rødbjerg, BMR 1611	162
060104 sb 202: Denarii from Møllegård, BMR 1235	162
060104 sb 264: Denarii from Karlshøj/Trommeregård, BMR 2225	162
060104 sb 351: Denarii from Hebro, BMR 3567	162

060106 sb 150: Denarii from Bukkegård, BMR 1171	163
060204 sb 82: Denarii from Bedegård, BMR 2506	163
060204 sb 94: Roman coins from Duegård NVN, BMR 3354 (denarii unless otherwise indicated)	163
060205 sb 33: Denarii from Sandegård, BMR 1371	163
060205 sb 198: Denarii from Rævekulebakke, Grave E	164
060205 sb 288: Denarii from Hundshalegård, BMR 3166	164
060302 sb 124: Denarii from Ndr. Mulebygård, BMR 3227 and 2812	165
060303 sb 190: Denarii from Vestergård, BMR 1672	165
060305 sb 70: Denarii from Smørengegård, BMR 1469	165
060305 sb 144: Denarii from Smørenge, BMR 766	167
060305 sb 151: Denarii from Lilleborg, BMR 24	176
060305 sb 223 and 251: Denarii from Tornegård Syd/Brede, BMR 2656 and Lillevang Øst, BMR 3495	176
060305 sb 405: Denarii from St. Smørengegård, BMR 1697	176
060305 sb 554: Denarii from St. Smørengegård NV, BMR 3550	177
060403 sb 74: Denarii from Sylten I, BMR 789	177
060403 sb 74: Denarii from Sylten II, BMR 789	177
060403 sb 93. Denarii from Sorte Muld, BMR 1191	179
060403 sb 93: Denarii from Sorte Muld Syd/Paradisgård, BMR 3141	183
060403 sb 93: Denarii from Fuglesangsageren, BMR 2649	183
060403 sb 96-97: Denarii from Højemark, BMR 1092, 2510 and 265	183
060403 sb 107: Coins from Brændesgård, BMR 1653	184
060403 sb 160: Coins from Engegård, BMR 2280 and 3185	184
060403 sb 135: Coins from Dalshøj, BMR 1639 (east of Højevej)	185
060403 sb 166: Denarii from Biskopenge VI, BMR 790	186
060403 sb 168: Denarii from Sylten IV, BMR 1077	187
060403 sb 169: Denarii from Sønderhøj, BMR 802	189
060403 sb 175: Denarii from Kanonhøj, BMR 1430 and 2650	189
060403 sb 182: Denarii from Biskopenge V, BMR 1760	190
060403 sb 191: Denarii from Nr. Fuglesang, BMR 2353	190
060403 sb 195: Denarii from Biskopenge 3B, BMR 1795	191
060403 sb 263: Denarii from Biskopenge 9, BMR 3314	191
060405 sb 144 and sb 207: Denarii from Krogegård I, BMR 2153 and 2252	191
060405 sb 201: Roman coins from Agerbygård, BMR 1523	192
Possible Subærati	192
Denarius imitations	193
Pierced denarii	194
Roman bronze coins	195

Indices	197
174 sites with Roman coins, in geographical order	197
174 sites with Roman coins, in alphabetical order	200
Abbreviations	203
Bibliography	205

Acknowledgements

The present volume focuses on the finds of Roman coins from Bornholm, and it aims to present and discuss the many new finds made in the last three decades. Coins registered in the National Museum, Royal Collection of Coins and Medals after 2010 are not included in the present study. The study is an attempt to see the Roman coins primarily in their local context, but also as part of a wider perspective of international connectivity. I have had three groups of readers in mind: one interested in the archaeology of Bornholm, southern Scandinavia and the Baltic area in the Roman and Germanic Iron Ages, another interested in the distribution of Roman coins, and a third interested in methodologies of detector archaeology and the special problems posed by an empiric material which is both in and out of contexts.

To do so I have ventured into several subjects that are outside my comfort zone, and this would not have been possible without generous help and good advice from many friends and colleagues.

I would like first of all to thank Finn Ole Nielsen, the archaeologist responsible for the antiquities of Bornholm, and his staff at Bornholms Museum for never-failing support and much practical help, and his predecessor, Margrethe Watt, a pioneer in detector archaeology and scientific approaches to settlement archaeology, who not only made her personal database on detector finds from Iron Age settlements available for study, but also gave much good advice and great support throughout this work.

Special thanks go to those who produced the empirical basis for this study: the many amateur archaeologists of Bornholm. During endless hours they have surveyed the fields with their metal detectors, meticulously registering all finds and handling them with such care. Their work has not only increased the number of finds from Bornholm enormously, but they have also opened possibilities unthought of before. The collaboration between amateur detectorists and the authorities represented by Bornholms Museum has worked two ways: Bornholms Museum has in some cases directed detectorists to sites known from reports from the 19th century for reinvestigation and attempts to locate exact positions of for example hoards, but in other cases Bornholms Museum has investigated hitherto unknown sites located by detectorists. This reciprocity has markedly enriched the value of the material, and without the metal detectorists this book could not have been written.

The work on this volume was made under a strict time limit, and I fully realize that I am touching upon many issues that ought to be discussed more fully. I do, however, hope that this presentation of the many new finds of Roman coins from Bornholm within the frames of their cultural, spatial and chronological contexts will be a stimulus for other researchers to dig deeper into the issues here hinted at and to include this material into wider discourses on Iron Age archaeology and Roman numismatics.

The distribution maps presented in the present study were drawn by mag.art. Michael Vennersdorf, harvesting all relevant information on the registration of finds from the archives of Bornholms Museum and 'translating' old coordinate systems into digital coordinates. The maps of the Ibsker settlement complex were based on the material digitized as part of the Sorte Muld Project and generously put at our disposal by Bornholms Museum. The remaining material was digitized for the present work. All finds registered with coordinates were included on the sitemaps in order to provide an impression of the find density on the site in comparison with the number of coins finds. Finds other than coins are normally represented by a small light grey dot, but in some cases it was decided to highlight specific finds of other types. Please note that the number of coins on the distribution map may be lower than the total number of coins found on the site, as some coins were not registered on site. All maps are oriented with north upwards. I am grateful to Michael for our good collaboration and to Farumgaard Fonden, who provided the funding necessary for this essential work to be done.

It was not possible, and perhaps not desirable, to reproduce photos of all Roman coins from Bornholm. I have chosen to focus on the 'oddities' among this vast number of finds (rare types, broken or reworked coins, imitations etc.), and present only a few examples of coins from most sites, in particular coins not illustrated in previous works. Unless otherwise indicated photos were made by Tine Bonde Christensen, to whom I am most grateful for help, and myself. Unless otherwise indicated coins are reproduced in scale 2:1. Extra illustrations and photographs were generously provided by both professional and amateur archaeologists from Bornholm, and Margrethe Watt allowed me to use the chronological map produced for her forthcoming map as basis for Fig. 17. I am extremely grateful to all individuals and institutions for this valuable help.

Line Bjerg, Michael Märcher and Michael Vennersdorf read and commented on sections in the early versions of the manuscript. Margrethe Watt read and commented intensively on both the contents and the English language of the entire text thus saving me from many errors. The peer review was made by a most distinguished scholar, Richard Reece, who not only recommended the text for publication, but even sent me comments and corrections to the whole text.

Helle Damgaard Andersen made some last minute proofreading and Tine Bonde Christensen cross-checked the bibliography and corrected find lists. I am most grateful to all who helped me, and I apologize for the remaining errors and linguistic infelicities, for all of which I am to blame.

Many new catalogues and studies have been published within the last decade. In particular the new find lists from Poland are of vast importance for this study, but also Dymowski's laudable attempts to collect information on illegally recovered detector finds from Poland should be mentioned. My work has benefited greatly from these works. To my regret, some research which undoubtedly will be of importance for a full evaluation of the Roman coins finds in Barbaricum could not be considered for the present work. Two important works should be mentioned here: Kyrill Myzgin (Kharkov University) generously provided me with the summary of his unpublished Ph.D.-dissertation on Roman coin finds within the Černjachov Culture, which are in many ways comparable with the material from both Poland and southern Scandinavia. The vast material from Sweden is currently being re-evaluated by Lennart Lind (Stockholm) for his forthcoming volume *Roman denarii found in Sweden and their European context*, which will replace his fundamental works from 1981 and 1988, adding among others information on more than a thousand coins not included in the first volumes. The manuscript was finished in January 2012. A few references to new finds and literature were added during proofreading, but otherwise no attempt was made to update the manuskript.

Foreword

The life cycle of a coin is long – one might even argue that its existence as a coin is only a minor part of the recycling of metal. The present investigation covers the later part of the Roman coin's existence: its arrival in Bornholm, its use there, and its deposition in and recovery from the soil.

Coin finds are evidence of connections between human beings. The coins were brought from one place to another by someone, and there was a reason to do so. Any object acquires new properties when moved from one cultural context to another, and the meaning of the Roman coin in the Danish Iron Age context no doubt differed greatly from its original significance. The Roman denarius was meant to be used as a coin in a monetary economy. Having left the area where the denarius was recognized as coin, it assumed new meanings. But: what where those new meanings? How was the denarius perceived in non-Roman communities? Which purposes did the coin serve?

The present work is a heavily empirical study of the Roman coins in their new contexts and attempts to approach these questions inspired by the socio-anthropological approach in much current archaeological work that often claims to be a descendant of a Bourdieu'an 'Theory of practice'.

Coins do not make up the largest single group of finds from Iron Age Denmark. The importance of the numismatic finds is that this artifact group is better documented than any other archaeological finds. There are two reasons for this: first of all coins comprise the only archaeological type that has always been declared treasure (*danefæ*) when handed in to the authorities and therefore – ideally – always registered,[1] secondly finds of silver and gold coins have always attracted attention, so we have good knowledge of old finds even if the coins themselves have not been preserved to the present. Bornholm in some ways form an exception to the remaining areas of Denmark: even though the majority of the many non-numismatic finds from Bornholm are not declared treasure, the enthusiasm of the amateur archaeologists has ensured that also these finds have been accurately registered, thus greatly enhancing the research potential of the material.

The present work has been organized in two parts. The first part comprises the analytical chapters. In the first chapter I will set the scene with an introduction to Bornholm and the archaeological and numismatic exploration of the island. The second chapter will provide an overview of the finds of Roman coin types on the island. A short paragraph is dedicated to the finds

---

1 This currently applies to all coins struck before 1536, and until the beginning of the 21st century coins were declared *danefæ* if struck before 1648. Hoards of large precious metal coins are declared *danefæ* no matter the production date. There is of course always the fear of 'nighthawks', but through many years of collaboration the amateur archaeologists from Bornholm have proved themselves trustworthy.

of ancient (Greek as well as Roman) coins in Viking Age contexts and the implications for the interpretation of single finds of Roman coins on the island. The third chapter will discuss the comparative numismatic material found in the European Barbaricum, and the fourth chapter will attempt to evaluate the finds in their local contexts and propose some interpretations of the material. The empirical basis for the work, the sites with finds of Roman coins, are presented in the second part of the book in the form of a descriptive catalogue of all sites that have yielded finds of Roman coins until the end of 2010. The catalogue is followed by lists of Roman denarii from sites with multiple finds, list of finds of particular types and indices of sites. Unless otherwise indicated dates are AD.

CHAPTER 1

Introduction

Bornholm is an island, and a relatively small one with its only 588.5 km². This nature-given property has determined living conditions on Bornholm. The strategic position in the Baltic Sea is of prime importance. On a clear day the visibility is so good that even by the naked eye it is possible to scan the sea from the southern tip of Scania to modern Germany. On a foggy day, however, raiders may sneak close to Bornholm or even go ashore before being discovered.

The sea offers a highway leading in all directions. It is no coincidence that Bornholm Museum houses a marvelous collection of *ethnographica* brought home by sailors from the Seven Seas. But the sea is also restricting, and those remaining on the island have led a secluded life. Likewise the story of Bornholm in the Iron Age presents a dichotomy between on the one hand local tradition and on the other hand an exotic influx, both reflected in the material culture. Roman coins obviously belong to the latter, but once imported into the island, they became part of the local culture. The use and meaning of the coins should be interpreted accordingly, in an interaction between the local and the foreign.

The landscape of Bornholm is characterized by the geological division of the island into two main zones. At the northern part of Bornholm the hard granites formed during the Precambrian era result in a dramatic landscape with deep valleys. On the southern part (very roughly speaking the west-east division line runs from modern Rønne to Nexø) the younger sandstone formations have resulted in a softer, but still undulating landscape which ends in the southeastern tip of the island with its famous beaches of white sand created by the eroded sandstone.

Archaeology of Iron Age Bornholm

From antiquarians to archaeology

The history of Roman coin finds in Bornholm is intimately linked the history of archaeological exploration of the island as a whole.[2] In fact, some of the first reports of archaeological finds deal with coins. The rich archaeological area near Svaneke was named The Field of Gold (*Guldageren*) already in documents of the 16th century, and several reports mention finds of Roman gold coins from what is today known as the Ibsker settlement complex (cf. below). The fate of these early finds cannot be traced, but some may have ended up in the King's possession. The last two entries on Late Roman coins in the handwritten inventory of gold 'medals' in the collection of King Christian V (1646/70/99) describe two solidi 'found in the soil at Borringholm [Bornholm]. Aº [anno] 169 ' – the year is incomplete, but it must refer to a date in the 1690s.[3]

---

2   Lund Hansen 2010 summarized the developments of Iron Age archaeology of Bornholm.
3   Breitenstein 1944, 1 and 68-69 no. 27.

Modern archaeological research on material from Bornholm was founded by Emil Vedel (1824-1909), who was appointed prefect (*amtmand*) of Bornholm in 1866. He soon took an interest in archaeology, and from 1870 he published several articles of the prehistory of Bornholm. He is known for his distinction between the Pre-Roman and Roman Iron Ages in Northern Europe, based on his analysis of Iron Age burials on Bornholm. His publication *Bornholms Oldtidsminder og Oldsager* from 1886 became seminal, and he continuously updated and supplemented his work in a series of later publications.[4] Most of Vedel's publications were based on material and information obtained in close collaboration with a local school teacher, J.A. Jørgensen (1840-1908). Vedel left Bornholm to take up a new position in Sorø on Sealand in 1871, and after that he participated in the field work only during short holidays. Meanwhile Jørgensen stayed on the island until his death, and he became the eyes and ears of Vedel, who published his observations.[5]

Vedel originally divided the Iron Age of Bornholm into three main phases (early, middle and late).[6] He dated the phases by comparison with material from other areas: for example the fibulas found in the latest cremation burials (*brandpletter*) and the inhumation burials from Kannikegård and Pilegård were compared to types found in the Thorsberg Moor dated *c.* 300 AD, and he therefore suggested that the *brandpletter* ended around 350. The shift from the early to the middle phase of the Iron Age was characterized by the arrival of new artifact types and dated *c.* 500. From the middle phase of the Iron Age Vedel noted the finds of solidi, gold bracteates and gold foil figures (*guldgubber*). He associated them with settlements, among which Smørenge, Sandegård, Sorte Muld and Sylten were the most important.[7] While numerous graves soon became known from the early phase of the Iron Age, only a few burials from the middle phase were known to Vedel, apart from the 163 discovered at Bækkegård in 1876.[8] Vedel stressed the continuity (culturally as well as ethnically) from the Bronze Age onwards, but was aware that the cultural development was influenced by objects and ideas derived from regions further south. He also noted the differences between finds from the Baltic Islands (Öland, Gotland and Bornholm) and the remaining part of Southern Scandinavia, and suggested that the two main areas of Southern Scandinavia were served by different parallel routes towards south. The beginning of Vedel's 'late' phase, characterized by the Viking Age tortoise brooches (*skålformede spænder*), was dated to *c.* 750 and would thus today be labelled Viking Age.

In his later work Vedel revised his terms in the light of new discoveries and research. The Iron Age was divided into two main phases: Early and Late. The Early Iron Age was sub-divided into Pre-Roman, Roman and Germanic-Roman phases.[9] It was followed by the Late Iron Age, divided into three sub-phases. The first was characterized by objects in the so-called Animal Style of the Germanic or Migration Period, although Vedel noted that 'animals' were rather few in the material from Bornholm. Vedel was reluctant to date the transition between the Early and Late Iron Ages, but suggested that it would fall in the mid-5th century.[10] The 'Germanic Style' was followed by the 'Irish Style' and the 'Carolingian Style'. Together the latter two styles covered the period *c.* 700-1050.

It is important to note that although Vedel's analyses on Iron Age material were based primarily on burial types and artifacts found in burials, notably fibulas, his main work was more comprehensive, listing and discussing sites and objects from all periods and types from Bornholm.[11] Vedel noticed some settlement areas, which he identified by the thick layer of black soil with pottery, animal bones, charcoal etc., and in collaboration with Jørgensen he made the first recorded excavations on classic sites such as Sorte Muld and Smørenge.

The work of Vedel was followed by a long period with limited interest in the Iron Age archaeology of Bornholm. Ole Klindt-Jensen (1918-1980) was next in line to play a role in the archaeology of Bornholm. His main work, *Bornholm i Folkevandringstiden* from 1957, described the results of his excavations of settlements (Dalshøj and Sorte Muld), fortifications (Gam-

---

4   Vedel 1886 and 1897.
5   Nielsen 2006.
6   Vedel 1873 and 1878.
7   Vedel 1878, 113-114 repeated in 1886, 187 and Tillæg XIIA.
8   Described in Vedel 1878.
9   Vedel 1890, 28.
10 Vedel 1890, 36.
11 Vedel 1886 and 1897.

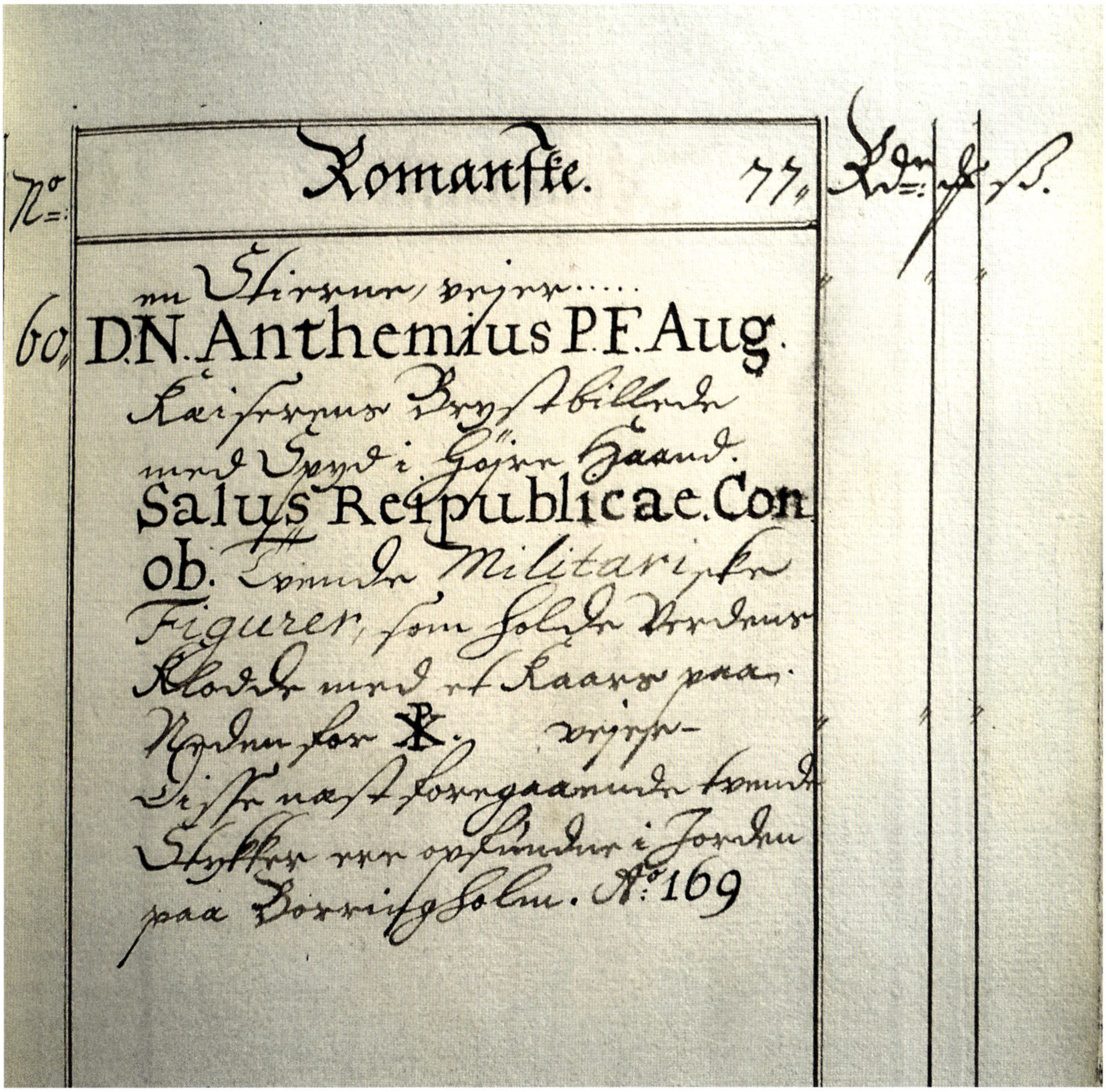

Introduction

Fig. 1. The last two entries on Roman coins in the collection of gold 'medals' belonging to King Christian V are described as finds from Bornholm: "Disse næst foregaaende tvende Stykker ere opfundne i Jorden paa Borringholm. Ao 169 ". The coin, published by Ramus 1816 as Anthemius no. 3, may be identical with the coin from Christian V's collection, as suggested by Fagerlie 1967, cat. 164.

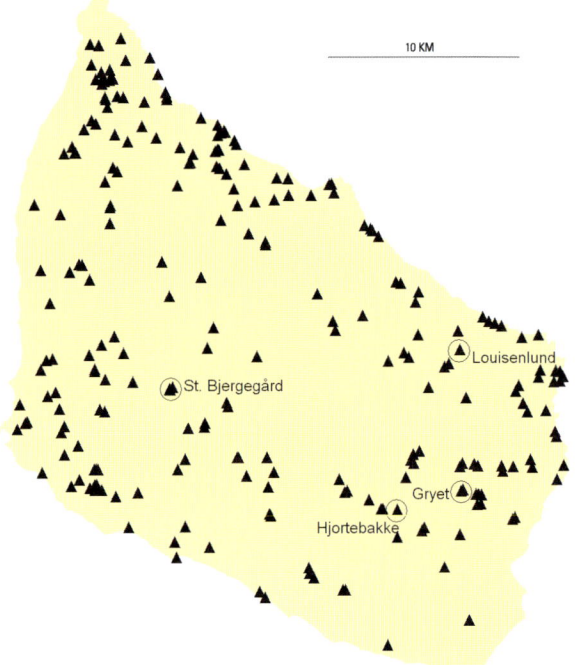

Fig. 2. Distribution of bauta in Bornholm. Four sites with large numbers of bauta have been marked out. Map by Michael Vennersdorf based on information from Finn Ole Nielsen/Benny Staal, Bornholms Museum 2012.

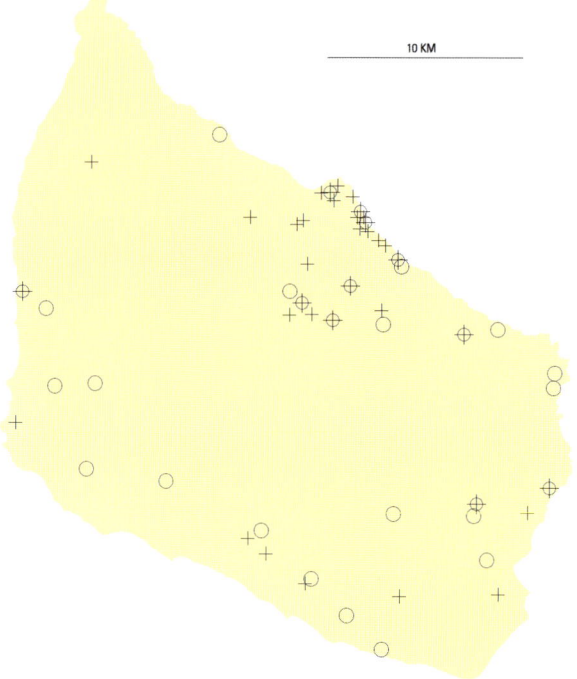

Fig. 3. Distribution of cemeteries, 375-750 AD. Map by Michael Vennersdorf based on information from Finn Ole Nielsen, Bornholms Museum 2012.

leborg in Almindingen) and cemeteries (Mandhøj, Bøgebjerg), and he aimed at including the results into a wider cultural historical narrative of the Migration Period of Bornholm.

After the publication of the volume on the Migration Period Klindt-Jensen continued work on the burials and excavated 1446 graves from the period *c.* 50 BC to AD 450 (Late Pre-Roman Iron Age to Early Germanic Iron Age) at Slusegård. The excavations took place during the years 1958-64, but the five-volume publication was only completed by his co-workers in 2010. The project has therefore become a combination of a total excavation of a major cemetery reflecting a documentation level of the period *c.* 1960 and publication standards changing over time from 1978 to 2010.

Numerous cemeteries and burials from the Iron Age and Viking Age have since been excavated and burials still dominate the publications of Iron Age archaeology in Bornholm.[12]

The chronology of the burials may seem of little relevance for the study of the Roman coins on Bornholm as only three burials, all from period C1b or C1b/C2, have yielded coins. Yet the chronological framework based on seriations of the grave-goods from the many burials forms the backbone for the understanding of the cultural development as a whole. The material from Slusegård and Ndr. Grødbygård formed the core of the burials used by Lars Jørgensen when defining the sub-phases of the Late Roman and Early Germanic Iron Ages of Bornholm.[13] The work was based on a seriation of the material, including pottery as well as fibulas. It arrived at conclusions which are much in line with the relative chronology built up by Bech using basically the same method on the ceramic material from Slusegård.[14]

---

12 Most recently Heidemann Lutz 2010, a monographic study of Late Roman Iron Age burials and the evidence for connections across the Baltic to Mecklenburg-Vorpommern.

13 In particular Jørgensen 1989.

14 The two chronologies were recently confronted by Heidemann Lutz. She prefers Bech's chronology for the ceramic material, but when working with detector material a chronology built on pottery alone is of little use. Nevertheless, the differences between the two chronologies are in minor details that are not directly relevant for the present work. Heidemann Lutz 2010, 34-43.

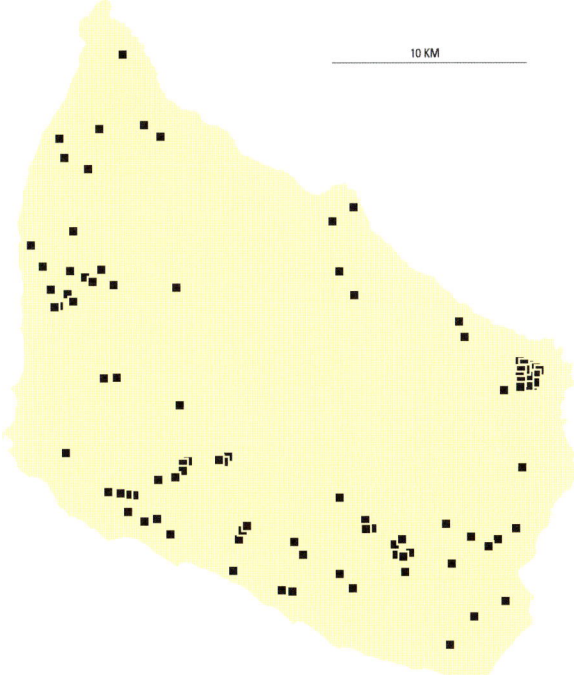

Fig. 4. Distribution of settlements 375-750 AD. Map by Michael Vennersdorf based on information from Finn Ole Nielsen, Bornholms Museum 2012.

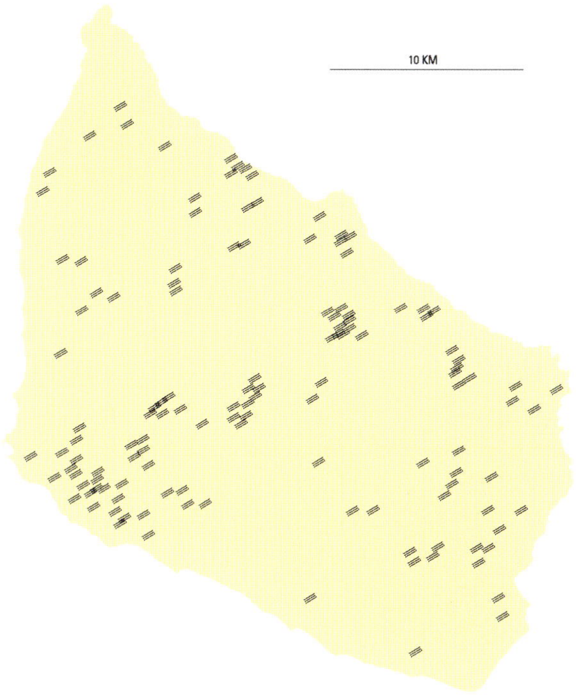

Fig. 5. Remains of prehistoric field systems. Note the remains of field systems at Rønne Plantation, close to the area where the two denarius hoards Robbedale and Udmarken were found, and the field systems near Borresø and Lilleborg in Almindingen. Map by Michael Vennersdorf based on V. Nielsen 2000, fig. 172.

The chronology of fibulas and other metal objects from the burials serve to date the detector finds of similar types, even though most detector finds derive from settlements rather than burials. While the production date of most Roman coins is known with relative accuracy, the context of the coins, that is the other metal objects found with metal detectors, can only be dated with reference to objects dated within the framework of the closed burial contexts.

Traditional archaeological excavation is still essential for the understanding of a site, but since the late 1970's non-intervention archaeological methods have increasingly been applied. Prominent among these are detector surveys, often carried out by amateur archaeologists, but it is important to note that they have often been supplemented by systematic soil sampling and phosphatic analysis, for example in connection with the so-called 'Black Soil Project',[15] by air reconnaissance and most recently by magnetometer surveys.

Iron Age Bornholm

Today, archaeological evidence from Iron Age Bornholm presents a picture of a densely inhabited island. Settlements and burial grounds have been located over most of the island. Throughout the last centuries BC the inhabitants were cremated, but during the Roman Iron Age inhumation gradually took over to become the dominant burial rite. There are, however, no sudden or profound cultural changes. On the contrary, burial grounds are being used continuously over several centuries as shown by the clear horizontal stratigraphy at several sites. In many places burials were marked by still visible cairns or *bauta* (monoliths). The bauta have been dated variously from the Bronze Age to the Viking Age. Recent investigations seem to favour a date in the Germanic Iron Age, thus making the bauta near-contemporary to the deposition of the Roman coins.[16]

During the 4th century (corresponding to the Late Roman Iron Age, and the transition between Danish Iron Age periods C to D) the number of registered burials drops significantly in Southern Scandinavia. This tendency is also seen in the material from Bornholm, but there are relatively more burials from this

---

15 Watt 2009.

16 Based on investigations and restoration works taking place in 2011. I thank Benny Staal for sharing this information.

period preserved on Bornholm than in other areas.

While some burial grounds are still visible in the modern landscape, most of the settlements are only known by indirect evidence such as black soil, crop marks or objects found in the plough layer, and they are consequently much harder to interpret and date than the burials. It seems safe to say that many sites were continuously inhabited, often over a very long period lasting several centuries, or they were re-inhabited at short intervals. Agriculture was of course the primary means of subsistence, but many of the settlements investigated during the Black Soil Project also produced evidence of smithing, and, for example, at Sorte Muld a row of loom weights were found *in situ* in 'House II'.[17] Two particularly large and rich sites stand out and will be discussed more fully: the Ibsker settlement complex and Smørenge. In addition there are a number of medium size sites (among others Agerbygård and Sandegård). Most sites, however, are relatively small in size and seem to consist of only one to two farmsteads, and it is argued that the pattern of dispersed single farms known from post-Medieval times in Bornholm may go back to the Iron Age settlement pattern.[18]

Actual Iron Age buildings are very hard to identify without excavations exposing the postholes dug into the subsoil, and few have been excavated. Klindt-Jensen revealed a sequence of houses from the Pre-Roman Iron Age to the Migration Period (his terminology, probably late 1st century BC to 4th/5th century AD) at Dalshøj and some house remains at Sorte Muld.[19] The excavations following the discovery of the first Fuglesangsager Hoard in 2001 brought forward evidence of several phases of houses in use from the mid-2nd century to the first half of the 7th century.[20] The buildings are rectangular with normally two rows of inner posts carrying the roof. Smaller outhouses are found in connection with the longhouses. Walls were constructed in wattle-and-daub technique, and several sites have yielded remains of burnt daub reflecting the constant danger when using open fires in these light constructions. While remains of houses destroyed by fire thus appear during surveys, other building remains would rarely be recognized, as unburnt daub and timber normally disintegrate without leaving traces.[21]

In addition to the settlements, fortified retreats were situated on higher terrain. Unfortunately, few investigations of the fortifications have been undertaken, and many questions about them remain unanswered. Most importantly the period of use remains uncertain. It seems that the retreat at Rispebjerg may have been in use around AD 200, Gamleborg in Paradisbakkerne[22] and Lilleborg may have been used during the Early Germanic Iron Age, while Gamleborg in Almindingen seems to have been established during the earlier part of the Viking Age. Borgen in Rø Plantage is un-dated. Several of the fortifications are situated in areas that today are forested, where trees and scrub obstruct the view. But in the same areas there are ample remains of prehistoric field systems. Both the fortifications and (in particular) the field systems are extremely hard to date and need not be contemporary. But together they indicate that the land use during the Iron Ages may have differed significantly from modern usage.

The gold foil figures are considered to be connected with ritual activity. With more than *c.* 2500 figures, the central part of the Ibsker settlement complex, Sorte Muld must have played a significant role, but figures are found in smaller numbers on several other settlement sites in Bornholm, notably sites which, also by other standards, stand out as special places.[23] Sacrifices of valuables have also taken place outside the settlements in the form of weapon sacrifices (Balsmyr and Knarremose, both with finds from Roman and Early Germanic Iron Age) and several gold deposits.[24]

---

17 Klindt-Jensen 1957.
18 Jørgensen 1991; Watt *in press*.
19 Klindt-Jensen's interpretation of the building remains at Sorte Muld as an L-shaped house met with severe criticism from the first review of his book by C.J. Becker in 1958, and no later excavation has supported his suggestion.
20 Sørensen 2009.

21 Watt 2006, 2009 and 2010.
22 Klindt-Jensen 1957, 152-156.
23 Watt 2009b (with references).
24 Klindt-Jensen 1957, 79-83 on weapon sacrifices; the finds from the moors in Bornholm were most recently discussed by Nørgård Jørgensen 2008, 104-110. The gold depositions were mapped by Jørgensen 1991a.

Roman coins on Bornholm

The first reports

One of the first to assess the coin finds from Bornholm in general was Christian Jürgensen Thomsen (1788-1865).[25] He claimed that there were four coin groups dominating the find spectrum of the island: Late Roman solidi, Cufic coins, English and German coins from the years around AD 1000, and finally low value coins struck in the period from 1241 to the middle of the 14th century. According to Thomsen these four groups were never found mixed with each other. Each of them reflected a period of crisis (assaults or war), where valuables had been deposited in the ground for safe-keeping. It is noteworthy that the solidus finds were numerous already in the early 19th century as one of the main groups known to Thomsen. He described the group as consisting of coins struck in the period from Arcadius to Anastasius (383/408-491/518), and noted that the majority had been dug op on a meadow called Sylten, famous for its many gold finds.[26] He suggested that the solidi had come to Bornholm from Constantinople *via* 'southern Russia' (he probably had the northern Black Sea coast in mind) to the Baltic.

The oldest coin from Bornholm, however, was the then only known denarius from Bornholm, struck by Marcus Aurelius and found on the Lilleborg castle mound.[27] Thomsen referred to parallels for this coin in the finds of Antonine denarii from the coastal area of Southern Sweden.

Half a century later Swedish archaeologist Oscar Montelius discussed the coin finds. He could list three denarius hoards found at Borresø, Udmarken and Robbedale as well as three single finds of denarii. The number of solidus finds had grown to a total of 67 solidi from 11 different finds.[28] The significant growth in numbers of finds continued, and in 1895 Peter Hauberg listed 12 sites with denarius finds from Bornholm.[29] The total material consisted of 498 denarii, of which the majority still derived from the three hoards (Hauberg listed the coins from Udmarken as three finds), but there were only six single finds of denarii. By then solidi had been found on 20 sites. Among the 112 coins 13 were single finds, the remaining coins derived from seven hoards.[30] Nine of the ten hoards listed had been found in the half-century from 1840-1890.

Hauberg discussed the Roman coins from all Scandinavia as an entity. Denarii were widespread, and Hauberg considered it likely that the mass influx came from the areas of modern Austria/Hungary along the Vistula, Oder and Elbe rivers. According to him the many denarius finds were the result of peaceful trade between the Empire and Barbaricum, and the end of the influx was caused by trade being interrupted by the Marcomannic Wars (*c.* 166-180). Hauberg noted that solidus finds were concentrated on the Baltic Islands, and the influx must have come from the Vistula area, the only area with finds comparable to the ones in Scandinavia. The coins derived from tributes from Constantinople to Goths and Huns. He suggested that trade in the Baltic seemed more connected to Bornholm and Öland than to Gotland after the division of the Roman Empire into an eastern and a western Empire in AD 395.[31]

In a series of articles initiated by Niels Breitenstein all previous finds were summarized, and thanks to his thorough archival studies he was able to describe old finds not included in Hauberg's lists.[32] He arrived at a total of 46 finds plus lists of coins known only from archival information. Denarii totalled 19 finds, again including the three previously mentioned hoards: Udmarken, Robbedale and Borresø, thus adding nine new finds to the material presented 50 years earlier by Hauberg. Solidi had been found on 27 sites comprising 17 single finds and 10 hoards, a small increase compared to Hauberg's numbers.

Breitenstein noted that the majority of the denarii were much worn, and he noted the 'late' character of the denarius hoards with reference to the famous work of Swedish historian Sture Bolin.[33] He did not doubt that the denarii were deposited as a consequence of war and unrest on the island, but claimed

---

25 Thomsen 1827.
26 Cf. below on the Ibsker settlement complex.
27 Thomsen 1827, 392-393 on NM I inv.no. CCCXLII.1. The coin cannot be identified today.
28 Montelius 1869, 8-11 nos. 72-78 and 24-25 nos. 216-227.
29 Hauberg 1895, 6-7.

---

30 Hauberg 1895, 24-25.
31 Hauberg 1895, 40-44.
32 Breitenstein 1944 on the finds from Bornholm.
33 Bolin 1929, who did not discuss Bornholm individually.

that the lack of finds of denarii together with solidi implicated that they had been deposited before the solidus influx began. The wear on the other hand indicated a late deposition, and he therefore suggested that the denarii were deposited in the 4th century. The solidi were closely related to the finds from on the one hand Gotland and Öland (although, according to Breitenstein, with a relatively larger part of western issues than these areas), and on the other Pommern and Mecklenburg. He therefore suggested that Bornholm acted as a transit point between the Continent and Southern Scandinavia.[34]

In the period between Breitenstein's compilation from 1944 and the subsequent one made by Anne Kromann and covering the period up to c.1980 only 29 Roman coins were found on Bornholm.[35] The coins derived from seven finds. The largest find was the solidus hoard discovered during Klindt-Jensen's excavations in Dalshøj.[36] Investigations on the Lilleborg castle mound added seven denarii to the previously known three denarii.[37] The remaining coins were single finds. One denarius came from an archaeological excavation of an Iron Age house in Nexø,[38] while the remaining coins were stray finds. Thus the find pattern until c. 1980 remained substantially similar to that of the previous years. However, changes were under way, as is obvious when reading the introduction to Kromann's coin list. She explicitly mentioned that the (then) recent finds a siliqua hoard from Gudme on Funen (c. 300 coins) and the Smørengegård hoard on Bornholm (c. 500 coins) were left out of the list, and she later published separate papers on both these hoards.[39]

Changing find patterns, detector archaeology 1980-2010

The number of finds has grown dramatically since the introduction of the metal detector among amateur archaeologists in Denmark.[40] Bornholm has been impacted on a spectacular scale and has proved ideal as a laboratory for assessing the use of new methods and in particular for evaluating the efforts of the many amateur detectorists. The size of the island is limited, and the whole island is under the authority of one local museum with a very small but stable archaeological staff. This means that all finds from the island since the beginning of detector archaeology have been registered in ways that are comparable throughout the period, and the generosity of the staff towards other scholars and students alike make information easily accessible. Furthermore Bornholm is extremely rich in archaeological sites as well as in amateur archaeologists. The latter are well organized in the group Association of Amateur Archaeologists on Bornholm (*Bornholmske Amatørarkæologer*) and have an excellent collaboration with the museum. This organization and collaboration (and I believe a certain amount of friendly competition among the detectorists) ensure that developments in surveying techniques are spread rapidly, and field registration is very good.[41] 'Detector tourism' and 'night hawking' have till now been kept to a minimum thanks to the good organization of the amateur archaeologists and the vigilance of the local society.

Margrethe Watt was responsible for the archaeology of Bornholm in the early 1980's. She initiated cooperation with the amateur archaeologist, and her approach has been decisive for the development of detector archaeology not only on Bornholm. She urged the detectorists to register the find spot for each individual object within a field, and Bornholms Museum undertook instruction of the detectorists as well as practical help with setting up coordinate systems for the registration. With the development of cheap GPS technology most detectorists are today pinpointing finds with this system, but the 'old' coordinates can be digitized and used along with the new measurements.

Some sites have been surveyed continuously over a long period, and sometimes the surveys have led

---

34 Breitenstein 1944, 82-83.
35 Kromann 1983-4, finds no. 52-58.
36 Kromann 1983-4, find no. 58; Klindt-Jensen 1957; Horsnæs 2009, 251-252 no. 27a.
37 Kromann 1983-4, find no. 52; Mørkholm 1969.
38 Kromann 1983-4, find no. 53. FP 3278.
39 Kromann 1988 (Gudme III Hoard); Kromann & Watt 1984 (Smørenge Hoard).
40 Horsnæs 2010a, 32 fig. 7.

41 News about the activities of the Association is often published in the periodical *Guldgubben* (articles from back issues available at www.dbabornholm.dk). Finds are also often presented on privately owned webpages. It should be noted that metal detector surveys are often supplemented by ordinary naked eye surveys.

Fig. 6. Until the development of cheap GPS technology detectorists marked find spots with numbered plastic spoons during the surveys. The plastic spoons did not interfere with the metal detectors, but facilitated the site registration of all finds after surveying. The method is an example of an operational and practical low-budget solution. Photo René Laursen.

to follow-up excavations. In cases where excavations have been undertaken we must consider that coins found in the top soil after the excavations have not only been moved around by agricultural machinery, but they have sometimes been removed from the excavation area and subsequently backfilled in approximately – but not necessarily exactly – the same area. Finds from the topsoil in previously excavated areas should therefore be considered as finds from the general area, although they have been plotted from the coordinates measured at time of recovery.[42]

Detector archaeology on agricultural areas does not produce finds of objects lost on the surface. It basically recovers objects torn from their original archaeological context by modern agricultural activity. The finds are still there, but the original context is irreparably damaged. The penetration depth of the metal detectors varies enormously according to a multiplicity of factors including soil composition, humidity, artifact type (chemical composition and size), orientation, and of course the type of the detector. However, with the exceptions of a few larger hoards, the ordinary detector will rarely register signals of objects still *in situ* below the modern plough layer.[43] In this respect detector surveys can be considered non-destructive, as they recover objects that have already been dragged from their primary contexts and would otherwise be lost to archaeological research.

Watt has discussed methodological considerations in regard to metal detector surveying in several works.

---

42 The same problem of displacement is of course relevant on sites where pre-metal detector excavations have taken place, for example Dalshøj.

43 Metal detectors penetrating deeper into the subsoil are available, but rarely used by amateur archaeologists.

Crossing boundaries

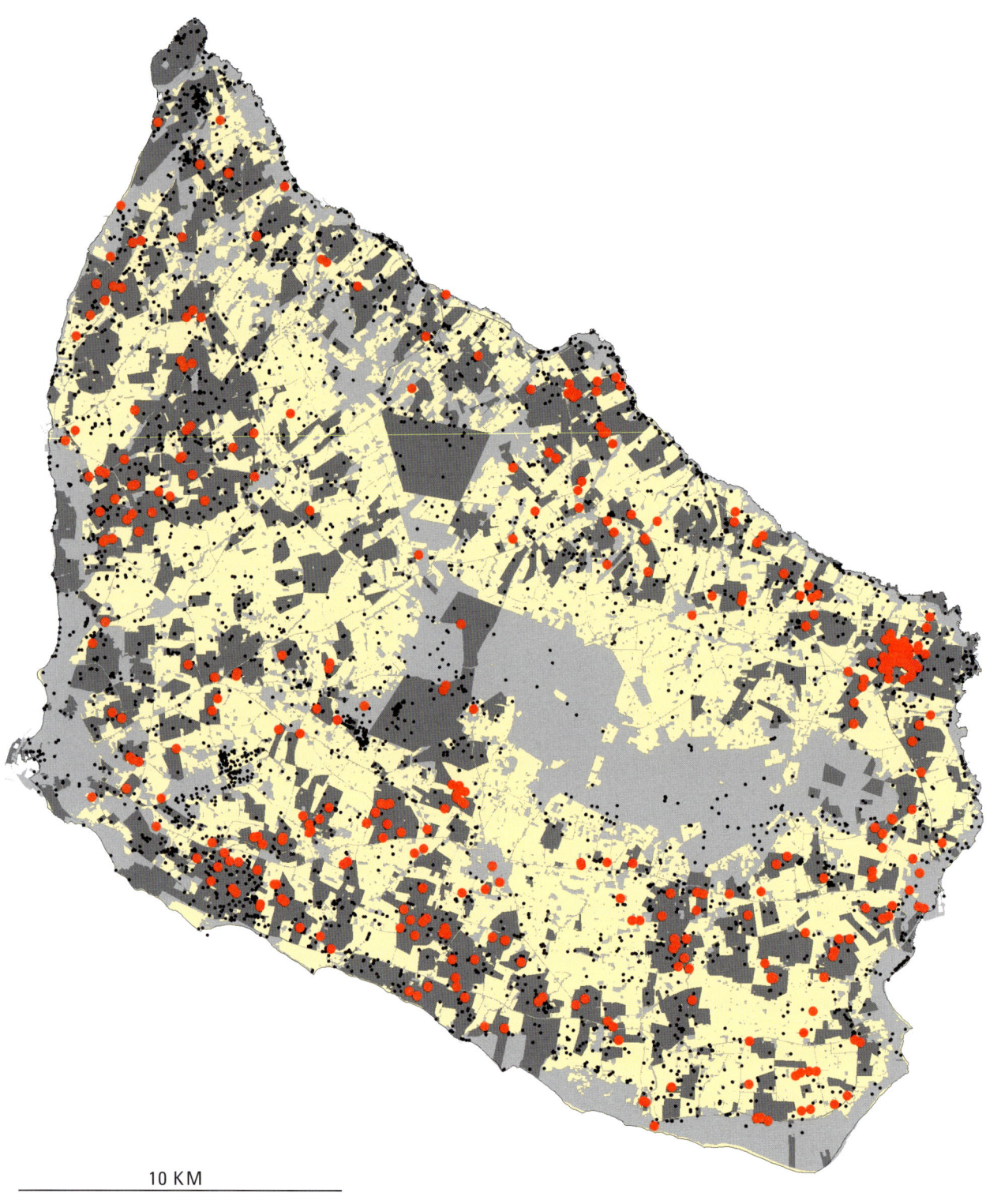

Fig. 7. The map gives a bird's eye view on the frequency of coin finds in relation to estates with a museum file (in dark grey). Areas that cannot be subject to metal detector surveys (forests, urban areas) are marked in light grey; areas with a potential for metal detector surveys are beige. Black points: sites defined in the national register (the so-called 'sb number'); red dots: coin finds.

Introduction

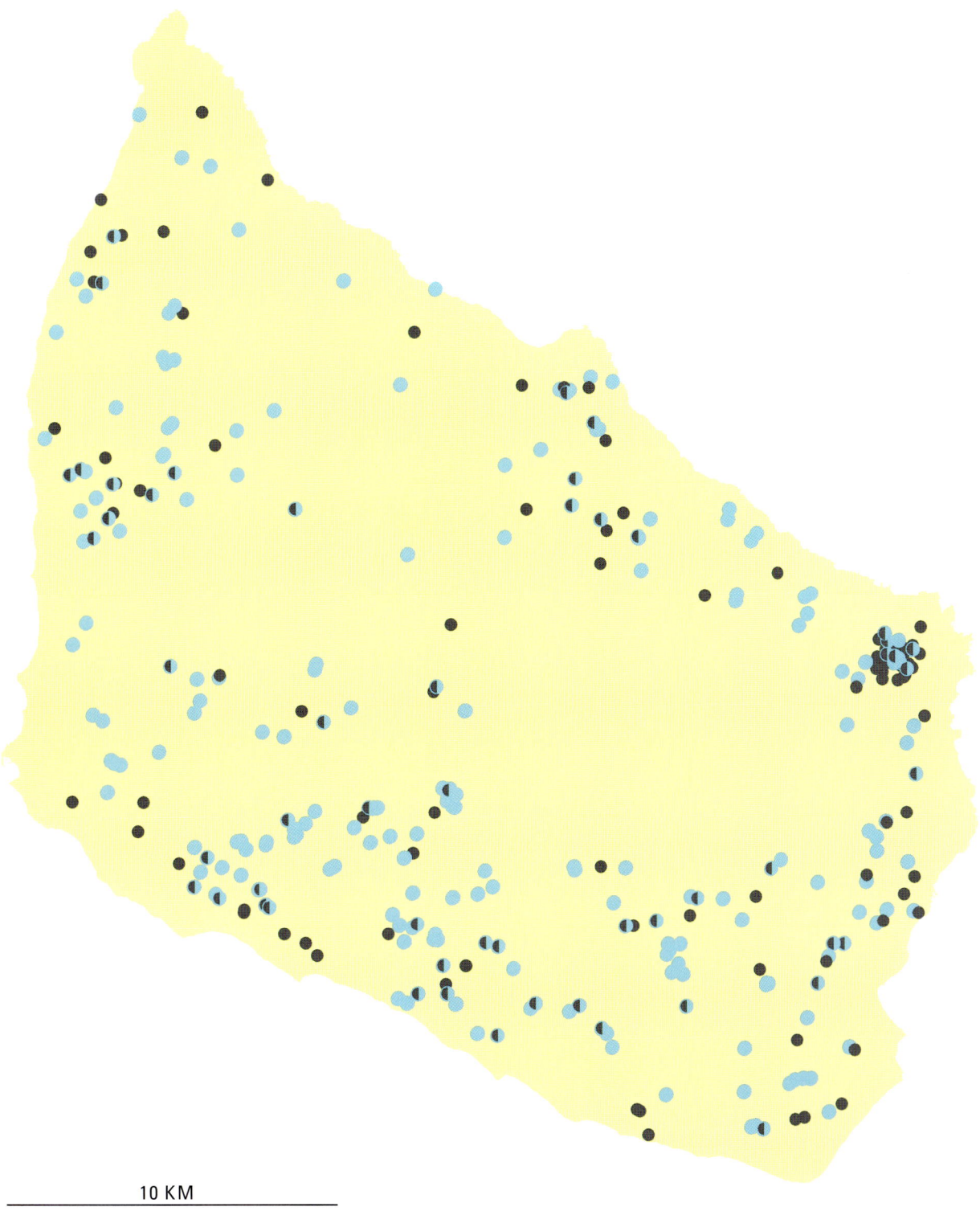

Fig. 8. Sites with one or more Roman coins (struck until c. 600) in grey and one or more Viking Age coins (struck c. 600-1130) in blue. A lower number of sites with at least one coin from each of the periods are marked with both grey and blue. A closer look at the sites with material from both Roman/Germanic and Viking Age reveals that many of them are in fact sites dominated by one of the two periods and the bi-coloured signature is based on some coins from one period and only a single one from the other. This is the case with several sites in the Østerlars area, dominated by Viking Age settlements, but with the occasional inclusion of a single Roman coin. The map demonstrates the shift in settlement pattern from one period to another.

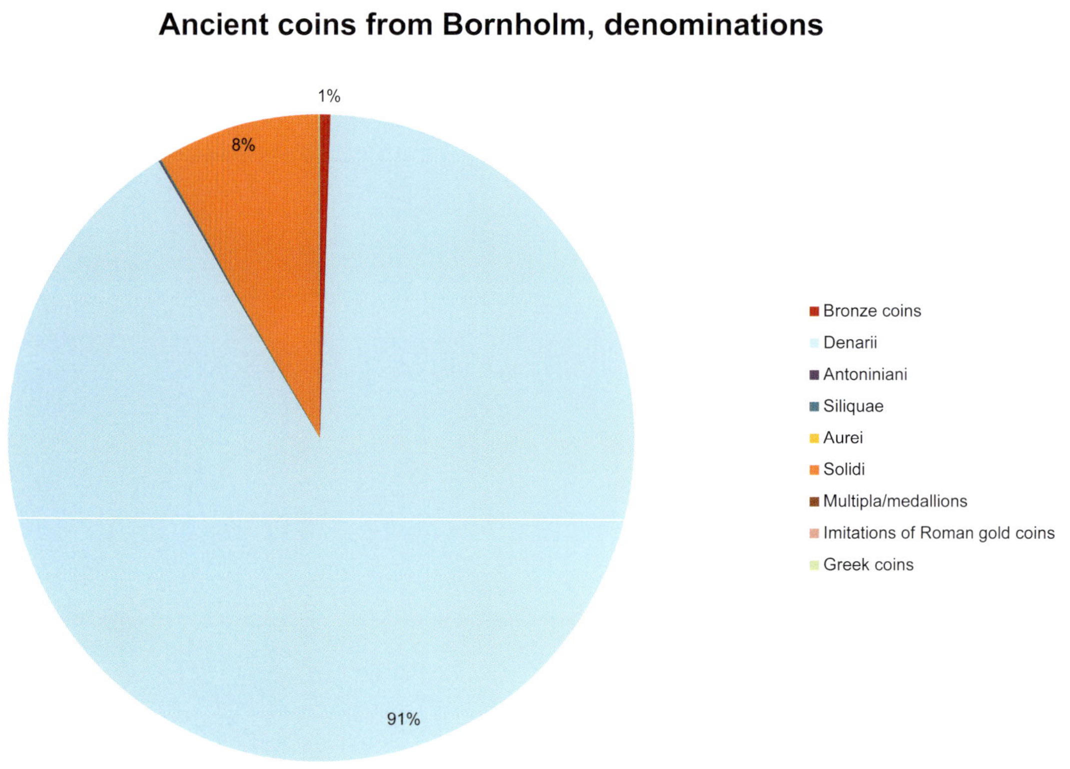

Ancient coins from Bornholm, denominations

- Bronze coins
- Denarii
- Antoniniani
- Siliquae
- Aurei
- Solidi
- Multipla/medallions
- Imitations of Roman gold coins
- Greek coins

1% / 8% / 91%

Figure 9. Distribution of denominations of Roman coin finds from Bornholm registered in the Royal Collection of Coins and Medal until the end of 2010. More than 90% of the coins are denarii struck between AD 64 and the early 3rd century (Compare Horsnæs 2010a, 40 fig. 12).

Her research projects included phosphate analysis and assessments of preserved culture layers on the settlement areas that make up the majority of the productive sites and have set a standard for this development in archaeology. She noted the differences in object types found using various methods: non-metallic objects are naturally under-represented in areas that have been investigated only by metal detectors, but there are also obvious differences in the chronological spectrum between objects found during detector surveys of the plough soil and objects found during excavation. The detector finds normally derive from culture layers that have been destroyed by ploughing, and hence represent younger phases of a settlement than the material found during excavation of the underlying culture layer.[44]

It seems that the number of finds from a site being surveyed annually is gradually decreasing, but it is also obvious that it takes more than a decade to empty the plough layer. Some fields have been surveyed for more than 25 years (Smørenge, hoard area), and they are still producing finds, even if numbers are decreasing. It has, however, been noted by some detectorists that the proportion of small and fragmented objects becomes markedly higher as time goes on. New and more sensitive metal detectors may be credited for that, but also the individual detectorist's growing experience must be taken into account, as well as the possibility that the plough layer is gradually being emptied for finds.

Abrupt changes in this gradual decrease of finds as well as of the size of the finds are often caused by the farmer's decision to change the type of plough employed, with the effect that hitherto untouched parts of the culture layers are destroyed.

In some cases a field has been surveyed with meager results, even in an area where many finds were expected. It later turned out to be caused by the finds being still *in situ* below the plough soil, but a change in way the field was worked – a plough reaching a bit deeper

---

44 Watt 1997; 1998; 2000; 2006; 2009; 2010.

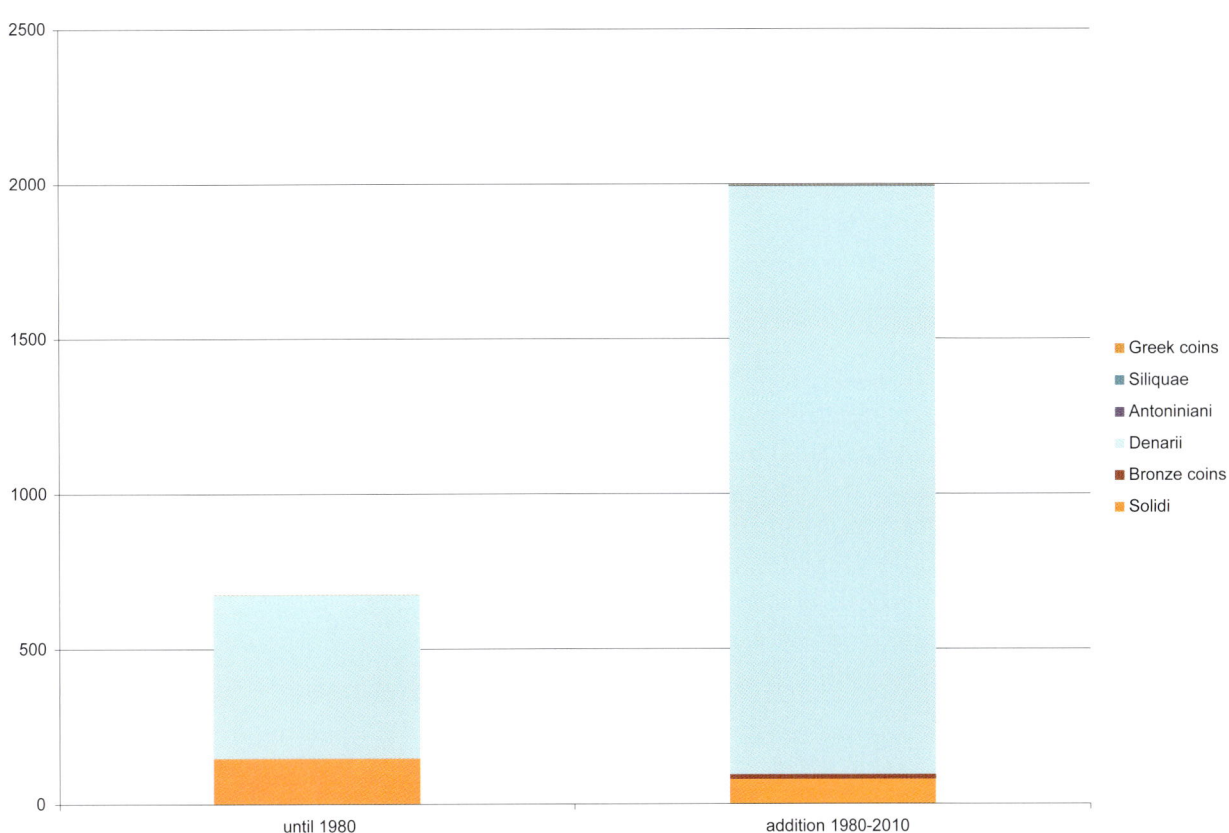

Fig. 10. The number of Roman coins found on Bornholm before and after the beginning of detector archaeology. The diagram reveals the change in both the volume of finds and in the composition of denominations (Compare Horsnæs 2010, 37-38 figs. 9-10).

than before – suddenly produced many new finds.[45] Watt's research has demonstrated that during the last c. 30 years the thickness of intact well-preserved culture layers has decreased rapidly.[46] This is the lamentable downside of detector archaeology: it saves only the last tiny bit of information on the culture layers lost to archaeological excavation. The fact that more and more finds are made with metal detectors is therefore a sad symptom that modern agriculture gradually rips away evidence of the past. No detector finds in a field may therefore be either evidence of no occupation in the past, or on the contrary an indication that culture layers are still preserved intact below reach of present machinery.

To evaluate the distribution of finds it is important to know whether we are actually discussing the distribution of finds or just the extent of the surveyed area.

The surveys are undertaken by volunteers as their hobby. Finds are registered, but we rarely have a systematic registration of fields that have been surveyed without producing finds, nor of the frequency of the intensity of the surveys. However, Watt has given indications of the survey frequency of the sites within the Ibsker complex,[47] and the rhythm with which finds are being handed over to the museum can indicate the frequency of surveying.

A comparison between the distribution of properties with one or more identified archaeological sites and the distribution of coin finds has revealed close correspondences. Furthermore it is obvious that the distribution of coin finds is heavily influenced by the visibility of an area, in the sense of whether it is possible or not to survey (Fig. 7). We face a situation that when looking at the map of Bornholm – or any other area – on a regional scale, the distribution of coin finds may be used as evidence for survey activity! This is of course seriously questioning the validity of

---

45 This was the case on one of the fields within the Ibsker complex, vividly described by experienced detectorist Klaus Thorsen.
46 Watt 2009, 25.
47 Watt 2009, 33 fig. 4, status 1999.

regional distribution maps as a means to understand the distribution of coin use through history: The areas without coin finds are not areas without depositions or coin use, but areas that have not (yet) been surveyed.

To gain a more valid picture of the distribution (presence/absence) of one artifact type, *in casu* the Roman coins, it has to be compared with the distribution of other types, or with coins from other periods. In the present work the mapping of all sites one or more coins struck before *c.* 1130 has been used as a means to overcome lack of exact registration and information on survey frequency. The coins have been divided into two distinct chronological groups, 'Roman' (struck until *c.* 600) and 'Viking Age' (struck *c.* 600-1130). In this way it is possible to demonstrate that there is only a partial overlap of find spots from these two periods, leading to the inevitable conclusion that the numismatic evidence can be used to argue for a quite distinct displacement of some sites from the Iron Age period to Viking Period *(Fig. 8)*.

It is very fortunate that a considerable number of the sites with multiple finds of Roman coins were included in the Black Soil research project undertaken 1996-99 under the guidance of Margrethe Watt. When possible the numismatic finds have been compared to the evidence produced by this project. The project included phosphate analysis of a large number of systematically collected soil samples from the plough layer of *black-soil sites* as well as soundings into the underlying culture layer to assess its composition and depth. Finds collected by wet sieving of the soil samples were indicative of the possible date range of the individual site. The project revealed close correspondence between the distribution of detector finds from a settlement and the extent of the area with high phosphate values. The original extent of the most frequented part of a settlement is likely to correspond to these. But there is a danger of circular argument: many of the detectorists used the farmers' phosphate maps as well as the black soil areas as guides to localize sites. These areas have therefore been chosen for surveys, and the expectation of 'rich' finds from these sites may have led detectorists to survey them intensively and hence to produce more material from these sites than other areas.

The intensive detector activity means that the number of coins known today is four times larger than the number known 30 years ago, and similarly the number of sites with Roman coins has grown from 52 to *c.* 170.[48] New finds are continuously being made with an average of 50-75 Roman coins from Bornholm every year.

Until *c.* 1980 only denarii and solidi were known from Bornholm. Now a few specimens of other denominations have been found, but the general pattern is still the same: denarii dominate the finds, while Late Roman solidi are also known in relatively large numbers. The number of finds of denarii has, however, grown much faster than the number of solidus finds. Roman bronze coins make up for *c.* 1% of the total number of coins, while antoniniani/radiates, siliquae and Greek coins are known from one or a couple of specimens each and are practically invisible in *Fig. 9*.

Approaching the finds

Coin registration

The coin finds have come to our knowledge mainly as a result of the Danish *danefæ* (treasure trove) legislation.[49] The present study is based on a database containing 2675 coins struck before AD 600 found on Bornholm and registered in The Royal Collection of Coins and Medals (The National Museum) until the end of 2010.

The coins have been registered in as much detail as possible. From a numismatic point of view this means that the coins have been identified according to the type numbers of *Roman Imperial Coinage*, which have been applied when possible. Otherwise notes have been made as to possible types; for example some of the Antoninus Pius types cannot be assigned to a specific year of issue due to wear of the obverse legend, but the reverse motif is readily identified and the coin can therefore be assigned to one of a number of possible types. In many cases, however, the state of preservation (or even the disappearance of the individual coin) has prohibited any assignment on a more detailed level than the reign of an emperor.

The type numbers for the earliest finds of denarii have been harvested from the coin lists published by

---

48 Exact figures of the number of sites are hard to give, among others because of the uncertainties of the old finds.
49 Horsnæs 2010a, 13-16.

Introduction

Breitenstein (1944) and Kromann (1983-4). Until the early 1990's Anne Kromann identified and registered all Roman coin finds and her unpublished identifications of the finds have been used. Her death in 1996 created a backlog in the *danefæ* work in the Royal Collection of Coins and Medals. Therefore most of the coins found since the early 1990's as well as the more recent finds were identified by me.[50]

A catalogue of the Late Roman solidi from Denmark including Bornholm, with illustrations of the recent finds, was published in 2009, and reference will be made to this work.[51] A full catalogue of the denarius finds is however not publicly available and is outside the scope of the present work. Furthermore a printed catalogue of denarius finds from Bornholm may create false impressions of a static situation, while in reality new finds are being made continuously. I have therefore decided to include lists with basic information of the denarii from sites with multiple finds. The lists include type number and weight, while information on the varying state of preservation of the individual coins (i.e. whether the coin is fragmented, melted, reworked etc.) is only mentioned in special cases.

Three factors must be considered in an evaluation of the preservation of the coins: The first is the post-production changes (reworking, wear or other damages) inflicted on the coin before deposition, both deliberately and as the result of use. Wear is an indication of the frequency of handling, but not necessarily of duration of the period of use: A heavily worn coin must have been handled considerably more than a fresh coin, but I am reluctant to equate freshness of a coin with a quick deposition. The fresh coin may have been kept in a safe and untouched environment for an extended period before deposition as can be seen by some of the denarii from dated contexts at Gudme.[52] Reworking or damage are directly connected to the use of the coins. The finds of partly melted denarii have sometimes been interpreted as preparation for re-use as raw material, and thus a deliberate reworking of the coins. In several cases, however, the denarii that have been destroyed by heat have been found in areas where burnt daub indicates that one or more buildings have been destroyed by fire. In these cases the melting of the denarii is almost certainly accidental.

Fig. 11. Melted denarii from the Sylten IV site in the Ibsker settlement complex. FP 4674.49, FP 4674.52, FP 4674.53, FP 4699.10.

The second factor comprises the corrosion, fractures and discoloration happening after deposition. The importance of the distinction between wear and corrosion cannot be underestimated.[53] While the coin

---

50 Coins with inventory numbers *c*. FP 5600-8500.
51 Horsnæs 2009.
52 Horsnæs 2010a, 99 fig. 49 bottom rows.

53 Frey-Kupper *et al*. 1995 have presented a laudable attempt to categorize wear and corrosion. I have however not used their categories throughout, but intuitively described the wear and corrosion of the denarii with words that largely follow their descrip-

Fig. 12. Four denarii with similar surface preservation from the Biskopsenge 9 site in the Ibsker settlement complex. FP 8105 and FP 8266.1-3.

is worn during use, corrosion is an important post-depositional influence on the coin, but not the only one: discoloration of the surface is for example seen on the denarii interpreted as a small hoard from the Biskopenge 9 site in the Ibsker settlement complex, while coins from other hoards may present a smooth silvery surface with spots of bright green copper compounds. In some sites more denarii than usual are fragmented, and I suspect that some chemical action from the soil has made them fragile, resulting in more breaks. De-

narii found in two or more fragments, often many years apart, are clear evidence that coins were broken in the soil rather than deposited as fragments. The post-depositional effects on the coins may be a guide to the interpretation of the deposition circumstances. When a group of denarii from a metal rich site present the same characteristics in surface preservation (corrosion, discolouration), and the coins furthermore differ in surface preservation from other silver objects from the same site, it indicates that the coins were preserved in the same microenvironment, a single deposition or hoard, until recent disturbance.

A third factor that has to be taken into account is the changes inflicted on the coins after modern recovery. This is particularly important for the many large productive sites that have been surveyed again and again. In these cases denarii (more often than other denominations) have been found over a long period, beginning in the early days of detector archaeology in the 1980's. Each inventory number in the register of The Royal Collection of Coins and Medals corresponds to at least one delivery of *danefæ* – normally handed over from Bornholms Museum once a year. It is today very evident that the post-recovery treatment of the coins has changed considerably over time. Coins have been handled by the finders, staff from Bornholms Museum and staff from the National Museum. Finders have been encouraged not to attempt any other cleaning of their finds that the blowing away of loose dust or rinsing in clean water that enables the finder to make a basic identification of the find. No professional cleaning or restoration work is normally undertaken before the finds are declared treasure. But while many coins, in particular those interpreted as belonging to hoards, were professionally cleaned and restored by the National Museum in the 1980's, denarii found after the early 1990's have rarely been subject to professional cleaning (exceptions being coins used for exhibition). The result is that even coins that most probably derive from the same hoard, may look very different today (*Fig. 13*).

The lack of professional cleaning may be a problem because acids from fertilizers etc. are still affecting the surface of the finds. On the other hand, the possibility of comparing the surface of finds made several years' apart including corrosive products and dirt may give hints as to the contexts of the coins before recovery.

tion of denarii on pp. 10-11.

Introduction

Fig. 13. Denarii from Sorte Muld hoard cluster, from left: FP 6453.5 and 2 (obverses), found in stack, now separated, cleaned and restored; FP 7253.2 and .4 (obverses), washed but not professionally cleaned; FP 8088.1-2 found in stack, un-cleaned. Note the difference in appearance.

Site registration

The site registration has generally been made to the highest possible level of precision. Very little reliable information is available for some of the old finds, sometimes only the name of the parish or general area is known. Contrary to this, recent detector finds have been registered not only with a specific site name, but most of the finds have even been registered with geographic coordinates in the field. When working with detector finds it is important to acknowledge the level of precision of the measurement in the field. The measurements are always in two dimensions. They were initially made using ordinary tape measures recording the find spot in relation to basic lines laid out for the individual site. Any archaeologist will appreciate that the level of precision by this method will have an uncertainty of at least a couple of meters. One might consider the GPS measurements to be of higher precision, but this is normally not the case with the hand-held GPS used by the amateur archaeologists. Only when measurements are made by professional high-precision tools – which are rarely done outside planned excavations – can we expect a higher accuracy. This of course means that while the method is extremely well adapted to identifying clusters of objects recovered over in some cases more than 20 years, it is of less use when discussing the exact position of particular objects in relation to each other.

The site names and the site registration numbers present a picture which is not always clear-cut. Archaeological sites in Denmark are registered by a 6 digit code according to the former three-level administrative division of Denmark into region (*amt*), district (*herred*) and parish (*sogn*). Bornholm was an *amt* characterized by all site numbers beginning with the digits 06. Within each parish all sites have consecutive numbers (sb no.). Together the site number and sb number should ideally provide a unique identification of each site. The archive number in Bornholms Museum (BMR no.) is usually unique to one site, followed by a serial number (x-no.) applied to each individual find. The inventory number of the Royal Collection of Coins and Medals (FP no.) is added when the coin is registered in the collection. In case more than one coin is handed in at the time, the FP no. is followed by a serial number.

Normally a site is named after the farm owning the land where and when the site was identified. But the find density in Bornholm is so great that in many cases several sites have been identified within the area owned by one farm. In these cases sites have normally been named after the relative geographical position (north, south etc.) or they have been called area 2, 3 etc. There are however examples where two farms situated in different parishes carry the same name. This is due to the fact that farm names often derive from for example the topographical situation of the farm (for example Bækkegård = Farm at the Brook). It is an understandable, but unfortunate source for confusion and misunderstandings. Another source of misunderstanding is the unavoidable administrative division of the same archaeological site into several

Crossing boundaries

Fig. 14. All sites with Roman coin finds. The six-digit area code refers to the parish, the so-called 'sb number' is the unique identification of the site within the parish. For the individual sites within the Ibsker settlement complex (grey square), see figs. 53-54. Insert: Bornholm's position in the Baltic area.

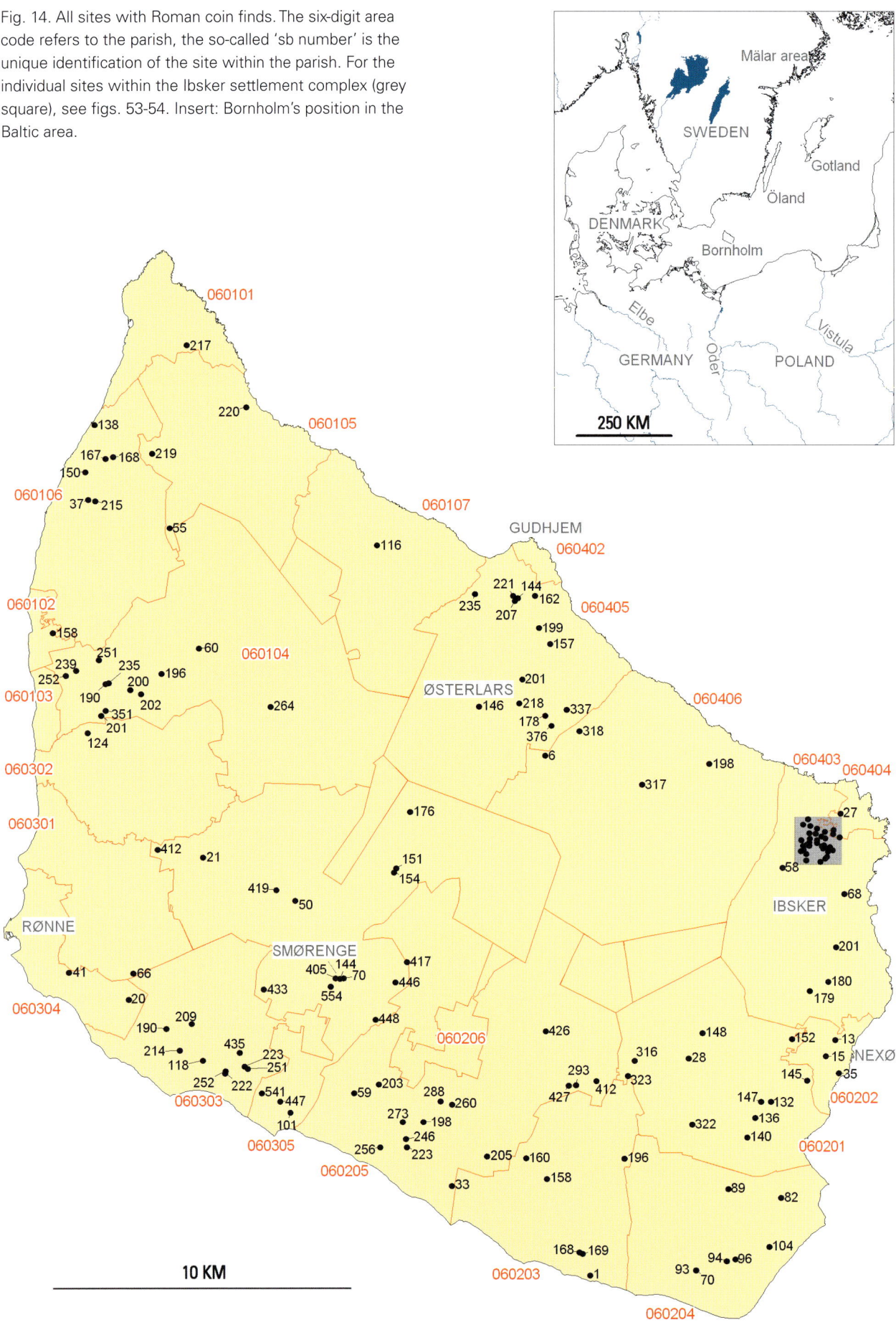

BMR and/or sb registration numbers as well as different place names in cases where the extent of the archaeological site stretches over property belonging to several owners. I have tried to avoid confusion by listing all registration and inventory numbers as well as alternative site names.

The geographical distribution of Roman coins

Roman coin finds as known in 1944 were a few denarius hoards, a few solidus hoards and some single finds, often with little exact information on find circumstances. Finds were known mainly from Ibsker and from an area between Østermarie and Gudhjem and more sporadically from the southwestern corner of the island.[54] Today the number of finds in Ibsker has grown enormously, and one could hardly have foreseen that the single denarius from Smørenge known to Breitenstein would grow to almost a thousand. The cluster around Østerlars has become much more manifest, and so have two areas on the western coast. The scatter of sites with Roman coins on the southern part of the island is also growing continuously, and most recently the number of inland sites seems to be growing.

There are, however, still areas without finds. Large parts of Bornholm that today are forested were not always so. Most of the forest is in fact quite recent: Almindingen was planted as the result of a decision taken by the central government in 1799, and large parts of the inland areas had before then been used as grazing. Remains of Iron Age field systems are, however, still visible in several places in the now forested areas, which clearly shows that at some point – which is hard to date with certainty – at least parts of this area was settled *(Fig. 5)*.[55] The Iron Age fortifications in Bornholm furthermore indicate that vegetation in several places must have differed significantly as present day forestation obstructs the view from many sites. Until now detector archaeology has concentrated on farmlands, while the forested areas have not been surveyed; with the increasingly heavy machinery used in modern forestry archaeological remains in these areas have become acutely threatened.

As described above, the overwhelming majority of the many new finds is due to amateur archaeologists surveying with metal detectors.[56] In practice most detecting is undertaken on soils that are regularly ploughed. The use of metal detector is not allowed at or close to a protected heritage site, nor is it possible to use metal detectors on publicly owned areas. These areas would therefore appear devoid of finds on a distribution map. Other areas have not been surveyed for practical reasons: detecting is impossible in most urban areas, proximity to underlying bedrock may affect detecting, and it is hard to achieve good results in areas that are not relatively level and open *(Fig. 7)*.

Detectorists are amateurs in the true sense of the word: for them detecting is a hobby, done for the love of it. Detectorists are guided by their own fancies and their great enthusiasm, and they are not necessarily covering areas that archaeologists would like to investigate. Ideally the fields should be covered systematically and each survey should be registered, including information of date, climate, crop types and other factors that might influence the result of the survey. Fortunately, amateur archaeologists have often volunteered to take part in systematic surveys, but smaller survyes undertaken on a private initiative do not always live up to the strict requirements of professional surveys. While amateur archaeologists report their finds, fields without finds are rarely registered. This means that absence of finds may be real in the sense that no objects have surfaced, but it may equally well demonstrate that the area has not been surveyed (yet!).

Attempts have been made by Margrethe Watt to register and publish survey intensity within the Ibsker complex, and not surprisingly most finds were made on the most densely surveyed areas.[57]

Then can we use distribution maps of Roman coins on Bornholm at all? There will always be elements of doubt, but it is considered that provided strict methodologies are applied the material acquired during detector surveys is more reliable than the early, accidental stray finds. One way to escape the danger of circular arguments based on the accumulation of finds from a popular site is to compare one artifact type, *in casu* the Roman coins, with other finds: in

---

54 Breitenstein 1944, fig. 91.
55 Nielsen 2000.
56 The use of metal detectors is legal in Denmark on privately owned areas – provided that the owner has given his/her permission. On the Danish *danefæ* legislation see Horsnæs 2010, 13.
57 Watt 2006, 151 fig. 6; 2009, fig. 4.

Crossing boundaries

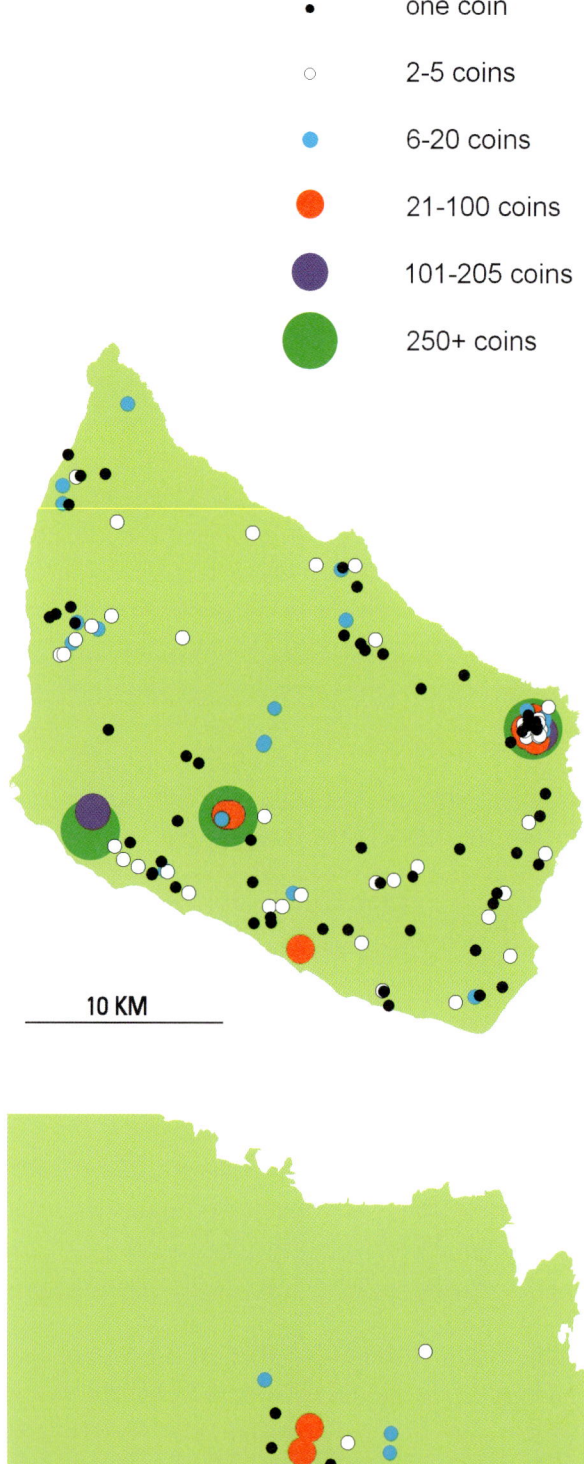

Fig. 15. Distribution of Roman coins on Bornholm. All types and denominations. Insert: The Ibsker settlement complex.

the present volume the distribution of Roman coins is compared on an overall level to the distribution of coins struck in the period *c.* 600-1130.[58]

The number of coins known from Bornholm of the period *c.* 600-1130 ('Viking Age' coins) is somewhat larger than the number of Roman coins. Viking Age coins have been found on 237 sites.[59] Only 57 of these sites have produced Roman coins as well, demonstrating significant differences in the distribution pattern of coins from the two periods. But even the 57 sites with coins from both periods do not form a closed entity on the contrary they can be divided into two distinct groups: Most sites with multiple finds of Roman coins have yielded only one or a few 'Viking Age' coins, and coins struck before the early 10th century dominate among these *(Fig. 8)*.[60]

On a site level the distribution of Roman coins is compared to the distribution of other finds from the same site – other object types contemporary to the Roman coins as well as the later numismatic finds. In this connection the numismatic material takes a special place as the most representative object group from a productive site, because coins struck before 1536, contrary to other object types, are always declared *danefæ*, no matter the number of finds from the site or the state of preservation of the individual object.

A final word of warning is the well-known fact that finds from archaeological surveys rarely provide a sample identical to the one recovered during excavations of the same site. The Black Soil Project has amply demonstrated how material from metal detector surveys can interact with material recovered during traditional surveys, soil sample analysis, and excavation to produce a more coherent picture of not only the individual site, but also supplement the interpretation of sites known only through detector surveys.[61]

Chronology

The date of the Roman coins is normally given in ab-

---

58 Viking Age coins from Bornholm were discussed by von Heijne 2004.
59 von Heijne 2004 enumerated 149 sites with finds of coins from the period until 1130. In Fig. 8 her figures has been updated with finds handed over to The Royal Collection of Coins and Medals and registered until the end of 2010.
60 Preliminary discussion in Horsnæs 2012.
61 Watt 2000; 2006; 2009.

Fig.16. Systematic metal detector survey at Sorte Muld undertaken by members of the Association of Amateur Archaeologist at Bornholm. Photo Kai Pihl.

solute dates, but their contexts are discussed within the frames of a relative chronology. On an overall level the chronological phases of Iron Age Bornholm have been correlated with the phases of the remaining parts of Denmark and the same terminology is used.[62] In previous works on the Iron Age of Bornholm the phases have been termed differently, and when comparing with material from neighbouring areas of Barbaricum it is important to 'translate' the different phases. The extensive exchange of objects allows for correlations of the phases from one area to another. It is however also important to keep in mind that the absolute dates of the archaeological phases to a large extent have been built on an interpretation of the relationship between the Roman imports (notably the coins themselves) and locally produced objects found in single burials in Barbaricum, hence a danger of circular arguments.

The 'post-Roman' coins are touched upon when found in connection with the Roman coins. They have not been studied individually for this publication, and in general only very broad chronological assignments are given. During the Viking Age the earliest coin finds in Bornholm are Sasanian type drachms and Umayyad dirhams, but the majority consists of Abbasid and in particular Samanid dirhams struck during the 9th and the first half of the 10th centuries, but often found in considerably later contexts. Pure dirham hoards are few and belong to the mid-10th century (a 9th century dirham hoard was found at Skovsholm, Ibsker, in September 2012).

In the late 10th century the influx of German coins started, and soon after the first English coins appeared. Throughout the 11th century the finds are dominated by German coins, but hoards continue to contain a certain number of old Cufic coins as well as some English

---

62   For a short introduction, see Horsnæs 2010, 25-27.

coins.[63] Anglo-Scandinavian and Danish coins are less common.[64] In the earliest part of this period hoards often contain considerable amounts of *Hacksilber* as well as coins, while the 11th century is characterized by a growing number of 'pure' coin hoards. It is, however, evident that as regards monetary practice, Viking Age traditions die hard on Bornholm.[65]

Coins struck during the 12th century are rarely found.[66] I have therefore decided to group all coins, Oriental/Cufic as well as Western, struck in the period from *c.* 600 to *c.* 1130 under one heading: 'Viking Age coins', following the division suggested by Heijne (2004) – while strictly speaking it should be called 'Viking Age and Early Medieval coins'. The lumping together of all coins struck until *c.* 1130 is a matter of convenience, shrouding the fact that during the long period up to *c.* 1130 profound changes took place on all levels of local society as well as in Northern Europe as a whole: This affected settlement patterns, import routes, burial practices etc. and not least the coming of Christianity to Bornholm. From a numismatic point, however, these changes are still to be studied on a local level in light of the manifold increase in the number of finds from Bornholm that have taken place since *c.* 1980.

Coins struck in the period from *c.* 1130 until 1536 have been labelled 'Medieval coins'. In the material from Bornholm this group is very small compared to

---

63 Moesgaard 2006 on two unusual hoards dominated by English coins.
64 von Heijne 2004, in particular, 88 and 158-160 and fig. 6.23. See also chronological list of finds (dated by coin *t.p.q.*) pp. 215-219. The Nørremølle Hoard found 2006 (*t.p.q.* 1024) was published by Ingvardson 2012.
65 Compare von Heijne 2004, 72 fig. 5.6 and 128 fig. 6.7. For the monetization of Denmark in the Early Medieval Period see Ingvardson 2010, a case study based on the material from Sealand. The situation on Bornholm is however not wholly compatible with that area. Though seriously outdated Skovmand 1942 still provides the best overview of Viking Age hoards in Denmark. For example, a mixed hoard of the advanced 12th century was found in Østermarie panish in autumn 2012 (Grinder-Hansen & Märcher 2013).
66 On a overall level this is consistent with the pattern in the remaining parts of present Denmark, cf. most recently Ingvardson 2010 with references.

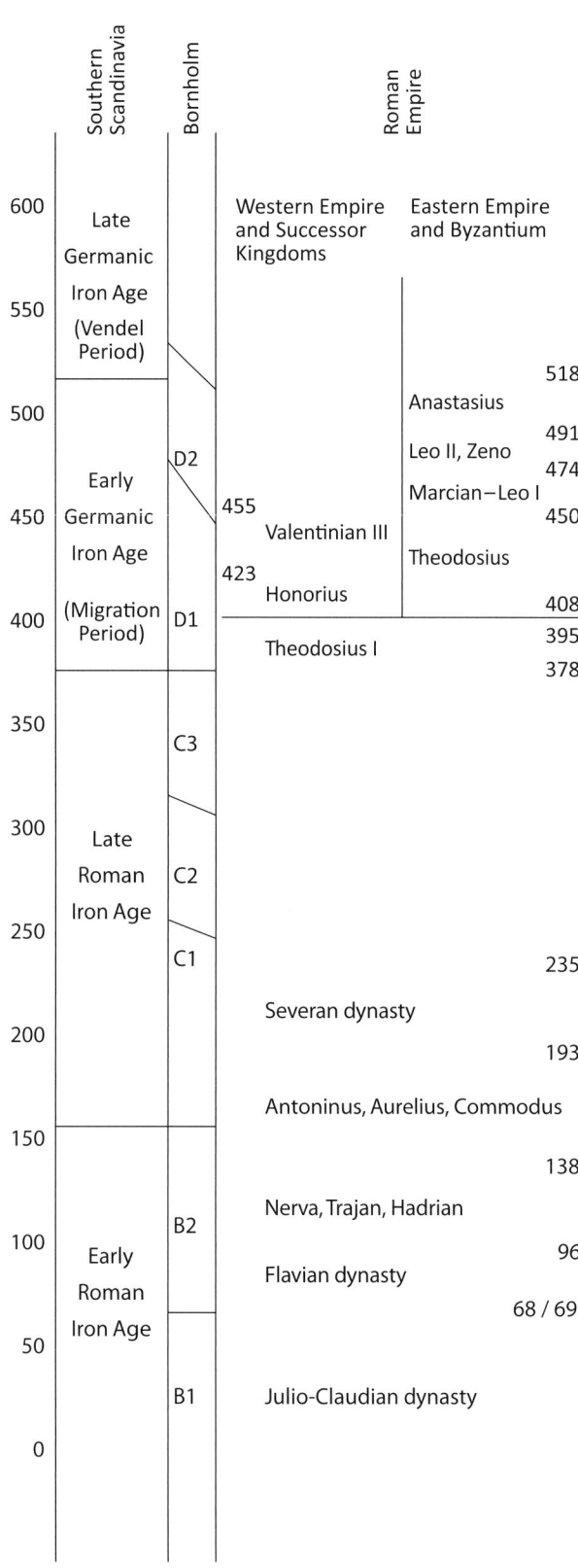

Fig. 17. Iron Age and Viking Period phases in Northern Europe (Drawing by Pia Brejnholt, based on chonological table developed for Watt *forthcoming*, re-produced with permission).

other parts of Denmark, where in particular finds of the so-called 'Civil War coinages' are abundant.[67] The majority of the 13th century coins have been found at two localities: a hoard found at Skrivergade,[68] and the Lilleborg Castle mound with series of single finds.[69] More recently, coins struck at the mint in Lund in the first half of the 14th century are found in increasing numbers on detector sites. Still, 'Medieval coins' are comparatively rare: only *c.* 100 sites are listed of which *c.* 60 sites have yielded only a single coin from the period.[70] Two theories have been proposed to explain the apparent lack of finds of 'Medieval coins'. One is the choice of the detectorists themselves, who often have been guided by published lists of Viking Age hoard finds and/or by the settlements recognized because of the characteristic black soil. The other is a question of survival, as it seems that many Medieval sites may be overlaid by their modern successors and thereby inaccessible to detector surveys.[71]

Coins struck after 1536 are only mentioned in particular cases, as the administrative practices of the *danefæ* legislation excludes the registration of single finds (stray finds) of small denomination coins struck after 1536. Therefore the distribution of finds of coins struck after that date is not representative for coin circulation.

Hoards and single finds – problems of interpretation

The traditional numismatic division into two major find types – hoards and single finds – is useful for studying for example coin circulation and coin use. The material becomes more valid when a distinction is made between hoards and single finds, as one hoard with many specimens of an otherwise unusual type may distort the overall picture. A very good example is the case of the Gudme III siliquae hoard from Funen that contains more than 90% of all siliquae found in Denmark.[72]

The division of the finds into hoards and single finds is based on an interpretation of the deposition circumstances: in common numismatic terminology a hoard is defined as one deposition of two or more specimens often (but not always) as the result of a conscious decision, while single finds are more often seen as accidental losses; still, there are many examples of an accidental loss of a 'hoard' (for example a lost purse) as well as conscious depositions of single finds. Finds retrieved during detector surveys have put this traditional division of deposition types under pressure, and we need to address the problem of many coins deriving from one site. Swedish scholars have used the expression 'hopade fynd' (literary translation: accumulated finds) when describing concentrations of finds, but it seems to me that the expression is not accurate enough, as it may be mixed up with 'accumulated finds' used as a term to define a context of many coins or other objects being deposited little by little in for example a votive context. The metal rich sites produce several types of finds: many coins that may derive from one or a number of conscious depositions of one or several coins that have been torn from their original contexts and later perhaps mixed up with other coins that derive from single accidental losses. The situation becomes even more complex when considering that the coins need not be the sole objects from a deposition: 1st millenium hoards are depositions of precious metal, whether in the form of coin or other objects types.

As long as a 'pot of coins' is found *in situ* the interpretation is straightforward, as it is in the situation when many coins of the same type are found within a relatively restricted area where no other finds have been made. The excavation of the ploughed up Orup Hoard (in Sealand) has demonstrated that the 'relatively restricted area' may indeed be quite large: over 100 denarii were found over an area covering more than 1600 square meters. No trace of the original deposition was recovered, but no other finds were made within the excavation area in spite of sieving of the soil, hence there are good arguments for an interpretation of the denarii as a single hoard.[73]

On Bornholm there are few productive sites where Roman coins have surfaced as the only object type, on

---

67 Grinder-Hansen 2000.
68 *DMS* II; 32 no. 96, *t.p.q.* 1280-1285. Furthermore two small hoards both *t.p.q. c.* 1200 have been found at Rø and in Rønne: *DMS* I, 302 no. 62 and 303 no. 63.
69 Mørkholm 1969, cf. also below.
70 Preliminary figures based on registrations in Fund & Fortidsminder; compare with the *c.* 170 sites with Roman coins and *c.* 235 sites with Viking Age coins.
71 I thank Margrethe Watt and Michael Vennersdorf for discussions on this problem. Coin use in Bornholm during the 2nd millennium is the theme of a project carried out by Michael Märcher 2013-2015.

72 Horsnæs 2010a, 138-144.
73 Horsnæs 2010a, 79-80 with further references.

the contrary in most cases they have appeared along with numerous other finds. Here arguments become increasingly complicated, and it is important to acknowledge that there is no easy way out. To be able to interpret clusters of coins found during detector surveys as the remains of a scattered hoard it is necessary to combine a number of different parameters:

- similarities of coin types and/or dates (is it possible or even likely that this combination of coins would have been hoarded?)
- similarities in conservation (is it possible that these coins have been kept under similar conditions for a long period?)
- distribution of the finds (is it likely that so many coin depositions should be made within a small area? Or on the contrary: is it possible that a single hoard should be spread over such a vast area?)
- time span of recovery (were many coins and/ or other objects made of precious metal found within a short period of time, for example during one or very few field surveys?)

The answers to these questions will often be subjective rather than measurable and involve experience as well as local knowledge.

The problems of interpretation are illustrative: can we distinguish between series of single finds (or single depositions) of coins and larger depositions containing a sometimes considerable number of coins within the same area as numerous other finds?

I would maintain that in many cases it is difficult if not outright hazardous to attempt any strict division between single finds and hoards. I am inclined to acknowledge the uncertainties rather than press the material unduly. In the present work I therefore decided to avoid distinction between denarii from hoard(s) and from single finds in the quantitative analyses of material from the large sites.

On sites such as Sorte Muld and Smørenge I am in no doubt that at least one major hoard and some single finds have been recovered, but I cannot set a clear-cut division line between the coin scatter from the hoard(s) and the single find(s). It is useful to examine the difference in the surface preservation of coins from the Smørenge hoard(s) and other denarii from Smørenge both coins from the same field as the hoards and coins from neighbouring areas. It has been possible to demonstrate that coins from the Smørenge hoard(s) have characteristics that differ markedly from coins found on the neighbouring field,[74] but it is necessary to acknowledge that the hoard area has also produced coins that compare best with coins from the neighbouring field, as well as coins that cannot with certainty be placed within one group or the other. It is also useful to note that denarii with traces of secondary heating have been found on the same field as the Smørenge hoard(s) and probably should be regarded as part of yet another context *(Fig. 18)*.

It is interesting to note that pierced coins from Smørenge have been found at some distance from the hoard(s). Similarly, the two pierced denarii from Sorte Muld are found far from the centre of the hoard cluster. (See also discussion in Part II, below).

The most problematic finds are probably not the large hoards containing for example more than hundred coins. But many denarius hoards from northern Europe are much smaller, containing perhaps only a dozen denarii. If ploughed up and scattered over an area of more than 50 x 50 m a small hoard will only be detected in circumstances comparable to the find situation of the Orup Hoard, where there are no 'background finds' – no other coins of the same period, and even better: no other finds at all.

While it is very hard to establish which denarii originally belonged to a hoard in an area with other denarius finds, it becomes increasingly difficult to establish the original composition of a hoard if it was a mixed hoard (consisting of both coins and other valuables) found on a site with many other objects. In these cases neither a study of surface preservation nor the coin structure are of any help. One such case is the Nr. Fuglesang Hoard (the Frennegård/Hallbrøndshøj site in the Ibsker complex) containing both denarii and other valuables. In this particular case we can interpret the finds of a number of objects as deriving from the same deposition because of the observations in the field (the finds appeared during one and the same survey), knowledge of the ploughing pattern of this particular field, and the distribution pattern of the finds.

Several settlements have produced a small number of denarii found scattered over a very large area, and they would often be described as single finds (stray finds). Yet, in some cases there is a single pair of de-

---

74 Horsnæs 2006b.

narii preserved in a stack, or one or more denarii that have a corrosion pattern with the central part of (one of the) faces of the coin being brighter and less corroded than the rim area. This pattern is characteristic of coins that have been in a stack that only recently has been taken apart *(Fig. 19)*. This may be caused by a small stack of denarii being split by the tossing around of the archaeological material in the plough layer during agricultural works. If other denarii from the same site have markedly different surface preser-

– the type in question in the hoard. This may in consequence lead to unfortunate circular arguments. The assignment or exclusion of a single coin to a hoard may change the date of the hoard considerably and create a domino effect at the interpretative level. This uncertainty at the first level of registration and interpretation of a find must therefore always be kept in mind. The arguments for the assignment of Roman coins to hoards on sites with multiple finds are presented and discussed in Part II.

Fig. 18. Stacked and partly melted coins from Smørenge. FP 6646.21. (top, c.6 coins) and FP 6646.22 (buttom).

Fig. 19. Two denarii from Bukkegård with discolouration indicating that each must have been preserved in soil close to another coin. FP 6463.1 and FP 7238.2.

Terminus post quem and deposition date – a difficult relationship

The production date of a coin is normally better known than that of any other archaeological find. Therefore the deposition of a coin or an assemblage of objects, as well as of an archaeological layer, is often based on a coin date. The numismatic *t.p.q.* (*terminus post quem*: time after which) is defined as the earliest possible production date of the latest coin in the assemblage. But when the coin *t.p.q.* assigned to for example a coin hoard becomes a figure in a long list of dates, it has an unfortunate tendency not to be interpreted as 'the earliest possible deposition date' (*terminus non ante quem*), as it should be when quoted in other literature, but to become *the* deposition date. As a consequence, Roman denarii struck in the period

vation and/or are found at a very large distance from the stacked coins this may be an indication that the settlement has produced both single depositions/losses and small hoards of two or a few coins.

The term hoard is thus based on an interpretation of the individual finds, and the interpretation must be based on a study of all aspects of the coins. Both the inherent information drawn from the coin type and date, and the surface preservation of the individual coin must be taken into account; and an analysis of the coins in their contexts and the spatial distribution must be undertaken. Failure to do so may result in coins being ascribed to – or not ascribed to – a hoard exclusively because we expect to find – or not find

AD 69-193 are often registered as finds from the Roman Iron Age in Denmark in accordance with the production date, but there are numerous instances where a Roman denarius has been found in a context that is considerably later than the coins. The fact that *some* denarii stayed above ground in Barbaricum centuries after their production date in Rome means that dates based on numismatic material alone may be misleading. As will be shown this is certainly the case in Bornholm.

CHAPTER 2

Coins

Denarii

The overwhelming majority, more than 90%, of the Roman coins from Bornholm are Imperial denarii. The earliest coin may be a subæratus stuck in the name of Tiberius and found during detector surveys of the Sylten II area in the Ibsker settlement complex.[75] It is the only denarius from Bornholm that may have been struck before the Neronian coin reform.[76]

Nero is represented by two specimens of the post-reform IVPPITER CVSTOS issues only,[77] and Vitellius and Otho are represented by one denarius each. The Vitellius coin is a detector find from a newly discovered site at Vedby SV,[78] while the Otho denarius was found at Brogård on western Bornholm in an area with possible burials. The latter is mounted in

Fig. 20. The earliest Roman coin from Bornholm. Subæratus, Tiberius RIC 26, found on Sylten II in the Ibsker settlement complex, FP 6074.1.

an unusual rim.[79] Flavian coins are represented by 41 denarii, and there are five denarii struck by Nerva. Thus a slow rise in find numbers only begin during the reigns of Trajan (121 denarii) and Hadrian (239 denarii) to peak during the reigns of the Antonine emperors. Antoninus Pius struck at least 711 of the denarii from Bornholm, and issues of Marcus Aurelius have been found in almost the same numbers: 713 denarii. Calculating the number of coins per year Marcus Aurelius becomes the most prolific issuer of the finds from Bornholm. This pattern contrasts with the remaining parts of Denmark, where the coinages struck during the reign of Antoninus Pius are slightly more common. To the coins assigned to either of these two emperors should be added 33 Antonine denarii that cannot be ascribed to either emperor: Many

---

75 060403 sb 74; BMR 789x606: FP 6074.1; the coin belongs to *RIC* (2nd ed.) type 26, originally minted in Rome 14-37 AD, w. 1.59 g. *AUD* 1999, 271. Cf. also below on the daing of subærati.

76 Butcher & Ponting 2005 have argued the the 'Neronian reform' in reality is a series of complex changes in the Roman mint. Here the traditional distinction between coins struck before and after AD 64 has been maintained for the sake of simplicity.

77 One from the Udmarken hoard(s), the other a detector find from Sylten 2.

78 060105 sb 55; BMR 2674x7: FP 8150.1; *RIC* (2nd ed.) type 109, Rome AD 69.

79 060104 sb 251; BMR 2374x5: FP 6409; *RIC* (2nd ed.) type 12, Rome AD 69. Horsnæs 2002b.

Crossing boundaries

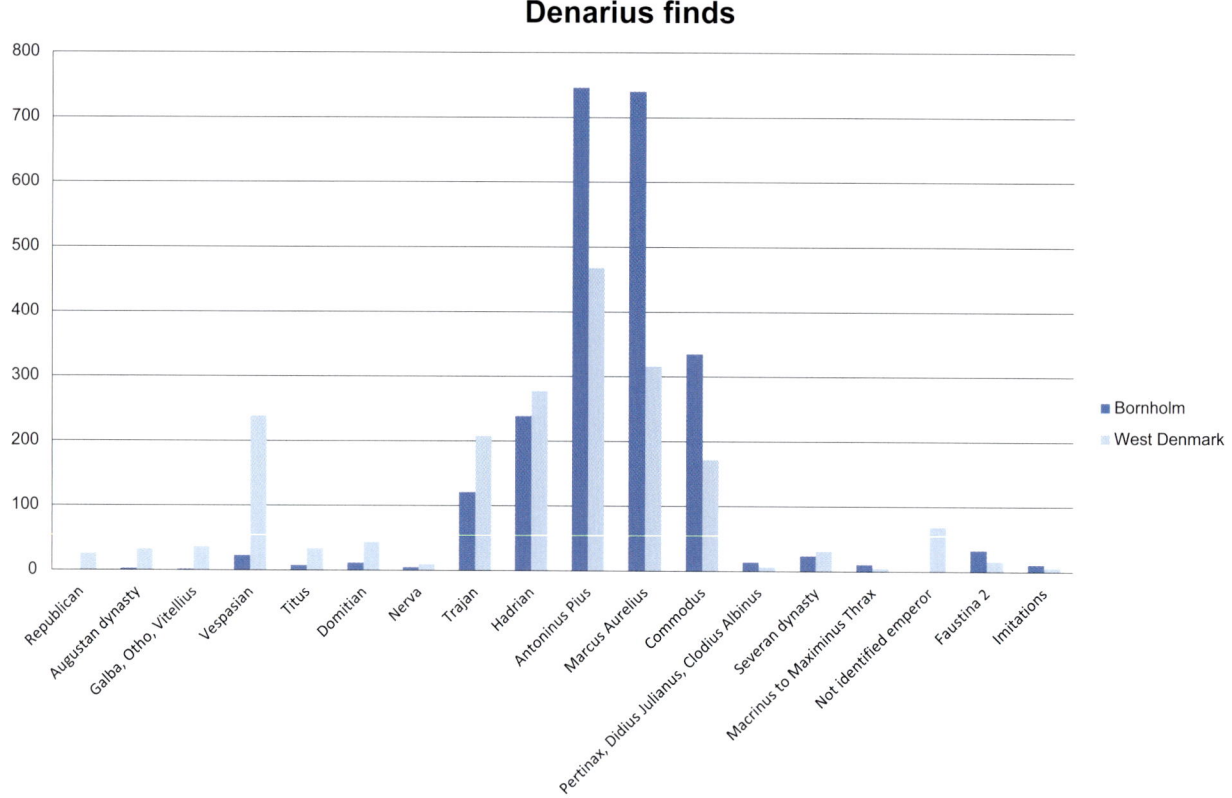

Fig. 21. A. Denarius finds from Bornholm, B. Number of denarii per year in Bornholm, compared to the remaining parts of Denmark. On Bornholm the number of early Imperial coins is negligible, and within the Antonine period the find numbers peak later (cf. Horsnæs 2010, fig. 63 and 66).

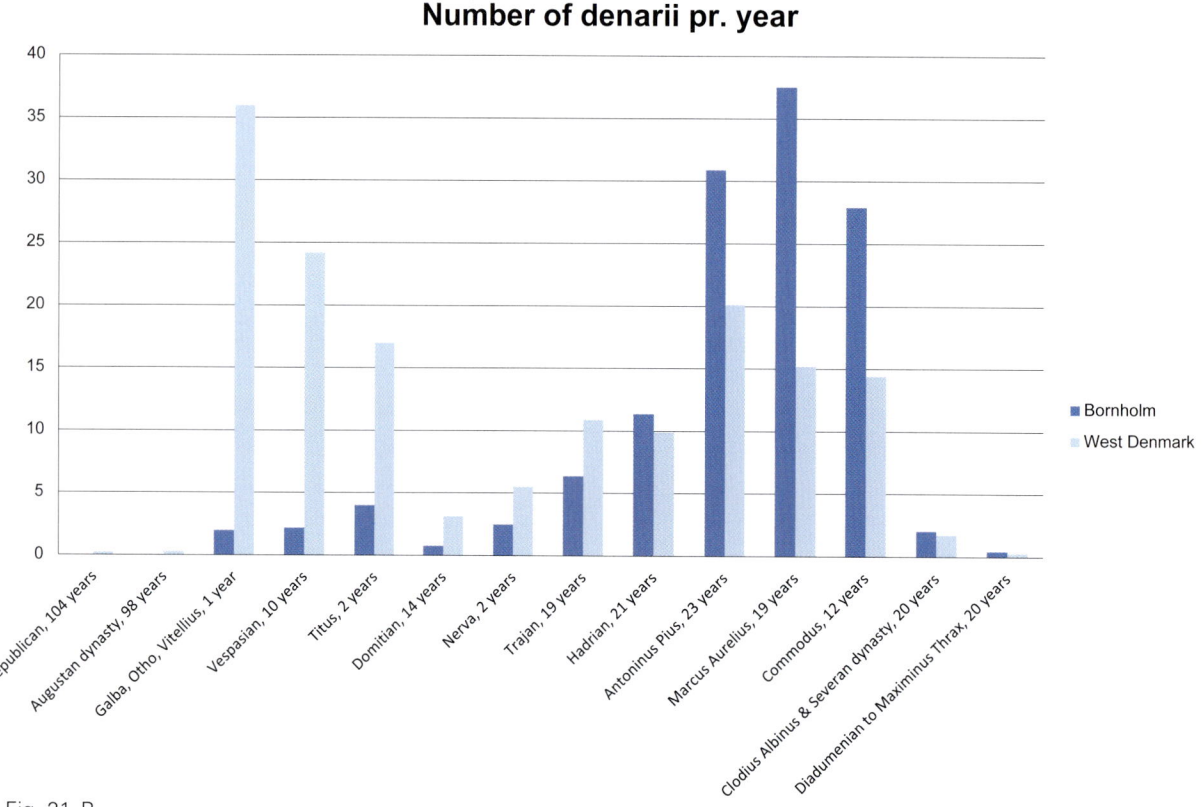

Fig. 21. B.

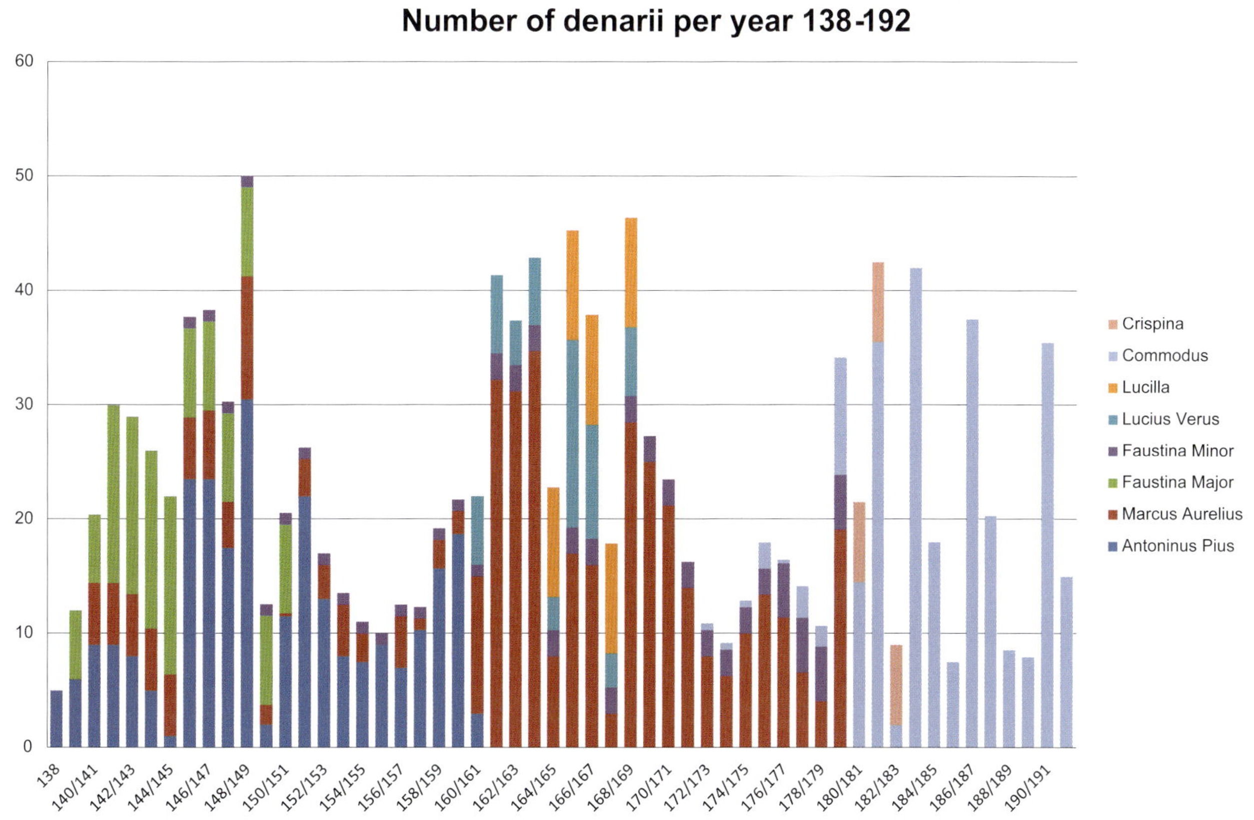

Number of denarii per year 138-192

Fig. 22. Chronological distribution of denarii struck by Antonine emperors from Bornholm (compare Horsnæs 2010a, 128 fig. 67, based on the same principles).

of them carry the portrait of Faustina Minor, others the portrait of Marcus Aurelius as either *caesar* or *augustus*. Commodus is represented by 335 denarii and thus a slightly lower number of coins per year than the preceding emperors.

After the end of the Antonine dynasty in 192 AD the number of denarii from finds in Barbaricum rapidly decline. The period until the end of the Severan dynasty is represented by 41 denarii; but in fact more than half (22) of the Severan coins belong to the first four years of Severus' reign (193-196 AD), while only four denarii can be dated safely within the 20 year period 197-217 AD.[80] The latest denarius issues (Diadumenian to Maximinus Thrax, 217-238 AD) are represented by 12 denarii. This is clearly a much lower number than during the Severan dynasty as a whole, but – although not statistically valid – the 12 coins struck in the two decades 217-238 AD present a small growth in the number of coins per year in comparison with the only four coins from the two decades 197-217 AD. It underscores that the drop in number of denarii found in Bornholm began during the reign of Commodus and came to an almost complete halt after the first years of Septimius Severus' reign, around 196 AD.

Compared to the remaining parts of modern Denmark the denarius finds from Bornholm are chronologically extremely concentrated in the Antonine period, with a smaller number of coins from the reigns of Trajan and Hadrian. A 'Flavian peak' is prominent in finds from Jutland and Sealand but almost totally absent in finds from Bornholm.[81]

The large number of denarii struck by the Antonine emperors present huge variety. Most issues are represented by only one or two specimens. The most common type found on Bornholm is the Antoninus Pius type *RIC* 137, struck in 145-161 AD (cover photo). 14 specimens have been registered (a little less than 2% of the number of coins struck for Antoninus Pius), but no die identical coins have been identified.[82] The

80 The remaining coins are four denarii struck for Julia Domna of undated issues, lost denarii ascribed Septimius Severus, or badly preserved coins that cannot be type identified.

81 Horsnæs 2010, figs. 50 and 70.
82 Searching for die identical coins has not been an is-

specimens are distributed all over the island: four derive from the Smørenge hoard area (sb 144), five come from four different areas in the Ibsker settlement complex, two were found in the Robbedale Hoard, two come from minor sites (Hundshalegård SV and Vellensbygård Syd 2), and one is an early find without provenance. It was a common and widespread type also outside Bornholm.[83] Similarly, the most common Diva Faustina Major issue in Western Denmark and a type commonly found in Barbaricum in general,[84] is known in eight specimens from Bornholm: two from the Robbedale Hoard, five from the Smørenge Hoard area, and one from the Ibsker complex.

In order to identify possible influx periods, the Antonine issues have been inserted into the diagram, *Fig. 22*, and compared to the similar diagram for the remaining parts of Denmark.[85] The comparison shows that in spite of the difference between denarius finds as a whole, there is, as mentioned, a consistency between the two areas regarding finds of Antonine denarii. Of course the number of Antonine denarii, and in particular the issues of Marcus Aurelius, is somewhat larger in Bornholm, but the sudden shifts from a year with many finds to one with few, for example Antoninus Pius' issues of 148/149 compared to 149/150, must be caused by differences in number of types produced in the Roman mint, and thus by the differences in annual mint output. In this way the chronological distribution of the finds from Bornholm support the view that the denarii in Barbaricum were drawn from a stock of circulating coins rather than reflecting special issues made for export directly from the mint.

Chronological composition of denarii from sites with several finds

Only the three early finds of denarius hoards from Borresø, Udmarken and Robbedale come from sites where no other denarius finds have surfaced. Several more hoards have been discovered, but in all cases they may be 'contaminated' by denarii not deposited as part of the hoards; hence it has proved impossible to make clear-cut distinctions between denarii from one or more hoards and single finds from the same site. Though is it sometimes possible to argue that one or a group of denarii from a site could not be part of a hoard from the same site, this is difficult to prove. Excluding those coins that possibly did not belong to a hoard from statistic analysis may also create a false pattern and lead to circular arguments. The chronological structure of the three above-mentioned denarius hoards has therefore been compared with the structure of *all* the denarii from each site that has produced more than 10 denarii (large and medium sized assemblages). Likewise the chronological structure of all denarii from small and medium size assemblages (in practice all denarii except the finds from Ibsker, Smørenge and the Robbedale and Udmarken Hoards) taken together have been compared to the finds from sites with more than 10 denarii.

The comparison has revealed a remarkable consistency in the chronological composition of finds from Bornholm. As already noted the denarius material as a whole is quite 'late', with less than 20% pre-Antonine denarii and less than 50% pre-Aurelius coins. The two large hoards from Robbedale and Udmarken are together with the coins from Smørenge among the latest assemblages: in these sites only *c.* 15% of the denarii are pre-Antonine, and little more than 40% of the coins were produced before the beginning of the reign of Marcus Aurelius in AD 161. The material from the Ibsker complex as a whole has yielded a slightly larger number of pre-Antonine denarii (*c.* 22%) as well as a larger number of coins struck before AD 161 (*c.* 54%). The chronological composition of the total number of denarii from medium size and small size assemblages taken together fit the same pattern. Slight oscillations are only seen in few sites with a small number of finds, and are therefore apt to be caused by statistical uncertainties.

Subærati

Subæratus is here used as the common denominator for denarii struck on what is essentially a bimetallic blank, consisting of a core of bronze covered by a thin layer of silver.[86] Subærati are known almost since the beginning of coinage. In Rome they were probably

---

sue in the present work.

83   Five specimens are known from the remaining parts of Denmark.

84   Antoninus Pius type RIC 351; discussed by Lind 1988, 191.

85   The diagrams have been built up according to the same principles for dividing the undated issues (the Antoninus Pius COS III and COS IIII, the issues in the name of the empresses etc.) over a span of years.

---

86   Other common terms are: plated denarius, fourrée.

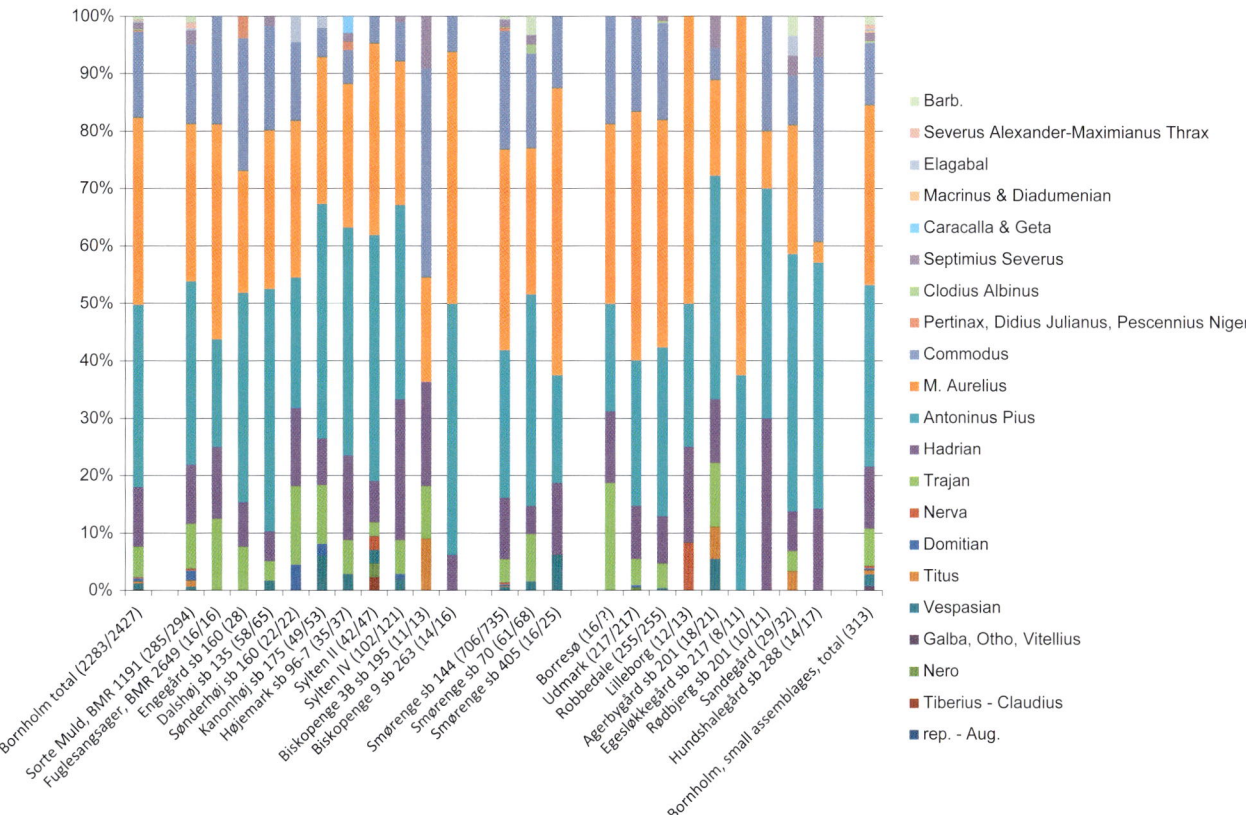

Fig. 23. Chronological composition of all denarius finds from Bornholm compared with sites with: A. Sites from Ibsker parish with +10 denaranii; B. Sites from Smørenge; C. other sites with +10 denarii; D. Total of all sites with <10 denarii. In parenthesis: number of denarii in diagram/total number of denarii from the site. In general c. 10% of the coins have not been identified. In most cases this is due to bad state of conservation. In the case of the Borresø Hoard we do not know the original number of coins from the hoard. In order to facilitate comparison of the chronological structure of finds from Bornholm with finds from other areas the unidentified denarii are not included in the diagram.

produced both within the official mint (die identities between subærati and regular denarii), and in other places. In particular the subærati minted in Augusta Raurica near present-day Basel are well researched, and they present types used in the official mint from AD 134/138 to the end of the 2nd century. Still, the dies and the die-links between the coins produced in the workshop prove that they must all be dated within the period 195-210.[87] It is therefore clear that the subærati may be considerably younger than the date indicated by the coin type/legend.

A number of different production techniques have been suggested. Several thin section analyses of subærati have revealed distinct differences between the bronze core (also known as *anima*), the silver surface and between them an eutectic layer of fused bronze and silver, probably resulting from a mechanic application of a silver foil on top of the core (like the wrapping of chocolate coins!). Analyses of the Augusta Raurica blanks and subærati alike, however, presented a gradual transition from the bronze core to a surface made of a silver alloy with a considerable content of copper, and it is suggested that the blanks were silvered using a relatively simple reflow technique (*Aufschmelzverfahren*), where the thin foil of the silver alloy was placed on a blank by means of a flux and heated until it melted onto the blank.[88]

It is generally acknowledged that it must have been almost impossible for the ordinary user to tell whether a coin was a subæratus or a regular denarius: the surface colour of the two would have been identical, and although it is suggested that the average weight of a subæratus would be slightly lower than the normal weight of a denarius, the deviations in weight among regular issues was so large that it would pass unnoticed. Even today, only metallurgical analysis of

---

87 Peter 1990.

88 Peter 1990, in particular 28-29.

Fig. 24. Possible subærati. Coin flaked into a thin silver shell with adhering bronze, FP 5448.4; coins with bronze core visible underneath the silver surface, FP 6241 and FP 6266.1; thin bronze cores of subærati, FP 8108.11 and FP 8108.12; heavily corroded and flaking coin, FP 8491.10.

a well preserved coin could reveal that it is not silver all through.

It has been possible to list 33 possible subærati, corresponding to 1.4% of the total number of denarii from Bornholm, distributed over most of the island. The major sites such as Smørenge and the Ibsker complex have both yielded specimens.

Many of the coins classified as subærati are quite badly preserved. There are a number of cases where the relatively well preserved silver surface of the subæratus is cracked open and offers a good view to a heavily corroded core. I assume that these subærati may have been produced by wrapping good silver foil around the bronze core. I other cases we have coins were the silver (or silver alloy) surface is altogether worn away, leaving only a very lightweight bronze core. Still, the motif – in particular the portrait on the obverse – is visible, albeit heavily worn.

Implications

While studying the denarius finds from the Przeworsk culture settlement in Jakuszowice (northern part of Małopolska/Little Poland), Aleksander Bursche noted a very high number of subærati among the material. At Jakuszowice 109 Roman coins were found: 101 were denarii, of which 26% were identified as subærati. During excavations three denarii were found in dated primary contexts of the 'jüngere römische und spätrömische Kaiserzeit'. The remaining Roman coins were 45 coins found during excavations but outside primary context and 61 coins found during metal detector surveys in an area measuring more than 200 x 75 m, 60 m distant from the excavation area.[89] All coins were, however, deemed to belong to the same phase as the above-mentioned context dated coins and were interpreted as single finds.

Bursche suggested that there is a difference in the proportion of subærati depending on the deposition circumstances, subærati being much rarer in hoards than among single finds (or rather: single depositions) from settlements. The reason for these differences

---

89   Distance measured from plan in Bursche *et al*. 2000, fig. 3.

should be sought in the sources for the coins found in Barbaricum: hoards deriving from large tribute payments in the wake of the Marcomannic wars, while single depositions derived from small scale exchange, where the 'Barbarians' were likely to be cheated by the Romans.[90]

The fact that Jakuszowice is so far the only published site with such a high proportion of subærati is, according to Bursche, explained by the difficulties in recognizing subærati, in fact Jakuszowice the *only* site in Barbaricum where a significant number of denarii have been subject to metal analysis. This may result in the number of identified subærati being lower than the actual figure, a problem that also applies in the case of Bornholm: Even though it has been possible to identify some subærati in the material there is a serious risk that in particular some of the well preserved subærati have escaped notice during registration.[91] I believe that the very large differences in the surface colour and texture seen on denarii from the same site most often reflect post-depositional changes caused by the soil composition, but it is certainly possible that also the inherent properties of the metallic composition, for example the fineness of the silver, is causing or accelerating corrosion and other post-depositional changes.

It has not been possible to verify whether subærati have a different distribution pattern from silver denarii. Robbedale is the only preserved denarius hoard where the coins are safe from mixture with single finds of denarii, and the fact that the denarii from the Robbedale hoard are very homogeneous lends some support to Bursche's view. Yet, a single subæratus was indeed noted among the coins of the Robbedale hoard. The photos of the cleaned and restored coins from both the Sorte Muld 1988 and the Smørenge 1983 hoard excavations present homogeneous pictures, but it is not possible to make clear distinctions between coins from these hoards and single finds, and it must be stressed that coins classified as subærati have been found at Smørenge, both in the hoard area (sb 144), and on the neighbouring field (sb 70).

Denarius imitations

Among the denarii it has been possible to identify 13 so-called Barbarian imitations.[92] There are considerable differences between them, and they probably represent various production areas and/or traditions, but none of them has been linked by die identity to known specimens. Three of the imitations are very heavy and dark (blackish green), but some of the coins ascribed to official issues looks much the same. One of the very dark imitations presents an obverse based on a Marcus Aurelius or Commodus portrait, and a reverse based on the Apollo Moneta issue of Commodus (*RIC* 205, AD 190); the legend is illegible. Another of the same texture is only partly preserved and cannot be identified exactly, but carries a female portrait and a distorted legend. Both were found on the Skovgård settlement.[93] A third specimen with a similar colouring is based on an Antoninus Pius prototype with a reverse showing a female figure (SALVS?) making an offering from a patera over a lighted altar and with a cornucopia(?) in left hand. The legend is illegible.[94]

A single imitation presents only a faint shadow of what may have been an obverse portrait that has been hammered flat. The reverse seems to be based on a prototype of a seated person facing left. Most important are the illegible legends, which on both obverse and reverse consist of the letters T and I alternating.[95]

Three imitations were found during the excavation of the Smørenge Hoard: two are based on Faustina

---

90   Bursche 1996b, 39; 2011, 70.
91   It was not possible to review all denarii from Bornholm within the timeframe of the present work, and no specific gravity testing or metallurgical analysis has been carried out. Moreover, as noted above (Chapter 1), the majority of the coins found since the 1990's have never been professionally cleaned/conserved, a fact which seriously affect the possibility of identifying subærati.

92   Again it must be stressed that this number is a minimum. Several unidentified imitations may hide among the many uncleaned and/or heavily worn denarii. A hybrid is has been counted among the imitations, although it might be Roman: From Sorte Muld (Ibsker) 060403 sb 93; BMR 1191x1764R, FP 6920.1, Antoninus Pius *RIC* 115-6/ Trajan *RIC* 119.
93   060104 sb 235; BMR 2001x97; FP 5810.1 and 2001x110; FP 6082.1.
94   Sønderhøj Syd (Ibsker) 060403 sb 169; BMR 802x178; FP 6546.3.
95   Sorte Muld (Ibsker) 060403 sb 93; BMR 1191x1516R; FP 6688.10.

Fig. 25. Imitations of denarii. Very dark imitations: FP 5810.1, FP 6082.1, FP 6546.3; very thin imitation with non-sensical legend: FP 6688.10; imitation with distorted legend: FP 5965.

Fig. 26. Fragment of denarius imitation with cuts from Smørenge, FP 6930.20.

Fig. 27. Slashed denarius from Sorte Muld, FP 5464.46.

Minor and one on a Commodus prototype.[96] The neighbouring field in Smørenge has since then yielded a single imitation with a distinct Marcus Aurelius (Caesar?) portrait and a more schematic reverse with a standing female (Providentia holding globe and cornucopia?). Both legends are distorted.[97] Finally an imitation of a Commodus/Aequitas with illegible legends was found in the Robbedale Hoard.[98]

The last group is comparable to European imitations with recognizable portraits, although no die links to any of the published specimens have been identified. The possible production dates of the imitations run from late 2nd to mid-3rd centuries.[99]

Reworked denarii

Many denarii are fragmented when found, but the breaks are not results of deliberate reworking of the coin. As shown by the examples where fragments of the same coin have found during surveys, the frag-

---

96 Kromann & Watt 1984, 34, however, only two Faustina Minor imitations were mentioned in the register of The Royal Collection of Coins and Medals. One of the Faustina Minor imitations was published in Kromann & Watt 1984, 33 fig. 7.21. The coins have not been restudied.
97 060305 sb 144; BMR 1469x108; FP 5965.
98 060304 sb 20; FP 636.180. Jørgensen 1900, 40 fig. 3; Breitenstein 1944, 7-33, no. 2.180 and fig. 4.
99 The imitations have been discussed by several scholars, notably Lind, Stribrny and Peter, cf. short summary in Horsnæs 2010, 135-138 and most recently Bursche 2011, 19-23.

mentation must in general be regarded as post-depositional changes of the coins.

Deliberate cutting of Roman denarii is very rarely seen.[100] A fragment of a Marcus Aurelius (imitation) from Smørenge has suffered deep criss-crossing cuts of the otherwise wholly illegible reverse, and some parallel cuts on the obverse.[101] A denarius from Sorte Muld struck for Julia Domna has two deep, parallel cuts across the portrait of the empress. Furthermore the edges of the coin have been filed down.[102] The cuts may be probes, but other possible explanations, such as deliberate mutilation of the portrait, cannot be left out.

The most common reworking of the Roman denarii is a pierced or punched (drilled) hole. The piercing can be distinguished by the metal being pressed out from one side, but preserved as a small bulge on the other side. It is often possible to see that the piercing has been made from the obverse of the coin. The punched or drilled hole is often much more regular, and characterized by a sharp cut.

In one case the hole was filled in with silver, while another coin has a hole filled with bronze. In the latter case the surface of the bronze indicates that it was broken, and it is interpreted as the remains of a partly broken off bronze rivet. A denarius from Dalshøj/Ibsker is slightly flattened around the hole, and it is probably another trace of a loop that had been riveted onto the coin. The use of loops fastened with rivets is attested from western Denmark. The best dated case is that of a siliqua (produced 340-351 AD) from the female burial at Torstorp Vesterby (Sealand) dated in period C3.[103]

Less commonly the coin is entirely preserved, but has been inserted into a mounting. A denarius found at Brogård (western Bornholm) was mounted in a silver frame with a now broken off loop. In this case the the loop is positioned above the head, but this was not the case in a parallel example from the Skovgårde cemetery in Sealand.[104]

A denarius struck by Antoninus Pius (or perhaps Hadrian) found at Mulebygård has been hammered flat on both sides of the imperial portrait. It is possible that the hammering was a preparation for mounting of the coin. The reverse present an unidentified motif.[105]

The position of the hole/loop in relation to the portrait of the coins is remarkable: the hole is placed above the head on four denarii, on eight coins it is in front of the head,[106] and on eight denarii the hole is placed behind the head. The only position completely lacking is a hole placed below the portrait. Thus there seems to be no arguments to interpret the reworking of the coin as an attempt to use the imperial portrait as a particular image. The die position of the denarii is most commonly 6 or 12; therefore both the obverse and the reverse motif would be seen 'lying down' if the coin was suspended from something.[107] The evidence seems self-contradictory: On the one hand the fact that the piercing is almost invariably made from the obverse would indicate that the obverse was the more important motif for the one who pierced the coin. On the other hand, the imperial portrait would rarely be seen upright when the coin was suspended. In fact upside-down would be the only way the emperor would *not* be seen, but from other areas there are examples of piercings made below the head of the emperor,[108] so the lack of this position in the material so far recovered from Bornholm may be purely accidental. Perhaps this contradiction can tell us that the non-Roman who pierced the coin had some

---

100 A badly preserved silver coin was initially interpreted as a denarius. It was quartered and pecks have been cut into the edges (a small part has been secondarily broken off). The coin was found on the Vellensbygård NØ site, where all other material is dated in the Viking Age and Medieval Period. The pecking is a Viking Age phenomenon, and if the coin indeed can be identified as a denarius, it must have been cut and pecked in the Viking Age. However, the identification of the coin as a denarius fragment is not convincing, it has therefore been left out of the discussion of the denarii. 060303 sb 207. BMR 2361x113, FP 6853.1, w. 1.06. Photo: Horsnæs 2010, 445 fig. 11.
101 060305 sb 144, BMR 766x825, inv.no. FP 6930.20.
102 060403 sb 93, BMR 1191x769, inv.no. FP 5464.46.
103 Horsnæs 2010, 169.

104 Parallels in Western Denmark: Horsnæs 2010, 167.
105 060302 sb 124. FP 7628.1, BMR 2812x143.
106 Including one denarius with portrait l., FP 7392, where the hole is thus on the left side of the portrait; and one denarius found on Dalshøj 2011 and not registered until 2012.
107 The same pattern is visible in Western Denmark, where only one of eight reworked denarii had been mounted in order to present the Imperial portrait correctly.
108 For example a denarius from Bregentved, Funen, cf. Horsnæs 2010, 167-168 and fig. 91.

Crossing boundaries

Fig. 28. Pierced denarii, FP 5044.6, FP 5228.3, FP 5459.1, FP 6646.13, FP 6693.1, FP 7106.2 (opposite page, left), FP 7260, FP 7271.2, FP 7392, FP 7422.1, FP 8087.2, FP 8295.2 (opposite page, right), FP 8295.4, FP 8437.1 (above).

sensation that the portrait was the more important face of the coin, and therefore instinctively turned this side up when piercing the hole. But still the image had so little meaning for the onlooker that no attempt was made to make it hang upright.

We do not know where the reworking of the coins took place. Pierced denarii are found widely dispersed in Barbaricum and seem to be a non-Roman phenomenon. The very simple techniques employed required no special skills and could have been done almost anywhere, including Bornholm.

The geographical distribution on Bornholm of the reworked denarii is somewhat odd. It is no surprise that a considerable number were found in the two areas with the largest number of denarius finds. Eight of 21 reworked denarii were found within the Ibsker settlement complex and four derive from Smørenge. It is more surprising that there are five reworked coins from the cluster of settlement sites between Hasle and Klemensker (060401) and three from the recently located settlement sites in the inland area of southeastern Bornholm (in the border area between the Bodilsker and Åker parishes 060201 and 060205). The denarii found on the fields of Glasergård and Brogård are the only examples where a reworked denarius may cautiously be connected to a possible burial site.[109]

Fig. 29. Denarius from Dalshøj Nord III/Engegård, Ibsker, with filled-in hole. FP 7254.3.

Fig. 30. Denarius from Ndr. Brændesgård, Ibsker, with remains of rivet. FP 8473.1.

Fig. 31. Denarius from Dalshøj, Ibsker, area around hole is hammered flat. FP 6551.6.

Fig. 32. Denarius from Brogård inserted into silver mount. FP 6409.

None of the reworked denarii can be safely connected to hoards: no pierced denarii were part of the Robbedale Hoard, nor are they represented among the 12 preserved denarii from Borresø.[110] 16 of the

---

109   060405 sb 376.

110   Breitenstein 1944, 33-35; Klindt-Jensen 1957, fig. 128.

Crossing boundaries

Fig. 33. Denarius from Mulebygård hammered flat on both sides of portrait. FP 7628.1 (obverse and reverse).

original 217 denarii from Udmarken were studied by Breitenstein, and none were reworked. The remaining coins were originally described only in very general terms as much worn, and we have no way of determining whether any of them had been pierced or not.[111]

Two denarii from the Sorte Muld site are pierced. Both are unusual types: one is a hybrid subæratus (possibly a barbarian imitation), the other is unusually late: it was struck by Severus Alexander. Both were found more than 50 m from the densest cluster of denarius finds, which must be interpreted as the probable deposition area of the denarius hoard. Similarly, the two pierced denarii from Smørenge are among those picked up furthest away from the cluster of coins. They were both found more than 100 m from the denarius hoard excavated in 1983, and also lack the surface characteristics of the denarii from the densest cluster of finds.

Burials with coin finds show that the reworked denarii (as well as later Roman coins) have been worn as beads in necklaces, mostly but not exclusively in female burials. Other functions, for example as dress ornaments, are possible.

Denarii in graves

Coins are rarely found in graves. In spite of the very large number of Iron Age burials excavated and published only three examples are known from Bornholm.[112] All were found in cemeteries on the southern

---

111 Breitenstein 1944, 5 no. 1.
112 There are a few cases (Brogård, Stangehøj/Glasergård) where the find circumstances of a single denarius suggest that it cannot be excluded that it derived from a burial – or in more general terms: a cemetery, but the evidence is highly uncertain and cannot lead to conclusions at present.

Fig. 34. The coins from Rævekulebakke. Photo Bornholms Museum

part of the island.[113] In two of the cases the burial was dated in the later part of period C1b (mid-3rd century), based on analysis of pottery from the burials. The last burial, Rævekulebakke, contained a number of objects, but no pottery. Therefore a dating to period C1b/C2 is based on the coins, the latest of which was struck by Severus Alexander in AD 223.[114]

The three coin graves are of outmost chronological importance as they show that some denarii were un-

---

113 The relevant sites were discussed by Heidemann Lutz 2010, 225-226 and Karte 70.
114 Heidemann Lutz 2010, 329 with references.

doubtedly present in Bornholm from the mid-3rd century. This is in agreement with the remaining parts of Denmark. But while there are examples of coin graves from C2 and C3 in Sealand and Funen, these have not been found in Bornholm. Why? One obvious reason is that coins are among the very rare object types from burials in general, and that the number of known burials on Bornholm drops significantly after the mid-3rd century, though a limited number of smaller cemeteries *are* known. A second reason may be that the coin types found in C2 and C3 burials from Sealand and Funen (aurei, Barbarian imitations, siliquae) have not been encountered in Bornholm, and therefore were not available in the area in periods C2 to C3.

Denarii from other dated contexts

During Klindt-Jensen's excavations at Dalshøj a denarius was for the first time found in an archaeological context. It was a denarius struck by Marcus Aurelius found in the floor level in the western part of Dalshøj House A, and interpreted as belonging to an Early Germanic Iron Age (Migration Period) phase of the house.[115] The same may be inferred for another denarius found outside the house, but it must be stressed that neither of the coins seems to derive from a closed context.

A denarius struck by Commodus was found on a settlement site in Nexø (1973) in a layer with pottery, animal bones and burnt daub. A fragment of a bone comb from the layer is dated in 'the Late Roman Iron Age or later'. Among the pottery no fragments are characteristic of either the Early Roman or the Early Germanic Iron Ages. This layer is overlaid by a layer of burnt material (stratum 2) and the top layer (stratum 1) that *mainly* – but not exclusively – contained material from the 'later part of the Early Iron Age', i.e. the Roman Iron Age. The context date of the denarius is therefore most probably the Late Roman or perhaps the Early Germanic Iron Age.[116] An unidentified denarius was found in a pit during excavations at Vasagård (1988/1993). The pit contained Iron Age

Fig. 35. Denarius found inside House A, Dalshøj. FP 2273.18.

material; among the finds were sherds of relatively thin-walled pottery with a blackish surface, as well as a decorated fragment of a lighter ware with a high hatched bulb and low furrows, similar to material dated by Jørgensen in the Early Germanic Iron Age (his phases 7-8).[117] Thus the earliest possible deposition date for this denarius would be in the second half of the 4th century, but possibly even somewhat later. Nothing excludes deposition more or less at the same time as the solidus hoard from Vasagård, but it is clear that the there is no connection between the denarius and the hoard.[118]

The fact that there are only three context-dated single finds of Roman coins from settlement excavations reveals the difficulties encountered when attempting to discuss the possible period of use of the denarii. First of all there are few coins from archaeologically well defined contexts, secondly context-dates estab-

Fig. 36. Fragment of decorated ware from pit VAS III at Vasagård, scale 1:1. Photo Bornholms Museum.

---

115 Klindt-Jensen 1957, 17 fig. 14,4 and fig. 11 no. 21. FP 2273.18.
116 Kromann 1983-84, 113-114 no. 53 (ill.), where the house with the Roman coin is dated in the Viking Age/Early Medieval Period. I thank René Laursen who found the description of the archaeological layers in the original excavation note books preserved in Bornholms Museum.

117 Jørgensen 1989.
118 The denarius was lost, and all notice of it disappeared from archives. I thank Finn Ole Nielsen for the information deriving from his personal excavation diaries.

Crossing boundaries

Fig. 37. Siliquae from Brændesgård, FP 5236.3 and Agerbygård, FP 8500.1.

lished by non-numismatic material result in quite a broad time span: The denarii were found in layers/pits that belong to either the (Late?) Roman Iron Age (Nexø) or the Early Germanic Iron Age (Dalshøj and Vasagård), covering the years *c.* AD 200-550 in terms of absolute chronology.

Siliquae

Roman silver coins struck after the Constantinian reforms in the early 4th century are normally called siliquae. They are not commonly found in Barbaricum.[119] It is therefore a bit surprising that two specimens have appeared in Bornholm. Both belong to late 4th century issues of the western mints and both are clipped in the manner commonly seen on finds from Britain.[120] One coin was furthermore pierced and has the remains of a possible loop.

While the Late Roman siliquae from the Western mints are very common in Britain, they constitute an emerging class of finds in Barbaricum. Until recently few finds were noted, but during the last years several new specimens have appeared. No less than seven

Fig. 38. Solidi from Højemark, FP 8096.6, and from Sønderhøj, FP 8162.5.

specimens appeared as part of a *Hacksilber* hoard found at Høgsbrogård near Ribe in 2009,[121] but there are also new finds from Gudme and northeastern Sealand,[122] and the first specimen from Scania (southern Sweden) appeared in late 2010.[123] While the coins are struck in the late 4th century they are invariably found in contexts from the late 5th or perhaps early 6th century in Denmark and northwestern Europe.

Solidi

Solidi have been found on more than 40 sites in Bornholm. The number of finds is growing continuously, but at a much slower pace than the finds of denarii.[124] In 2008-2010 two new finds appeared, both from sites belonging to the Ibsker complex: A Theodosius II solidus

---

119 Horsnæs 2010a, 138-144.
120 From Brændesgård 5-6 area, Ibsker, 060403 sb 107; BMR 1653x52: FP 5236.3. W. 0.75 g. Unidentified emperor and mint. Clip factor 4 (Guest 2005); and from Agerbygård, Østerlars. 060405 sb 201; BMR 1523x732: FP 8500.1. W. 0.70 g. It was probably struck in Milan (397-402 AD) by Arcadius or Honorius, cf. Guest 2005 no. 708 or 724. Clip factor 4.

121 Feveile 2010.
122 Gudme area II (Funen): FP 8470.4; Nordgårde (Sealand): FP 8251.1.
123 Aspeborg 2012.
124 Full catalogue of finds known until 2008 was published as Horsnæs 2009.

Coins

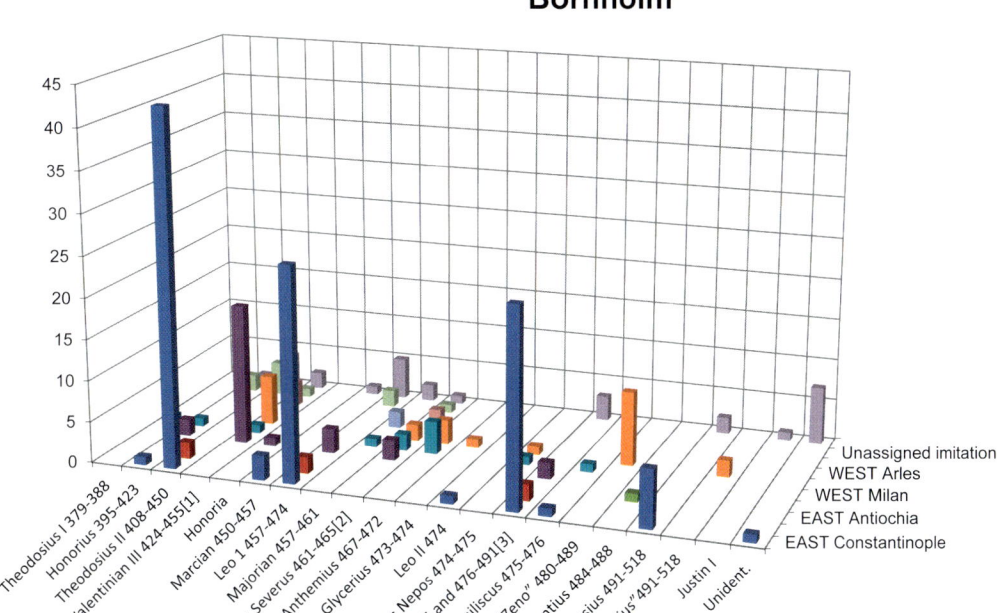

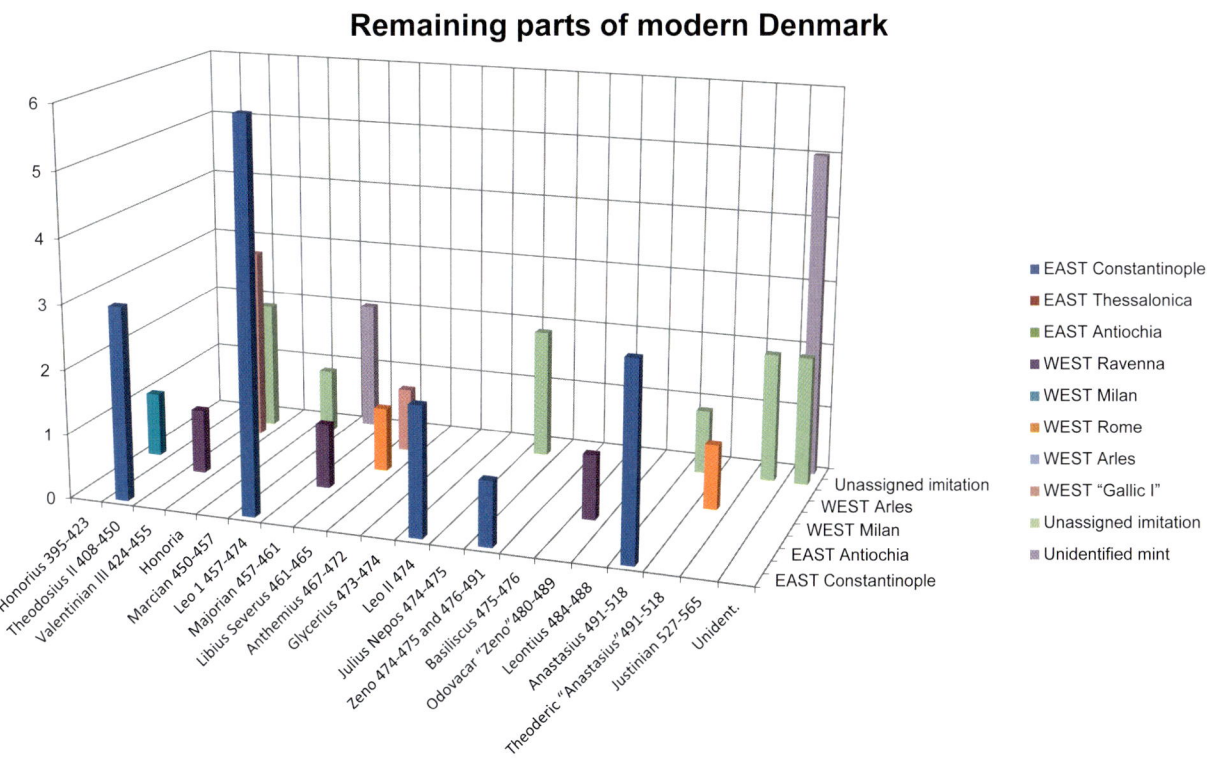

Fig. 39. Diagrams illustrating the distribution of emperors and mints of Late Roman solidi found on Bornholm compared to finds from the remaining parts of present-day Denmark. Note the differences in the absolute number of finds.

struck at Constantinople in 430-440 AD was found at Højemark in an area that had already produced two solidi.[125] An unidentified solidus from Sønderhøj was heavily damaged; it was bent and deliberately beaten flat.[126]

Furthermore two old finds should be added to the hitherto published find lists: A solidus was found near Bekkegård in Klemensker parish in the 19th century and is known only from archival evidence,[127] and a gold coin was found west of Stensgård and sold to a goldsmith around 1945. The goldsmith declared that is was a Chinese coin, which is highly unlikely. There are finds from both Iron Age and Viking Age in the area, and it cannot be excluded that the coin was a solidus.[128] Including these additions the total number of solidi found on Bornholm has reached 225 and almost doubled since the publication of 129 solidi in Fagerlie's seminal work on Late Roman solidi.[129]

Half the Late Roman solidi were struck in the mint of Constantinople and only *c.* 1/3 were struck in various western mints. Non-imperial or even Barbaric issues are rare. The number of coins from the first half of the 5th century is relatively high, but also the reigns of Leo and Zeno are well represented.

Most of the hoards from Bornholm are relatively small and it is therefore hard to put much weight on similarities and differences. The two largest hoards, Soldatergård with 36 solidi and Saltholmgård with 29 solidi, both have a preponderance of solidi struck by Theodosius II, Leo I, and Zeno in the mint of Constantinople and a numismatic *t.p.q.* after 491 AD, but also the smaller hoards have Constantinople as the most prolific mint and present a large chronological spectrum covering most of the 5th century.

The Fuglesangsager I and II hoards are the only finds with a very narrow chronological spectrum of the coins and there are several die links within the Fuglesangsager I hoard. They are also the only hoards that have an numismatic *t.p.q.* (435 AD) theoretically allowing a deposition date before the mid-5th century, but in these cases the most commonly used chronology of the Nordic bracteates found with the coins raise the deposition date to at least the second half of the 5th century, and possibly even later.[130]

Reworked solidi

The majority of the solidi are extremely well preserved. Only few have been reworked: either by transforming the coin into a piece of jewellery, by piercing or drilling a hole or by adding a loop, or by cutting up the solidus into smaller pieces.

Twelve solidi have a pierced hole. They derive from five different hoards and one single find. The Saltholmgård hoard from Ibsker parish has yielded six pierced coins out of 29 solidi in the hoard. In all six cases the holes seem to be pierced from the obverse, and on five of the six coins the hole is positioned in the lower half of the obverse.[131] The Dalshøj hoard produced one solidus with a pierced and refilled hole,[132] and also one of the solidi found recently in the area close to the position of the Dalshøj hoard has been pierced.[133] It is possible that this coin may have belonged to the hoard.

The Kåsbygård, Soldatergård and Almindingen/Ravnebro hoards have each yielded a single pierced solidus. The Kåsbygård (one out of 14 solidi)[134] and Soldatergård (one out of 35 solidi)[135] coins were pierced from the obverse above the portrait. The coin from the Ravnebro hoard (one out of six solidi) had a relatively large, pierced hole above the imperial portrait, but the hole had been refilled.[136] The possible single find from 'a field at Svaneke' of a solidus with a small pierced hole left of the portrait cannot be more exactly provenanced.[137]

The position of the holes varies. The majority of the solidi of the Saltholmgård Hoard were pierced from the obverse below rather than above the imperial portrait, and the single find from Dalshøj was pierced from the reverse above the head of the figure of Constantinople and thus below the imperial portrait. The

---

125 060403 sb 96: FP 8096.6, *RIC* 257; cf. Horsnæs 2009, 251 nos. 25 and 25b.
126 060403 sb 169: FP 8162.5.
127 60104 sb 60; Vedel 1886, 385.
128 060305 sb 21. I thank René Laursen from Bornholms Museum for making me aware of this find.
129 Fagerlie 1967.

130 Axboe 2002.
131 Breitenstein 1944, figs. 28-54.
132 Kromann 1983-84, no. 58.1; Horsnæs 2009, 251-2 no. 27a.
133 Horsnæs 2009, 253 and fig. 3.29.
134 Breitenstein 1944, 58-61 no. 23.6, fig. 60.
135 Breitenstein 1944, 46-52 no. 21.35, fig 27.
136 Breitenstein 1944, 66-68 no. 26.5, fig. 74.
137 Breitenstein 1944, 74 no. 36, fig. 83.

examples of cut solidi have been found in Gudme[139] and most recently in the Høgsbrogård Hoard of hacksilber from southern Jutland.[140] It is most likely that the gold coins have been cut in order to use the gold as means of payment in a weight economy.[141]

A number of bent solidi have been found, and more may have existed, as it is possible that coins from old finds may have been straightened out without note being made of it. The bending may have happened as accidental post-depositional change. In some cases, however, it is certain that the coins were deliberately bent. A good example is the coins (as well as the bracteates) from the Fuglesangsager Hoard I which were bent in order for them to be inserted into the rolled up silver dish that contained the gold objects.

Antoniniani

The antoninianus (or 'radiate') was created as a silver double denarius and was intended to circulate as such, but the silver content quickly dropped. In areas far from the *Limes* antoniniani are rare, and normally appear in unusual or even dubious contexts.[142] The two antoniniani from Bornholm have, however, been found during detector surveys on productive sites. One derives from the northernmost of the sites within the Ibsker complex, Engegård, with material from the Roman and Early Germanic Iron Age.[143] The other antoninianus derives from Duegård VNV,

Fig. 40. Antoniniani (radiates): FP 6559.5 and FP 7620.3.

majority of the remaining specimens, however, have a hole above the portrait.

The six solidi from the Fuglesangsager I hoard have been mounted with a beaded rim and a loop eye. The loops, as well as the beaded rims, are closely comparable to the fittings of the Nordic bracteates of the same hoard. Apart from these only the single find of an unusual Theodosius I solidus from Østermarie is fitted with a loop.

The fact that solidi are rarely reworked into jewellery is in stark contrast to the finds from other parts of Denmark. It is evident that gold coins must have played another role in Bornholm.

Five cut-off fragments of solidi have been found, and three coins have traces of attempted cutting.[138] Similar

---

138   1. Smørengegård. Site 060305 sb 70. FP 6693.14. BMR 1469x259. Horsnæs 2009, 246 no. 16 and fig. 3:15.
   2. Smørengegård. Site 060305 sb 405. FP 6993.15. BMR 1697x158. Horsnæs 2009, 247 no. 18 and fig. 3:19.
   3. Dalshøj. Site 060403 sb 135. FP 6364.5 and FP 7727.5. BMR 1639x303. Horsnæs 2009, 253 no. 276 and figs. 3:30-31.
   4. Kirseløkkegård. Site 060405 sb 157. FP 220/NM I 19452. Horsnæs 2009, 254; photo Klindt-Jensen 1957, 234 nr. 11 and fig. 198
   5. Sorte Muld. Site 060403 sb 93. FP 5464.52, attempted cutting. Horsnæs 2009 fig. 3:26
   6. Sandegård. Site 060205 sb 33. NM I C 336-344 contain two solidi with attempted cutting. Horsnæs 2009, 242; photo Breitenstein 1944, 69-70 nos. 28.3-4 and fig. 78-79.
139   Horsnæs 2009, fig. 3:36-37.
140   Feveile 2010.
141   Horsnæs 2010b, 439-440.
142   Horsnæs 2010a, 162-164.
143   060403 sb 160: BMR 2280; FP 6559.5: Gallienus, RIC V.i.83, 253-260.

Crossing boundaries

Fig. 41. Recent finds of Roman bronze coins: FP 6922.3, FP 6931.5, FP 8269.1 and FP 8314.2 (right).

a settlement area with finds dating from the Late Roman Iron Age through the Viking period. Other finds include seven Roman denarii, a fragment of a Cufic dirham and a Haithabu coin.[144] In these two cases it is likely that the antoninianus could be seen as part an Iron Age influx.

Base metal coins

Roman bronze coins are rare on Bornholm, only 15 specimens are known, equaling only 0.5% of all Roman coins.[145] The number of bronze coins compared to denarii is considerably lower than the number from Western Denmark, and both the chronological and contextual distribution differs somewhat from the bronze coins found there.[146]

All bronze coins are recent finds, and most of them have appeared on productive sites, but unfortunately none of them derives from a closed and datable context. There are relatively more of the early senatorial issues compared with the material from Western Denmark (six senatorial coins and five coins of the late 3rd – 4th centuries). Only one Byzantine bronze coin is known, and as there are no examples of Byzantine bronze coins in archaeological contexts elsewhere in Denmark, it is interesting to note that this coin was found in a modern urban environment, and as such it was most likely a modern loss.[147] The material from Bornholm is certainly less contaminated by modern collector's coins or tourist's souvenirs than what is the case in the remaining parts of modern Denmark, and strengthens the view that while bronze coins were not popular in non-Roman communities, *some* Roman low denomination coins (bronze coins as well as antoniniani) did arrive in Barbaricum during the Iron Age.

144 060204 sb 94: BMR 3354; FP 7620.1-5 (two denarii, un-identified antoninian, dirham, penning), 8017.1-3 (denarii), 8475.1-2 (denarii).
145 See list of 'Roman bronze coins', p. 195
146 Horsnæs 2006a and 2010a, 160-162.

147 Justin II, 20 *nummi*, struck in Nicomedia, year 5 = 569-570 AD. The coin was found in Allinge, without details on the find circumstances: AUD 1991, 225; Horsnæs 2006a, no. 118 (ill.).

Coins

Fig. 42. Bronze coin with trimmed rim probably struck in the late 4th century. FP 6995.3.

Fig. 43. Tablet shaped weight cut out from sestertius struck by Maximinus Thrax. FP 5464.49.

Fig. 44. Halved sestertius. FP 6372.6.

Reworked base metal coins

No less than three of the bronze coins were reworked in antiquity: two were cut and trimmed,[148] to obtain a form similar to tablet-shaped weights commonly found on all productive sites, and it has indeed been suggested that they were re-used as weights.

A heavily worn sestertius found in the Ibsker complex was halved.[149] Finds of halved (and quartered) sestertii is a well-known phenomenon in the northwestern periphery of the Roman Empire, where they were probably used as legal tender in periods with a lack of small change.[150]

Ancient coins in Viking Age contexts

The rarity of dated depositions has been stressed several times. Yet in some cases it is possible to demonstrate that an Ancient coin has appeared in a context that undoubtedly belongs to the Viking Age.

The hoard from Kongens Udmark near Vestermarie consisted of a large number of Cufic dirhams, at least three Haithabu half-bracteates, 21 German, one Polish and two Italian coins, and probably six Byzantine miliarenses of the mid-10th century (931-969). Finally there was a single Roman denarius,[151] and no less than 1284 g silver in the form of jewellery, (*Hacksilber*) and ingots.[152] The coin *t.p.q.* of the hoard is 967/8 (Galster) or 973 (von Heijne), making it one of the earliest Viking Age silver hoards with coins found on Bornholm. The hoard was deposited in a clay pot 1½ *alen* (c. 90-95 cm) below surface, and there is no doubt that the denarius had been deposited with the Viking Age hoard.[153]

---

148 From Vestergård, 060303 sb 190. BMR 1672; FP 6995.3 (unpubl.) and from Sorte Muld, 0604030 sb 93, BMR1191x829R; FP 5464.49: Horsnæs 2006a, no. 47.
149 060403 sb 93. BMR 1191x1425R; FP 6372.6: Horsnæs 2006a, no. 38.
150 Chantraine 1982, 25-33; Kemmers 2006, 86.

151 FP 224. Trajan RIC 315, 114-117.
152 Skovmand 1942, fig. 28.
153 060305 sb 50 (Pindeløkkegård). FP 224 and 396: Skovmand 1942, 127; Breitenstein 1944, 38 find no.

The Store Frigård hoard found between Østermarie and Østerlars consists of more than 1000 German coins, and a considerable number of English, Danish and Cufic coins, as well as 52 blanks and finally a single Roman denarius.[154] It was deposited after 1106 and it has been considered the latest hoard of Viking Age character. The hoard was deposited in a clay pot with a flat bowl used as cover.[155]

The Lillegærde hoard was discovered by metal detector surveying in the spring of 1989. To date 124 coins and some *Hacksilber* pieces belonging to the ploughed up hoard have been found during excavation and repeated surveys of the site. Some of the coins were found within the remains of a pottery vessel, and the excavations revealed that the hoard was deposited within a Viking Age settlement.[156] The hoard consists of mainly German and English Viking Age coins, but there are also Cufic coins, a Byzantine coin of the 10th century and some Danish 11th century coins. The coin *t.p.q.* of the hoard is 1048.[157] Within the coin scatter a Hellenistic drachm was found.[158] The coin was compared to *SNG Cop* 977, a posthumous (3rd century BC) Alexander issue of uncertain mint (Greece or Macedonia); it was even suggested that this coin is die linked to the specimen from Bornholm.[159] Greek coins are rarely found in Denmark, and all other finds are made in circumstances where it seems most likely that the coin has been lost recently. In this respect the drachm from Lillegærde is unique. While the Roman denarii from the

Fig. 45. Alexander drachm from the Lillegærde Hoard. FP 4989.1.

previously mentioned Viking Age hoards have not been reworked, the drachm has rim notches and pecks. This is highly unusual among Ancient coins, but a regular feature on Viking Age silver objects including coins imported from the areas to the south and southeast of Bornholm.[160] The pecks and notches therefore indicate that the coin was in use in the Viking Age. It may have travelled north together with the Cufic dirhams and/or the Byzantine coin from the hoard.

The three Viking Age hoards containing an Ancient (Greek or Roman) coin have all been found in areas which from a numismatic point of view are dominated by Viking Age material.

Two other finds have been mentioned as possible Viking Age finds including earlier material. At Nr. Sandegård not far from Store Frigård and Lillegærde detector surveys have yielded at least 93 Viking Age coins and some *Hacksilber* from a settlement area. The finds have been interpreted as a hoard, with a preliminary numismatic *t.p.q.* of 1027.[161] Within the 'hoard area' a single denarius was found. It is very worn and broken, but not pecked or otherwise reworked. It therefore seems hazardous to ascribe the denarius to the Viking Age hoard until a detailed spatial analysis of the finds from the site has been undertaken.[162]

The 'Poulsker Find' is an assemblage of coins previously in Fyns Stiftmuseum (today Odense Bys Mu-

---

   5; Galster 1980, 33-39 no. 14 and tav. 26, 14.29; von Heijne 2004, 5.97.
154 FP 1701. Hadrian *RIC* 262, 134-138.
155 060406 sb 318. Galster 1929 (publ.); Skovmand 1942, 165; Galster 1980, 135-169 no. 48 and tav. 26, 48.1198; von Heijne 2004, cat.no. 5.135. For an even later mixed hoard see now Grinder-Hansen & Märcher 2013.
156 060405 sb 197: FP 4989.1-4 and 6-17; 5138.1-7; 5241.1-5; 5460.1-5; 5798; 6362.1-4; 6857; 7635.1-7; 8351.1-7; 8398.1-72, and x200-203 (not registered). Kromann & Jensen 1993; von Heijne 2004, 329 find 5.126.
157 von Heijne 2004, 329.
158 FP 4989.1: AUD 1991, 227 fig. 2.2.
159 Kromann & Jensen 1993, 74. Same type as Martin Jessop Price 1991: *The Coinage of Alexander the Great and Philip Arrhidaeus*. Zürich – London, no. 862. Weight (4.05 g) and axis (12) correspond with the specimens quoted by Price 1991, 170.

160 Ingvardson 2012.
161 060405 sb 199. von Heijne 2004, cat.no. 5.128. The date was based on 30 coins ascribed to the hoard, but already then younger coins had been found on the site. No analysis of the spatial distribution of the coin finds has been made. Since the research undertaken by von Heijne the number of coins found at Nr. Sandegård has risen considerably.
162 FP 6846.1: fragment of a Marcus Aurelius struck for Divus Antoninus Pius, RIC 436 or 438.

Fig. 46. The denarius from Nr. Sandegård, found near the Viking Age hoard scatter. FP 6846.1.

The finds of Roman denarii in Viking Age contexts are few, but they reveal that a single or a few denarii may have been discovered and reused in a silver economy at least until the early 12th century as evidenced by the Store Frigård Hoard. The find of a single Roman denarius in a site otherwise dominated by Viking Age material therefore cannot be taken as evidence for an Iron Age phase of the site. In this case it is imperative that all material from the site (coins as well as other object types) is studied as an entity.

seer), where it was kept with a note saying that it was 'found in Poulsker parish in 1838'. The assemblage consists of nine coins. One is a Roman denarius (Marcus Aurelius, *RIC* 225var), the remaining ones are Viking Age coins: an 8th century Abbasid dirham, one Danish, two English and four German coins of the first half of the 11th century.[163] The Viking Age coins are of types commonly found in hoards on Bornholm, and also the denarius might well derive from Bornholm, but the evidence of all the coins' being (part of) a single hoard is scanty: strictly speaking the note about the provenance only tells that the coins derive from Poulsker, not that they were actually found together. The 'Poulsker Find' will therefore not be discussed further.

Examples of Roman coins mixed into much later Viking Age hoards are known in a number of cases in the Baltic area, normally with only one or a few Roman coins in much larger hoards, except for the Oxarve Hoard from Gotland with 79 Roman denarii.

Recently a list of 39 Viking Age contexts from Poland with one or more Ancient coins was compiled by Anna Zapolska together with a short list of similar finds from other countries. She noted the distribution within a Baltic zone (by her defined as all lands surrounding the Baltic Sea from Finland to Germany) and she suggested, as did Galster before her,[164] that the Roman coins may have come from Viking Age casual finds of denarius hoards in the area.[165]

---

163   Now in the Royal Coll. of Coins and Medals, inv. FP 4176: Poulsen 1982; von Heijne 2004, cat.no. 5.49, here the find is interpreted as a hoard.
164   Galster 1929, 285.
165   Zapolska 2007. The suggestion that the denarii from Viking Age (in Continental terminology Early Medieval) hoards from Poland might represent a backflow from Gotland seems unnecessary.

CHAPTER 3

Bornholm in a wider context

To understand the role of Roman coins in Bornholm it is important first to examine if and how finds from Bornholm differ from those of other areas.

As we have seen there is an almost complete dominance of only two coin types – denarii from the 2nd century and Late Roman solidi from the 5th century. Less than 1% of the Roman coins are of other denominations and/or dates. In this respect the only area with a comparable domination of denarii and solidi is the island of Gotland, and to a lesser degree Öland and the Mälar area in Mainland Sweden.[166]

The remaining parts of Sweden present an uneven distribution of Roman coins (*Figs. 47-48*). In particular the denarii are concentrated on relatively few coastal areas of southern Sweden, where most finds are hoards. Single finds of solidi are scattered a bit more with several single finds in the – largely agricultural – inland area between Göteborg and Stockholm and a small concentration in Medelpad,[167] but finds from the southern coast dominate.

Gotland and Uppåkra are the two most important areas for detector archaeology in Sweden. From these areas there are large numbers of single finds of denarii, and the lack of single finds of denarii in other parts of Sweden may be due to the lack of metal detector investigations. In particular the areas with finds of Roman gold coins or other import types are likely to reveal denarii once investigated with the use of detectors.

The number of base metal coins is very low in Öland and Gotland (compared to total number of finds), but slightly higher on the mainland.[168] In addition the

---

166 The intensity of investigation of certain areas at the expense of other is an important reason for the concentration of finds in relatively few areas of Sweden. This was the case with the Mälar area (Callmer 1976) as it is for Gotland and Uppåkra in Scania.

167 Wiséhn 1992. It should be noted that the small group of finds from Medelpad share characteristics with the material from Denmark rather than the material from the Baltic islands.

168 Sweden has produced a total of *c.* 160 base metal coins. The finds of Roman bronze coins from northern Sweden were recently discussed by Inger Zachrisson (2010, distribution map fig. 1), but I believe that a very large number of them must be regarded as secondary finds. I therefore disagree with her on several points: For example a considerable part (34 of the 90 Roman base metal coins from Northern Sweden discussed by her) derive from the 'hoards' from Storsjö, Härjedalen (+12 coins, dated from 221/205 BC to 1603/12 AD) and Stora Glamsarvet, Dalarna (107 coins, dated from the 3rd century to the Osmannic Empire) which cannot be regarded as anything but (pre-)modern collections. Furthermore, the composition of the finds from Bergsbyn, Västerbotten (12 coins of the 3rd and early 4th centuries and one plated Gaius/Lucius imitation) and Boda, Dalarna (11 coins, Late Roman, Byzantine and Greek), is unusual, although not impossible.

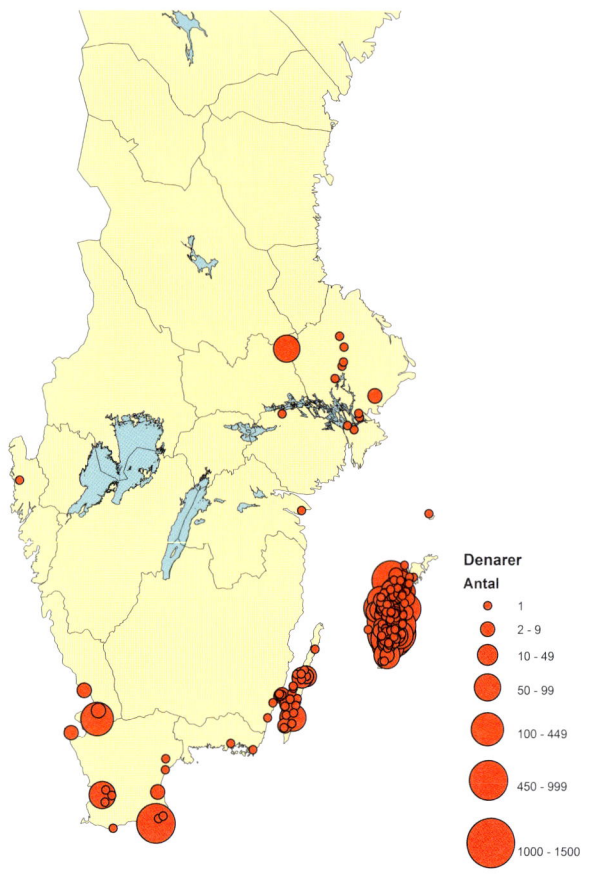
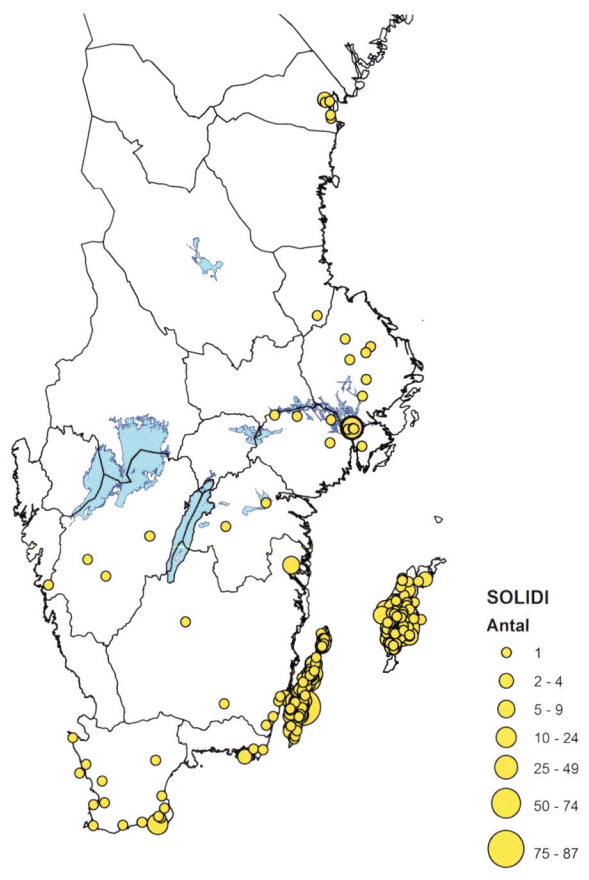

Fig. 47. Distribution of denarii in Sweden (Map by Kenneth Jonsson, status 2011).

Fig. 48. Distribution of solidi in Sweden (Map by Kenneth Jonsson, status 2011).

Mainland has produced a few gold coins from the 1st to 4th centuries as well as the recent find of a western siliqua from the late 4th century.[169]

In the parts of Denmark west of Øresund there is a much higher number of finds of aurei and early solidi, as well as a growing number of siliqua finds of both eastern and western mints.[170] However, a considerable number of these finds derive from the 4th century horizon of Gudme and central Funen. This region is long recognized for its close contacts with southeastern Europe,[171] and the very high number of finds here reflects this privileged position.

In the remaining parts of Denmark low denominations and coins from the 3rd and 4th centuries make up 1-2% of the total material. This figure is comparable to areas southeast of Denmark. A considerable number of bronze coins, antoniniani, aurei and pre-395 AD solidi have been found in present-day Poland, indeed Bursche discussed 1246 coins (from 837 finds) produced in the 3rd and 4th centuries.[172] But compared to the estimated finds of more than 60,000 denarii in the Vistula basin, and the far more than 70,000 denarii mentioned as the probable total number of finds from Poland, the 3rd and 4th century coins make less than 2% of the total number of Roman coins from Poland. There are, however, important differences within the different Polish landscapes:[173] The

---

169 Aspeborg 2012.
170 Horsnæs 2010.
171 Alföldi 1935; Werner 1988.
172 Bursche 1996.
173 When discussing the distribution of archaeological types I have decided to use the modern political regions throughout this work. In areas with dynamic changes of the extent of an archaeological culture through time, there is a danger of a circular argument when describing the find of a coin as belonging to one or another culture. Because of the often considerable time gap between the production date and deposition date in Barbaricum, the deposition of the individual coin (hoard) may have taken place within either one or another archaeological culture depending on the (often unknown) deposition date.

distribution maps in the recent and updated find list from Pomerania, Silesia and Mazowia/Podlachia,[174] as well as the somewhat older catalogue of finds from Małopolski,[175] clearly show that the proportion of 3rd and 4th century coins (antoniniani, bronze coins and pre-395 AD gold coins) are lower in Pomerania and Mazowia than in the more southwesterly parts of Poland.[176]

Within the Ukrainian Barbaricum (the Černjachov Culture)[177] *c.* 1200 sites with a total of 26,000-30,000 Roman coins have been found. According to Magomedov only *c.* 2-3% of the coins were struck in the 3rd and 4th centuries.[178] More recent research has revealed that more than 20% of the coins from single finds belong to the 3rd-4th centuries, but it seems that denarii take a much more prominent position among the hoards.[179]

In other parts of Barbaricum there are clear indications that the closer to the Empire, the higher the number of Roman coin finds – but the number of denarii in relation to base metal denominations is decreasing markedly when approaching the Empire. This is very evident in the material from the Czech Republic and Slovakia. In spite of a very high number of coin finds, there are few denarii.[180] Outside the

---

This is not a pressing issue in Bornholm, but on the Continent shifting boundaries of archaeological cultures are quite common. Bursche 1996, 11 suggested relative stabiblity of the archaeological cultures found within modern Poland in the period 230-375 AD. An attempt to evaluate the differences of the coin finds within the Wielbark and Przeworsk Cultures based – it seems – on these borders was presented by Ciołek 2008.

174 Ciołek 2007 and 2008; Romanowski 2008.
175 Kunisz 1985.
176 Compare Bursche 1996, folding map: low intensity of finds in Debczyno Group and Wielbark Culture, except for the Lower Vistula area, with high find intensity.
177 According to Line Bjerg (pers.comm., 2011) no Roman Imperial coins have been found within the Bosporan Kingdom.
178 Magomedov 2008, 172.
179 Myzgin 2011. I thank Kirill Myzgin for access to the manuscript of this paper and the summary of his dissertation (Myzgin 2010) on the Roman coin finds of the Černjachov Culture (in Ukrainian).
180 Militký 2010.

Limes we thus see a gradual decrease in percentage of base metal coinages, from a quasi-monetary economy along the Limes to the almost complete absence of base metal coinages in the Baltic islands.[181]

The peculiarities of the find spectrum from Balticum are visible when comparing the denarius and solidus finds with finds of the the same denominations in other regions.

Let us first take a look at denarii and solidi separately and proceed to compare the results in order to examine whether they are two disparate phenomena or two different images of the same.

Chronological composition of denarius finds from Barbaricum

Important regional differences soon appear in the chronological composition of the denarius finds. Most denarius finds from Bornholm are dominated by Antonine denarii, but very often we see a 'topping up' consisting of one or a few denarii from the early 3rd century. The end-coin of an assemblage/hoard of (mainly) 2nd century denarii therefore often seems to have been added somewhat haphazardly and has little importance for the evaluation of the assemblage as a whole.

The overall picture from Bornholm presents the predominance of Antonine denarii. There is normally less than 20% pre-Antonine and less than 20% Severan or later denarii in an assemblage from Bornholm. The number of coins pr. year peaked during the reign of Marcus Aurelius. Several factors thus combine to give an impression of a chronological structure of the material from Bornholm which is late in comparison with the remaining parts of Denmark. Only few and relatively small closed contexts from western Denmark have a chronological composition with less than 20% pre-Antoninus coins, and it is interesting to note that the deposition of those contexts are dated considerably later than the production period of the denarii. That applies to Gudme IV (hoard with denarii and siliquae, *t.p.q.* 365 AD), Nydam (context *c.* AD 300), and Dankirke Vest II (*t.p.q.* 276 AD).[182]

---

181 As noted already by Hedeager 1978.
182 Horsnæs 2010a, 130 fig. 68.

Crossing boundaries

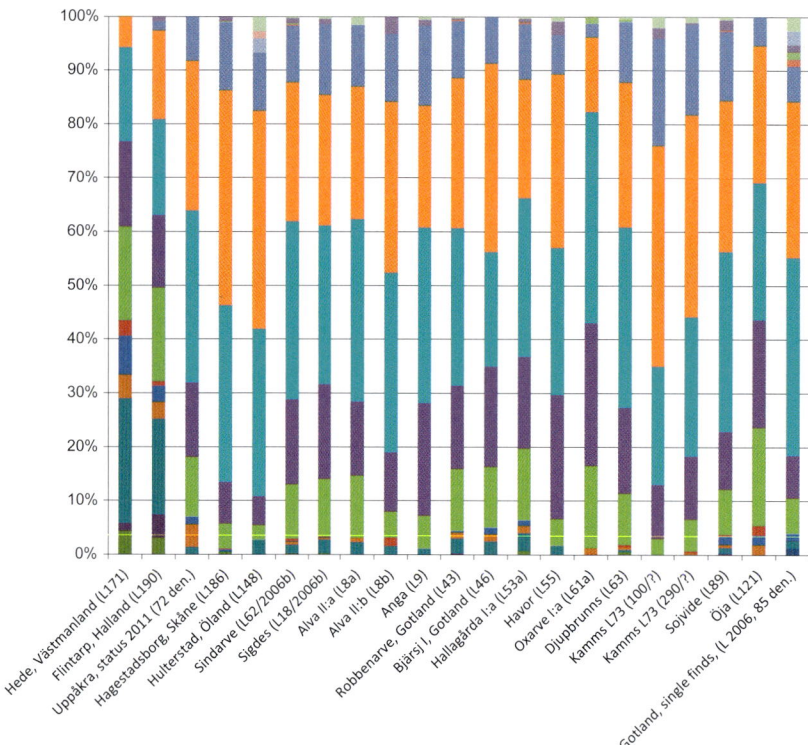

Fig. 49. The chronological distribution of denarius hoards and assemblages in Sweden (L = Lind 1981 cat.no.; L 2006 = Lind 2006; L 2006b = Lind 2006b). The figures from Uppåkra are based on the unpublished finds list of 72 denarii identified by Ulla von Wowern and Lennart Lind. I am most grateful to both of them for permission to use their material. The material from Uppåkra furthermore includes one denarius of Julia Mamaea and three bronze coins (Lind, pers. comm. 2011). The Mälar Valley area, which is otherwise rich in archaeological material from the Late Iron Age/Migration Period, and relatively rich in solidi (cf. below) has produced only a small number of single finds of denarii and is not represented in the diagram.

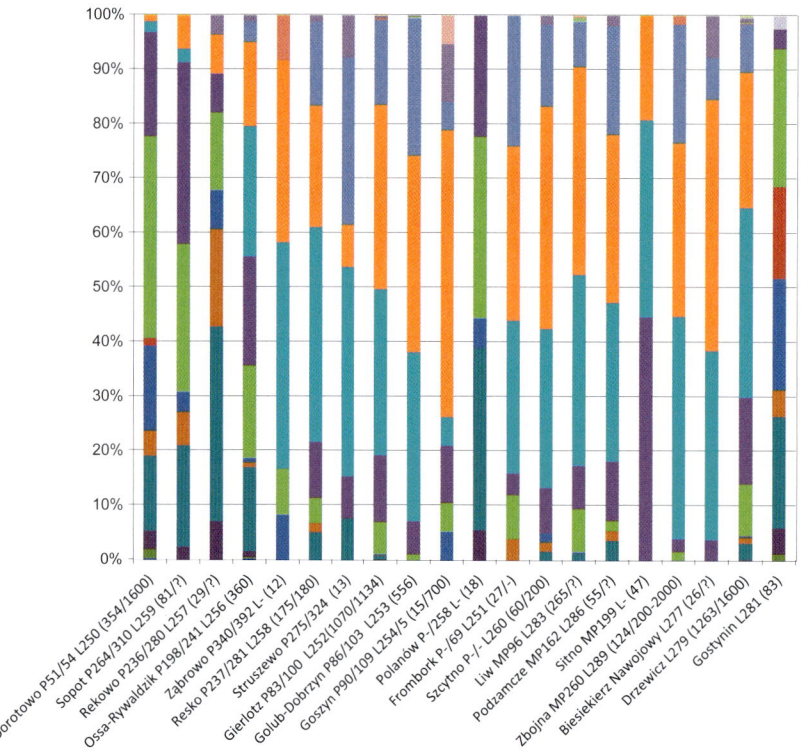

Fig. 50 A. The chronological distribution of denarius hoards and assemblages in Poland.
A. Pomerania, Mazovia and Podlachia (L = Lind 1981; P = Ciołek 2007; MP = Romanowski 2008).

Bornholm in a wider context

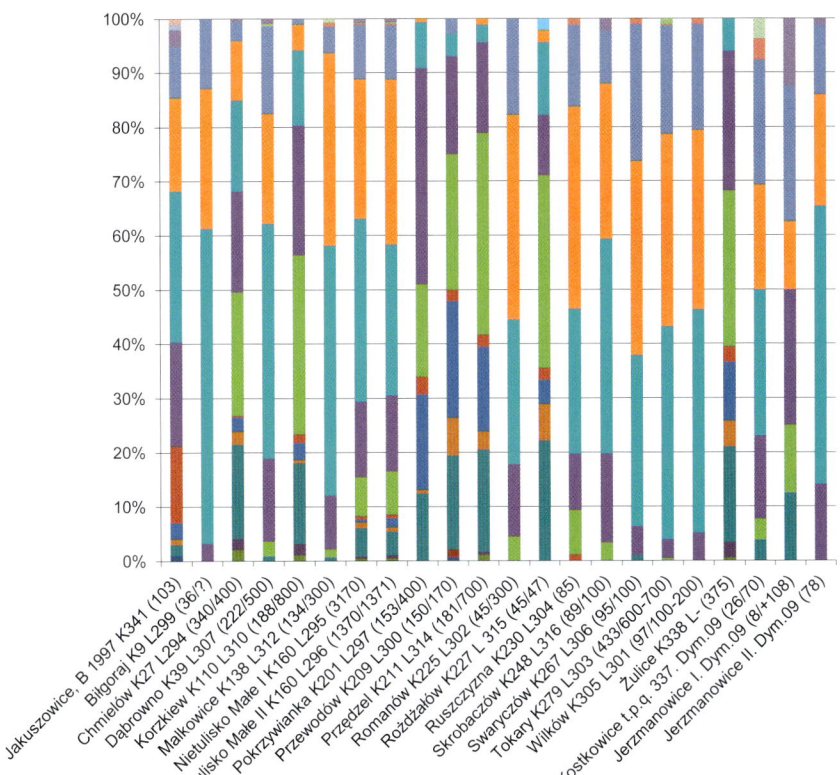

Fig. 50 B. The chronological distribution of denarius hoards and assemblages in Poland.
B. Little Poland (B 1997= Burche 1997; Dym 09 = Dymowski 2009; K= Kunisz 1985; L = Lind 1981)

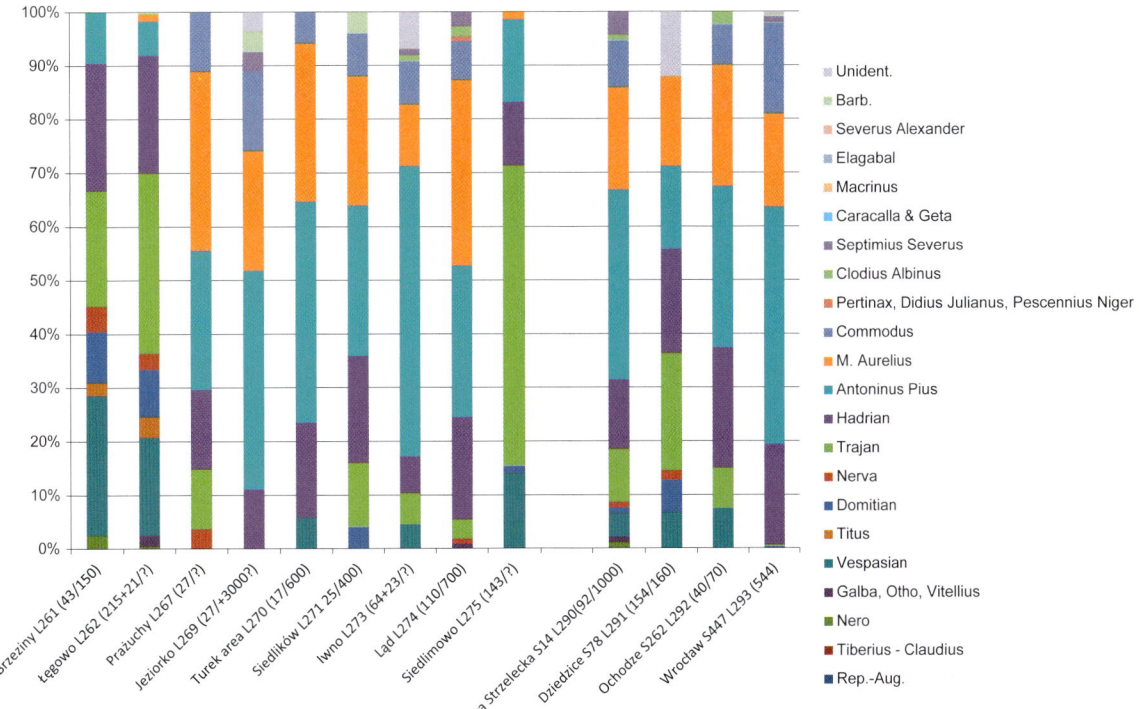

Fig. 50 C. The chronological distribution of denarius hoards and assemblages in Poland.
C. Greater Poland and Silesia (L = Lind 1981; S = Ciotek 2008b)

Looking towards modern Sweden *(Fig. 49)*,[183] the denarius hoards from Öland (Hulterstad) and Scania (Hagestadsborg) are not only the finds closest to Bornholm geographically, but their chronological structures also compare very well with the finds from Bornholm.

The overwhelming majority of Roman denarii from Sweden have been found on Gotland. A considerable number of denarius hoards have been known for a long time, but as Gotland is the only area in Sweden (except for Uppåkra site) that has been surveyed systematically with the use of metal detectors, there are also many single finds.[184] The chronological structure of the material is internally consistent, but with an average of around 30% pre-Antonine coins, 30% Antoninus Pius, 25% Marcus Aurelius and 15% Commodus (and later) in the hoards, the overall chronological composition seems to be slightly earlier on Gotland than on Bornholm. A few contexts are more closely comparable to the material from Bornholm, notably the Kamms find, but this find is unfortunately badly known and its composition is uncertain.[185]

Uppåkra near modern Lund in Scania is the most important productive site in Mainland Sweden to have been surveyed systematically with the use of metal detectors. Uppåkra was without doubt an important centre in Late Roman and Germanic Iron Age Scania. It has been the subject of a major research project including both excavations and systematical metal detector surveys. The finds include several types of finds that can be compared to the finds from Sorte Muld, notably die identical gold foil figures.[186] The chronological composition of the single finds of denarii from Uppåkra compares well with the material from Gotland, but the relatively small hoards from Ledøje and Lærkefryd in Sealand may also be quoted as comparative material. Ravlunda in eastern Scania is another site of importance for the understanding of the material from Bornholm and it is currently subject of archaeological field work. The site has produced a denarius hoard (*t.p.q.* Clodius Albinus) found before 1776 and some 'Byzantine' coins, among which one struck by Julius Nepos, Nordic gold bracteates and gold foil figures. The recent investigations have so far produced two denarii.[187]

The hoard from Hede in Västmanland is so far unique in Sweden, and with almost 80% pre-Antonine denarii the composition of the hoard is best compared to the earliest denarius hoards from Western Denmark (Råmosen, Orup).

The area of Barbaricum that stretches between the Baltic Sea and the Black Sea is very rich in Roman denarius finds.[188] Thousands of denarii have been found, mainly in hoards which often contain much larger numbers of coins than are found in Scandinavia.[189] Unfortunately much of this important material is fragmentary. Often only a part of the coins from a hoard has been preserved, or the composition of the hoard is known purely from literary sources. Still, the material is so important that all hoards with a substantial number of identified types have been inserted into diagrams comparable to the ones made on the material from Scandinavia.[190]

Poland *(Fig. 50A-C)* has produced a number of hoards with a very early composition, i.e. 75% or more pre-Antonine coins. A smaller group has 50-75% pre-Antonine coins, but the majority of the hoards have less than 50% and often less than 30% pre-Antonine coins. In the 2nd to 5th centuries AD Poland is divided into a number of archaeological cul-

---

183 Lind 1981 and 1988 are fundamental studies of denarii in Sweden, and Lind's collection of denarius hoards from Barbaricum is still valid for many areas. Lind has announced a forthcoming research entitled: *Roman denarii found in Sweden and their context*.
184 Östergren 1981 and 1986; Lind 2006; Jonsson 2010, 11 with distribution map of single finds of denarii in Gotland fig. 2.
185 Note that the coin identifications by Lind give a 'later' structure of the find than the list provided by Montelius.
186 Watt 2004 and *forthcoming*.

187 Von Heijne 2010, 16-17 with references.
188 Except the West Balt Culture area, cf. however Zapolska 2009 on the denarius finds from the southernmost part of this area.
189 Lind 1988, 185-190.
190 Cf. also diagrams on finds from northern Germany in Horsnæs 2010, fig. 69. I am consciously parting from the assumption that the information of the chronological structure of a hoard is representative for the hoard as a whole, even though only a part of it has been preserved. If a deliberate sorting of the coin types has been undertaken, for example by a coin collector, it would tend to preserve the most unusual types and/or the best preserved specimens, but I believe that it would have few chronological implications.

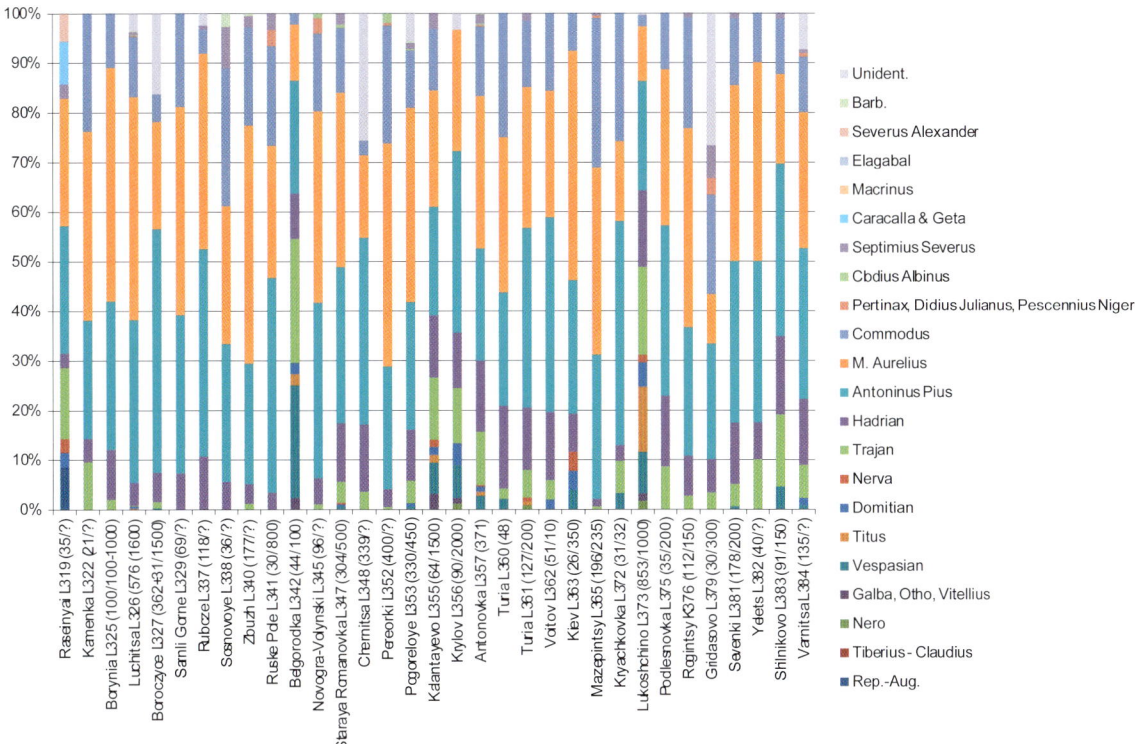

Fig. 51. The chronological distribution of denarius hoards in the former USSR, as listed by Lind 1981: Lithuania (L 319), Belorussia (L 322), the Ukraine (L 325-376), Russia (L 379-383) and Moldavia (L 384).

tures. The Wielbark and Przeworsk cultures are the most prominent among them, and the river Vistula acts as a borderzone between the Przeworsk Culture to the west and the Wielbark Culture to the east and around the Vistula estuary at the Gdansk Bay.[191] The area thus defined as Wielbark Culture has a relatively higher number of 'late' denarius hoards than the Przeworsk areas west of the Vistula line. The lower Vistula River and estuary are among the richest areas for Roman coin finds in modern Poland, but there is a much lower find density in the remaining coastal areas towards the Baltic Sea; in particular east (West Balt Culture), but also west (Debczyno Group) of the Vistula's outlet into the Baltic Sea.[192]

Denarii completely dominate the finds of Roman coins from the Ukraine *(Fig. 51)*, and they are recorded as found very often in contexts of the second half of the 3rd and the 4th centuries AD.[193] Denarius hoards from Ukraine are normally of a very 'late' composition: 22 of 27 analysed hoards have less than 30% pre-Antonine denarii, and only the two earliest hoards have 65% pre-Antonine denarii.

During the 2nd century the Great Hungarian Plain was a non-Roman pocket between the provinces of Pannonia and Dacia. Significantly the composition of the majority of the denarius hoards from the Great Hungarian Plain[194] is closely comparable to the hoards from Ukraine, Poland and Scandinavia. They are surprisingly homogeneous and also surprisingly 'late', when compared to material from the border are-

---

191   Bursche 1996, 11 and distribution map.
192   The recent corpora of finds from Pomerania, Silesia and Mazovia/Podlachi provide easy access to finds from these areas: Ciołek 2007 and 2008 and Romanowski 2008. Finds from Małopolski were collected by Kunisz 1985. Denarius hoards were listed by Lind 1981, and coins produced in the 3rd and 4th centuries by Bursche 1996.
193   Magomedov 2008. I would like to thank Kyrill Myzgin for sending me a summary of his analysis of Roman coins from the Černjachov Culture (Myzgin 2010), the present analysis is however based on the find numbers in Lind 1981.
194   The so-called 'Sarmathian territory' as defined by Farkas & Torbágyi 2008. The analysis of the chronological composition of the hoards was based on Lind 1981, cat.no. 398 (Kecel 2 Hoard) and figures taken from Farkas & Torbagyi 2008.

as both north (the Czech Republic and Slovakia) and south (for example the Siret River in Romania, see below) of Hungary. Many of the hoards are relatively small, but the material also includes the large Kecel 2 Hoard, known for among other things a large number of Barbaric imitations of denarii that have been die linked with finds from other areas in Barbaricum.

Contrary to the evidence from Hungary the denarius hoards from the Czech Republic (Bohemia) all have an 'early' composition,[195] and similarly the single finds of denarii from Bohemia present a relatively 'early' composition with almost 60% pre-Antonine coins.[196]

The recent catalogue of denarius hoards with the latest coin in the period from Trajan to Balbinus found in present-day Romania enumerates almost 200 finds with a total of 25000 denarii.[197] Romania is a good example of the differences found between areas inside (or periodically inside) the Roman Empire and those outside the Empire. The composition of the denarius hoards from Provincia Dacia (here based purely on the denarius finds from the area enclosed by the Carpathians) is markedly different from any area in Barbaricum. The hoards in general have an 'early' composition, but they cannot be readily compared to the hoards from Barbaricum. More importantly there is a lack of uniformity in the chronological structure of the hoards, and the latest coin of each hoard has a much greater significance for the overall chronological composition of the hoards from Provincia Dacia than of those from Barbaricum.

A very high number of denarius finds were made in the border zone of the Provincia Dacia just east of the Carpathians, in the Siret River valley. Here most of the hoards closing with a coin of Marcus Aurelius (or later) contain 40-70% pre-Antonine denarii, no matter what the date of the latest coin, while the hoards with an earlier end-coin naturally have a somewhat earlier composition. The only 'late' hoard has a very unusual combination of more than 50% coins of Septimius Severus and only 11% pre-Antonine denarii. Based solely on the information drawn from the composition of the denarius hoards, the Siret Valley differ significantly from both the neighbouring area within the Roman province and from the adjacent zones of Barbaricum, almost as if creating an independent regional zone.

The results of the analysis of the chronological composition of the denarius finds in Barbaricum with end-coin of Marcus Aurelius or later have revealed the existence of two major and quite distinct groups: One consists of 'early' hoards and assemblages with a majority (often more than 60%) of pre-Antonine denarii. In areas far from the Limes this group becomes increasingly rare. It comprises almost half the finds from northern Germany,[198] a slightly smaller proportion in Poland (notably in the southern and western parts of the country), the earliest finds from Denmark,[199] as well as the Hede and Flintarp Hoards from mainland Sweden. In the remaining parts of Sweden and Poland, on Bornholm, in the Ukraine, and perhaps more surprisingly in the Hungarian Plain this early group is almost absent.

Theories regarding the outflow of denarii from the Roman Empire have focussed on two main causes: economy (trade) and Roman policy (payment for peace at the frontier). Today it seems that most scholars have rejected the monocausal theories and regard Roman denarii to have come to Barbaricum for several reasons, and discussions more often concern the outflow date. In several papers Aleksander Bursche has argued for an outflow starting during the reign of Marcus Aurelius and ending soon after the Severan reform that lowered the silver contents of the denarius significantly, at any rate before 240 AD, after which date he considered denarii to be no longer available within the Empire.[200] Lennart Lind, on the other hand, considered it possible that denari withdrawn from circulation by Roman authorities were kept in deposits until they were paid out to Barbarians in the late 3rd or even 4th century.[201] Neither of the theories can be positively proved or disproved, but I find it difficult to believe that stocks of good quality silver survived intact within the Roman Empire throughout the various political and financial crises in the 3rd century.

---

195 Militký 2010 has been used to evaluate the credibility of earlier find surveys and the list of denarius hoards in Lind 1981.
196 Militký 2008, Taf. 1-2.
197 Deperot & Moisil 2008. An analysis was made of finds with 50 or more denarii identified by emperor.

198 Horsnæs 2010, figs. 69a-b.
199 Horsnæs 2010, fig. 68.
200 Most recently summarized in Bursche 2011, 70-71.
201 Lind 2006b.

The combined evidence from Scandinavia suggests that the first influx of 2nd century denarii took place in the early 3rd century (the Illerup weapon sacrifice) and that *some* of the denarii of the same period of production were not deposited until the 6th century.

The overall view on the denarius hoards with mainly 2nd century issues indicates that there are two major groups of denarius hoards in Barbaricum. It seems possible to relate these groups to two main outflow periods. An early outflow phase mainly affected the Rhine area and fed the Barbarian societies settled within modern Germany, but it also reached modern Poland in significant numbers and on a smaller scale Jutland and Sealand in Denmark and the southwestern part of Mainland Sweden.[202] It resulted in a high proportion of denarius hoards and assemblages with an early composition (more than 70% pre-Antonine denarii). A continuous 'topping up' of these 'early' hoards is possible, as can be seen by the occasional inclusion of single coins that are considerably later than the main part of the hoards.

A later and numerically larger outflow mainly affected the area from the Baltic to the Ukraine. Looking at the geographical distribution of the 'late' denarius hoards it is tempting to suggest the possible existence of a 'corridor' in the Hungarian Plain, through which denarii were redistributed to the Ukraine (specifically the Černjachov Culture around Kiev) and Poland. This suggestion is supported by the well-established connection between southern Scandinavia (in particular the centre at Gudme in Funen) with, on the one hand the Hungarian Plain and on the other the Černjachov Culture.[203] Numismatic evidence confirms these connections, in particular the presence of Barbarian imitations of denarii in the Kecel Hoard that are die identical with finds from other parts of Barbaricum,[204] and the distribution of gold imitations of Roman coins.[205] Still, this somewhat simplified suggestion is not fully satisfying. For example it does not explain why all denarius hoards in the Hungarian Plain, except the Kecel Hoard, are relatively small compared to the material in the Ukraine and Poland.

This later outflow of denarii was an eastern phenomenon and it had few parallels in the west. The sporadic occurrences of hoards with a late denarius composition in northwestern Europe (Germany and Belgium) derive from contexts that have been dated considerably later (late 4th to late 5th centuries) than the production period of the denarii, as for example the Laatzen and Lengerich hoards, and the denarii from the Childeric burial. These late contexts in Western Europe have in their turn been ascribed to a reflux of 2nd century denarii from more distant areas in the east rather than a direct influx from the empire.[206] The Laatzen hoard from northwestern Germany furthermore contained Barbarian imitations of denarii of the SALVS AVGVSTVS Group that are die-identical with imitations from both the Kecel hoard in Hungary (another hoard with a late composition) and from Gotland,[207] thus linking it even closer to this eastern group of material.

Modern Poland constitutes a 'border zone' between the two areas. There is a considerable, although not dominant, number of hoards with an 'early' composition particularly in the southern and western part of the country comparable to the area defined as Przeworsk Culture,[208] while the material from the northern and eastern part of the country have characteristics in common with the finds from the Ukraine and the Baltic area.

Without independent archaeological dates for the contexts of the denarii is it very hard to be specific about the circulation period of denarii in Barbaricum. The deposition date is most often established by a *t.p.q.* date of the denarii, but denarii found in contexts with other datable material can be used to double check the numismatic dating of the denarius hoards. It turns out that the independently dated denarius finds often belong to the period from the advanced 3rd to the mid-5th century. This is the case for several context-dated finds in Denmark.[209] Analyzing the relatively few context-dated denarius hoards/assemblages from other areas in Europe we find that the denarius composition in these contexts is com-

---

202 The Flintarp Hoard in Halland.
203 Werner 1988.
204 Stribrny 2003, in particular map 3.
205 Horsnæs 2013.

206 Alföldi & Stribrny 1998, 43 on the denarii from Childeric's grave. The discourse was developed by Martin 2004 that also included the denarii from 4th to 5th century burials in northwestern Europe as the result of a reflux.
207 Stribrny 2003.
208 Bursche 1996.
209 Horsnæs 2010a.

Crossing boundaries

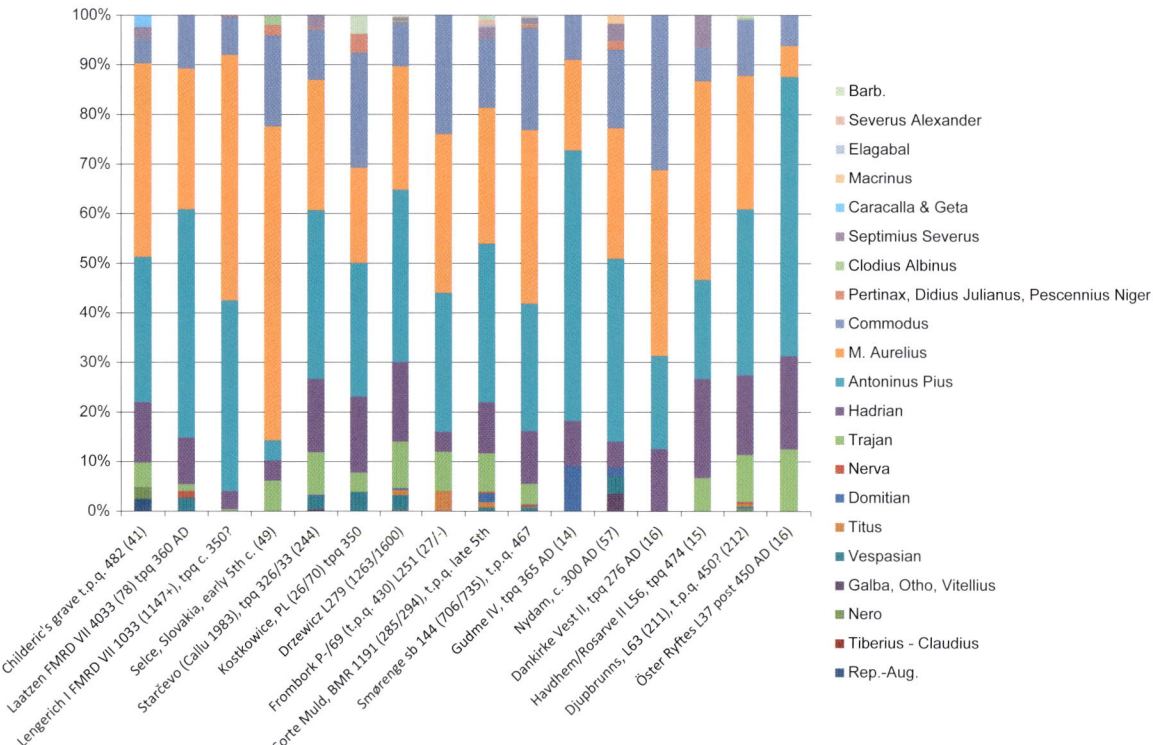

Fig. 52. Chronological composition of denarii from hoards dated in the 4th and 5th century. The date is based on the presence of later Roman coins (often solidi) or datable non-Roman objects. The Djupbrunns and Öster Ryftes Hoards contained Nordic gold bracteates. Note the overall similarity between the hoards found in northwestern Europe and those from central/eastern Europe. Childerich burial: Alföldi & Stribrny 1998; Laatzen: FMRD VII no. 4033; Lengerich: FMRD VII 1033; Selce: Kolníková & Pieta 2009, 122 and tab. 5 (dated in the early 5th century because of a silver fibula in the hoard); Starcevo: Callu 1983; Kostkowice: Dymowski 2009; Frombork (Frauenburg): Ciolek 2007, no. 69.

parable to the composition seen in the 'late' denarius hoards.[210]

Percentages of pre-Antonine coins do not vary according to the date of the final coin of the hoard no matter whether it was struck during the reign of Commodus or a singleton struck by a Severan or even later emperor. The *t.p.q.* date indicated only by the latest coin therefore conceals the fact that the deposition of the hoard may have taken place much later.

---

210 There are cases, where coins of different denominations are listed in different coin lists, sometimes even without cross references. There are also cases, where a find has been interpreted as several hoards because of uncertainties of the composition. This is the case of the Starčevo Hoard, which was interpreted as two separate hoards; cf. most recently Vasić 2001. In addition to the material analyzed and presented here (*Fig. 52*) Myzgin 2011 mentions two denarius hoards with coins from the 4th century and 14 mixed hoards consisting of coins of the 1st-3rd centuries and other objects from the 4th-5th centuries.

The analysis of independently dated denarius hoards thus reveals that they have been deposited in the mid-4th century or later, no matter where in European Barbaricum they were found. There is therefore good evidence to suggest that even a considerable number of the single-type denarius hoards with a 'late' composition were deposited more than hundred and perhaps more than two hundred years after the production date of the latest coin. Thus the final coin has no significance for the deposition date of denarius hoards with a 'late' composition.

Regional differences within the 'late' or 'eastern' denarius group

Over and above the consistency in the chronological composition of the 'late' denarius hoards and assemblages, there are still variations from region to region with Bornholm and southern Sweden providing the overall latest composition of denarius finds, while the composition of most of the hoards from Gotland (30% pre-Antonine and 10% post-Antonine) compare better with the finds from Ukraine, Poland and the Hungarian Plain.

Within even such a small region as Bornholm it might be possible to discern minute differences between on one hand the Smørenge site and the two hoards from Robbedale and Udmarken, and on the other hand the Ibsker complex and the remaining parts of the island. Similarly, it is possible to see minor differences in the composition of the various denarius hoards from Gotland. Both the differences from region to region and the differences between individual hoards/assemblages within the small regions indicate that the denarii did not arrive as the result of a single major influx event. There must have been a series of successive arrivals of denarii, beginning in the 3rd century. This suggestion does not exclude the possibility that denarii arriving as part of hoards were subsequently split up and redistributed within the region. The over-all similarity between assemblages of the 'late' group over much of Barbaricum and the vast distribution of die identical imitations of Roman coins indicate that the denarii may have circulated within Barbaricum for an extended period. It is therefore impossible to propose one single route carrying denarii from Rome to Bornholm.

Solidi in the West Baltic area

It has long been acknowledged that the solidi from the Baltic islands (Bornholm, Öland, Gotland) as well as the Mälar Valley in Mainland Sweden and Pomerania in northern Poland form a specific and unique group[211] and indeed present an extraordinarily high number of precious metal deposits seen in a European context.[212]

The solidi from the Baltic area are characterized by relatively good preservation, few examples of reworking,[213] and a predominance of coins from the Constantinople mint. Joan Fagerlie noted several examples of die links between coins from the different regions within the Baltic, not only between the areas in Southern Scandinavia, but she was also able to link no less than five solidi found in Pomerania with coins from Scandinavian finds.[214]

Having established the similarities and even the uniqueness of the finds from the Baltic area the internal differences between the regions within the main area should be noted. The differences are first and foremost in the end-dates: The hoards from Öland end with issues of the years 475/6 AD, and the single finds follow the same general pattern, although a few later single finds should be noted. In the remaining areas, however, there is also a considerable number of solidi struck in the period until the end of the reign of Anastasius.

Various explanations for the chronological differences have been proposed. Joan Fagerlie was convinced that the solidi came to the islands via Pomerania. At first they came from the Vistula estuary, but during the reign of Anastasius the route shifted to the mouth of the Oder. This suggestion was based on the shift in distribution of hoards. Hoards with the final coin struck in the period 457-490 concentrated around the Vistula River, while hoards with the latest coin struck in the period 491-526 were found along the coastline towards the Oder.[215] Fagerlie suggested that solidi flowed northwards from c. 450, at first to Öland, where the largest number of internal as well as external die links was identified. From Öland the coins were redistributed to other areas. For some rea-

---

211 Fagerlie 1967 is still the most important study with references to earlier works; an excellent summary of discussions following her work can be found in Östergren 1981, 4-6; additions to Fagerlie's find lists have been published by Westermark 1983 (Sweden and Denmark) and Horsnæs 2009 (Denmark); discussion by Metcalf 1995. Some new finds have been noted since 1967, in Denmark the number of solidi has almost doubled, but the explosion in the volume of material seen in the denarius finds on both sides of the Baltic Sea is not equalled by the new solidus finds, and the nature of the evidence today is not much different from the solidus material available to Fagerlie. Finds of Late Roman precious metal hoards including coins throughout Europe have been collected by Hobbs 2006 with references to earlier works, and some of the hoards were published with more detailed coin lists by Depeyrot 2009.
212 Hobbs 2006, figs. 18-21 and 29.
213 Fagerlie 1967, 137-144.
214 Fagerlie 1967, 112-136 and 167 n. 6.
215 See distribution maps in Hobbs 2006, fig. 19-20. The chronological shift was also noted by Ciołek 2010, 384-385.

son the influx to Öland stopped around 475 AD, and Gotland took over the role as main distributor to both Mainland Sweden and Bornholm. Frans Herschend made a specialized study of the gold from Öland and Ola Kyhlberg used the finds from Helgö in the Mälar Valley as a starting point for a discussion.[216] For both scholars the solidi were but one factor in a gold economy where the major role was played by unminted gold. Herschend argued that unminted gold had been imported to Öland since the 3rd century as payment for wool, while the solidi came directly to the island with small bands of soldiers returning from military service on the Continent. Kyhlberg, on the other hand, argued that the solidus hoards had been assembled on the Continent. They were brought from the coasts of Poland and Eastern Germany to the Mälar area, Öland and Bornholm, and came secondarily to Gotland via one of these areas. Compared to the Baltic islands, the Mälar Valley has produced a relatively low number of solidi, but the area is rich in other gold finds, and Kyhlberg argued that this gold derived from recycled solidi.

The geographical distribution of the finds and the *t.p.q.* date of the hoards based on the latest coin have been the most important factors in the discussion of the Baltic group of solidus finds. Two other factors need to be considered more closely: one is the distribution of the mints represented in the hoards, and the other is the condition of the individual coins when found, in particular whether they were reworked or not. Both factors are however very difficult to evaluate on a European level, as many finds are preserved to the present day only in the form of verbal descriptions.

The date of the beginning of the influx must naturally be placed after the production date of the earliest issues in the beginning of the 5th century AD. The deposition date of a single find still cannot be dated more closely than the date inherent in the coin itself, but considering the very long structure of most of the solidus finds from the Baltic area it seem possible to narrow down the date of the influx period. No solidi have been found in hoards that can be dated before the mid-5th century. The only hoards with such an early coin *t.p.q.* are the ones from Fuglesangsager in the Ibsker complex. They are quite atypical for the material in the Baltic area, and the Nordic bracteates from these hoards indicate a deposition date no earlier than *c.* 500 AD. The material from Öland as a whole has the earliest numismatic *t.p.q. c.* 475 AD. All other solidus hoards from the Baltic area must be placed in or after the reign of Anastasius at the earliest.

As is the case with the denarii is seems unlikely that all solidi arrived in Balticum as the result of one import event: In spite of the relatively high consistency within the material, there are some notable differences between the compositions of the different hoards. The material from Pomerania is of prime importance, but unfortunately many of the coins are now lost and known from verbal description only.[217] Of *c.* 850 solidi found in hoards only 358 coins could be identified by emperor and of these only 48 could be assigned to a mint. Among the single finds 26 solidi could be identified by mint.[218] The earliest material derives from the hoard(s) from Trabki/Klein Tromp in the westernmost part of Pomerania, where gold coins were found on at least three different occasions.[219] The earliest coin from the site is an aureus struck during the reign of Gordian III and there are also some late 4th century solidi, but the majority of the coins are solidi struck during the first half of the 5th century and the numismatic *t.p.q.* is provided by the coins of Valentinian III (425-455 AD). The Karlino Hoard of only five solidi seems mainly to belong to the same chronological horizon, but the end coin was struck by Leo I (457-474 AD). Half the coins of the Radostowo Hoard (9 of 18) were struck by Theodosius II (408-450 AD), but again the end coin is slightly later: in this case it is a solidus struck by Basiliscus (475-476 AD). The large Mrzezino Hoard on the contrary consisted of only one coin struck before the mid-5th century, while *c.* 130 of the *c.* 150 coins in the hoard were reported to belong to the reign of Anastasius (491-518 AD) or imitations thereof. Only the Karsibor Hoard has a very 'long' chronology containing a single coin issued by Honorius (395-423 AD), while the remaining coins belong to the reigns from Theodosius II to Anastasius. The dates of the single finds are more evenly distributed throughout the 5th century and

---

216 Herschend 1980; Kyhlberg 1986.

217 Ciołek 2007; 2009 and 2010.
218 Ciołek 2009b, 219-220, tabs. 2-3; 2010, tabs. 2-3.
219 Ciołek 2007 (nos. 352-354 with references) listed the material as two hoards and a single find, but there is so close correspondence between the coins as to suggest that they derive from one and the same hoard.

the latest coins belong are issues of Anastasius. When the mints are known Constantinople always takes a prominent position.

The material from Sweden is better preserved and much more varied. It has long been recognized that the material from Öland – both single finds and hoards[220] – consists of almost exclusively coins struck in the period from the late 4th century to *c.* 475 AD, with few additions in the form of single finds from the 6th century. Hoards from Gotland[221] as well as the Helgö (Lillön) Hoard[222] from the Mälar area have a longer span than the hoards from Öland: the earliest coins are from the reigns of Honorius/Arcadius but the latest coins are issues of Anastasius or even Justinian I.

While the chronology of the hoards have been much discussed, less weight has hitherto been put on the mint distribution, but it seems that in spite of the dominant position of Constantinople, the western mints play a more prominent role in Öland than is usually acknowledged. Herschend suggested that this was caused by the lack of coins from the last quarter of the century where the Constantinople mint acquired a more dominant position after the break-down of the western Empire around 475 AD.[223] In the two largest hoards from Sweden, the Botes (Gotland) and the Helgö (Lillön, Mälar area) hoards, as well as in the material from Bornholm, western mints are as well represented in the last quarter of the 5th century as they were earlier.

The general pattern is one of similarities between the material from Gotland and the Mälar area (the Helgö Hoard) with the composition of the Radostowo Hoard and the single finds from Pomerania. The Pomeranian Karlino and Trabki Hoards with early end dates on the other hand seem to compare better with the material from Öland.

The Smiss Hoard and the Övede Hoard (Gotland) both have a considerable number of very late solidi and can best be compared with the Karsibor and Mrzesino Hoards from Pomerania.

Two small hoards including solidi of the 5th century have been found on the southern coast of Scania. Unfortunately, they have both been lost. One was found around 1780 in Gyllerup. It was a mixed hoard consisting of an unknown number of solidi, a chain with pendant and pieces of gold. The majority of the solidi was said to derive from the reign of Leo I, but also the reigns of Zeno, Julius Nepos and Anastasius were represented.[224] The other hoard were found in 1817 in Målen and consisted of two solidi (one of which struck in Italy 443-444 AD) and four gold bracteates.[225]

Most scholars assume that the coins arrived in the Baltic area by waterways ending in the Vistula estuary. This seems to be the most logical (and economical) explanation, but the influx route is almost impossible to assess. There is no trail of 5th century solidi through Europe to be followed like the pebbles of Hansel and Gretel. On the contrary, solidus finds from central Europe tend to disappear in the third quarter of the 5th century,[226] exactly the period relevant for the influx to the Baltic. In the Italian Peninsula a number of solidus hoards dated in the period 425-526 AD have been found, and – when known – the mint distribution in the Italian hoards tend to be related to the (relatively few) hoards from western Europe.[227] The western issues always occur in larger relative quantities in the hoards found in western and central Europe than in the Baltic.[228] It is therefore unlikely that

---

220 The hoards analyzed are Fagerlie 1967 nos. 50, 86, 99, 115 and no. 40 with additions in Westermark 1983.

221 The hoards analyzed are Fagerlie 1967 nos. 122, 135, 137b and no. 130a-b with additions in Westermark 1983.

222 Fagerlie 1967 no. 6, Fagerlie suggested that this hoard had come via Gotland, and counted it among finds from this island.

223 Herschend 1980, 148.

224 Balling 1966, 74 no. 33.

225 Balling 1966, 71 no. 22.

226 As most recently summarized by Prohászka 2009 (Hungary); Bodzek 2009 (southern Poland).

227 Hobbs 2006 with distribution maps. A more detailed discussion in Ungaro 1985, 53-56. A relatively high number of coins from western mints can also be seen in the Sovana Hoard from northern Italy. I thank Fernando López Sanchez for access to his forthcoming catalogue of this hoard. The Reggio Emilia Hoard is described by Ungaro as an exception with only eastern mints represented and furthermore consisting of Late Antique and Barbarian jewellery. Sanchez regarded it to be an Oriental import.

228 Unfortunately, the mint composition of many solidus hoards remains unknown. The most extensive coin lists including information of mint distribution

the Scandinavian/Baltic hoards were assembled within the Western Empire or in the Successor Kingdoms.

The majority of the solidi found in the Baltic were minted in Constantinople, by far the most productive mint in the 5th century, but coins from western mints are always present in the ensembles from the Baltic areas. It is therefore unlikely that the solidi travelled directly to the Baltic area from the mint of Constantinople.

The mint composition of solidus hoards from the Eastern Empire is hardly ever known,[229] but there *are* examples of solidi from western mints found within the Eastern Empire so we cannot exclude that the hoards travelling north were formed here.

Another possibility is that the ensembles were formed *en route* outside the Empire, but the complete lack of comparative material from anywhere between the Eastern Empire and the Baltic makes this hypothesis purely conjectural.

The solidus finds in the Baltic region forms a closed group that is relatively easy to define in both time and space: an influx period lasting no more than half a century feeding the coastal areas from Pomerania to the Mälar region. Contemporary finds in Barbaricum outside this area form a different and somewhat diffuse picture. The number of coins in this group is much smaller and consists of small assemblages or even single coins spread over a geographically much larger area. Many of these coins are reworked into jewellery often by adding a loop and sometimes even a rim to the coins. While coins from the Constantinople mint are still common, a relatively higher number of coins from western mints are found outside the Baltic region. In western Denmark there is even a group of imitations not ascribed to any of the mints of the Western Empire of the Successor Kingdoms. It seems that the 5th century coins of this group continue a tradition of reuse of Roman coins in Barbarian contexts initiated no later than the 4th century with Constantinian coins, and in the later 4th century with the use of Roman medallions and imitations of them.

While the coin import into the Baltic region came to a rather abrupt close, the situation in the west differs significantly. The 5th century tradition dwindles, but there are occasional single finds of Byzantine coins of Justin and Justinian scattered around central and northern Europe, and few specimens appear in Scandinavia as a whole. In Western Europe the relatively few finds of 5th century solidi seem to herald the post-Antique period of the Successor Kingdoms with small scale use of gold coins and a generally decreasing number of coin finds.

The geographical definition of the two regions with diverging uses of Late Roman and post-Roman solidi is complicated because of several examples which cross the boundaries. The Fuglesangsager hoards from Ibsker are examples of western ensembles within the Baltic region. The coins from the hoards are earlier than other solidus finds from Bornholm, and in particular the loops and rims mounted on the coins reflect material from Western Denmark rather than from Bornholm.[230] Furthermore the 'bracteate paradox' is even more acute in Bornholm than in other parts of southern Scandinavia. The typologically earliest bracteates carry motives inspired by or imitating portraits and reverse motifs on coins and/or medallions of the middle or second half of the 4th century,[231] but these coins are not readily available anywhere in Scandinavia apart from Gudme and its surroundings. Morten Axboe suggested that the unfinished and discarded bracteate from Sylten should be evidence for a local production of bracteates in Ibsker.[232] Considering the intensive detector activity and the very high number of finds on Bornholm in general, the relatively low number of bracteates is a bit surprising: In southern Scania and eastern Sealand for example the bracteates outnumber solidus finds greatly.[233] The relatively low number of finds on Bornholm seems to contradict Axboe's theory, but it is on the other hand remarkable that while several of the finds have yielded die identical bracteates, there are no certain die identities between bracteates found on Bornholm and from other areas.[234]

The solidi from the Childeric burial in Tournay on the other hand are characteristic of the Baltic group, and thus conform to the suggestion that the denarii from the burial came from the east. In fact the ar-

---

are Kent 1994, lxxxviii-cxvi and Iluk 2007, 148-166.
229 Hobbs 2006, 9.

230 Horsnæs 2009, 239.
231 Axboe 2001.
232 Axboe 2009.
233 Helgesson 2002, fig. 1.
234 A possible exception being the bracteate fragment from Smørenge, Axboe 2011 on IK 606.

gument may be taken one step further, namely that both the solidi and the denarii from the burial may be part of the same influx from the east, and thereby the same eastern connection as seen in the jewellery from the burial,[235] even though the different denominations appear not to have been directly associated within the burial.

The two western siliquae from Bornholm may also be part of an exchange with the west, but based on the present evidence – two single finds of coins without possibility of dating the contexts – this is hard to ascertain.

After the end of the main influx of solidi to the Baltic area the more sporadic exchange with western areas may have continued. The only substantial find of 6th century solidi is the Smiss Hoard from Gotland. It consists of 20 small gold objects and 25 solidi ranging in time from Honorius to Justinian I (represented by seven coins) and Theodebert (one coin). The appearance of the solidi from the Smiss Hoard differs from the majority of solidus finds in the Baltic area: several of the coins are heavily worn and others are pierced. Perhaps the few occurrences of 6th century coins in the Baltic area can be understood as a part of a possible western influence post-dating the end of mass influx of solidi to the Baltic, in particular in the light of the single coin struck by the Merovingian king Theodebert present in the Smiss Hoard.[236]

Bornholm – a stepping stone or a final destination?

The questions is whether Bornholm was foremost a recipient of coins that never left it again or whether a much larger number of Roman coins passed it *en route* to somewhere else? Did the coins come directly to Bornholm from Pomerania or did they first pass through other of the areas within the Baltic circulation zone? Looking at a geographical map it is evident that Bornholm is not situated on a direct line from Vistula to Öland/Gotland. A detour was required. Was it convenient for example to pass Bornholm for taking in of fresh water or for trade?

The intense contacts between the Baltic islands, parts of the Swedish Mainland and Pomerania visible in the coin distribution is paralleled in the fibula material, but the fibula types furthermore demonstrate that the islands were part of a network which included also the Balt cultures of present-day Lithuania, Kaliningrad and eastern Poland.[237] This aspect is wholly absent when looking only at the numismatic finds and warns us that wider studies of interregional connections and routes cannot be based on one artefact type only. Although an investigation of this kind falls outside the scope of the present work, a few remarks centred on the routes in the western part of the Baltic area should be made.

It seems impossible on the basis of the numismatic material alone to argue whether the Vistula area fed all the other areas in the Baltic zone independently of each other in a series of bilateral connections, or whether one of the areas received material that was shipped on to other parts of the zone. Are the coins found on Bornholm for example those left over after the ships sailing on to Mainland Sweden, Öland and/or Gotland?

There are several instances where objects believed to have been produced in Pomerania but found on Bornholm are mentioned as evidence for connections between Bornholm and Pomerania,[238] but I have encountered less material from Gotland/Öland/Sweden found on Bornholm.[239] On the basis of the numismatic material I will suggest for the present that the coins most often came directly to Bornholm *via* the Vistula area.

Gotland is often described as being in close connection with the Mälar Area, and Fagerlie suggested that

---

235 Perin & Kazanski 1996.
236 Arne 1931 on the first finds of solidi and gold objects. Fagerlie 1967 no. 122, quotes later finds of solidi and mentions finds of two denarii and a pieces of bronze on the site; Östergren 1981 no. 123 mentioning a total of 20 gold objects from the same field. A large solidus hoard containing 6th century coins was found in the middle of the 19th century in Briesenbrow, Brandenburg, see FMRD XI, 2003. Solidi found in the late 2011 and possibly belonging to the same hoard included another specimen of a Theodebert coin, http://www.spiegel.de/wissenschaft/mensch/0,1518,807352,00.html.

237 Bitner-Wroblewska 2001.
238 For example the distribution of boat graves (Seehusen 2010) or Balt spears from the 4th-5th centuries found in Balsmyr (Nørgård Jørgensen 2008, 110).
239 This may be a coincidence – or sheer lack of investigations from this point of view.

the Helgö Hoard should be regarded as part of the Gotlandic material. Connections between Bornholm and Öland are possible, and we should not overlook the possibility that Bornholm, the eastern coast of Scania and Öland acted as an exchange zone. This is to some degree supported by the distribution of Roman coin finds on the Scania coast and the position of Ravlunda. But to get a firmer grip on the possible routes of interconnectivity within this zone we are in serious need of up-to-date studies on a broader range of objects and/or other cultural features.

CHAPTER 4

Coin usage on Bornholm

Find density

The number of Roman coins found in Bornholm is almost equal to the number found in all remaining parts of Denmark put together. With 2675 Roman coins from an area of only 588.5 km2, Bornholm is probably the single region outside the Empire that has the largest number of Roman coin finds per km². The number of sites in Bornholm is naturally lower than the rest of Denmark, c. 170 sites with Roman coin(s) compared to the c. 360 sites in the remaining parts of Denmark, but the site density naturally becomes much higher, and an average site yields more coins in Bornholm than in Western Denmark. Apart from the very large central places (Ibsker, Smørenge), there is a considerable number of middle size sites with more than five Roman coins – Sandegård, Agerbygård, Egesløkkegård and Rødbjerg/Tornbygård, but even a quick look at the distribution map of Roman coin finds in Bornholm reveals that there are many sites represented with two to five coins. Many sites, however, yielded only one Roman coin. In this way it seems that the redistribution, the flow of Roman coins, from nodal points (central places) to secondary or small sites is much greater in Bornholm than in other areas. But before drawing such a conclusion it is necessary to take a look at the two areas that are most closely comparable to Bornholm: Gotland and northeastern Poland.

Bornholm and Gotland not only share the position in the Baltic Sea, but more importantly the old sites with finds of hoards have been systematically re-investigated during Majvor Östergren's pioneering research in the 1970's and since then detector surveying of sites have been continued in Gotland. This has led to an impressive number of single finds from Gotland,[240] but the density of denarius finds from Gotland is still somewhat lower than from Bornholm (Gotland: 6500 denarii from 3,184 km² compared to Bornholm: 2426 denarii from 588.5 km²). It is quite possible that the higher number from Bornholm is due to the large number of private detectors who have spent endless hours here, compared to the detector investigations on Gotland.

Northeastern Poland is not readily comparable with Bornholm and Gotland as the registration of recent finds made by private detectorists is undertaken on private initiative. Still, a significant growth in coin finds from these areas has been registered since the turn of the millennium, and it seems fair to guess that the find density in these areas is in reality much higher than hitherto believed.[241]

The differences in the approach to detector archaeology as well as in national legislation between different areas are therefore of enormous importance for

---

240 Lind 2006.
241 Compare for example the distribution maps in Romanowski 2008 with the ones in Kubiak 1979 and the ones in Ciołek 2007 with the ones in Ciołek 2001.

Contexts

In spite of the high number of finds, very few Roman coins from Bornholm have been found in traditional closed contexts. This applies to coins found in single burials and in closed context during excavations of buildings or pits. In the three burials with coin finds from Bornholm the denarii were found in positions that indicate that they were most likely deposited in a purse made of organic material. They should therefore be seen as part of the dead person's (at least in two cases: the dead man's) personal belongings, rather than as part of a special deposition made in connection with the burial ritual.[242] The few closed settlement contexts have helped us suggest possible deposition dates, but the nature of the finds gives little more information on the possible use of the coins. The pit with the denarius from Vasegård for example contained various ceramic sherds, but it is not possible to say whether it was a conscious deposition or just the rubbish swept away. To be able to develop a more coherent discussion of the single finds we badly need more coins found in their primary deposition context.

The overwhelming majority of the finds have been made since the introduction of the metal detector in the exploration of the archaeology of Bornholm in the early 1980's. This is the most striking single factor in the review of the sites producing Roman coins. Although the scientific potential of these finds are great, they must be handled differently from the coins found in closed contexts.

Most of the recent detector finds of Roman coins are denarii deriving from sites identified as settlements by other find spectra or observations from the sites, whether they be other detector finds, small-scale excavations, crop marks visible by air photography or elevated phosphate values.

The vast distribution of settlements with Roman coins should be noted. There is a very large number of settlements with a small numbers of Roman coins on each site, and these settlements are distributed throughout the island. On roughly the northern half of the island a few intensively surveyed areas (Ibsker, Østerlars, Vang and Hasle) have yielded many sites. On the southern part of the island sites are situated more closely to each other, and what until recently would seem to be a coastal phenomenon, with many sites situated within 2 km from the coastline, is now changing, for example several recently located sites in the inland area between Nexø and Åkirkeby that have yielded finds of denarii. The apparent lack of sites in other areas is probably a reflection of the lower survey intensity in those areas. As argued above (Chap. 1) the distribution of coin finds therefore only tells us where coins have actually been found. Absence of finds probably indicates a lack of detector surveys rather than an absence of coins.

Detector finds as well as excavations reveal an impressive longevity of many settlements. The Ibsker settlement complex, for example, has produced finds from the Pre-Roman Iron Age to the Early Middle Ages. Roman coins, in practice 2nd century denarii, often surface among material dominated by finds from the Early Germanic Iron Age. There are even examples where one or a few denarii are found with material dominated by Viking Age coins. Sites where non-numismatic finds are dominated by objects from the Roman Iron Age are on the contrary quite few.

There are, however, numerous methodological problems involved in this assertion. Watt has demonstrated how the archaeological material varies according to which type of site it came from (settlements/graves) as well as to different retrieval methods (naked eye survey/detector survey/excavation) and according to the estimated erosion level of the settlements.[243] Likewise, the precision with which different object types can be reliably dated is of great importance for the evaluation of the detector finds: no other objects can be dated as precisely as the production dates of the coins. The production date of the denarii belong within the time frame of either the Early Roman (including the reign of Antoninus Pius) or the Late Roman Iron Age (from the reign of Marcus Aurelius onwards), while the Late Roman solidi would be placed within the Early Germanic Iron Age. The dating profiles of the major denarius sites peak in the Late Roman-Early Germanic Iron Ages or slightly later; while two of the medium size sites as regards denarius finds, Agerbygård and Sandegård, peak within the broader period Early Germanic Iron Age-

---

242 As also noted by Heidemann Lutz 2010, 225-226.

243 Watt 2006.

Viking Age.²⁴⁴ The dates of the material found during detector surveys alongside the Roman denarii indicate that the deposition date of the Roman coins took place somewhat later than the production date.²⁴⁵ More specialized studies of other types of material would hopefully help clarify and validate these assumptions. It would also be very useful to distinguish between short-lived and long-lived settlements. Without analysis of all available material from a site this is rarely possible, but the general impression is one of stable and long-lasting settlements *or* of repeated reoccupation of the same sites at short intervals.

It is on the other hand possible to postulate some displacements of the settlements from the period with finds of Roman coins to the period with finds of Viking Age coins, as only a relatively small part of the sites have both types. Among the sites with multiple finds of both periods it is furthermore possible to see that there is a tendency that most of the Viking Age coins belong to the first waves of Oriental imports: Sassanian drachms, and dirhams of the 8th and 9th centuries, while the more commonly found coins of the 10th and 11th centuries (Samanid dirhams and German and English coins) are rarer on sites with several Roman coins.²⁴⁶

Hardly any of the recent detector finds have been made on sites with no other finds. As mentioned, almost all coins have been found on sites with settlement related finds, and there is good reason to see denarii as settlement indicators. Most exceptions to this rule are old single finds without precise provenance. The two 'old' hoard finds of denarii from Robbedale and Udmarken have been found in areas that have not been subject to detector archaeology, and no traces of settlement activity have been noted. On the other hand prehistoric field systems have been mapped in the area, and it is therefore highly likely that these hoards may also derive from settlements rather than from an isolated areas.

I am quite convinced that a large number of the denarii found on the settlements are to be considered single finds in the sense that they were either lost or deposited one by one. It is more difficult to say whether the depositions were accidental or conscious and to discuss how the coins were used before deposition. Here detector archaeology reveals one of its weaknesses.

Coin finds within the settlements

The Iron Age houses on Bornholm were built of light timber and clay structures. Very few houses with a preserved ground plan have been excavated. Sometimes all that is left of the structural remains of a settlement are a few undated postholes and pits dug into the subsoil and/or remains of burnt daub found in the plough layer. While is it clear that most of the finds of Roman coins have been made on settlements, it is much harder to define the distribution of the coins in relation to building. The few cases are, however, revealing. The recent excavations at the Fuglesangsager site has demonstrated that the house was relatively small with three pairs of internal roof posts, characteristic of contemporary houses in other parts of Denmark. Both here and in the earlier excavation at Dalshøj gold hoards including Late Roman solidi had been deposited in clear connection with and just outside the building. It should be noted that the hoards were found in connection with relatively small houses apparently without traces of livestock, similar to finds in Gudme and other prosperous sites with imports found in connection with smaller houses, interpreted as possible 'private' halls.²⁴⁷

In the nearby Sylten IV site a dense cluster of partly melted denarii has been found in an area with remains of a burnt down house. Excavation did not establish the original position and size of the house, but there can be little doubt that the coins could only have been so heavily affected by the fire because they had been kept inside the building. Also several other sites have yielded both remains of burnt daub and denarii affected by excessive heat, leading to the suggestion that house fires in the Iron Age were a common cause for both coins and other valuables to have been abandoned.²⁴⁸ In other situations we can be fairly cer-

---

244 Watt 2006.
245 Taking away the denarii from the dating profiles would augment this tendency rather than the opposite as it seems that denarii from detector surveys have regularly been classified in the Roman Iron Age phase.
246 Horsnæs 2012.

247 Sørensen 2009, 141.
248 The experimental burning down of a reconstruction of an Iron Age house produced a maximum tempera-

tain that a dense cluster of denarii on a site are the remains of a buried hoard, but there are no examples where the deposition can be directly connected with a contemporary building, and we can therefore not be certain whether a hoard would be deposited within the house, in its vicinity or perhaps further away, close to a fence or an outhouse. Much more extensive excavations (and some luck) are needed, but we must remember that when a larger number of denarii appear as detector finds, they are remnants of disturbed coin hoards and an indication that the cultural layers have already been destroyed by modern activities. If the hoard had been hidden below surface (whether inside or outside a building), only the lowest levels of postholes and/pits from the settlement would be preserved once the hoard has been ploughed up.

The heavy stone foundations used for constructions of Iron Age houses in Gotland are much easier to recognize than the lightly built houses on Bornholm. Östergren therefore was able to conclude that there was a close connection between finds of coin hoards and settlements, and she was able to demonstrate that in several instances a hoard had been discovered inside a building.[249] Her research supports the interpretation of the majority of the coin finds from Bornholm as material deriving from settlements.

There are examples of medium sized sites where both denarii and solidi have appeared, but it is evident that the two denominations did not necessarily belong to the same contexts. In Vasegård and Egesløkkegård it is possible to argue that the solidi were deposited as hoards, while denarii from the same site were single finds. The material from Sandegård is more difficult to interpret as numismatic finds from all periods are distributed across the site without any specific clusters pinpointing disturbed hoards. However, both the finds made in the 19th century and the considerable number of detector finds of gold from the western part of the site indicate the presence of one or more gold hoards on the site. The seemingly haphazard scatter of material on Sandegård may indeed be partly caused by the no less than three, all very minor excavations undertaken on the site, of which only the latest (from 1990) can be approximately localized within the fields; but the disturbance caused by these excavations does not explain the fact that the coins are evenly scattered over such a large area.

Also on Agerbygård there is a very wide scatter of all coin types, but here there is a tendency that the Roman coins are found in a broad almost 100 m long band along the E-W road that runs alongside the part of the site that has been subject to investigation, while most of the (relatively few) Viking Age coins were found more than 50 m to the south closer to the nearby Østerlars church. The Medieval coins were scattered all over the site although no less than six of 14 coins were of the same type, struck by Magnus Smek in Lund after 1332. The trial excavation of long but narrow trenches undertaken in 1996 seems to have left no impact of the distribution of later detector finds.[250]

Hoards

For many years the majority of the denarii from Bornholm derived from three hoards only: The Robbedale, Udmarken and Borresø Hoards. While examining some of the large productive sites we have encountered an impressive number of new finds that may be interpreted as hoards: the Smørenge hoard(s), the hoards from the Ibsker settlement complex (Sorte Muld, Sylten IV, Nr. Fuglesang, Biskopenge IX), and the possible hoards from Store Smørengegård (Guldhullet) and Hundshalegård.

The Robbedale and Udmarken Hoards were almost certainly pure single type denarius hoards, and it is possible to interpret the finds from Sylten IV, Biskopenge IX and Hundshalegård similarly. Among these the Robbedale Hoard was the only one to be found together with remains of the original container, but the pottery fragments were unfortunately not preserved. Thus the 'pure' denarius hoards can only be dated by their inherent numismatic *t.p.q.*

---

ture of 1126 degrees C, more than enough to melt silver, Rasmussen 2007, 69. Remains of burnt houses are normally much 'richer' in material than other sites, probably because the disastrous event prevented salvage of the objects inside the building.

249 Östergren 1981, 15-16. The houses in Gotland are built on heavy stone foundations (nicknamed 'Giants' tombs') and much easier to recognize on the surface than the light structures in use on Bornholm.

250 The soil was backfilled into the original section of the trenches, pers.inf. Margrethe Watt.

The Smørenge Hoard may be interpreted as a single hoard deposited in two small pottery jars, and it is almost certain that the Anthemius solidus (struck 467-472 AD) found 15 cm from the jars was part of the hoard.[251] Likewise it is very likely that the Valentinian III/imitation solidus that was found attached to a denarius at Sorte Muld was part of the large Sorte Muld Hoard.[252] In both cases the hoards contained an overwhelming number of 2nd century denarii but a numismatic *t.p.q.* for the deposition date late in the 5th century was provided by the associated solidi.

As noted above, I am convinced that – apart from the hoards mentioned – both the Sorte Muld and Smørenge sites have yielded a considerable number of single finds and/or small hoards of denarii. This is based on the extremely large area with denarius finds, the marked differences in the surface preservation between the denarii found within the densest cluster of finds and those from more peripheral areas. This is particularly noticeable by the presence of a number of partly melted stacks of denarii at Smørenge, as well as the interesting distribution of reworked coins quite far from the centre of the main hoard scatters on both sites.

If we accept that Smørenge and Sorte Muld were both mixed hoards consisting of denarii and at least one solidus in each site, we must also consider the role of the other solidi that have been found on both these sites. In Smørenge there are several solidi, of which all except the one from the 1983 excavation were found more than 60 m from the hoard clusters. Sorte Muld on the contrary has produced five solidi within the cluster of denarii, as well as some solidi found further away. Comparative interpretation of the finds would suggest that while the Smørenge hoard contained one solidus only, the Sorte Muld hoard must have contained at least the five solidi from the cluster.

The hoard from Borresø was associated with gold spiral rings, but these are unfortunately of little help when trying to establish a non-numismatic *t.p.q.* for the deposition. The hoard from Nr. Fuglesang was also a mixed hoard consisting of denarii as well as silver and gold in the form of rings or ingots. The possible hoard at Guldhullet/Store Smørengegård contained among other things three small gold figures and gold bracteates. The find is thus dated in the late 5th or more probably in the 6th century, but we cannot in this case be certain that the denarii found in the area were part of the hoard. The coins seem to be spread over a larger area, and the site should perhaps rather be interpreted as part of a cumulative votive deposit.[253]

The gold hoards with solidi can be divided into three groups. Only a few hoards contained only coins: Buddegård (9 solidi), Ravnebro (six solidi) and Spagergård (seven solidi). The Dalshøj Hoard (17 solidi) probably belongs to this group, but it was already scattered when found, and more recent finds of solidi and other gold fragments from the area may or may not belong to the same hoard. Likewise we cannot exclude that it contained other elements as well.

The remaining hoards (Fuglesangsager I and II, Saltholmgård, Kåsbygård, Sandegård) can be described as mixed hoards containing Late Roman solidi as well as local objects of gold. The other object types are most often spiral shaped ring gold and ingots. In general, jewellery (gold beads with filigree, pendants and finger rings) is less common, but gold bracteates, beads and pendants were the main components in both hoards from Fuglesangsager. A single bracteate fragment came from the Sandegård Hoard.

Isolated finds?

While almost all denarii can be related to settlements, the situation is slightly different when looking at the solidi. Some gold hoards have been found in areas with no other contemporary finds. This may of course be due to a lack of investigation of the area in question, but in several cases hoards are found in topographic positions that indicate that they may have been deposited deliberately in an isolated area. This applies to the Buddegård Hoard found on a field near a pond, and to the now lost solidus from Bekkegård that probably derived from the same property as a large gold hoard found on various occasions on the edge of the moor, Balsmyr,[254] 300-400 m north of one of the two weapon sacrifices from Bornholm from the Late Roman Iron Age.[255]

---

251   The second cluster of denarii excavated in 2000 may or may not be part of the same hoard.
252   FP 5464.50; Horsnæs 2009, 250 find 24b.

253   Laursen & Watt 2011.
254   060104 sb 60; Klindt-Jensen 1957 and fig. 137. Gold hoard now in National Museum Prehistoric Dept. inv.nos. 19774-6, 20127, 20156-7, 20180-1.
255   060104 sb 59; Klindt-Jensen 1957, 79-82; Nørgård

Other hoards appear to be deposited in areas that may be considered on the one hand as boundary zones, but on the other hand as sites connected with a crossing from one place to another. Such an explanation may fit the Saltholmgård hoard found under the side stone of a prehistoric dolmen at the south side of the stream that has been suggested as the southern limit of the Ibsker settlement complex.[256]

The Ravnebro/Almindingen hoard was likewise found close to some small lakes in Almindingen and with a place name indicating the presence of a crossing ('Raven's Bridge'). The Kåsbygård hoard was found just south of the stream Askebækken, near the old crossing of the stream at Brandsvad Bro, with an interesting double description in the name (*vad* = ford and *bro* = bridge). Also the Spagergård hoard found *c.* 1.5 km west of Østerlars, 'in a heathery area east of the Spagergård' may belong to this group.[257] It is possible that this area was close to the stream Spager Å passing east of Spagergård. The toponym Spager-Bro *c.* 0.5 km east-northeast of Spagergård indicates the position of the crossing of the stream. So far no other finds can be related to the Spagergård hoard.

The Soldatergård hoard, consisting of 36 solidi, is the largest solidus hoard from Bornholm. It was discovered already in 1850-51 on a level field while removing some stones. The site is situated not far from Vasegård where a small solidus hoard was found on an Iron Age settlement, but at present it is not possible to tell whether it was connected to this settlement.

The early single finds of solidi are very difficult to evaluate. They are sometimes the only finds from a site, and re-investigations of these sites as well as other sites with single finds of gold objects are difficult and time consuming to undertake, as the descriptions of the old find spots are rarely precise. It is therefore not possible to ascribe these old finds to either a settlement or suggest that they are smaller hoard depositions in a liminal area. We must remember that the intrinsic value of a single gold coin would be high enough to be considered a valuable deposition in its own.

Coin influx to Bornholm c. 500 AD, an alternative suggestion

Time

The review in Chap. 3 shows that both as regards denarii and solidi there are differences in the combination of finds between eastern and western Europe and in both cases Bornholm is placed in an eastern context. The denarius finds from Bornholm can be compared to finds from a vast geographical area reaching from the Ukraine to the Baltic. Comparable solidus finds are however only found within a restricted coastal area within the Baltic area. While there are differences in some of the cultural expressions between these areas, the solidus finds testify to sea routes connecting them. The influx of solidi and the use of them must have happened within a relatively short period, perhaps as little as a half century.

The influx period of the denarii on the contrary must have started in the 3rd century as evidenced by the few finds from single burials. There are no dated primary contexts for denarii after the early 6th century which suggests that the denarii disappeared from use simultaneously with the solidi, and thereby creating a *terminus ante quem* for the influx of the denarii. Although dangerous, this argument *e silentio* cannot be wholly avoided when discussing the Roman coins in Bornholm. The relatively low number of coins from contexts dated in the 3rd century is intriguing and may point to a relative rarity of coins in this period, perhaps as exotica. The large coin influx into Funen, the Brangstrup/Danceny (or perhaps rather the Gudme/Černjachov) horizon of the 4th century, completely bypassed the Baltic. The very few 4th century coins from Bornholm cannot be used as argument for an influx in the same period: The two siliquae are of western mints and have been secondarily clipped, and the closest parallels for them have been found in contexts of the late 5th or even 6th century in other parts of Denmark and northwestern Europe. The bronze coins of the same period belong to the most ubiquitous types from the Roman Empire and circu-

---

Jørgensen 2008, 107. A snake head ring from the gold hoard belongs to Bechmann's type 39c, traditionally dated in period C2, and it is thus somewhat earlier than the solidus, cf. also Ethelberg 2000 with discussion of the snake head rings and lists of finds (note that his lists do not include rings from hoards).

256 060403 sb 68. FP 475. Breitenstein 1944, 52-58 no. 22; Klindt-Jensen 1957, fig. 131; Horsnæs 2009, 248-249 no. 22.
257 060405 sb 146. FP 216. Breitenstein 1944, 66 no. 25; Horsnæs 2009, 254 no. 36.

lated widely long after the breakdown of the western Empire.

Among the relatively few dated contexts of denarii in Bornholm several are placed in the Germanic Iron Age, and some have been dated by solidi in the late 5th/early 6th century. Looking at the general descriptions of the finds of other object types from detector sites it seems that quite a large part of the denarii from detector sites in Bornholm most probably belong to a chronological horizon that can be dated within the Early Germanic Iron Age.

Within the area where we encounter what can be termed the 5th century solidus horizon (the Baltic islands, the Mälar area, and probably the eastern coasts of Scania) solidi are accompanied by a very high number of denarius finds and a very low number of other Roman coin types.

The intensity of the influx of denarii over time are hard to establish, but it seems fair to suggest that the major influx of denarii to the Baltic islands may have arrived together with the solidi in the late 5th or even early 6th centuries. Suggesting that a considerable part of the denarii came during a short and intense period will naturally have consequences for the understanding of the use and meaning of the denarii in Bornholm.

Source

The coin influx into the Baltic area can be traced back to the Vistula estuary. Fagerlie's suggestion that the export area changed from the Vistula to the Oder in the latest part of the 5th century is founded on the chronological structure of the Karsibor Hoard only. There is, however, little other evidence to support it. Some finds dating back to the 5th century have been made at Wolin, but there is little evidence for any major settlements with foreign connections in that area.[258] It therefore seems – for the time being – safer to suggest that this hoard was the result of coastal connections within Pomerania originating from the Vistula area.[259]

The majority of the coin finds from Pomerania cluster around Gdansk and along the right bank of the Vistula River. In the latter area we find the two important archaeological sites, Weklice (Iron Age cemetery and settlement) and Janow Pomorski (identified as the Viking Age *emporium* Truso) that testify to the importance of the area throughout the first millennium, and to the possibility of locating a centre of redistribution and trade responsible for the outlet of solidi towards the Baltic.

'Hortfundhorizont'

An important prerequisite for hoarding is, however, often overlooked: the ability to create a surplus that could be saved in the form of precious metal. Suggesting that the majority of denarii and solidi from Bornholm belonged to the same chronological phase would mean that the period of deposition is contracted to little more than half a century, beginning in the second half of the 5th century and ending probably within the first quarter of the 6th century. The reason for this sudden influx of relatively large amounts of precious metal has not been satisfactory explained. Lars Jørgensen believed that a surplus of agricultural product (mainly cattle and/or hides) was exported in return for the goods,[260] but he failed to explain who needed the products, and he did not take into account the parallel growth in precious metal coins in the finds from Gotland and Poland. It must be stressed that the 'large amounts' of precious metal in the Baltic areas is seen in relation to the amounts of precious metal recovered in Bornholm from the immediately earlier and later periods of the Iron Age. On a European scale the *finds* of gold coins from the 5th – early 6th centuries in the Baltic area are unique, but Late Roman and Early Byzantine literary sources reveal that much larger sums of money in the form of gold, coins or other valuables were available, both on the private level, as for example the yearly income of a single Roman senator which was far larger than the amounts in gold found in the Baltic area, and on political levels as indicated by the recorded sums paid out as tribute.[261]

---

258 Bogucki 2010.
259 The unfortunately badly recorded Mrzezino Hoard (Ciołek 2007, no. 225) is ample evidence that this area was receiving material also in the latest phase of the solidus influx.

260 Jørgensen 1991. It should be noted that Jørgensen regarded the denarii as belonging to the Early Germanic Iron Age rather than the Late Roman Iron Age.
261 One among several examples is the treaty signed at the battle at Chersonese in 447. It included among

This coin influx however coincides with the apparent climax of the central sites at Ibsker and Smørenge, and the majority of the finds have been made there. Both sites have yielded impressive hoards, and there are several indicators that they played significant roles in the communities. The Sorte Muld hoard was deposited in a central part of the site in an area with finds of weapons and close to the slightly later deposition of gold foil figures. The centre of the coin hoard cluster is situated at the corner of a quasi-rectangular structure (up to 40 x 30 m in size) visible on the geomagnetic survey map, but not yet verified during excavation.[262] Furthermore, the largest known find of gold foil figures has been made on Sorte Muld in an area only *c.* 30 m from the denarius cluster. It is possible that both the Sorte Muld coin hoard and the gold foil figures belonged to the religious sphere. If meant as a religious sacrifice recovery of the hoard was never intended.

The Smørenge hoard(s) was deposited a bit to the north of the area yielding the largest amount of ordinary settlement material, but still within an area with building remains. It was much closer to the centre of the settled area than the sacrificial site west of the settlement, and the other more distant sacrificial site at Guldhullet to the southwest. Considering the size of the hoard – probably the largest denarius hoard found in Denmark as regards the number of coins – and the particular character of the Smørenge site as a whole, we cannot exclude that the hoard should be interpreted in line with the two sacrificial sites as a possibly ritual deposition.

The two large centres have been tentatively related to the fortifications or 'Fluchbürge' at Gamleborg in Paradisbakkerne *c.* 4 km from Ibsker and Lilleborg in Almindingen at almost the same distance north of Smørenge. In the latter case it was recently confirmed that the Medieval castle of Lilleborg must have had an Iron Age forerunner coexisting with the main phase of the Smørenge site, while the connections between Ibsker and Gamleborg are of a more conjectural nature.

Why hoarding?

Both Breitenstein and Klindt-Jensen followed Bolin and other Swedish scholars, when they discussed hoards in relation to the theme 'war'. They were convinced that hoards had been hidden during periods of unrest. Klindt-Jensen suggested that the denarius hoards, of which he knew only one example associated with other objects namely the Borresø Hoard, had been deposited some time after the production period (late 1st to early 3rd centuries), but still before the beginning of the Migration Period (according to Klindt-Jensen in the late 4th century). The gold hoards were later, as shown not only by the numismatic *t.p.q.*, but also by the local objects in the hoards. The three hoards from Soldatergård, Spagergård and Almindingen were regarded as hidden by people taking refuge in these, according to him, unhospitable places.[263]

Östergren summarized the many theories regarding the reasons for hoarding and – more importantly – for not recovering hoards: war, piracy, internal crisis and emigration.[264] Conflicts, whether internal or imposed upon a society by outsiders in the form of piracy or war, are seen as a main instigator for hoarding, but natural phenomena (climate changes and pandemics) were also mentioned. The different theories do not stand alone, but may be interacting, and various backgrounds have been suggested. All interpretations however rely on the same empiric material, interpreted by using various theoretical frameworks. These theories have in common a profane approach to the concept of hoarding, and take into consideration only the economic value of the hoard.

Ritual depositions

More recent approaches suggest that the concept of hoarding should be examined from a wider range of perspectives, including various types of religious or culturally defined depositions. In these cases a hoard needed to stay buried. It is therefore important to note that the Roman coins were most abundant in those centres which are also characterized by the find of gold foil figures. Both coins and figures are characterized by being small objects in precious metal carry-

---

other things(!) an annual tribute of 2,100 pounds of gold to be paid out to Attila and Bleda by Theodosius II. This amount alone equals 151,200 solidi, if paid in coin, cf. Guest 2008.
262 Lund Hansen *et al.* 2009, 184-185.

263 Klindt-Jensen 1957, 156-162.
264 Östergren 1981, 35.

ing an image of a human figure. Is it possible to imagine that they were used for the same purposes? They definitely did not belong to the same chronological horizon, but could the gold foil figures be taking on a role formerly filled by the coins?

After suggesting a religious background for the depositions of the gold in liminal areas as well as the largest denarius/gold hoards inside the settlements, it is time to turn to the old finds of denarius hoards. The Borresø Hoard could certainly be explained as a religious deposition in the lake next to what might have been the main(?) fortification of the Germanic Iron Age on Bornholm, Lilleborg. The two other hoards were both found in outlying fields in the 19th century, but information is too scanty to draw safe conclusions as to their Iron Age contexts. Surface reconnaissance has identified prehistoric field systems in the areas, suggesting a settlement pattern different from the pre-modern period. The areas are badly investigated and not favourable to detector surveys; parts of the area have even been dug away in connection with exploitation of gravel. Still, it would be extremely interesting if future field work could contextualize these two hoards.

The 6th century

The lack of coin influx into the Baltic area after the early 6th century could suggest that the local communities suffered an economical set-back. This appears not to be the case. The analyses of the total material from productive sites undertaken by Margrethe Watt show that the quantity of other find-groups did not dwindle as the coins disappear, on the contrary, material from both settlements and burials indicate that life went on – at least relatively – unaffected.[265] Lars Jørgensen argued for the Early Germanic Iron Age as a transitional phase with significant changes in the settlement pattern from village-like structure (based on the large collective cemeteries from that period) to central places as Ibsker in combination with dispersed single farms. The precious metal in the hoards belonged to this transitional phase and gave way to wealth displays in the rich warriors' graves from the later part of the Germanic Iron Age. To Jørgensen, the transition was also one of a change of external relations from a focus on the Baltic zone to more western contacts with upcoming Successor Kingdoms such as the Franks.[266] His view may be supported by the interpretation of the gold coins from northern Europe as the result of two distinct routes: the eastern route feeding the Baltic area and a less massive, but more long-lived western route including the post-Anastasian solidi. Gold did become rare during the 6th century. Not only the solidi disappeared, but also the other types of gold objects known from the hoards of the 5th and early 6th century. The sole locally produced gold objects are the gold foil figures, and in spite of the huge number of figures known from Bornholm, in particular from the Sorte Muld, the production of them demanded very little raw material in comparison with the weight of the solidi and the Nordic gold bracteates.

It is very likely that the finds reflect a primacy of the centres in the influx and hoarding of wealth, which was then re-distributed to secondary centres and more ordinary settlements. The permeability from the centres to the minor sites is however much greater than on Funen, where the mass of coins seems to be less extensively redistributed.[267] Roman coins have been found in Gotland on sites that were later to become a *thing* site,[268] but in Bornholm the large central places went out of use towards the end of the first millennium, and there seems in general to be little continuity in use of Iron Age sites after that period.

Raw material

There are no natural deposits of silver or gold on Bornholm. All precious metals had to be imported, so even locally produced gold and silver objects demanded a supply of raw material. The 'raw material' theory creeps into the archaeological discourse; not because it has been proven that coins were re-used as metal deposits, but largely because of lack of other explanations. There are several sites where traces of smithing activities have been encountered, but even then finds of (partly) melted denarii from Bornholm

---

265 Watt 2000.
266 Jørgensen 1991.
267 Horsnæs 2010, 185. Future finds and research may of course change this picture.
268 Myrberg 2009.

cannot be used as an argument for the use of denarii as source of silver. The (partly) melted denarii have been found on sites where also the presence of burnt daub has been recorded. We must consider that the Iron Age houses were highly at risk of fires, and disasters must have happened regularly. The temperature reached at the burning of an Iron Age house would be sufficiently high to melt silver.

Much more research needs to be undertaken to evaluate the raw material theory. Naturally both silver and gold may have come to Bornholm in the form of coin, as suggested by Heidemann Lutz,[269] but there must have been other sources of precious metal, particularly for the gold: No gold coins produced before the very end of the 4th century has ever been found on Bornholm, yet locally produced gold objects antedating this time are numerous.

---

269 Heidemann Lutz 2010, 227.

CHAPTER 5

Conclusions

Lack of impact?

The finds of Roman coins demonstrate huge variations from one part of Denmark to the other. This applies not only to the volume but also to the nature and composition of the coin finds. The distinct features that characterise the material culture of Bornholm throughout prehistory and early history are well known. Hence it is no surprise that these characteristics also apply to the numismatic material in the Iron Age, where the island differed from other parts of what is now Denmark. While Roman coins came to Western Denmark from various sources as a result of a long series of 'import events', they seem to have arrived in Bornholm in great numbers over a relatively short period.

There is a chronological correspondence between coin influx and the growth of main centres in Bornholm in the Early Germanic Iron Age. It is fair to assume that the two are connected and to see the coins as a reflection of greater wealth at this period. The coins were usable in a pre-monetary economy – not as coins but as exchangeable objects (pre-weighed or stamped ingots) within a barter economy. The reason for this wealth is puzzling but it clearly affected the western Baltic area as a whole, while the cultures on the eastern coasts of the Baltic appear to have missed the influx of gold and silver. The question is how much the Roman coins were put to use in an already established tradition. That the gold coins entered into local use is evident as they were found in hoards together with for example gold jewellery, ring gold and small ingots (sometimes as a gold-silver alloy). Gold as a material was obviously more important than the shape of the gold objects. Denarii are sometimes found as pure denarius hoards, or can be mixed with gold either in the form of coins or as ingots.

The symbolic value of coins is difficult to assess, but it is remarkable that the Roman coins seem to have had surprisingly little impact on local society in the years around 500 AD. There are few examples from Bornholm of objects imitating Roman coins or use of coin motifs or stylistic elements traceable in local objects. On the contrary, the very few examples of local figurative art have no features taken over from the coins. The small gold male figures found recently at Guldhullet (Smørenge)[270] resemble some small – presumably contemporary – figures from Sweden and the Slipshavn hoard on Funen, and they are local or rather 'non-Roman' in their expression. The slightly later gold foil figures, found in great numbers on Bornholm, differ technically from the coins. Although certain motifs may echo Roman iconography[271] they also represent a

---

270   Laursen & Watt 2011.
271   Margrethe Watt refers to a gold foil figure that seems to carry a motif inspired by the Roman *signifer* type, Watt 2004, 209. Note, however, that the foil figures are dated to the Later Germanic Iron Age and thus after the period where Roman coins were readily available.

101

'local' tradition in the same way as the gold bracteates.

Ritual deposits in moors existed on Bornholm before the 5th century, but the sheer availability of precious metals in the form of coins may have increased the usage of ritual depositions. After the coin influx had ceased precious metals, particularly gold, became rare on Bornholm, and ritual deposition mainly consisted of the thin and very light-weight gold foil figures. The figures are, however, normally found on the sites where Roman coins had been abundant, and sometimes – as at Sorte Muld and Smørenge – the deposits seem to continue the tradition expressed by depositing the coins.

The prevailing interpretations of the Roman imports into Scandinavia in the 20th century were based based on a theoretical approach of *imitatio romana* assuming a profound Roman influence in all aspects of elite culture in the Late Roman Iron Age (Eggers' Period C).

Since the turn of the Millenium much research has focused on the concepts of 'middle ground theory', 'hybridity' and 'creolization' as interpretative tools for the understanding of the changing identities for objects and persons alike, and this theoretical framework has also made its way into Scandinavian archaeology.[272] The use of terms such as 'hybridity' or 'creolization', that characterizes the situations where persons of different backgrounds meet and coexist, are however inadequate as concepts for understanding the presence of Roman coins on Bornholm. The material culture represented by the archaeological finds from Bornholm does not support an interpretation of the island as a 'middle ground' where a hybrid culture could develop.

Looking at the coin finds from Bornholm a wholly different picture emerges. There is no reason to believe that the Roman coins were brought into southern Scandinavia by Romans directly from the mint. On the contrary all evidence points to the majority of the coins, 2nd century denarii as well as 5th century solidi, arriving in the late 5th or and some even as late as the early 6th century *via* non-Roman intermediaries. In the case of the 2nd century denarii this implies an extended period of circulation outside the Empire. The Roman impact as transferred by the coins was subtle. The coins were certainly imported objects, and they were probably recognized as 'foreign', but they were probably not seen as 'Roman' and they did not evoke a sense of Roman-ness on the inhabitants of Bornholm

The finds can better be understood within a framework of an 'appropriation theory': basically suggesting that the coins had completely changed their original meaning and were used in a way that was appropriate for the local community. There was no difference between the use of Roman coins and other objects made of precious metals. The coins have an intrinsic value, and they were clearly hoarded alongside local objects of precious metals. Hoarding of coins was possible only during a relatively short period simply because the coins were available at that particular time.

An assessment of detector archaeology

Detector archaeology is well suited for studies in bird's eye perspective. It is useful for the recovery of large amounts of material that can provide evidence to trace routes and changes over time. It has likewise made it possible to demonstrate redistribution from centres to middle size or smaller sites, and thus documenting a much wider use of single coins throughout the community than was ever imagined before the start of detector surveying.

It has been possible to suggest the existence of a 'Hortfundhorizont' in the late 5th and early 6th century, which is in some ways comparable to the situation in Funen in the 4th century, characterized by depositions of precious metal hoards, many probably of religious nature, both inside and outside the settlements/centres.

The pinpointing of finds by detector archaeologists has proved its value. Yet it is still difficult, and sometimes impossible, to define which coins (and other objects) were the result of single accidental losses and which had been deliberately deposited, perhaps as hoards.

Detector archaeology has brought to light enormous amounts of finds that would otherwise have been lost to research, and non-intervention methods as phosphate analysis and soil sample analysis have improved our understanding of many productive sites. Surprisingly little archaeological field work has been undertaken considering the vast number of finds, and the

---

272 An outspoken example in Ekengren 2009.

interpretation of the finds would no doubt benefit from targeted and large scale archaeological excavations of specific sites. Yet, it must be underlined that in many cases the original cultural layers have already been completely destroyed by modern argriculture: no strata are left between plough layers and subsoil. This means that all archaeological artefacts are today found in modern plough layers. It makes little sense to conduct excavations in these circumstances, but metal detector archaeology provides us with a last chance to recover information on our ploughed-up history.

A picture of different types of denarius finds on the same sites is emerging: Much worn coins that may tentatively be ascribed to hoards can be found close to other coins – and among them some reworked ones – that are less worn. It has been shown that the tossing around in the plough layer is destructive even for the massive and normally well-preserved denarii. In several instances where denarii have been broken it seems that the breaks were recent. The broken objects whose parts can be recombined give an impression of the distances over which the objects are being moved around by agricultural works.

While using this compilation of material it is important to remember that is it not the final nail in the coffin. Our knowledge of a detector sites is continuously evolving in a manner completely different from archaeological excavations. Once finished the excavated areas are most often backfilled and therefore inaccessible to other scholars, and they are only known (in ideal cases) through an excavation report. The surveyed fields are constantly rendering new material and interpretation will have to be adjusted accordingly.

CHAPTER 6

The sites with Roman coin finds

This section includes all the sites that until the end of 2010 had been registered as the find spot of one or more Roman coins. The first group to be described is the complex of sites in Ibsker parish forming a cluster between the modern town of Svaneke and the Romanesque church of Ibsker. The remaining sites will be listed in a counter clockwise sequence from Ibsker following the north, west and south coasts of Bornholm.

A Field of Gold - the central place in Ibsker parish

The toponym *Sorte Muld*, literally 'Black Soil' has become the name for a specific type of archaeological site: A *black-soil site* is an area where the soil is darker than the surrounding fields. The black soil is caused by the material, including charcoals, ploughed up from the underlying culture layers which are also rich in phosphoric acid. The *black-soil sites*, often referred to in English as 'productive sites', are rich in archaeological finds. Apart from describing this particular type of site, the name Sorte Muld is somewhat confusingly used both for the central part of the Ibsker settlement complex and for the complex as a whole. The confusion in itself dates back to the earliest finds from the area; hence it is not possible to prove beyond doubt the exact provenance of some of the solidus finds, where the find spot is named either Sylten (a name now used for one of the satellite sites, cf. below) or even more general 'Svaneke area'.

Sorte Muld is situated *c.* 1.5 kilometres inland from the town of Svaneke on the eastern side of Bornholm. In a 16th century source it was also known as *Guldagerenn*, 'the Field of Gold'. This alternative name proves that gold finds had been made from an early period onwards.[273] The status of Sorte Muld can already be inferred in the earliest archaeological studies by the fact that it was the first site to be mentioned in Vedel's section about settlement areas, with a description of the excavations undertaken in 1869 and 1884, as well as a short list of the most important finds.[274] Excavations were undertaken again between 1948 and 1953, when Ole Klindt-Jensen investigated building remains on both Sorte Muld and Dalshøj.[275]

The full potential of the site has, however, only been revealed by the surveys, excavations, and phosphate analyses undertaken continuously since the early 1980's. The investigations have shown that Sorte

---

273 Lund Diocese Manorial Court Roll 1569. For a general introduction to the site see Adamsen (ed.) 2009, in particular Watt (pp. 17-27) on the history of the exploration; Watt 2010, 564-567; Margrethe Watt is preparing a monograph on the Sorte Muld area (Watt *forthcoming*).
274 Vedel 1886, 399.
275 Klindt-Jensen 1957; reviewed by Becker 1958.

105

Crossing boundaries

Fig. 53. A: The Ibsker settlement complex with indications of the sb numbers of the individual sites. In grey: modern roads and other areas not accessible for metal detecting.

Muld is part of a much larger complex, consisting of the central area surrounded by a number of satellite sites. The Ibsker complex existed from the Roman Iron Age until it dwindled during the Viking Age. The main periods, as revealed by the detector finds, were the Roman and Germanic Iron Ages, while the Viking Age presence is more sporadic and tend to move away from the central area.[276]

---

276 See maps with distribution of dated finds in Adam-

The sites with Roman coin finds

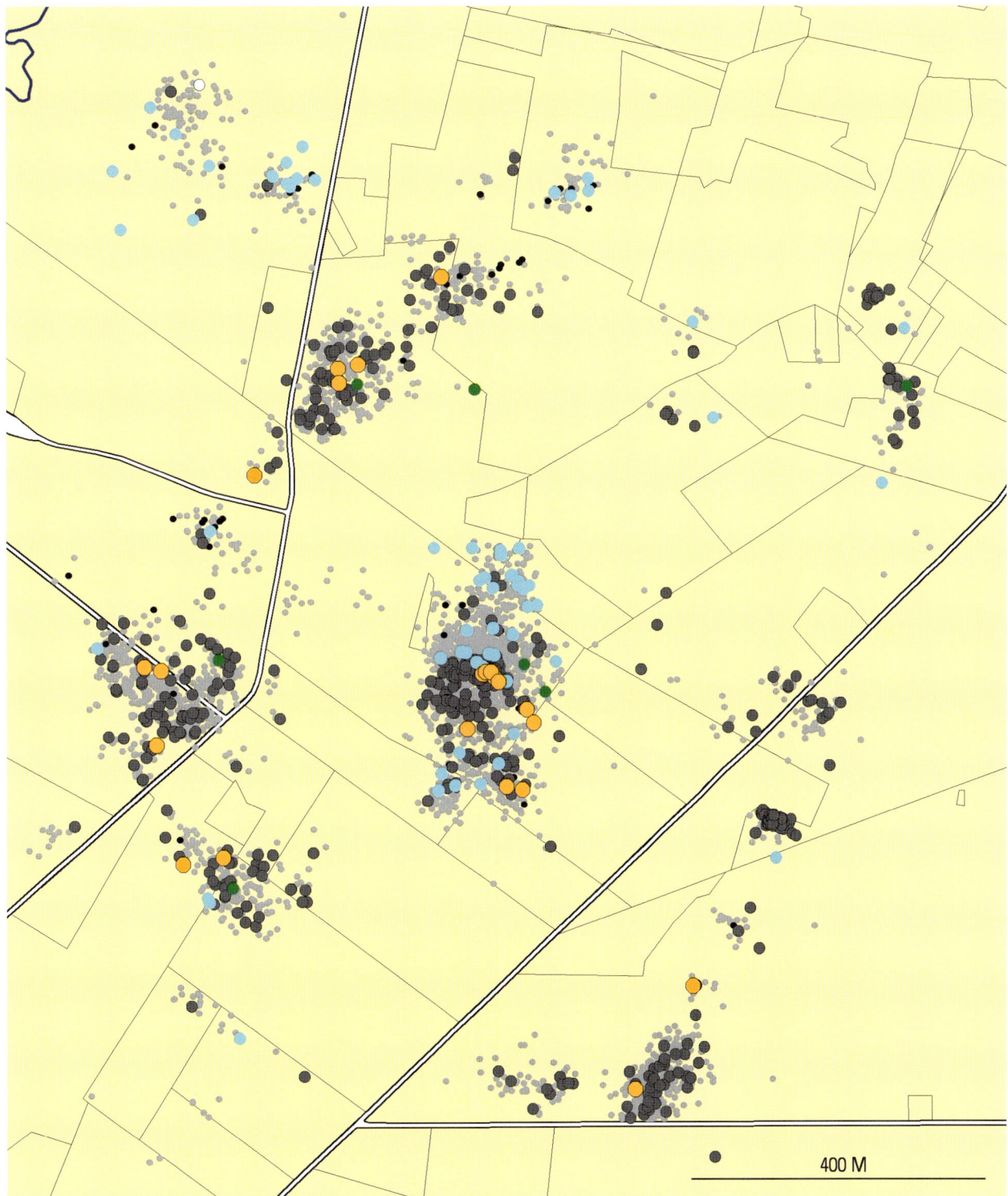

Fig. 53. B: Ibsker settlement complex. Distribution of finds. The dense cluster of light grey dots in the centre of the site marks the area with concentration of gold foil figures. Note that Viking Age coins are remarkably rare in the circle of sites around Sorte Muld, but some have been found on the central site itself – in particular in the northern part of it – and they have been found in some numbers in the peripheral sites. Legend: See fig. 55 (p. 101)

sen *et al*. 2009, 146-147. Note that the denarii have been plotted onto these maps according to production date, i.e. they are represented in the map with finds from the Roman Iron Age.

The Ibsker complex is connected to the sea via the old 'Krøblingevejen' track that can still be followed from Sorte Muld, passing Dalshøj and undulating towards the natural landing place at Vigen in

Fig. 54. The central part of the Ibsker settlement complex (note: north is to the left). The very dark soil is clearly visible, both on Sorte Muld in the centre of the photo and on Dalshøj with patches of surfacing rock (in the lower left hand corner). Photo: Martin Stolze, Bornholms Museum.

Svaneke, but there are other landing places in the area, in particular in the Frennemark area east of Svaneke, but so far few archaeological finds from the area have been made on any of them.[277] Topographically the area is enclosed by the streams Vase Å, with an outlet at Listed northwest of the complex, and the smaller Skovsholm Bæk with an outlet at Thygehavn southeast of the complex. The Saltholmgård hoard (cf. below) was found at a dolmen next to this stream. Cemeteries belonging to the main period of the complex have not been located within the area enclosed by the streams, but some bauta have been found in the coastal area northeast of the complex.[278] The Hintzegård site is situated near Ibsker Church, southwest of the Iron Age complex and clearly outside the ring of satellite sites. It is the only site of some substance in the vicinity of the Ibsker settlement complex, and it has yielded material mainly from the Viking Age.[279]

The Ibsker settlement complex has (until late 2010) yielded more than 900 Roman coins, which is the largest number of Roman coins from one area in Bornholm. The concentration of Roman coin finds from the settlement complex is even more striking, when comparing to other areas in the northeastern Bornholm, where Roman coins are practically absent. The description of the individual sites within the complex will concentrate on the numismatic material, but includes reference to other information relevant for the understanding of the coins in their contexts. The presentation will start with the central area, Sorte Muld itself, and the adjacent Fuglesangsager. It will proceed with the satellite sites, here described from the north counterclockwise.[280]

---

277 Lund Hansen *et al.* 2009, 186-187.
278 Seehusen 2009.

279 060403 sb 58. BMR 1530.
280 For additional information on Sorte Muld: Adamsen

Sorte Muld

After the initial investigations by Vedel, Klindt-Jensen excavated 800 square metres at Sorte Muld in 1948-49. The excavation took place *c*. 80 m north of the highest point of the field and uncovered the remains of what Klindt-Jensen interpreted as two buildings from the Migration Period.[281] It is significant that no Roman coins were noted during the excavations. Some years later, in 1953/4, a single solidus was found at the centre of Sorte Muld 'on the top part of the north slope', but there is no indication as to its exact location.[282]

Detector archaeology at Sorte Muld began in the early 1980's, and in 1985 the find of several gold foil figures prompted an excavation near the highest point of Sorte Muld, to the south of the former excavation. 600 square metres were excavated, and to retrieve as many of the very small gold foil figures as possible, all soil was wet sieved on the spot. The procedure resulted in a very high number of finds, including *c*. 2300 gold foil figures, around 85% of all known specimens, and an indication of the presence of a nearby cult centre. The cultural layer furthermore contained clay daub deriving from a building.

Continued surveys brought to light a dense cluster of denarii from an area a bit to the east of the 1985 excavation, and the material was quickly interpreted as the remains of a denarius hoard. Renewed excavations were undertaken in 1988 to establish the possible stratigraphy and extent of this hoard, but in spite of the many finds of denarii during the excavations, no trace of the original deposition was found *(Fig. 58)*.

The central area of the Ibsker complex[283] has until 2010 yielded 313 denarii, 15 solidi, two Roman bronze coins, 26 Cufic dirhams and 8 Late Medieval to Pre-Modern coins *(Fig. 55)*. Many of the coins have been found in the plough soil after the closing of the excavations, but the distribution pattern of the coin finds still reveals a significant cluster of coins, mainly denarii but also some solidi and even later coins, in the area investigated in 1988. The area of the gold foil figures has, however, not produced more Roman coins than other parts of the field, in spite of the thorough investigation. The area excavated by Klindt-Jensen can only be located approximately in relation to more recent field work, but is it clear that the find density of denarii in the area excavated by him was relatively low, and it is unlikely that he overlooked significant coin finds. It seems safe to conclude that many of the denarii from Sorte Muld derive from one deposition, a hoard that must have been deposited *c*. 30 m from the main cluster of gold foil figures. Within the centre of this cluster there are also five solidi, and one of them was found still adhering to a denarius *(Fig. 56)*.[284] Margrethe Watt suggested that the hoard consisted of not only denarii, but also at least one solidus. If this theory is right we may suggest that the solidi found within the centre of the cluster also belonged to this hoard.

The remaining coins are spread over a large area, where also numerous other finds have been made. The surface of most of the denarii from the central part of Sorte Muld is generally well preserved, although quite worn. The very worn condition renders legends legible only with difficulty. Very few of the coins are broken. The wear and absence of corrosion are the most easily recognizable common characteristics. After cleaning and conservation the coins are shining brightly. Unfortunately the cleaning of many of the coins has removed the dirt and patina of the surface that may be a clue to define whether other coins derive from the same context or not.

The same characteristics apply to the denarii from the areas Sorte Muld Syd and Fuglesangsager. It has been possible to identify two fragments from the same coin found years apart on the Fuglesangsager *(Fig. 57)*.[285]

The distribution of Roman coins as well as objects in general crosses field boundaries and thereby individual ownerships: denarii have even been found in the adjoining fields of Paradisgård (5 specimens) and Fuglesangsager (16 specimens). The scattered finds include both denarii and solidi, as well as a small number of more recent coins.

(ed.) 2009, and – most importantly – Watt *forthcoming*.
281 Klindt-Jensen 1957, 18-26. Some of his interpretations were immediately questioned by Becker 1958.
282 Klindt-Jensen 1957, 184 and 159 fig. 135 top; Fagerlie 1967, find 204, cat. 343; Kromann 1990, 114 no. 56 (ill).; Horsnæs 2009, 250 no. 24a.
283 060403 sb 93. BMR 1191 (Sorte Muld), 2649 (Fuglesangsager) and 3141 (Sorte Muld Syd/Paradisgård).
284 Solidus FP 5464.50 (x830Ra), see photo in Horsnæs 2009, 235 fig. 3.25, and denarius FP 5464.23 (x830Rb) Antoninus Pius or M. Aurelius (Caesar).
285 BMR 2649x20/FP 6403.2 and x225/FP 7034.2.

Crossing boundaries

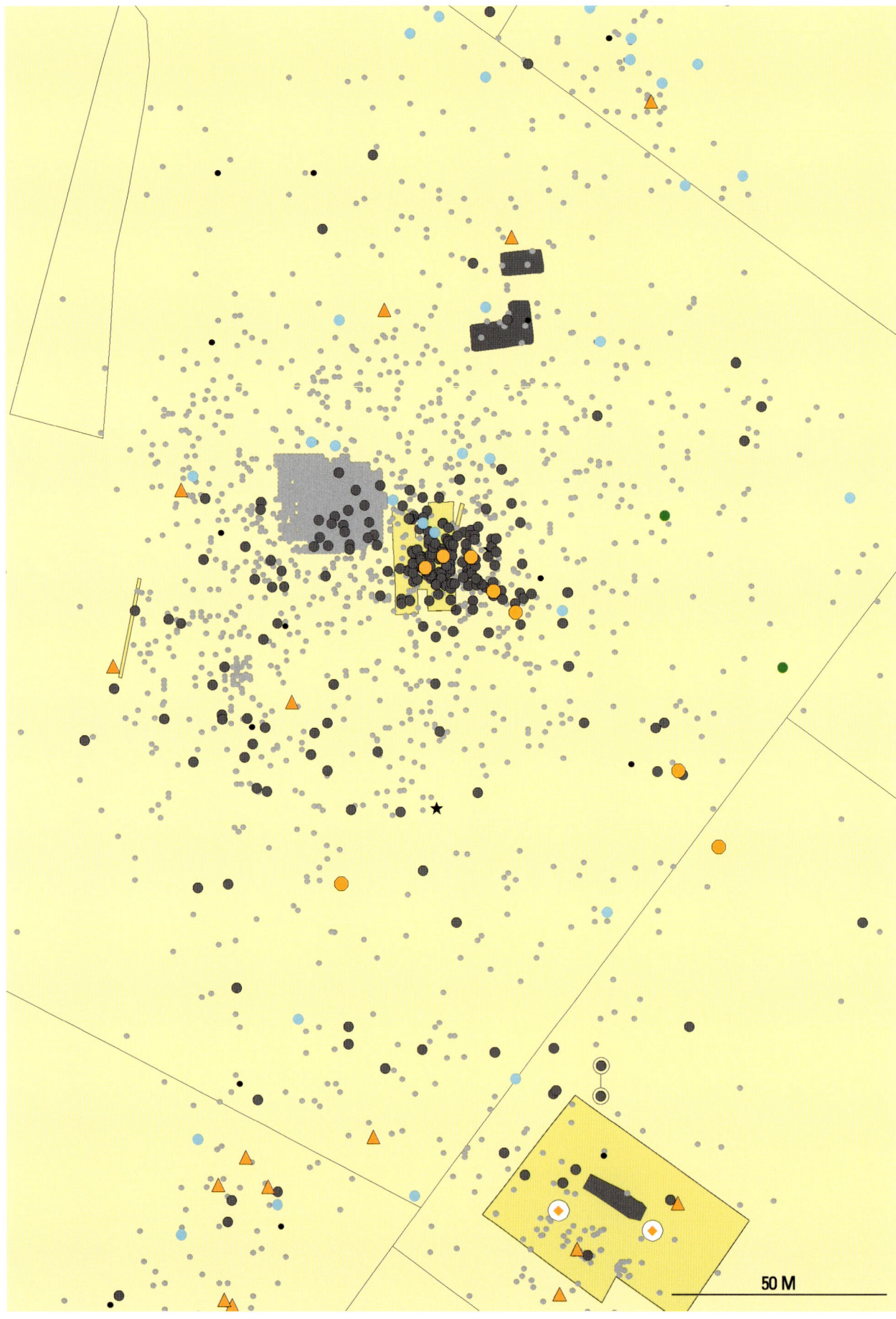

50 M

- Denarius
- Solidus
- Bronze coin
- Ring gold
- Fibula
- Other gold objects except gold foil figurines
- Denarius hoard
- Gold hoard
- Viking Age coin (struck 600-1130)
- Medieval coin (struck 1130-1536/1540)
- Coin struck after 1540
- Siliqua
- Coin struck after 1130
- Other object types
- Surfacing bedrock
- Excavation areas
- Two or more fragments of the same coin

Fig. 55. Distribution of finds from Sorte Muld superimposed on houses and trenches from the mid-19th century excavations: the houses are marked in dark grey, and excavation areas are marked in yellow. One of the trenches dug by Klindt-Jensen cut the area of denarius hoard, which at that time was not identified and may have been still in situ (after Klindt-Jensen 1957, fig. 9). The house and excavation limit of the Fuglesangsager site are in the southeastern corner (after Sørensen 2009). Note the position of the hoards in relation to the house. The excavation area of the cluster of gold foil figurines (in light gray) is situated close to the coin hoard, but there is clearly at least 10 m and probably more than the double between them. Scale 1:1250.

Fig. 57. Joining fragments of denarius from Fuglesangsager. FP 6403.2+7034.23.

Fig. 56. Solidus and denarius as found (attached) and taken apart. FP 5464.50 and FP 5464.23.

Fig. 58. Sorte Muld. Examples of denarii from the 1988 excavation area (BMR 1191). Scale c. 1:1. Photo Martin Stoltze, Bornholms Museum.

The sites with Roman coin finds

Fig. 59. Sorte Muld. Denarii from Sorte Muld Syd/ Paradisgård (BMR 3141): FP 6923.1, FP 7035, FP 7294.1, FP 7294.2, FP 8157.1.

The question is whether it is possible to distinguish between coins from the large hoard at the centre of the Sorte Muld site and coins from other depositions in the area?

Fig. 60. Sorte Muld. Denarii from Fuglesangsager (BMR 2649): FP 6844.1-4.

The results of the excavations of the hoards from Orup (Sealand) and Præstemosen (Funen) have demonstrated that coins from one hoard may be spread over quite large areas, but I am reluctant to believe that objects were moved more than 100 m from the original deposition area, and it is highly unlikely that coins have been moved across the modern field boundaries.[286] Therefore the finds from Paradisgård *(Fig. 59)* and Fuglesangsager *(Fig. 60)*, and most probably also a considerable number of denarii from the southern part of Sorte Muld itself, must be inter-

---

286   Horsnæs 2006b.

Crossing boundaries

Fig. 61. Fuglesangsager, hoard 1. Scale c. 1:1. Photo John Lee/Nationalmuseet.

preted as not belonging to the hoard from the centre of Sorte Muld. It is however not possible to draw a firm division line between coins from the Sorte Muld hoard and coins *not* from the hoard. It would be far too insecure: there is no unequivocal and clearly defined area without finds, nor is there a significant difference in the overall preservation of the coins.

The gold hoards from Fuglesangsageren

Two well defined gold hoards were recovered in the southern part of Sorte Muld, Fuglesangsageren. The first hoard was found during a detector survey and contained six looped solidi as well as bracteates and gold beads hidden inside a rolled-up Roman silver dish *(Fig. 61)*. The discovery was followed up by an excavation of the site. It revealed that the site had been in use from the transition from the Early to the Late Roman period and into the 7th century. Five superimposed buildings belong to consequitive phases (phases 2-6), typologically dated from the 5th to the first half of the 7th century. Both the first hoard discovered and a second bracteate hoard, consisting of five bracteates and a single solidus, had been deposited close by, but outside the buildings, and they are assumed to belong to its phase 4.[287]

Brændesgård

Brændesgård is located to the northwest of Sorte Muld.[288] The settlement area was first described by J.A.

---

287 Nielsen 2004, 74-75; Sørensen 2009. For the hoards see Axboe 2002 and 2009; Horsnæs 2002 and 2009, 251 nos. 24c-d.
288 Sb 107. BMR 1653. Watt 2009, 47-49.

Jørgensen in 1880, and it was re-located in 1982. Coin finds include nine denarii and a siliqua, as well as three dirhams and three German Viking Age coins, among which at least two belonged to the period around 1000. Finally, the area has yielded two Danish Medieval coins. Two, perhaps three, solidi were probably also found in this area.[289] The denarii show much variation in wear and surface preservation. One coin is broken, the five Antonine coins are quite worn, while the rare examples of post-Severan denarii are relatively fresh.

Other finds indicate continuous use of the area from Early Roman Iron Age to Viking Age, but the lack of Baltic Ware suggests that the settlement fell out of use before the later part of the Viking Age.

Brændesgård area II
Brændesgård area II is situated east of the Brændesgård site.[290] Viking Age material dominates this site, also seen in the numismatic material with 11 Viking Age coins, the youngest being a penning of Oluf Hunger struck in Lund (1086-1095). Only one denarius is known from this area.[291]

Engegård
Engegård is situated north of the central area of Sorte Muld and east of Brændesgård. It was mentioned by Klindt-Jensen as a settlement area with remains of a building from Roman to Early Germanic Iron Age, and his general observations were confirmed by Watt's investigations, where remains of burnt daub have been found, as well as pottery.[292] The site as a whole has yielded 28 denarii, an antoninianus,[293] and probably a Roman bronze coin.[294] Furthermore, there are five coins dated from the 15th-18th centuries, while the Viking Age and Medieval periods seem completely absent from this area.

The coins have been found scattered over a considerable area consistent with the distribution of other objects. The 28 denarii were found during 14 surveys of the two plots covering the Engegård site carried out during the period 2000-2010. The majority of the denarii are quite worn, and five were broken. A Commodus denarius features a filled-in hole *(Fig. 29)*.[295] The coins were found scattered over a large area, but it should be noted that the single solidus was from the area where traces of the still unexcavated house have been identified.

Recently two denarii were found in a new detector area southeast of Engegård (in direction towards Biskopenge, cf. below).[296]

Dalshøj
The Dalshøj site was discovered in 1949. In 1950-53 Klindt-Jensen excavated 1200-1300 square metres, an estimated 5% of the whole site *(Fig. 62)*.[297] The excavations uncovered remains of several phases of buildings and a cobbled area interpreted as a road passing west of the houses in the northeasterly direction. A denarius struck by Marcus Aurelius was found during excavation in the floor level in the western part of Dalshøj House A.[298] It was described by Klindt-Jensen as 'worn', but in reality this coin is less worn than the denarii commonly found on Bornholm. Another, and more worn, Marcus Aurelius denarius was found outside Houses A and B and at the same level.[299] Furthermore, four gold hoards were found in connection with the houses, but at a slightly lower level *(Fig. 63)*. One of the hoards, located just north of House A and 6 cm below the level of the house, consisted of at least 17 solidi.[300] The coins were not excavated *in situ*, but were found ploughed up and spread over 9 square metres. Northeast of House A a silver fibula and a small hoard of gold ingots were deposited *c*. 5 m from each other in the area with remains of several earlier houses, and were interpreted as belonging to the same

---

289 Registered as sb 106. Horsnæs 2009, 247-248 no. 20 and 250 no. 24a.
290 Sb 194. BMR 2155. Watt 2009, 49-50.
291 FP 8473.1, a very worn Antoninus Pius, type not identified.
292 Sb 160. BMR 2280 and 3185.
293 FP 6559.5; Gallienus, *RIC* 186 (253-260 AD), 3.43 g.
294 BMR 3198x4, unidentified.

295 BMR 3185x38. FP 7254.3.
296 Sb 276. BMR 3408. FP 7431: Antoninus Pius, *RIC* 17a, AD 139; Marcus Aurelius, *RIC* 252, 171-172.
297 Sb 135, BMR 1639 and sb 274, BMR 2156 (Ndr. Brændesgård). Klindt-Jensen 1957; Watt 2009, 41-44.
298 Klindt-Jensen 1957, 17 fig. 14,4 and fig. 11 no. 21. FP 2273.18.
299 Klindt-Jensen 1957, 190 and fig. 147,5. FP 2302.1.
300 Klindt-Jensen 1957, 186-190, fig. 7 no. 2 and fig 24 (position), fig. 146 (photo); Kromann 1990, 116-120 (photos); Horsnæs 2009, 251-252 no. 27a.

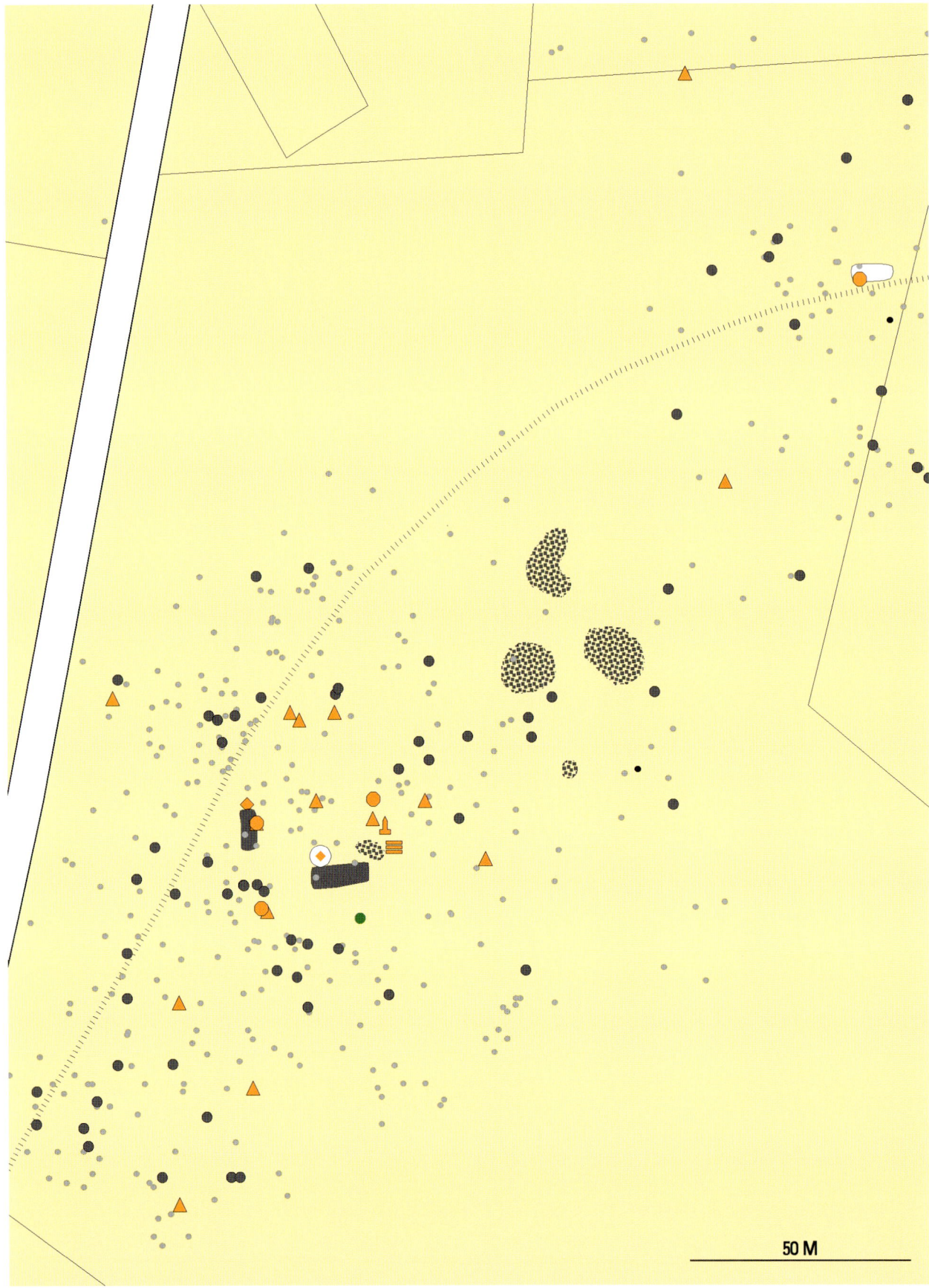

Fig. 62. Distribution of coins at Engegård and Dalshøj showing the excavated houses with gold hoards and the still unexcavated house and road identified by Klindt-Jensen (superimposed on the map Klindt-Jensen 1957, fig. 7). Note how the solidi found during detector surveys cluster near the houses. Scale 1:1250. Legends as Fig. 55.

The sites with Roman coin finds

Fig. 63. The gold hoards found on the Dalshøj site in the 1950s. Scale c. 1:1. Photo Nationalmuseet.

Crossing boundaries

Fig. 64. Distribution of coins at Kanonhøj/Sønderhøj. Scale 1:1250. Legends as Fig. 55.

phase as House A and the solidus hoard.[301]

It is clear today that the site is much larger than the area excavated by Klindt-Jensen, and stretches on both sides of the Højevej *(Fig. 62)*.[302] The larger, eastern, part of the Dalshøj settlement area has yielded 90 coins, of which 19, 17 solidi and two single finds of denarii, derive from the excavations in the 1950s. All

---

301   Klindt-Jensen 1957, 190 and fig. 24.

302   Watt 2006.

later finds are from detector surveys. The overwhelming part of the finds, 65 coins, are denarii, while there is now a total of 21 solidi, one sestertius[303] and three coins from the 16th-18th centuries. The western part of the site has so far produced only one denarius.[304] The chronological distribution of the coin finds – with a complete lack of Viking Age coins – supports Watt's suggestion that this area had been deserted by the Viking Age.[305]

The many denarii have been found spread over an area of the same size as the settlement itself. The state of preservation among them varies considerably: a few coins have been burnt, some are completely worn down in particular on the reverse where the motif is hardly visible, other have a bright silvery surface with some green corrosive product comparable to the coins from the hoard area of Sorte Muld, while others are relatively fresh. Fourteen coins have been broken, but none of the fragments join. A single denarius has a drilled hole and around it the surface is slightly flattened, probably from a loop riveted onto the coin *(Fig. 31)*.[306] The diversity shows that the denarii must derive from several depositions/losses.

The newly found solidi were discovered *c.* 20 m apart and at approximately the same distance from the excavation area. As they are found in the same general area as the excavated houses, it is possible that they once belonged to the hoard. The first detector find was a solidus struck by Honorius at Milan, a type that is so far unique in Bornholm. Two of the three remaining detector finds, a pierced Theodosius II and a cut Valentinian III are of types identical to coins from the Dalshøj Hoard, and particularly the Theodosius is of a type very common in Bornholm. The last solidus is a cut fragment of an unidentified 5th century coin.[307] The types of the detector finds do not contradict ascription of the coins to the hoard, but it should be noted that there were no cut solidi among the finds made in the 1950's.

The Dalshøj II area,[308] situated south of Dalshøj in direction of Sorte Muld, has so far produced only one denarius, but no less than 12 dirhams.[309]

Baunehøj and Kanonhøj/Sønderhøj

The area registered as sb 190 seems to consist of two small independent house sites. The Baunehøj site has produced four denarii,[310] two of which were stacked, and one solidus.[311] On Sønderhøj N there are four denarii, one German penning of the 11th century, one Erik Menved penning, and a klipping from the 16th century.[312] South of these a single denarius has been found at Sønderhøj.[313]

Brændesgård and Sønderhøj V *c.* 200 m to the west are also two small separate units within the same area.[314] Brændesgård has produced a denarius and a dirham,[315] while Sønderhøj V has produced three denarii.[316]

The Kanonhøj/Sønderhøj site has been registered under several headings due to the site's extension over land with different owners *(Fig. 64)*.[317] The Sønderhøj area (north of the road) has produced 22 denarii, a Roman bronze coin of the Constantinian period and a solidus, as well as a Medieval coin and a Danish coin of the 17th century *(Fig. 65)*.[318] Denarii were recorded eight times during the decade 2000-2010. They are quite worn, and differences in the surface preservation as well as the distribution all over the site suggest that they were not deposited together.

---

303   FP 6364.4; BMR 1639x299. Commodus *RIC* 494 or 523 (186-189).
304   Sb 274. BMR 2156x7. FP 8293: Marcus Aurelius for Lucilla *RIC* 482.
305   Watt 2006, 153.
306   FP 6551.6. Drilled hole behind head.
307   Horsnæs 2009, 253 no. 27b (photos). Note that the distance to the excavation area is here wrongly given as 200 m, it should be 20 m. The exact find spot within the field is not known for the earliest detector find of a solidus: FP 4703.

308   Sb 218. BMR 3065.
309   FP 6921.1: Antoninus Pius for Marcus Aurelius Caesar *RIC* 417a. Dirhams: FP 6363.1-4; 6845.1-5; 6921.2; 7081; 8476.
310   BMR 2261. FP 8098 and 8149.
311   FP 5604. Horsnæs 2009, 253 no. 31.
312   BMR 2507. FP 5815, 6077, 7032, 7293, 7849.
313   Sb 199. BMR 2739. FP 6076: Antoninus Pius, *RIC* 292e, 158-159.
314   Sb 170. Watt 2009, 52 and 55.
315   BMR 1219. FP 4677 and 7260. Watt 2009, 55 interpreted this area as a Viking Age site due to the finds of Baltic ware.
316   BMR 1641. FP 6550 and 7021.
317   Sb 169 and 175. BMR 1430x1-425; BMR 802x1-114; BMR 1219x8-11; BMR 2763x1-3; BMR 2650x1-4. Watt 2009, 52-55.
318   Sb 169. BMR 802.

Fig. 65. Denarii from Sønderhøj, FP 8162.1-4.

Fig. 66. Joining fragments of denarii from Kanonhøj. FP 7020+7765.3 and FP 8163.1.

The Kanonhøj area (south of the road) produced 53 denarii, two solidi, two German coins of the 11th century and four Renaissance coins.[319] The two areas, north and south of the road, clearly constitute one archaeological site cut by the modern road. The denarii are evenly distributed over both areas in close correspondence with other object types from the site, supporting the interpretation of the coins as a series of single finds. The denarii were found during 21 separate surveys taking place over two decades. During one detector survey two fragments of the same coin were found more than 30 m apart,[320] while two fragments of another coin were found during excavation of a trial trench in 1997 and during a survey in 2007 *(Fig. 66)*.[321]

East of the Højevej, the Højemark Nord area is possibly part of the same Kanonhøj/Sønderhøj site. Two denarii have been found here along with a few other objects.[322]

South of Kanonhøj/Sønderhøj the smaller Kanonhøj II site has yielded four denarii and a solidus, and a large number of other finds, including the gold pommel of a ring-sword, from the Early Germanic Iron Age. Two of the denarii (FP 6414.1-2) were found quite close to each other, while the third denarius and the solidus were discovered *c.* 40 m apart.[323] Even further away a single denarius appeared in 2010 along with few other objects on a new survey area at Kanonhøj Syd.[324]

319   Sb 175. BMR 1430 and 2650.
320   FP 8163.1/BMR 1430x590a+b.
321   FP 7020/BMR 1430x398 and FP 7765.3/BMR 1430x577.
322   Sb 217. BMR 3184. FP 6548 (Commodus, *RIC* 90 or 102, 184-185 AD) and 7255 (Antoninus Pius, probably *RIC* 360, 141-161 AD)
323   Sb 207. BMR 2508. FP 6414 (Hadrian, *RIC* 39, AD 118; Antoninus Pius, unidentified type (very fragmented); unidentified denarius; solidus Theodosius II, Constantinople, *RIC* 314. Horsnæs 2009, 254 no. 33) and 6797 (Trajan, unidentified type).
324   Sb 273. BMR 2509. FP 8294: Antoninus Pius, unidentified type.

The sites with Roman coin finds

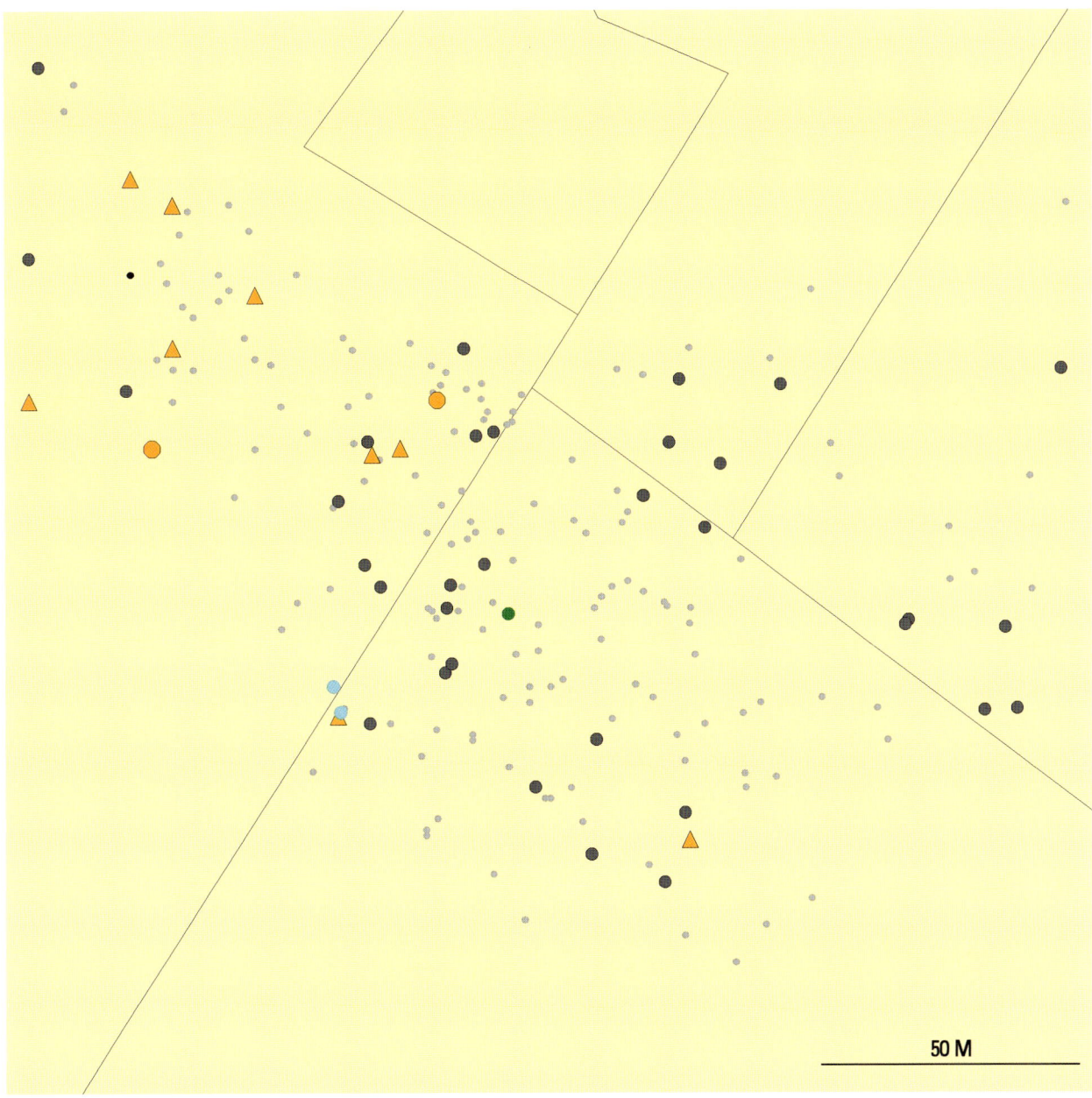

Fig. 67. Distribution of coins at Højemark. Scale 1:1250. Legends as fig. 55.

Højemark

Højemark is situated southwest of Sorte Muld. It was probably the find spot of one of the early finds of a solidus,[325] and Jørgensen already in 1880 recognized the site as a settlement with blackened soil.[326] Coin finds include 36 denarii, a Roman bronze coin,[327] and three solidi *(Fig. 67)*.[328] Furthermore, there are two dirhams and a German penning of the 11th century.[329] Again the coins have been found in the course of many surveys, the 36 denarii having been registered in no less than 16 batches. The coins are found scattered over the entire site. There is great variation in wear as well as corrosion, but one coin stands out as considerably less worn than any other coin, namely a pierced denarius

---

325 FP 378.
326 Sb 96 and 97: BMR 1092, 2510, 2651 and 2755. Watt 2009, 59-62.
327 FP 8314.2: 'Gloria exercitus' type with two soldiers and two standards (330-335).

328 Two struck by Libius Severus (the above mentioned FP 378 and FP 6090.2; Horsnæs 2009, 251 no. 25), and a recently found Theodosius II (FP 8096.6, unpublished).
329 FP 6244.4-5 (dirhams) and FP 7763.5 (German coin).

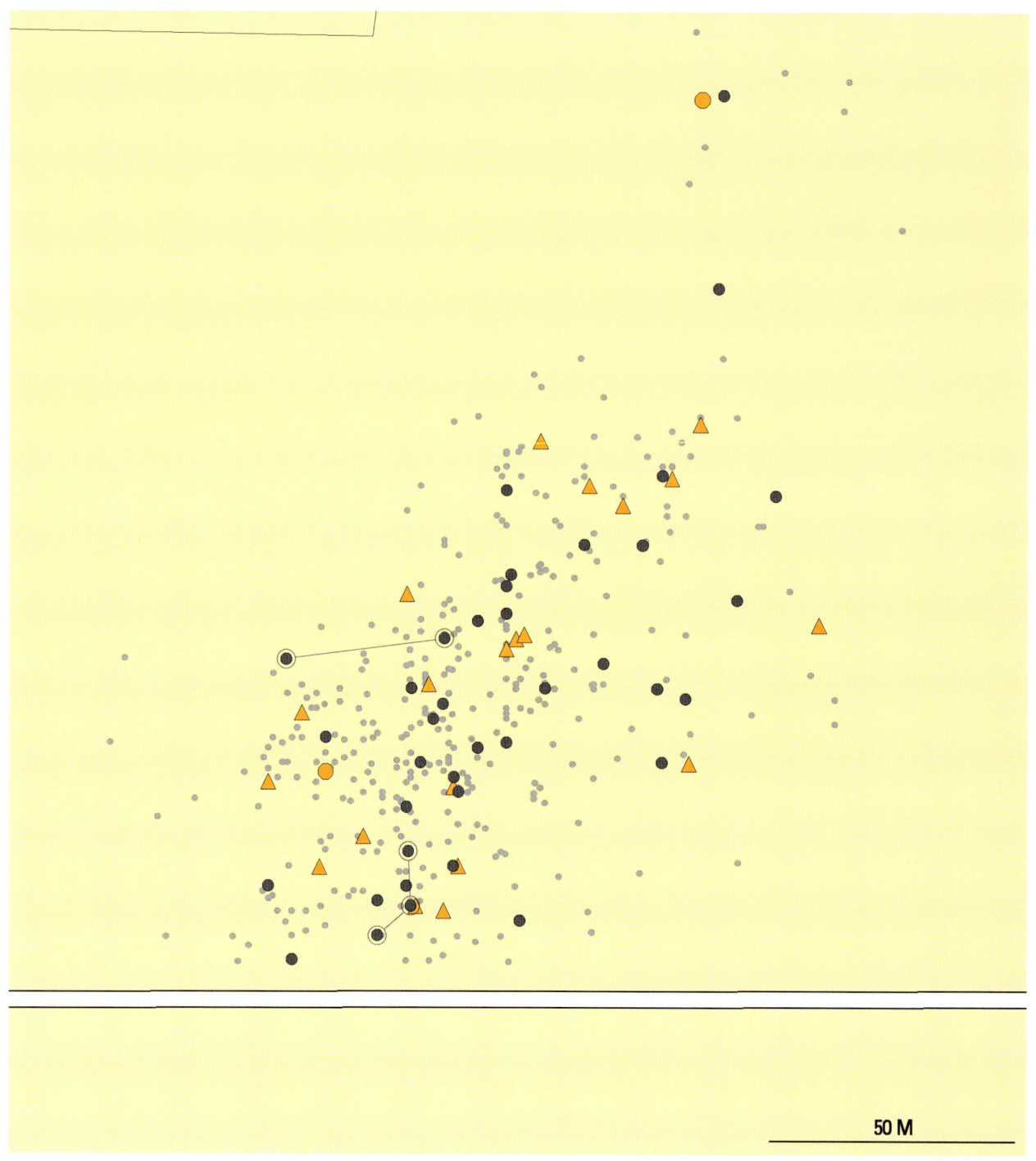

Fig. 68. Distribution of coins at Sylten II. Scale 1:1250. Legends as fig. 55.

struck by Caracalla. The piercing was made from the obverse, in front of the emperor's head.

A bit to the south of Højemark is the recently discovered site at Grydehøj (Stenskov) which has produced a decorated gold piece from the Roman Iron Age, fibulas of the Early Germanic Iron Age and two denarii.[330]

Sylten

Stricktly speaking the name 'Sylten' refers to a low-lying area south/southeast of Sorte Muld. Adjacent to this lies a number of individual sites. Although it cannot be ascertained beyond doubt that the 'Sylten' of the 18th and 19th century reports is identical to the area so named to-

---

330 Sb 206. BMR 3144. FP 6373 (Marcus Aurelius for Lucilla, RIC 781) and FP 6644 (Antoninus Pius, unidentified type).

day, it is possible that some of the old gold finds (nine solidi) from Ibsker Parish were found here.[331]

Sylten I and II have yielded a high find density, and the denarii have been found scattered on both sites.[332] During detector surveys 63 coins have been found in these areas (60 denarii, nine of which came from Sylten I, two solidi[333] and one coin struck by the Teutonic Order). The denarii from Sylten II *(Fig. 68)* include two unusually early coins, one subæratus struck in the name of Tiberius *(Fig. 20)* and one post-reform denarius struck by Nero. The material seems to contain a slightly higher number of fragmented denarii than the average for the sites in the Ibsker complex. It has been possible to restore several objects from fragments, in two cases the two, or three respective fragments that make up a single coin have been found several years apart *(Fig. 69* and coin list). Also the Medieval coin was found as two fragments five years apart.[334] It is possible that a solidus found in 1894 derives from the area of Sylten I and II as well.[335]

The localities Sylten VI and III are situated north of Sylten I-II. The sites are smaller, and they have yielded only a small number of finds. Among them are, from Sylten VI two denarii and a solidus,[336] and from Sylten III four denarii.[337]

The Sylten IV area first attracted attention because of the find of several denarii with traces of fire dam-

Fig. 69. Joining fragments of denarii from Sylten II. FP 4800.1+5454.6+5966.5 and FP 6240.28+6835.

age.[338] Excavations undertaken in 1988 revealed traces of a burnt down building dated to the beginning of the Early Germanic Iron Age (second half of the 4th century).[339] More than 120 denarii have been found on Sylten IV, and they thus make up more than half the total number of detector finds from this part of the complex *(Fig. 70)*.[340] Most of the denarii should be regarded as a hoard kept above ground inside the burnt down building, rather than a hoard hidden below the floor, as they have clearly been exposed to considerable heat: Among them are pieces of completely melted silver where a possible origin as denarii cannot be proved *(Fig. 71)*, as well as several coins where only slight traces of the original motif can be seen due to the heat damage *(Fig. 11)*.

There are, however, also a small number of denarii without any visible traces of fire, as well as two coins that are considerably younger than the burnt down building (a dirham and a Frederik IV 8 skilling of 1700). Some of the unburnt denarii were found

---

331 Sb 277. Breitenstein 1944, 62-66 find no. 24; Horsnæs 2009, 248 no. 21a-c and 23b.

332 060403 sb 74: BMR 789; Coin finds: FP 4675, 4700, 4701, 4782, 4800.1-4, 5068.1-6, 5069.1-2, 5330.1-4, 5454.1-8, 5600.1-2, 5812.1-4, 5966.1-5, 6045.1-2, 6074.1-3, 6240.1-3, 6433, 6549.1-2, 6835, 7029.1-3, 7435.-6, 8099.1-3, 8313.

333 Horsnæs 2009, 250 nos. 23a and 23c.

334 Unfortunately the find spots were not registered. A fibula produced in Southeast Europe around AD 600 was restored from six fragments found at intervals on Sylten II, cf. Callmer in Adamsen *et al.* 2009, 70.

335 Breitenstein 1944, 62-66 no. 24.3; Horsnæs 2009, 250 no. 23b.

336 Sb 189. BMR 2149. FP 5246 and 5461.

337 Sb 193. BMR 1716. FP 5067, 7951, 8311. Furthermore a Danish 2 skilling struck by Christian IV (1588-1648, type Hede 168) has been found: FP 5463.

338 Sb 168. BMR 1077. FP 4674.1-56; 4699.1-14; 5066.1-13; 5247.1-6; 5594.1-10; 7030.1-7; 8100.1-3; 8161.1-10; 8315.1-5. Among these coins are one Samanid dirham and one Danish 8 skilling of Frederik IV (1700).

339 Watt 2009, 67.

340 The exact number is hard to tell because of many melted coins and finds of melted silver that may or may not derive from denarii.

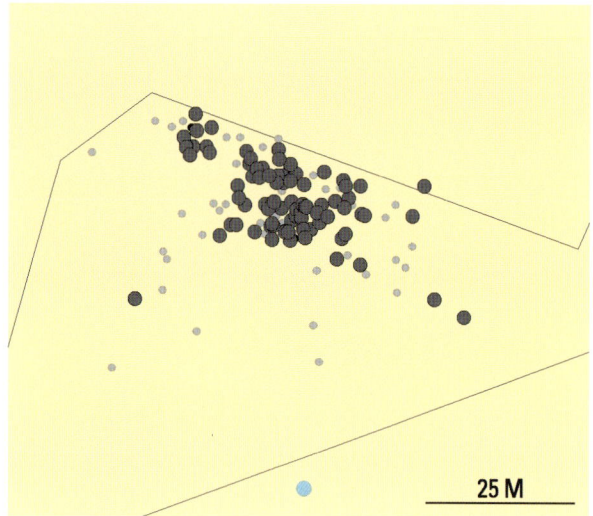

Fig. 70. Distribution of coins in Sylten IV. Note the extremely high find density in the area, comparable only to the find density seen in the central part of the Sorte Muld hoard cluster and the clusters of the Smørenge hoard(s). Scale 1:1250. Legends as fig. 55.

at some distance from the centre of the coin scatter, and it indicates that while the majority of the denarii derive from a hoard kept within the house, others are most probably single finds deriving from accidental losses.

From a methodological point of view it is interesting to note that the most recently found denarii from Sylten IV are in very small fragments. This may be due to modern metal detectors becoming more sensitive and thereby retrieving smaller fragments than earlier models. But it should also be noted that the plough layer by now seems to have been emptied of heavier objects (melted silver, denarii in stacks) that all were found during the first phase of detecting on the site.

Frennegård/Hallebrøndshøj area

North of the Sylten are the Frennegård sites located west of the Hallebrøndshøj dolmen.[341] The main area (sb 191) has produced only two denarii,[342] but it is possible that an early find of a solidus should also be assigned to this area.[343] In 1820 six German coins

Fig. 71. Melted silver from Sylten IV. FP 4699.14.

from the period around 1000 were found on a field next to the barrow.[344]

The northern part of the area, Nr. Fuglesang, has yielded five denarii as well as some silver ingots and half a gold bracelet. The surface preservation of the denarii is very homogeneous (quite worn, but hardly corroded). Several of these finds appeared on the same day within a restricted area. These are all arguments for an interpretation of this group of artifacts as a

---

341 Sb 191 (incl. sb 220). BMR 2353x1-30 and BMR 3308. Sb 214 (northern part of the area). BMR 2353x31ff. Watt 2009, 69.
342 FP 5998.
343 FP 1623. Breitenstein 1944, 77, no. 44 fig. 90; Fagerlie 1967, find 206, cat. 588; Horsnæs 2009, 253 no.

32.
344 Sb 79. Described in inventory of the Prehistoric Department, no. CCCXXI.

The sites with Roman coin finds

Fig. 72. Denarii from Biskopenge VI. FP 5972, 6268, 6840.1-3, 8007.1. Photos: Pia Brejnholt.

mixed hoard deposited together.[345] Rescue excavation of the area in 2004 did, however, not reveal building structures nor a possible place of deposition.

Biskopenge

The Biskopenge (literal translation 'Bishop's meadows') northeast of Sorte Muld designates a low-lying area with a number of smaller sites situated on slight elevations in the landscape. Two adjacent sites, Biskopenge VII and Biskopenge VI, are placed on the road passing Frennegård. Biskopenge VII has yielded three denarii,[346] while Biskopenge VI has yielded six denarii and a number of other objects.[347] The six denarii from Biskopenge VI are homogeneous: all are quite worn, but hardly corroded *(Fig. 72)*. A common deposition cannot be excluded.

Halfway between Biskopenge VII and VI on one hand and the central area of Sorte Muld on the other, a survey in 2009 produced a single denarius.[348]

The largest site, Biskopenge 1-2, is situated below the crossroads on the Korshøjevej. It has yielded a number of finds from Roman and Germanic Iron Ages as well as some Baltic ware, but so far no coins.

Biskopenge IIIa and IIIb are two small sites separated by a low lying area.[349] Biskopenge IIIa has produced three denarii,[350] while Biskopenge IIIb produced 12 denarii and a possibly melted denarius, a dirham, a heavily corroded Medieval/pre-modern(?) coin, and a 2-skilling from 1788. The denarii differ greatly from each other, both as regards wear and surface preservation. They are scattered over the whole site, as defined by finds of other object types *(Fig. 73)*.

---

345 Some of the finds presented in Adamsen *et al.* 2009, 21.
346 Sb 181. BMR 1761. FP 6375 (Marcus Aurelius, RIC 50, 161-162) and 6641 (Hadrian, RIC 113, 119-122 and Antoninus Pius, *RIC* 167 or 181, 147-149).
347 Sb 166. BMR 790. FP 5972, 6268, 6840.1-3, 8007.1.
348 Sb 264. BMR 3534. FP 7955.1: Hadrian, *RIC* Class A, 117-122 AD.
349 Sb 195. Watt 2009, 73.
350 BMR 1839. FP 5967.1 Hadrian *RIC* 202 (125-128); FP 5967.2 Antoninus Pius *RIC* 301 (159-160); FP 7421 Marcus Aurelius for Faustina Minor *RIC* 715 (161-164).

Crossing boundaries

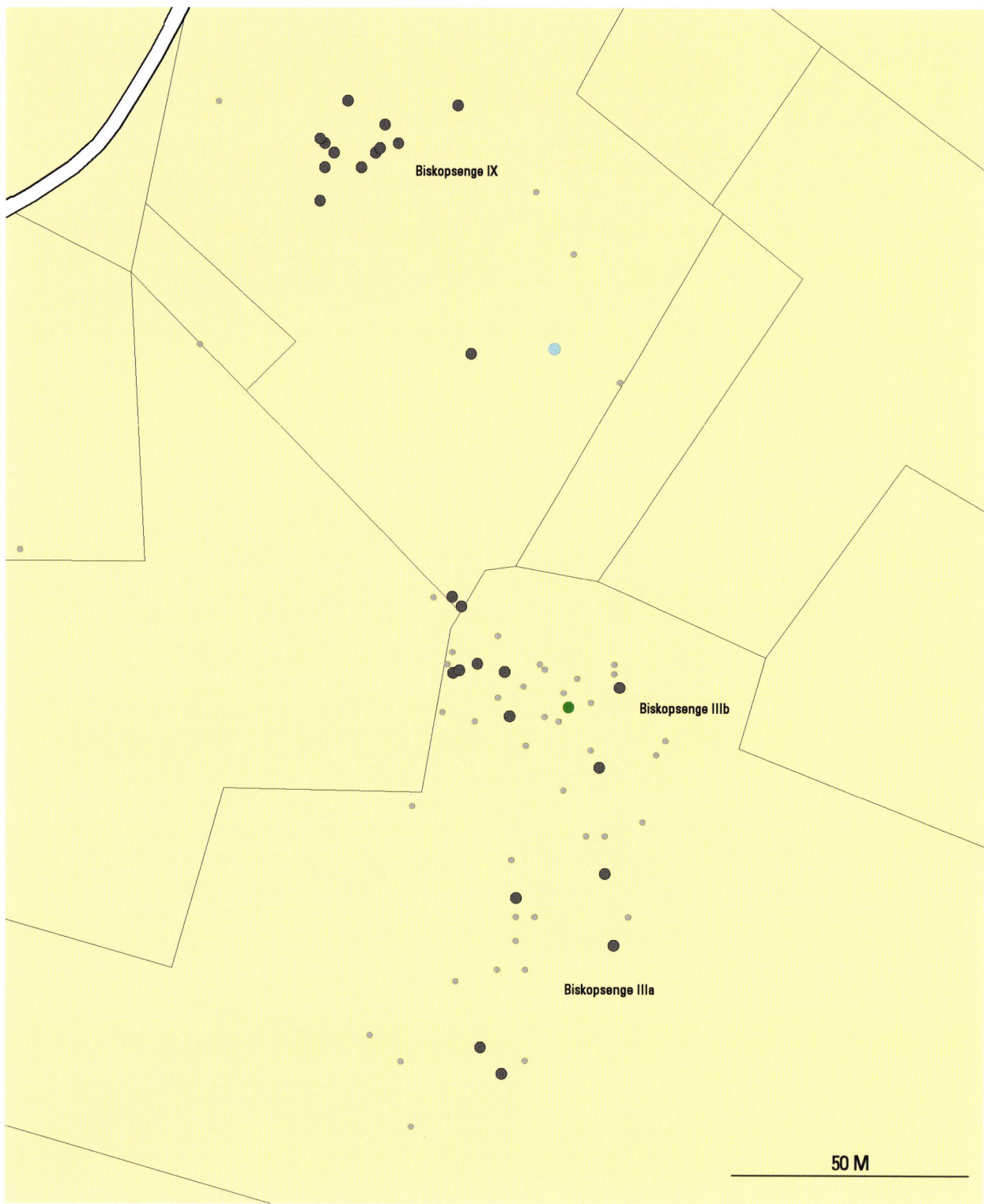

Fig. 73. Distribution of coins from Biskopenge III a-b and Biskopenge IX. Scale 1:1250.

Biskopenge IX is the northernmost of this group of sites, and although registered only in 2006, it has already produced 16 denarii as well as a single cut and pecked fragment of a German coin of the 11th century. The denarii are interpreted as the remains of a hoard *(Fig. 73)*. Only two of them are fragmented, and in both cases the fracture seems fresh. All the denarii present the same degree of wear, and they have the same kind of reddish coating of the surface. The coating is not seen on the German coin. It is therefore likely that the coating derives from the 'microenvironment' of the denarii, i.e. from some mate-

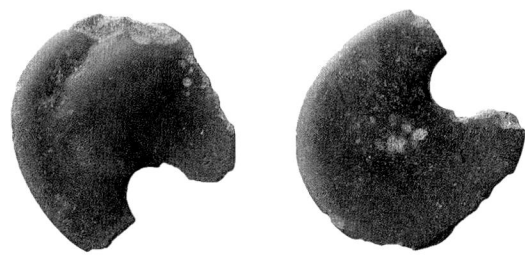

Fig. 74. Pierced subæratus(?) from Biskopenge V. FP 7049.4.

rial wrapped around them at the time of deposition (*Fig. 12*).[351]

A denarius with the provenance 'West of Biskopengen' found in 1950[352] could have come from an area not far from – or even identical with – the area Biskopenge V.[353] The latter site is situated halfway between Biskopenge III and Sorte Muld and it is thus located inside the circle of settlement sites surrounding Sorte Muld. Biskopenge V has produced a small number of finds including five denarii and a klipping struck by Christian II in Malmø (1518-1522). The denarii are very heterogeneous: a Hadrianic denarius is worn, but presents a bright and silvery surface, three Antonine denarii on the contrary have a dull brownish surface, while an unidentified and very light (0.88g) fragment seems to consist of mainly copper. It is heavily worn with a smooth almost water-rolled surface and may be the core of a subæratus. A large pierced hole is positioned at the chin of the emperor's portrait (*Fig.74*).

The Iron Age settlement complex – summary

There can be little doubt that the Ibsker settlement complex was the main central site on Bornholm for almost a millennium. How did it achieve this position? The many finds clearly indicate that the settlement complex was part of an interregional network, and it must have had access to its foreign contacts via the sea.

As can be seen from the distribution maps, Sorte Muld is enclosed by a circle of satellite sites. A few recent finds, however, indicate some infilling of the area between Sorte Muld and the satellites (notably sb 182, 264 and 215).

---

351 Sb 263. BMR 3314.
352 Sb 138. FP 2302.2: Marcus Aurelius for Lucilla, unknown type. Klindt-Jensen 1957, 238 find list 2 and map fig. 5, no. 8.
353 Sb 182. BMR 1760.

The majority of the sites in the Ibsker complex have produced considerable numbers of denarii. In a few cases, the clustering of the denarii renders an interpretation of them as (part of) a ploughed-up hoard probable. This interpretation is supported by similarities in the surface preservation of the coins, most clearly seen in the burnt hoard from Sylten IV. It is clear that even within areas where a considerable number of the denarius finds have been deposited together, there are some coins with a surface preservation that does not conform to the majority of the coin finds. A large number of the denarii are found widely scattered, but normally their distribution is congruent with finds in general. This suggests that they should be interpreted as a large series of single finds, perhaps in combination with some smaller hoards.

In some cases it has been possible to reconstruct denarii (or parts of denarii) from fragments found with very long intervals. Two important conclusions can be drawn from these finds: First of all it proves – what has hitherto never really been questioned – that the fragmented denarii have been broken *after* deposition. The fact that the relative number of fragmented coins differs from site to site may be caused *either* by the chemical composition of the soil rendering denarii from some sites more 'brittle' and thereby more apt to break than denarii from other sites, *or* it may be a consequence of archaeological layers having been tossed around in the plough layer for longer time at some sites than at others. The soil composition is probably a main factor for the preservation of the coins in general. The highly diverse effects of soil composition on the preservation of archaeological artifacts were convincingly demonstrated by Matthiesen,[354] and were inferred by previous studies of Roman denarii in Denmark.[355] Secondly, the spatial distribution of the fragments of the same coin shows how far objects may 'travel' as a consequence of repeated agricultural works on the site, and supports the view that even a considerable distance between two finds does not exclude the possibility that they were once deposited together.

The assemblage from Nr. Fuglesang, is interpreted as a mixed hoard of denarii, silver and gold. It is extremely difficult to identify a mixed hoard among a large number of other artifacts in a metal rich site. A 'pure' single type denarius hoard is much easier to

---

354 Matthiesen 2006.
355 Horsnæs 2006b.

Fig. 75. The Saltholmgård Hoard. Photo John Lee/Nationalmuseet.

identify, but even here we encounter considerable uncertainty in the cases where a metal rich site may have contained two or more denarius depositions of varying size.

This all leads to the somewhat discouraging conclusion that a definite distinction between material from a hoard and material deriving from series of single finds (or series of small hoards, or a combination of these!) is rarely possible. Arguments based on an initial classification of detector finds from a metal rich site into hoards and single finds can therefore only be used with extreme caution.

Viking Age finds from the Ibsker complex

Several of the sites in the Ibsker complex have produced a small number of Viking Age – Early Medieval coins, but there are also a few areas where the Viking Age coins dominate: in the northern part of Sorte Muld (in particular sb 218) and in the Brændesgård/Engegård areas just outside the circle of satellite settlements. In general this chronological distribution corresponds with other datable material from the Ibsker complex, and reveals that the finds gradually move away from the centre of the complex. Further away the Hinztegård site confirms that sites with an apparent chronological climax in the Late Germanic/Viking Age period are situated outside the complex. At Hinztegård a single denarius has been found, while there are 17 coins from the Viking Age.[356] The lack of denarii at the latest sites within the complex as well as at the closest site outside the complex proper is a clear indication that the denarii were no longer available for use – otherwise the good silver of the denarii would certainly have been exploited. It is hard to say exactly when the denarii disappeared from circulation. The denarii from mixed contexts show that they were in use for an extended period until the end of the Early Germanic Iron Age, but it seems that they had outplayed their role around the turn from the Early to the Late Germanic Iron Age, i.e. during the first half of the 6th century.

The Saltholmgård Hoard – marking a boundary?

In 1882 a hoard consisting of 29 Late Roman solidi and a large ingot of a silver-mixed gold alloy was found in a stone setting surrounding a Stone Age dolmen close to the Skovsholm Bæk (brook) southeast of the Ibsker complex. The structure of the hoard is closely comparable to the hoard from the Dalshøj House with several identical types, but although coins from both hoards can be die-linked to finds from other Nordic sites there is no die-links between

---

356   Sb 58. BMR 1530. FP 6434, 7498, 8090.

these two hoards.³⁵⁷ Since the small brook may have formed a ritual (rather than physical) limit between the Ibsker complex and its surroundings, it is possible that the Saltholmgård Hoard should be interpreted as a liminal sacrifice, enhanced by the deposition in connection with the prehistoric dolmen.

Outside the Ibsker complex

The almost complete absence of Roman coins from the areas surrounding the settlement complex is striking. The area west of the Ibsker complex is conspicuously void of finds, but the rich Viking Age finds from the southern part of the parish between Årsdale and Nexø show that in this case the lack of Roman coins is certainly not due to lack of investigation of these area.³⁵⁸ Among the many sites dominated by Viking Age material only three have produced Roman denarii. A single, extremely worn, denarius was found at Bækkegård in 1998, but there is no other indication of prehistoric occupation of the area.³⁵⁹ Further south a settlement area with finds from the Roman Iron Age to the Early Medieval Period at Rabækkegård has produced two denarii and a dirham.³⁶⁰ Furthermore, a third denarius from this location came to the National Museum via the estate of King Frederik VI in 1868.³⁶¹ In the same area an 11ᵗʰ century hoard was found during ploughing before 1875, and detector surveys located the find spot of this hoard some 30 m from the area with the two Roman coins found recently. The Rabækkegård Hoard consisted of mainly German coins of the 11ᵗʰ century (111 of 124 preserved coins) with a coin *t.p.q.* 1079.³⁶² Almost one km northeast of Rabækkegård, the last denarius from Ibsker parish has been found at Sejrshøj.³⁶³ The area has yielded some fragments of pottery from the Iron Age(?) and Viking Period as well as pieces of daub from a house.³⁶⁴

Other sites in Øster herred

The northern coastline of Bornholm has produced few Roman coins finds in Østermarie parish (060406), while a number of sites have been located in Østerlarsker parish (060405).

Single finds of gold coins without precise provenance have been made in both Gudhjem³⁶⁵ and Østermarie parish.³⁶⁶ Other finds can be located within the ownership of a single farm: two solidi from Kløvegård in Østermarie,³⁶⁷ one cut fragment of a solidus from Kirseløkkegård in Østerlars,³⁶⁸ and finally a hoard of seven solidi found east of Spagergård.³⁶⁹

No solidus has been found during detector surveys, but in addition to the few early denarius finds there is a number of recently discovered detector sites: Two isolated finds in Østermarie, and two concentrations of sites, one around Østerlars and the other in the area between Østerlars and Gudhjem.

One of the isolated finds in Østermarie is an old denarius find from Rynsegård of which no details are

---

357 Die links identified by Fagerlie 1967; summarized in Horsnæs 2009.

358 See for example the map in Naum 2008, 54 fig. 5 for the distribution of settlements, silver hoards and strongholds from the Viking Age and Early Medieval Period (drawn by F.O. Nielsen).

359 060403 sb 201. BMR 2717. FP 6087, Marcus Aurelius(?), perhaps struck for L.Verus? Type not identified.

360 060403 sb 179. BMR 1764. FP 6259 (Marcus Aurelius for Lucius Verus, *RIC* 463, AD 161) and 7005.1-2 (Commodus, *RIC* 90 or 102, 184-185; dirham).

361 NM I 21771, cf. *Aarbøger* 1868, 132, no. 89. Antoninus Pius, unidentified type.

362 von Heijne 2004, 326 no. 5.114 with further references.

363 060403 sb 180. BMR 1791. FP 7953. Antoninus Pius, *RIC* 179(?), 148-149.

364 In May 2011 the first denarius appeared at the important Viking Age site Munkegård (060403 sb 49) during detecting following a supplementary excavation in the spring 2011 at the site of one or more Viking Age *Hacksilber* hoard(s) with almost 1000 registered coins. I thank Benny Staal (BMR) and the finder Bent Gregersen for this information.

365 060402 sb 221. FP 591, Horsnæs 2009, 247 no. 19.

366 060406 sb 316. FP 22, Horsnæs 2009, 255 no. 38 and 060406 sb 134, NM I C 1547, Breitenstein 1944, no. 20. The latter was struck by Theodosius I, and it is the only Roman gold coin found on Bornholm struck in the period ante-dating the division of the Empire in 395 AD.

367 060406 sb 6. FP 260 and a lost coin, Horsnæs 2009, 255 no. 39.

368 060405 sb 157. NM I 19452, Horsnæs 2009, 254 no. 37.

369 060405 sb 146. Coins registered as FP 216, only one preserved today, Horsnæs 2009, 254 no. 36.

known.[370] The other is a detector find from Maglegård, a settlement area dated to the Roman Iron Age with finds of among other things cooking pits, daub, pottery, beads, loom-weights.[371]

Denarius sites around Østerlars

Near the solidus sites of Kløvegård and Spagergård mentioned above are six sites with denarius finds. The highest number of Roman coins has been found on the Agerbygård/Bakkegård settlement situated in an elevated position at the confluence of the two streams Præstebæk and Spagerå north of Østerlars. It has assumed special importance not only because of the large number of finds, but also because the archaeological field work undertaken on the site renders it useful as reference site for the Black Soil Project.[372] Watt's investigations revealed an area with very high phosphate values. Only part of the site situated south of the modern track has so far been surveyed. The distribution of the finds presents a marked cluster which is on the whole consistent with the areas with the highest phosphate values. According to excavated material, the earliest occupation of the site can be dated in the Early Roman Iron Age. Among the detector finds, however, only a few can be dated to the Pre-Roman and Early Roman Iron Ages. This is probably due to the culture layers from the Early Roman Iron Age still existing intact below the plough soil. The latest preserved layers probably belong to a house with a cobbled entrance/floor(?), dated to the transition from the Late Roman to the Early Germanic Iron Age (i.e. *c.* 375 AD). There is a peak in the number of detector finds in the Germanic Iron Ages and in particular in the Viking period, probably caused by the ploughing up of the culture layers from that period. There is a clear drop in the number of finds from the Medieval Period.

Coin finds total 52 ranging in time from 69/79 to 1569/1600 AD, among which 18 denarii and a siliqua *(Fig. 76)*. Comparing the numismatic material with the other finds from Agerbygård as presented by Watt some chronological discrepancies soon appear. The 2nd century denarii are not matched by the same abundance of other finds from the Early Roman Iron Age (period B), on the contrary, it is more likely that the denarii should be seen in relation to the finds from the Late Roman or Germanic Periods (periods C-D). The denarii have mainly been found in the northern part of the site, coinciding with the area with the highest phosphate values.

The denarii present differences in both wear and corrosion, and there is no obvious correlation between degree of wear/corrosion and exact find spot. It is therefore difficult to interpret them as the remains of a single hoard.

The number of dated finds from Agerbygård peaks in the Viking Age (c. 750-1066), while the number of finds from later periods declines. This is in contrast to the numismatic material. Relatively few Viking Age coins: only five dirhams (late 9th–mid-10th centuries) and seven western coins (end 10th–11th centuries) have been found. The Viking Age coins are concentrated in an area *c.* 50 m south of the majority of the denarius finds. Furthermore, no less than 14 Danish penninge (late 13th–early 14th centuries) and two Pomeranian *vinkenaugen* from *c.* 1400 have been found. This contrasts the apparent decline of the site in the Medieval period, and although the figure does not seem impressive in itself, it should be considered that coins from this period are in general much rarer than Viking Age coins in Bornholm. The Medieval coins are mainly found scattered in an area between the cluster of Viking Age coins and the modern road. Margrethe Watt suggests that the relatively high number of Medieval coins is caused by activities related to the neighbouring Østerlars church.[373] It is the largest round church in Bornholm, probably erected in the mid-12th century. Finally, the site has yielded two coins from the 16th century.

A single denarius has been found on another site named Agerbygård, closer to Østerlars and east of the road leading towards Gudhjem. This site also produced a hoard of partly melted silver objects, including a dirham, and sherds of Baltic Ware.[374]

East of Østerlars, Rytterbakken is another site included in the Black Soil Project. This relatively small

---

370 060406 sb 317. FP 676, Breitenstein 39-40 no. 8.
371 060406 sb 198. BMR 1657x41. FP 7513: Marcus Aurelius for Faustina 2, *RIC* 711.
372 060405 sb 201. BMR 1523. FP 4954, 5141, 5243, 5443, 5806, 6000, 6078, 6239, 6975, 7634, 7853, 8144, 8500, (x793 not reg.); Watt 2010, 568-571. Viking Age coins: von Heijne 2004, 327 no. 5.120.

373 Personal information, Margrethe Watt.
374 060405 sb 218; BMR 2207. FP 5465.1 Marcus Aurelius for Lucius Verus, unidentified type; FP 5456.2 dirham, cf. von Heijne 2004, 327 no. 5.119.

The sites with Roman coin finds

Fig. 76. Distribution of coins from Agerbygård/Bakkegård. Note the extremely high density of finds. Phosphate analysis proves that the site extended north of the road, but this area has not been surveyed. The original extent of the site must have been over 10,000 square metres. Scale 1:1250. Legends as Fig. 55.

site must have existed at least from the Roman Iron Age into the Viking Period, and it has been interpreted as a single farmstead. Coin finds are few, and comprise a single denarius and a sestertius, as well as an Arabo-Sasanian drachm, four dirhams, and a single klipping struck by Frederik II (1559-1588). Furthermore some clipped gold objects of the Germanic Iron Age have been found in the outskirts of the settlement/farm area.[375]

A pierced denarius of the Antonine period was found before 1915 together with an axe (*pålstav*), 58 beads and several fragments of beads, fragments of a small bronze ring and some fine ware pottery at Stangehøj (also called Glasergård). The composition of this assemblage may indicate that it derived from a burial.[376] The site Bækkegård/Glasergård 500-1000 m to the north was located in 2006 and has produced three denarii and a Medieval British sterling out of only 17 registered finds, suggesting that future surveys may bring forth a higher number of coins.[377]

Further to the east (across the boundary to Østermarie parish) a denarius was found in the Viking Age *hacksilber* hoard of Store Frigård. The hoard consisted of 1276 coins, jewellery and ingots discovered *in situ* within an earthenware jug while leveling the court-

---

[375] 060405 sb 178. BMR 750. Watt 2009, 109-111; FP 4801, 4994, 4996, 5245, 5603, 7852. von Heijne 2004, 329 no. 5.129.

[376] 060405 sb 163 and 376. NM I inv.no. C 16564. Breitenstein 1944, 45 no. 19.

[377] 060405 sb 337. BMR 3426. FP 8306 and 8540.

yard.[378] The denarius is quite worn, but still legible (Hadrian, *RIC* 262).

Between Østerlars and Gudhjem

The area between Østerlars and Gudhjem is very rich in archaeological finds, and the character of the finds as well as numerous toponyms reveal that the area probably had a special significance, in particular during the Late Germanic Iron Age and Viking Period.[379] In a settlement area at Nørre Sandegård *c.* 1.5 km from the coast a Viking Age *hacksilber* hoard, including almost 100 coins, has been found. A denarius was found within the scatter of the hoard.[380] The denarius was struck by Marcus Aurelius for Divus Antoninus Pius (*RIC* 436). It is fragmented (broken), bent and quite worn, but contrary to some (but not all) the Viking Age coins it is not pecked. It cannot be excluded that the denarius was deposited as part of the Viking Age hoard, a situation comparable to the Store Frigård Hoard mentioned above.

According to tradition, Eigil Regnarsen, *høvedsmand* to the Danish king Knut IV the Holy (1080-86), resided on the plateau overlooking Gudhjem. A series of Viking Age sites have been located, and Ancient coins have been found on three sites. The most important of these for Roman coins is Krogegård. Here a closed hoard (the Melsted hoard) of Viking Age coins and other objects in silver, including a Thor's hammer, had already appeared in the early 19th century. In 1880 Vedel received a single German coin from the 11th century from this hoard, but all other finds were lost. The exact find spot of the hoard was not described, but it was believed to be identical to the site, where detector surveying since 1993 and a trial excavation in 1995 has yielded 25 coins. No

Fig. 77. Krogegård. Denarius FP 6461.1.

structures were identified during the subsequent excavation. The majority of the coins were struck in the 11th century (22 German coins and one Danish coin struck by Hardeknud 1035-42), but there is also one denarius, one dirham, and one 16th century coin.[381] The denarius, which was struck by Trajan, is much worn and the type is not identified *(Fig. 77)*.

Another possible hoard area (Krogegård I) was located in 1994 *c.* 150 m southeast of the previous site and an excavation in 1995 revealed the remains of two burnt down houses and two pits. The plough layer has yielded several more finds, totaling 44 coins, both during and after the excavation. Again German coins of the 11th century dominate (25 specimens), but there are also eight dirhams and eight denarii as well as three Danish penninge of the 13th and early 14th centuries.[382] Except for the Roman denarii and the few later Medieval coins, all other finds are dated to the Viking Age. Hanne Wagnkilde suggested that Krogegård I (sb 207) should be interpreted as the primary hoard area and possible find spot for the Melsted Hoard, while the finds from Krogegård (sb 144) represent material transferred from sb 207 in connection with infilling of wet areas in the former meadows.[383]

The Krogegård sites have been surveyed by amateur archaeologist Klaus Thorsen for more than 15 years.

---

378 060406 sb 318. FP 1701 and NM II D 11305-19. Galster 1929 and 1980 no. 48; *DMS* 37 (denarius cat.no. 1201; von Heijne 2004, 331 no. 5.135.

379 Jørgensen & Nørgård Jørgensen 1997, 11 fig. 1: distribution of Late Germanic Iron Age cemeteries in Bornholm and fig. 3: cemeteries south of Melsted. Most recently Nørgård Jørgensen 2011 discussed the many cementeries found along the coast south of Gudhjem.

380 060405 sb 199. BMR 1853. Viking Age coins: FP 4805, 4990, 5064, 5242, 5589, 6846.2-11, 8175.1-14, and unregistered coins: x126-152(27), x161-5, and x191-3. Hacksilber: NM I 7090/90. Cf. von Heijne 2004, no. 5.128. The denarius: FP 6846.1.

381 060405 sb 144. BMR 2153. FP 5239, 5567, 6461 and 7496 (25 coins). Denarius: FP 6461.1. Galster 1980, 110 no. 34 on the Melsted hoard; von Heijne 2004. no. 5.106 and 5.124-125.

382 060405 sb 207. BMR 2252. FP 5574, 5997 and 7790 (44 coins). von Heijne 2004, no. 5.124-125. The site is still being detected, and the most recent finds made in late 2010 and early 2011 include three more denarii, FP 8924.1-3. I am grateful to Klaus Thorsen for information and photos of the newly found denarii.

383 Hanne Wagnkilde, unpublished excavation reports for BMR 2153 and 2252 (1995).

The sites with Roman coin finds

Fig. 78. The denarii from Krogegård (sb 207) are worn, but not much corroded or fragmented. FP 5574.1-4 (left) and FP 5574.5-7, FP 5997.1 (right).

According to him the denarii have been found scattered over such a large area that an interpretation of the denarii as part of a ploughed-up (Viking Age?) hoard is unlikely. The surface preservation of the denarii is, however, remarkably homogeneous: all denarii are much worn and have scratches caused by having been moved around in the plough soil, but they are hardly corroded *(Fig. 78)*. This applies to both the coins from Krogegård I and the so far single denarius from Krogegård *(Fig. 77)*. This homogeneity seems to contradict the spatial distribution of the finds, and it may be argued that they derived from the same deposition, lending some support to Wagnkilde's reconstruction of events. If she is right, it implies that material from the Viking Age hoard has been tossed around in the plough layer for almost two centuries, which may explain the very long distances between the finds! However, only a specialized study of the Viking Age material from the two sites may give a hint whether it is possible to interpret this material as deriving from one deposition. Even so it seems hard to evaluate whether the denarii also derive from this hoard, or – perhaps more likely? – from a small denarius hoard deposited in the same general area.

Crossing boundaries

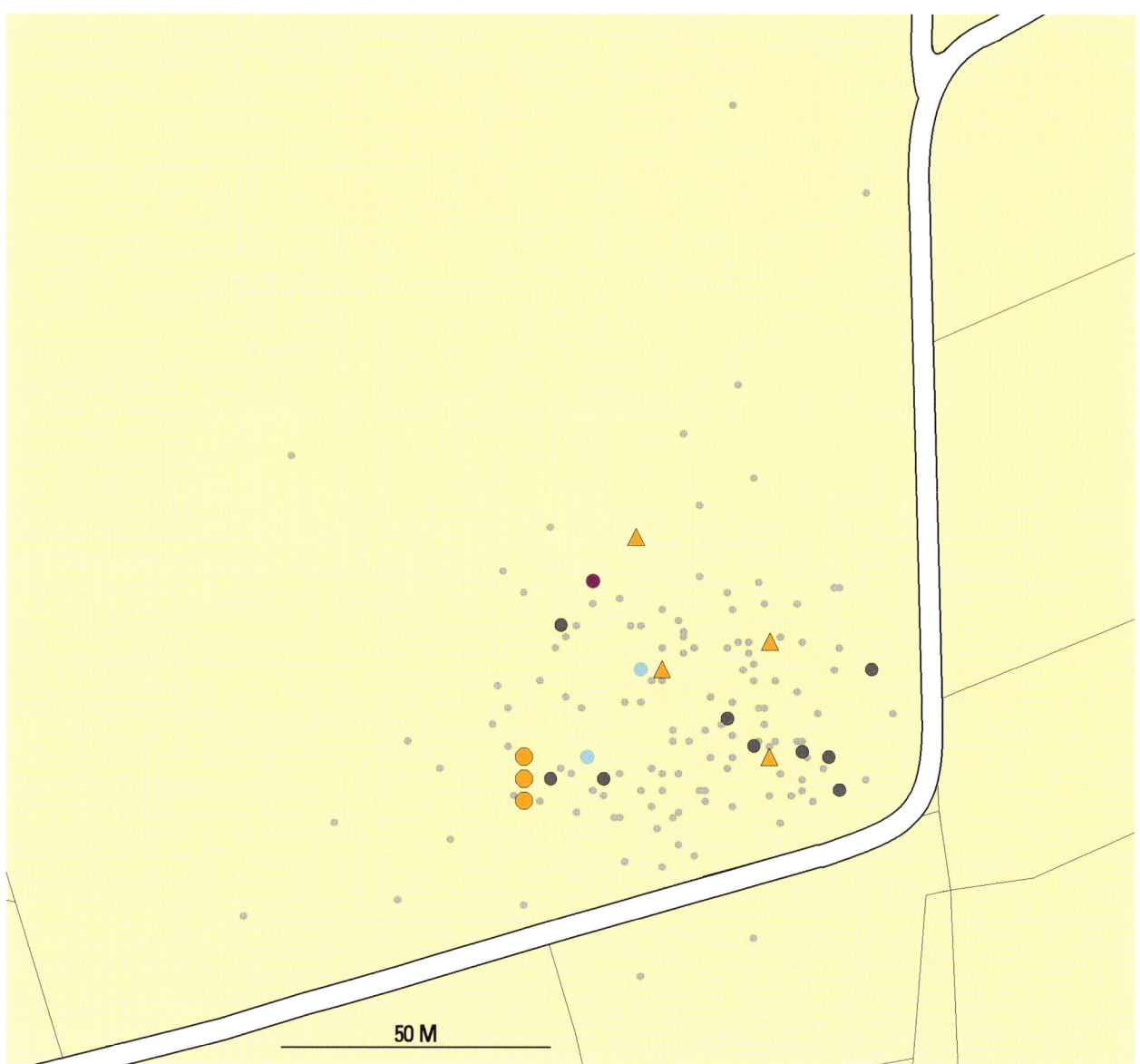

Fig. 79. Distribution of coins from Egesløkkegård. Note the position of the three solidi very close to each other, but in the periphery of the settlement area. Scale 1:1250. Legends as fig. 55.

Finally a third Viking Age hoard, namely the Lillegærde Hoard, has been discovered on the plateau.[384] To date 124 coins from this hoard have been found, with a numismatic *t.p.q.* of deposition AD 1048. A single drachm of a posthumous issue of Alexander the Great was found within the cluster of Viking Age coins *(Fig. 45)*. A comprehensive analysis of the spatial distribution of this hoard has not been made, so the exact position of the Greek coin is not known, but the coin is pecked and carries a considerable number of notches on the rim. Neither of these features is common before the Viking Age, so the attribution of the Greek coin to the Viking Age hoard is highly probable.

Just across Melsted Å (stream), less than half a km from the Viking Age sites at Krogegård, two denarii were found on a hillock at a grove north of Damaskegård. The coins were handed in to the museum

---

384 060405 sb 197. Kromann & Jensen 1993 (preliminary publication, then 89 coins had been found); von Heijne 2004, no. 5.126. FP 4989.1-4 and 6-17; 5138.1-7; 5241.1-5; 5460.1-5; 5798; 6362.1-4; 6857; 7635.1-2; 8351.1-7; 8398.1-72. The drachm is registered as FP 4989.1. Kromann compared it with SNG Cop 977 (uncertain mint, Greece or Macedonia, 3rd cent. BC) = Price 1991, no. 862 (uncertain mint, Greece or Macedonia, 325-310 BC).

Fig. 80. Denarius from Egesløkkegård with discoloration characteristic for a coin deriving from a small stack. FP 6924.2.

in 1890, but no other finds have been recorded from this area.[385]

In the opposite direction, towards Bobbeå (stream) west of Gudhjem, a probable settlement area at Lensgård Nord, discovered in 2002, has until now yielded two denarii.[386]

Northwestern Bornholm

The northern coastline between Gudhjem and Hammershus is rocky and forested, and therefore not favourable for detector archaeology. It is almost void of Roman coin finds. Only two denarii have been found on a small settlement area, Nyvang west of Rø, which has also yielded some pottery sherds tentatively dated to the Late Iron Age.[387] A Byzantine 20 *nummia* of Justin II (565-578) found in the town of Allinge should probably be regarded as a secondary 'tourist' coin.[388]

Egesløkkegård

The only site with a substantial number of Roman coins from the northwestern part of the island is Egesløkkegård. It is a settlement area southwest of Allinge situated on the eastern side of a hillock. The site overlooks the Kæmpeløkke Å (stream) that flows into the Baltic between Sandvig and Allinge a little more than 1 km northeast of the site. The site is known only from detector finds (a total of more than 180 registered objects), mainly from the Late Germanic Iron Age. Among the finds there are 18 coins: 11 denarii, three solidi, three dirhams and a klipping *(Fig. 79)*.[389]

The three solidi were found aligned within an area of 1 x 8 m in the western part of the site, and it seems fair to interpret them as a small gold hoard.[390] The 11 denarii have, however, been found scattered over a larger area corresponding to the general distribution of finds from the site. They are all badly preserved, most of them are worn or very worn and some in addition are corroded and/or have layers of incrustations, perhaps deriving from association with other metal objects. They do not have the characteristics of a single deposition (hoard), yet two of the denarii are corroded in a manner that indicates they have been deposited in stack *(Fig. 80)*.[391]

Between Teglkås and Vang

There are two significant areas in western Bornholm with a number of sites, several of which have multiple finds of Roman coins. In both cases the concentration of sites is caused by surface reconnaissance undertaken by an amateur archaeologist. The lack of finds in the surrounding areas may therefore be misleading, and surveys are needed to establish whether or not the proximity of sites in these two nuclei is part of a general pattern.

The northern cluster of sites is situated in Rutsker parish between Teglkås and Vang and along the modern main road between Rønne and Allinge-Sandvig.[392] The first find was the Kåsbygård Hoard discovered in 1839 while digging a potato clamp. The hoard is mixed, consisting of 14 solidi as well as a gold mount for a sword scabbard, a couple of gold spiral rings, a whole as well as a fragment of a gold bar.[393]

---

385 060405 sb 162. NM I C 762. Breitenstein 1944, 43-44 no. 16. Marcus Aurelius *RIC* 396 or 406 and Marcus Aurelius for Lucius Verus *RIC* 539.
386 060405 sb 235. BMR 3241. FP 6639 (Antoninus Pius for Diva Faustina Major) and 7390 (Marcus Aurelius for Faustina Minor, *RIC* 669).
387 060107 sb 116. BMR 1947. FP 7509: Domitian *RIC* 87, 89 or 92 and Marcus Aurelius *RIC* 138(?).
388 060105 sb 220. BMR 2005. FP 4972. Horsnæs 2006a, no. 118.

389 060101 sb 217. BMR 3140. FP 6462.1-2, 6924.1-6, 6996.1-4, 7237.1-2, 8152.1. Three recently found coins (x94-96), two dirhams and one klipping, have not yet been registered.
390 Horsnæs 2009, 240 no. 1.
391 FP 6924.2 and 7237.1.
392 Area surveyed by amateur archaeologist Bent Gregersen.
393 060106 sb 37. FP 3. Breitenstein 1944, 58-61 no. 23; Klindt-Jensen 1957, fig. 129; Horsnæs 2009, 240-241

Fig. 81. Uncleaned denarii from Rødbjerg. FP 5459.3 and 7241.1.

Fig. 82. Denarii from Nygård/Skovgård: FP 5471.1 and 5605.2.

Kåsbygård is overlooking the coast just south of the stream Askebækken, and near the old crossing of the stream at Brandsvad Bro. The hoard was found 'on a level field', but its exact position in relation to the farm was not noted. Later reconnaissance has located an area of black soil with pottery finds on the fields of Kåsbygård, and a small number of scattered metal objects, including a fragment of a dirham, has been found in the area.[394]

The Bakkegård site was recently located 500-1000 m inland from Kåsbygård and south of the stream, Askebækken. Bakkegård has so far yielded only one denarius and an Otto Adelheid pfennig dated around 1000, and presently it can hardly be properly interpreted.[395] The two sites Tuleborg/Almegård and Dalshøj/Krakken are situated 1.5 km north of Askebæk, on either side of the modern main road. Both sites have indications of settlement material from the Iron Age. Tuleborg/Almegård has produced two denarii, and a fragment of an unusually early dirham struck by Isdris I or II (AD 788-807).[396] Dalshøj/Krakken recently yielded a single double struck denarius.[397]

Bukkegård is situated halfway between these sites and Kåsbygård. Detector surveys have over a period brought to light seven denarii and a solidus[398] in an area with remains of cremation burials of the Roman Iron Age as well as Iron Age settlement material.[399] The denarii present differences between areas with a bright silvery surface and areas with a dull, dark grey surface characteristic for coins that have been stacked, and it is not impossible that they have been deposited together.[400]

A single denarius struck by Severus Alexander has allegedly been found in Vang before 1873. There is no recorded context for this coin, which is of unusually late date in comparison with most Roman coins from Barbaricum.[401]

---

no. 3.
394   060106 sb 183. FP 5476 (dirham fragment).
395   060106 sb 215. BMR 3280. FP 8107.1: extremely worn denarius of Antoninus Pius.
396   Sb 167. BMR 1734. FP 6052 and 6997. Denarii: Vespasian (- *RIC*) and unidentified fragment of a denarius

397   Sb 168. BMR 1876. FP 8482. Vespasian, unidentified type.
398   Horsnæs 2009, 241 no. 4. FP 6287.2/BMR 1171x39.
399   060106 sb 150. *AUD* 1993, 247 and 2001, 239.
400   It was not possible to present an overall mapping of the finds from Bukkegård. At least three of the denarii were found within an area of c. 12 x 12 m (FP 6287.1, FP 7238.1-2), but a fourth (FP 6463.1) seems to have been found more than 100 m away. The solidus is also found more than 100 m from the group of three denarii.
401   Breitenstein 1944, 44-45 no. 18. NM I C 1615.

Only few Ancient coins have been found in Olsker parish. There are only two denarius sites, and they are both situated in the westernmost part of the parish, close to the group of sites in Rutsker. Gl. Skovgård is situated *c.* 1.5 km east of the Tuleborg and Dalshøj sites. Here only a single denarius has been found on a field that has otherwise produced a few Medieval and Renaissance coins.[402] Vedby SV is isolated further inland at a distance from the former sites. The site had earlier been noted as a possible Iron Age settlement, but the first detector finds were only registered in 2009. They already comprise two denarii, a dirham and a gold pendant from the Early Germanic Iron Age, but an evaluation of this site must await further surveys.[403]

Between Hasle and Klemensker

Another concentration of denarius sites within a few square kilometers has been found in the hilly terrain just east of Hasle. It consists of eight sites in the western part of Klemensker parish and one site in Nyker parish.[404]

It is hard to make direct comparison between these locations. Rødbjerg/Tornbygård was for example among the first sites to be surveyed by detectorists in 1981, and in fact most of the sites in this area were mainly surveyed in the 1980's and 1990's, while the first finds from Hebro/Tornbygård II only 200-250 m from Rødbjerg were not made until 2009. Phosphate analysis and soil samples indicate that Rødbjerg, although a relatively small settlement, was continuously occupied from the Roman Iron Age to the Viking Age.[405] The site has yielded 11 denarii and one dirham.[406] Some of the denarii may originate from one deposition (i.e. a small hoard), as three of them were found in stack and a fourth was found close to these. A fifth denarius was found aligned with the former 30 m away, while two denarii were found in an area *c.* 100 m from the other denarii and *c.* 15 m apart. Two coins that have not been cleaned and restored both present a characteristic reddish surface layer *(Fig. 81)*.[407] It is, however, difficult to compare these with the other coins, the majority of which have been cleaned. In spite of the Roman coins dominating the numismatic material, the majority of the fibulas from the site are from the Late Germanic and Viking Ages.

The neighbouring site Hebro/Tornbygård II produced four denarii and some fibulas of the Germanic Iron Age all found during the same survey.[408] It is not a typical ensemble of denarii as the three identified coins are relatively late, but considerering that this is a newly located site additional finds may quickly alter the picture. Two of the denarii were reworked (one is pierced and one has a small punched hole). The very light fragment of a Crispina coin has an extremely worn and smooth surface. It seems to consist mainly of copper and should probably be interpreted as a heavily worn down *anima* of a subæratus. It is closely comparable to a denarius from Biskopenge V.[409] The state of preservation of the coins differs greatly.

From a numismatic point of view other sites in this area are dominated by Medieval material and have only a few Roman and Viking Age coins. This applies to the sites at Nygård/Skovgård and Mulebygård. Nygård/Skovgård is situated on either side of a track. It has been surveyed since the late 1980's. Excavation of trial trenches in the eastern part of the area in 1995 as well as soil samples examined as part of the Black Soil project confirmed the presence of intact culture layers from the Late Roman and Early Germanic Iron Ages.[410] The majority of the coins from the site, however, belongs to the Medieval period (late 13th-14th centuries) and a considerable number of them are concentrated in the eastern part of the area, where they may be related to building remains and finds of pottery of Siegburg type. 33 coins from the eastern part of the area (sb 235) include six denarii *(Fig. 82)* and four dirhams, as well as one coin from the 19th

---

402 060105 sb 219. BMR 1569. FP 4739, 4804, 4995, 6958. Denarius FP 4995.1 struck by Antoninus Pius for Faustina Minor, *RIC* 495a (III, 93), 146-161 AD.

403 060105 sb 55. BMR 2674. FP 8150.1-3: Vitellius *RIC* 2nd ed. 109, AD 69; Trajan *RIC* 118-135 var. with Salus(?), 103-111 AD; dirham, very worn and cut in half.

404 Sites in this area are surveyed by amateur archaeologist Kaj Pedersen. It should be kept in mind that the area has also produced sites from the Iron Age with no coin finds.

405 060104 sb 201. BMR 1611. Watt 2009, 83-84. *AUD* 1990, 199; 1995, 262; 1999, 266.

406 Dirham FP 7241.2 (x91)

407 FP 5459.3 (exc.no. x53) and 7241.1 (exc.no. x90)

408 060104 sb 351. BM 3567, FP 8295.1-4.

409 Cf. above: BMR 1760x11, FP 7049.4.

410 Watt 2009, 79-82.

Fig. 83. Denarii from Møllegård: FP 4983.1-2 (left), FP 5137, FP 5253.

century.[411] The earliest finds, however, come from the western part of the site (sb 190), which has in general been less productive than the eastern area. The smaller number of finds is reflected in only four coins, including one denarius found in two fragments *c.* 1 m apart.[412] An analysis of the fibulas from Nygård /Skovgård supports the evidence derived from the distribution of the numismatic material.[413] A small cluster of Early Roman Iron Age fibulas is situated in the western part of the site, while fibulas from the Late Roman and Germanic Iron Ages are distributed over most of the area where denarii have been found. Viking Age coins are rare and only dirhams are represented corresponding with the few fibulas from the Viking Age. It is suggested that the centre of the site may have moved from the western area towards east at the transition from the early to the late Iron Age, which would place the majority of the denarii in a Late Iron Age context. The preservation of the denarii differs considerably, and two of them are Barbarian imitations (*Fig. 25,* FP 5810 and FP 6082).

At Brogård, situated *c.* 800 m north of Nygård / Skovgård a single denarius has been found in a field which also yielded some gold fragments. It has been suggested that they might derive from burials, but there is no other evidence to support this except that the denarius was looped and mounted in a silver frame *(Fig. 82)*.[414]

An unusual denarius, struck by Diadumenian,[415] was found while ploughing at Sigård around 1875. The site was already then noted for finds of coins and jewellery, but no details as to the possible date of these finds were recorded. Modern detector surveys have so far yielded only a small number of finds, including four coins from the Viking Age to Early Renaissance Period, probably deriving from a settlement.[416]

The Møllegård and Hoglebjerggård sites are situated east of Nygård /Skovgård. Møllegård was surveyed 1984-1995 and the area was investigated as part

---

411 Skovgård sb 235 BMR 2001. FP 4985, 5144, 5244, 5471, 5605, 5810, 6082, 7386, (x145-147 not counted). AUD 1991, 225; 1995, 262; 1997, 246; 1999, 267. Note that no western Viking Age coins were found.

412 Sb 190. BMR 1640. FP 5255: dirhem and Christian IV (4-skilling); FP 5458: denarius (found in two fragments, *c.* one metre apart) and Christian II (klipping). AUD 1995, 262; von Heijne 2004, no. 5.16.

413 Horsnæs 2012 with distribution map by Michael Vennersdorf, based on information filed in Bornholms Museum.

414 060104 sb 251. BMR 2374. FP 6409. Horsnæs 2002b; Horsnæs 2010, 167 for examples with similar mounting.

415 FP 507, *RIC* 109 (IV,ii, 14), 217-218 AD. Breitenstein 1944, 44, no. 17.

416 FP 5472 and 6359. von Heijne 2004, no. 5.13.

of the Black Soil Project in 1999. Several finds have been made, in particular in an area around a burnt down building with pottery finds from the transition Late Roman – Early Germanic Iron Age. Few finds can be dated to that period, but they include some unusual objects that indicate high status or a special function of the settlement, among other things the *patrix* for a gold foil figure, a gold ingot and pieces of gold. Møllegård has yielded seven denarii, eight Viking Age coins and one Medieval coin.[417] The denarii differ greatly in state of preservation *(Fig. 83)*. Two (perhaps three) of them have been exposed to fire, and may thus be related to the burnt down building registered during surveying and soil sampling. The denarii are distributed over an area of *c.* 100 x 100 m.

The neighbouring site Hoglebjerggård has also produced remains of burnt daub and pottery from the Iron Age and Viking period. The number of finds registered from this area is relatively small; it includes among other things seven coins: three denarii, a dirham and three Medieval coins.[418] The two most recently found denarii were situated *c.* 20 m apart.

South of the parish border, two areas at Ndr. Mulebygård, discovered in 1999, are comparable to the sites in Klemensker.[419] The sites – probably representing two households – are known only from the detector finds and the blackened soil on the sites. The finds include several unusual objects, in particular from the Late Iron Age and Viking Age, such as gold and a Viking Age miniature sword. The numismatic material comprises 56 coins, among which there is an unusually high number of Medieval coins (35) compared to only seven Viking Age coins and seven Roman denarii. The two sites are comparable to Nygård/Skovgård (cf. above), where Medieval coins also outnumber coins from the Roman and Viking Age. The distance between the denarii is quite large, more than 100 m. Several of the coins are very worn. One is almost completely covered by corrosion material,[420] another is partly melted.[421]

Kistegård/Simblegård is an inland settlement site west of Klemensker.[422] The site has yielded four denarii found during two surveys, and six relatively early Cufic dirhams found during three other surveys.[423] The spatial relations between these finds have not been analysed. In 1939 a total of 28 mainly German Viking Age coins appeared in a gravel pit west of the modern farm. The coins have a numismatic *t.p.q.* in AD 1065.

The Karlshøj/Trommeregård site is situated on the road leading from Klemensker eastwards towards Årsballe and the Almindingen area, isolated from other sites with Roman denarius finds.[424] Four denarii and two dirham fragments have appeared during surveys that have produced objects from the Early Germanic to Viking Age along with pottery representing probably more than one farmstead. The coins are distributed over almost 150 x 30 m.

Gold finds are rare in the area between Hasle and Klemensker. One Late Roman solidus was found in Østre Byvang near Hasle before 1929, but no details about the find circumstances are recorded.[425] In the 19th century another gold coin is reported from the inland site of Bekkegård northwest of Klemensker.[426]

Southwestern Bornholm, between Rønne and Åkirkeby

Sites with Roman coins are numerous on the southern part of Bornholm, in the area dominated by sandstone. Most sites are situated south of the main road from Rønne to Nexø. One of the few exceptions to this rule is the cluster of sites around Smørenge.

---

417 Sb 202. Watt 2009, 76-78. AUD 1991, 225; 1993, 247; 1995, 263. See also von Heijne 2004, no. 5.11 and 5.61 (same site).

418 060104 sb 200. BMR 871 and 1536. FP 4707B, 4797, 6053, 6123. von Heijne 2004, no. 5.5. Denarii: Antoninus Pius *RIC* 177d and 200 (for Diva Faustina Major) and Commodus *RIC* 172.

419 060302 sb 124 (BMR 2812) and without sb (BMR 3227).

420 FP 6411.1 (2812x50).

421 FP 7106.2 (3227x47)

422 060104 sb 196. BMR 888. FP 5228 and 8481.

423 FP 6178, 6348 and 6973. von Heijne 2004, cat.no. 5.15.

424 060104 sb 264. BMR 2225 and 2238. FP 5993.1-4, 6371.1-2, 7786 (7 coins: 4 denarii, three dirhams). von Heijne 2004, no. 5.7

425 060102 sb 158. FP 1707. Horsnæs 2009, 240 no.2.

426 060104 sb 60. The coin is lost.

Crossing boundaries

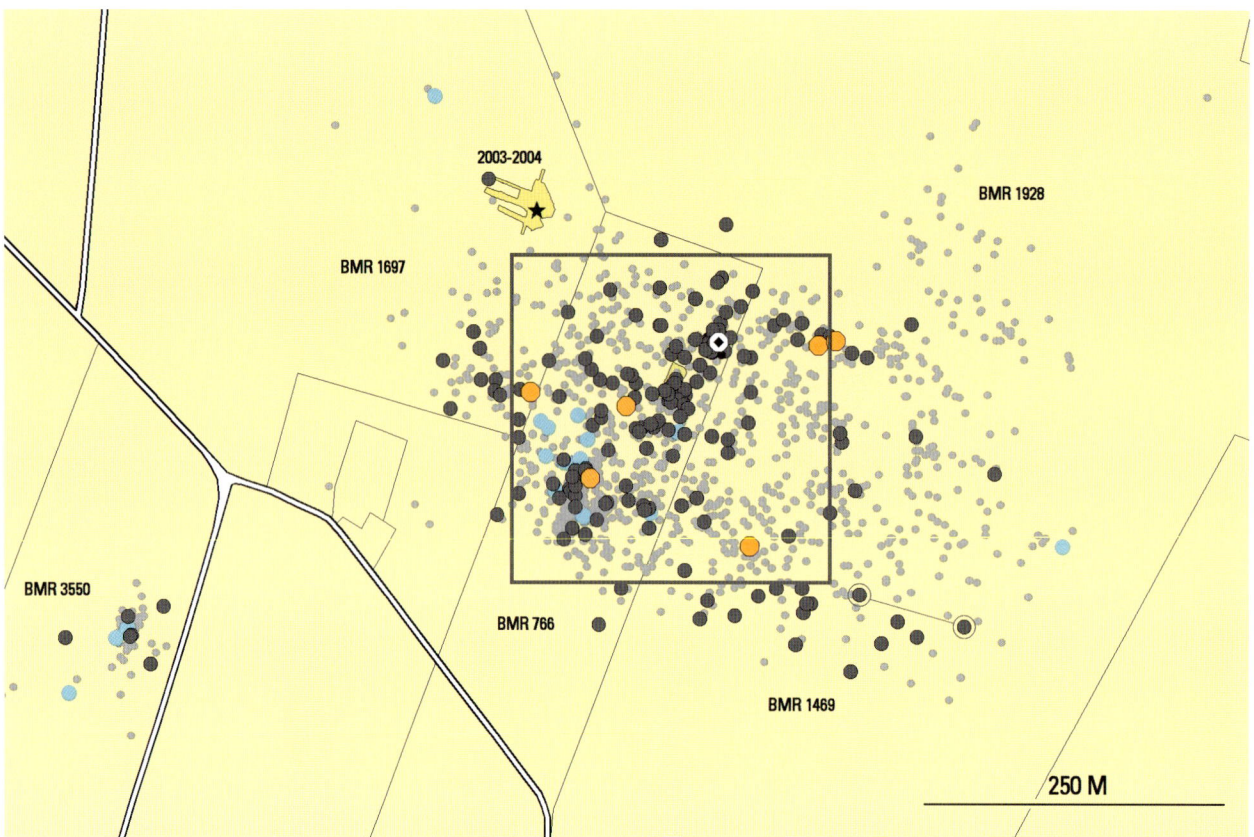

Fig. 84. Distribution of finds from the Smørenge complex. Guldhullet ('The Gold Pit') is situated almost 400 m west of the centre of the main site. The possible cultic area (with the impressive find of an enormous fibula) is marked with an asterisk northwest of the main site. Scale 1:5000. Legends as fig. 55.

Smørenge – settlement, hoard and cult site

Smørenge is situated between Lobbæk and Åkirkeby, c. 5 km from the coast.

Finds of gold from the area were mentioned as early as 1725, when Jakob von Melle described the find of twenty gold foil figures from a site that may be identical with the 'votive area', Guldhullet, close to Store Smørengegård (cf. below, sb 554/BMR 3550; *Fig. 84*). Vedel undertook the first excavations on the site in 1870, and he found remains of a settlement.[427] Two Roman denarii were found in 1877 and 1950, respectively.[428]

Detector archaeology began early at Smørenge, and in 1983 the discovery of 47 denarii within a restricted area led to the first rescue excavation with the aim of recovering a denarius hoard. The excavation brought to light part of the hoard still *in situ*. 313 denarii and two small ingots were found in the lower and still untouched parts of two small pottery vessels, surrounded by numerous denarii already scattered by the plough. Only 15 cm from the vessels a solidus struck by An-themius was found. The hoard was located within the line of wall posts from a house. No datable material was found in the post holes, but they cut into a culture layer with remains of a burnt down house from *c.* AD 200 and must clearly be younger than this *(Fig. 86-87)*. The coin hoard that probably also contained the Late Roman solidus found amidst the cluster of 2nd century denarii probably belong to the settlement phase represented by the younger house.[429]

In the following years the number of denarius finds from the field grew steadily and a second excavation took place in 2000 in an area *c.* 50 m southwest of the first *(Fig. 85)*. This excavation produced more denarii, all coins from the plough soil. Remains of wall posts and pits were visible in the subsoil, but none were dated. However, fragments of pottery from the Roman Iron Age were found in the plough layer.

Today the total number of denarii from this field has risen to 735. Most of the coins are heavily worn and present a bright lustre as well as some clear green

---

427 Vedel 1886, 394 and 400.
428 NM I C 2852; Breitenstein 1944, 41 no. 12.

429 060305 sb 144. BMR 766. Watt 1983; Kromann & Watt 1984.

The sites with Roman coin finds

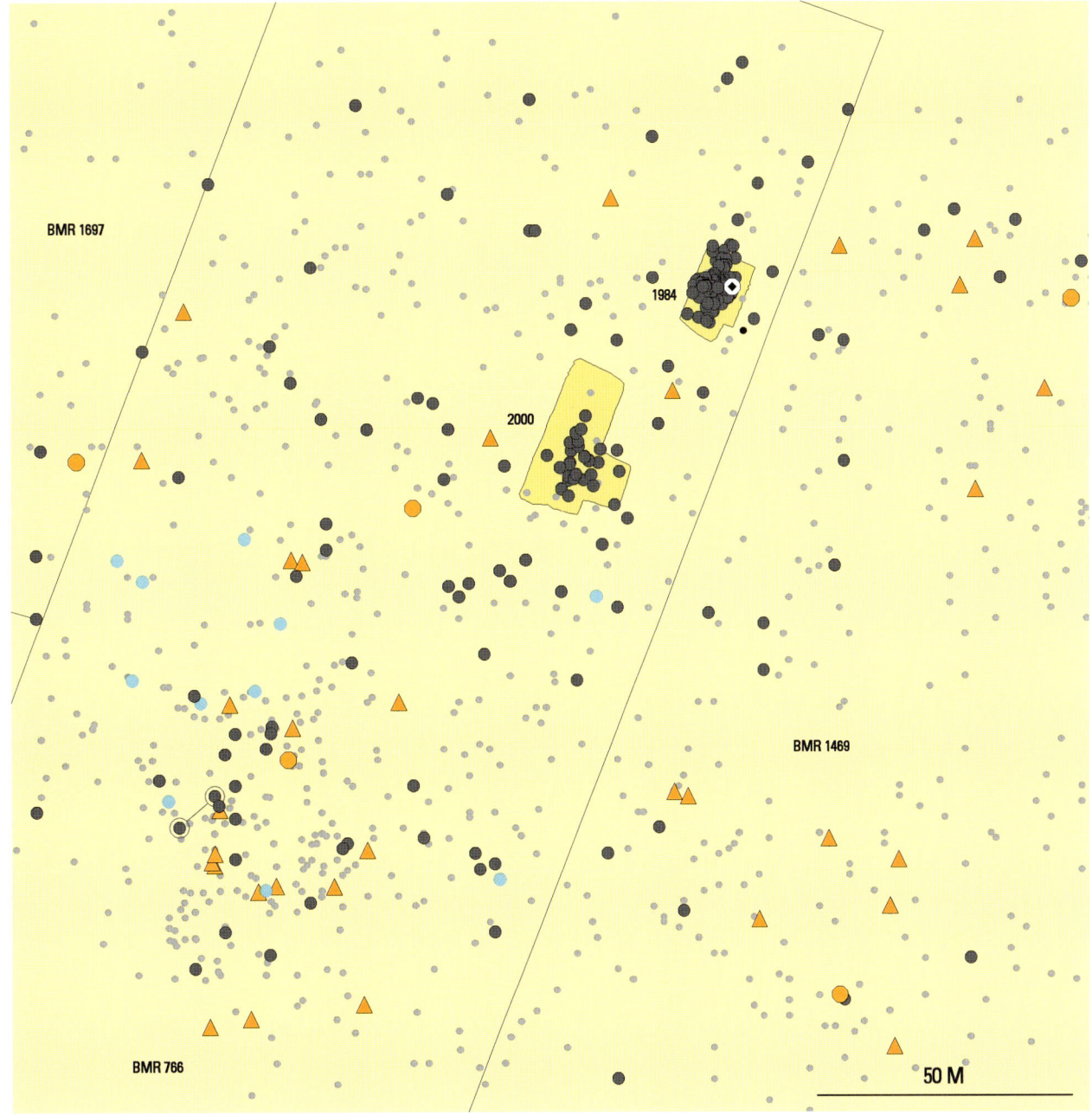

Fig. 85. Distribution of coins from the central part of the Smørenge site. The overall highest find density is in the southwestern part of the site, while the two denarius clusters are located outside this area. The thin lines mark the division of modern ownerships. Finds are evenly distributed on either side of the boundaries. Excavation areas (1983 and 2000) are outlined. Scale 1:1250. Legends as fig. 55.

spots. It is uncertain whether the two denarius concentrations excavated in 1983 and 2000 represent one or two denarius hoards. There is no difference in the material from the two excavation areas, neither in wear, corrosion or the internal structure of the finds. A division of the material into two hoards (rather than one) is based purely on the distance between the two main clusters of finds.[430]

A small number of other denarii found on the same area as the hoard scatters are less worn, but more corroded than the denarii deriving from the Smørenge hoard(s), and it is likely that they represent single depositions/losses or perhaps one or more smaller hoards. The surface preservation of these coins can be compared to the finds from the neigh-

---

430 I have previously argued for an interpretation of the material from the two clusters as the remnants of one hoard; Horsnæs 2006b, 102.

141

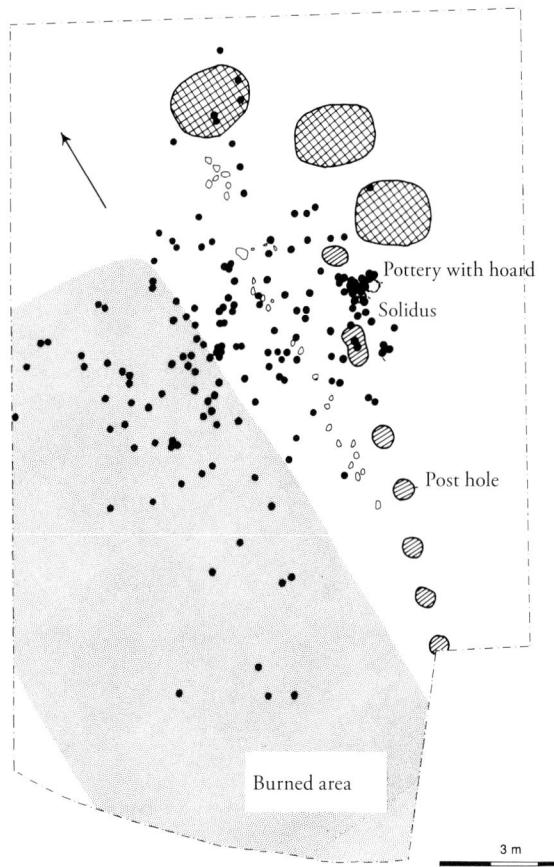

Fig. 86. Plan of the first hoard excavation at Smørenge (after Watt 1983, 34 fig. 4). Black dots: denarii.

bouring field (sb 70=BMR 1469, cf. below *Fig. 88-90*).

Two stacks containing partly melted coins have also been found on the same field. They were found c. 70 m apart and clearly outside the clusters of denarii belonging to the hoard. The distance between the stacks is so large that they can only tentatively be interpreted as coins that were once hidden in the burnt house from c. 200 AD.

In addition to the denarii five solidi have been found on this field. The Anthemius solidus struck in Milan (467-472 AD) that appeared during the first rescue excavation was interpreted as part of the hoard, thereby providing it with a numismatic *t.p.q.* The other solidi were found so far from the hoard(s) that they are probably not connected to it/them.[431] The area has furthermore produced 13 dirhams.

The Roman coins make up more than half the finds from this field, but the finds are not evenly distributed. The denarii are mainly found in the northern

---

431 Horsnæs 2009, 247 no. 17a-e.

Fig. 87. Smørenge. Denarii from the first hoard excavation, sb 144. Scale c. 1:1. Photo Nationalmuseet.

part of the field, where the hoard(s) is located, while the majority of other, mostly younger, finds derive from the southern part. This is also the area with the highest phosphate values, and this combination indicates that the main settlement area was in the southern part, and that the hoard(s) may have been buried on the periphery of the settlement. The central part of the settlement, i.e. the southernmost part of the field, has, however, also yielded a number of denarii. Here the coins are generally less worn than the majority of the coins from the hoard area, but it seems that the phosphor in the soil may be responsible for an aggressive etching of the surface of the coins *(Fig. 89)*.[432]

The adjacent field, just east of the one producing the hoard scatters, has yielded 68 denarii and four solidi *(Fig. 90)*. There are only three or four later coins: one dirham, two Danish coins (a klipping 1523-33 and a skilling from 1605) and a badly preserved bronze coin(?) of unknown date.[433] In this area denarii constitute less than 10% of the material *(Fig. 84)*. The denarii are very corroded and many of them are broken in the soil *(Fig. 90)*. The degree of wear varies. Two coins have a punched hole *(Fig. 28)*, and one of them was found in stack with two other denarii.[434] The ensemble of coins from this field are corroded in a manner similar to the minority of the scattered denarii from the hoard area (cf. above).

A recently discovered find made northwest of the hoard area has attracted attention as a sacrificial deposit containing among other things a unique and extremely large fibula, probably belonging to the Late Germanic Iron Age or Early Viking Age *(Fig. 84, BMR 1697 and Fig. 91)*.[435] This site has produced 25 denarii and two solidi. Most of the denarii are worn and corroded, and present a somewhat dull surface. Only a single one has a bright surface comparable to the coins deriving from the hoard(s). Five of the denarii are partly melted together, but the remaining ones show no traces of exposure to heat. In addition to the denarii this area has yielded two Late Roman

---

432 Horsnæs 2006b
433 060305 sb 70. BMR 1469. Solidi: Horsnæs 2009, 246 no. 16 and figs. 3.12-15.
434 FP 6693.1 and 6992.20 (in stack).
435 060305 sb 405. BMR 1697. Vennersdorf *et al.* 2006.

Fig. 88. Denarius with a thick layer of corrosion, from sb144/BMR 766, FP 6930.21 (x826).

Fig. 89. Denarius recomposed from two fragments, from sb 144/BMR 766, FP 6930.23 (x839) and 7057.28 (x967).

Fig. 90. Denarius from Smørenge, sb 70/BMR 1469, recomposed from two fragments found 74 m apart. FP 6992.16+8154.6.

Fig. 91. Denarii from area sb 405/BMR 1697, FP 7038.1-4.

solidi, one of which is cut,[436] and two dirham fragments.

Guldhullet ('The Gold Pit') at Store Smørengegård further away from the hoard site has produced several gold finds: bracteates, three small solid figures and several gold foil figures *(Fig. 84, BMR 3530)*. A subsequent excavation showed that no settlement remains were preserved, and the locality is tentatively interpreted as another sacrificial area, probably in connection with a natural spring. This site may be identical to the area with finds of gold foil figures mentioned by Jacob von Melle.[437] Apart from the gold objects it has yielded seven denarii, two dirham fragments and an Otto Adelheid pfennig.[438] The denarii from this area are characterized by a reddish coating, probably iron oxide from the nearby spring *(Fig. 92)*. In spite of the relatively large distances between the denarii I believe that they may be part of the same deposition. Dirhams from the same site do not present the same reddish coating.

Other inland sites

Three sites between Åkirkeby and Smørenge have been located recently and cannot as yet be fully evaluated. At Hullegård, only a single fragment of an Antoninus Pius denarius has been reported.[439] Mellemste Myrebygård has yielded more material, mainly from the Vi-

---

436 Horsnæs 2009, 247 no. 18 and figs. 3.18-19.
437 Laursen & Watt 2011.

438 060305 sb 554. BMR 3550.
439 060305 sb 448. BMR 3321, FP 7037.

The sites with Roman coin finds

Fig. 92. Smørenge. Denarii from sb 554. FP 8296.1-3 and FP 8296.6.

king Age, but also a denarius fragment and a Medieval coin.[440] Lundsminde (Skørrebro Øst) has produced a dirham fragment and a much worn sestertius of Antoninus Pius from a field with finds which include Iron Age pottery, fibulas, a weight and some gold.[441]

West of Smørenge, Almegård is another example of a recently discovered settlement area with a Roman denarius, a fragment of a Viking Age coin and some *Hacksilber*, as well as Baltic Ware.[442]

Close to Vestermarie a denarius and an Early Germanic Iron Age fibula have been found at a settlement at Pindeløkkegård.[443] The 'Kongens Udmark' Viking Age hoard was found in 1861 less than one km from Pindeløkkegård. The hoard is dated to the late 10th century, but there is no doubt that a single denarius was part of the Viking Age hoard.[444]

In the westernmost part of Vestermarie parish the settlement area at Sdr. Ellebygård is situated just south of Blykobbe Å (stream). Finds include material from the Viking Age and Early Medieval Period as well as six coins: a denarius (Marcus Aurelius), three German coins from late 10th-early 11th centuries, an English coin struck by Edward the Confessor (1042-1066) and one Danish penning from Lund 1332-1360.[445] Furthermore there is an un-confirmed report of a find of an unidentified gold coin from the area west of Stensgård. The area has yielded finds from both Iron Age and Viking Period, so it cannot be excluded that the coin was a solidus.[446]

Almindingen forest
Within the forested areas of Bornholm very few sites are known, yet remains of prehistoric field systems have been mapped. The lack of coin finds is probably caused by lack of detector surveys. Three sites with multiple finds of Roman coins hint at the potential of more finds to be discovered in the forested areas.

Lilleborg Castle mound
Investigations which have taken place over the last two centuries have resulted in numerous coin finds from Lilleborg. The first report of finds dates back to 1821, where 26 coins were recovered during the construction works undertaken by head forester Hans Römer.[447]

---

440 060305 sb 446. BMR 3189, FP 6566.
441 060305 sb 417. BMR 2079, FP 8269.
442 060305 sb 433. BMR 2661, FP 6088 (much worn denarius, probably Marcus Aurelius) and 6041 (Vi-

king Age coin fragment).
443 060305 sb 419. BMR 2157, FP 5233 (Antoninus Pius).
444 060305 sb 50 (Pindeløkkegård). NM I inv.no. 19602-20; FP 224 and 396: Skovmand 1942, 127; Breitenstein 1944, 38 find no. 5; Galster 1980, 33-39 no. 14; von Heijne 2004, 5.97. Denarius: FP 224. Trajan *RIC* 315, 114-117.
445 060305 sb 412. BMR 1524, FP 5059, 5256, 5599, and 5808.
446 060305 sb 21. I thank Michael Vennersdorf and René Laursen for information of this find.
447 060305 sb 151. Recent finds registered as BMR

Peter Hauberg investigated the site from 1876, and from 1887 he represented the National Museum during excavations.[448] Hauberg's excavations were restricted to the area inside the fortification. He concluded that the fortification had two building phases, and based on the Medieval coins found during the excavation he suggested that the first building activity took place in the mid-12th century.[449] He identified Lilleborg with the 'King's castle' known from literary sources to have been destroyed by the Slavic nobleman Jaromir of Rügen in 1257 while assisting the archbishop of Lund against the Danish king. Large amounts of burnt material were found during the excavations, and Hauberg concluded that the castle had been burnt down. Since then it has been used as quarry for building material, by among others Schweder Ketting, who in the mid-16th century used stones from Lilleborg to build a house with cellar and tower at Vallensgård and by Römer, who carried off 2-3000 cartloads of building material in the early 19th century. Without going into details, Hauberg mentioned that also Stone Age material and Iron Age pottery had been found on the castle mound along with Roman denarii.[450]

During the 1950s investigations undertaken by The National Museum and Bornholms Museum included sieving of the soil heaps left by Hauberg. A total of 162 coins were found during three campaigns.[451] In

Fig. 93. Denarii from Lilleborg. FP 8493.1-3.

1969 Otto Mørkholm presented a short article concentrating on the Roman coins from the Medieval castle mound, but enumerating a total of 266 coins, amongst which the overwhelming majority (257), were Danish coins dated in the period 1146-1286. Mørkholm assumed that the nine Roman denarii then known from the site could be regarded as a (part of a) denarius hoard found during the Medieval period, perhaps the Borresø Hoard (cf. below). He also claimed that the find pattern of the denarii, scattered throughout the area, revealed that the Roman denarii could be used as legal tender during in the 13th century, a suggestion that must today be refused, as they were not found *in situ*. A tenth denarius was found in the walls of Lilleborg in 1976.[452]

---

24. Inv.no. NM II CCCXLII, acquired 30/3 1821, included one denarius struck by Marcus Aurelius, *Antiqvariske Annaler* IV, 1827, 167 no. CCCXLII.f. The coin is now lost, but it was described as 'much worn'. Römer's investigations were described by Hauberg 1911, based on an eye witness account to Hauberg in 1876.

448 Inv.no. FP 1674 (and Bornholm Museum, historical dept. no. 7318): 74 coins found in the period (1822)/1882-1918; Hauberg 1911. The finds included two denarii, FP 1674. The first, struck by Marcus Aurelius for Divus Lucius Verus, was found 'outside the large house a little to the south of the foot path', the second was found in 1893 'in the courtyard west of the large house at the foot path'. On Hauberg and Bornholm, see Vesth 2006.

449 Hauberg 1911, 139.
450 Hauberg 1911, 147.
451 Excavations by the National Museum 1954: 32 coins, inv.no. FP 2420.1-32; 1955-6: 63 coins, inv. no. FP 2496.1-63 (among which four denarii); and investigations undertaken by Bornholms Museum (Olaf Olsen) in 1957: 67 coins, inv.no. FP 2542.1-62 (among which two denarii). Mørkholm 1969. The coins were found mainly while sifting the soil heaps left by Hauberg.

452 FP 3579, found '*i Lilleborgs ringmur*'. Kromann 1983-83, 113, no. 52.8. Kromann's list also included the nine previously found denarii from Lilleborg.

The sites with Roman coin finds

Fig. 94. Borresø.

In spite of the fact that Hauberg had already identified Neolithic and Iron Age material from his excavations at Lilleborg, the prevailing interpretation of the site has been one favouring a foundation *ex novo* of the castle in the Medieval period and its destruction by Jaromir only a century later. Mørkholm mentioned in passing that the Danish coins found on the site seriously challenge the traditional destruction date of Lilleborg. However, only a brief review of the dates of the Medieval material has hitherto been presented by Isler, who concluded that several objects were of types belonging in the second half of the 13th century or even into the early 14th century.[453]

During 2010 restoration work took place in order to reinforce the original walls of the castle. The clearing of the ground revealed hitherto untouched layers, and the workmen informed the Bornholms Museum of finds of several coins. These new finds included Danish coins from the late 12th and 13th century, as well as Roman denarii of the 2nd century *(Fig. 93)*. The total number of denarii from the Lilleborg castle mound has now risen to 13. The three denarii discovered in connection with the restoration works were all refound in soil heaps and it cannot be established exactly where they were found.[454] The coins were badly preserved and covered by burnt or corroded material.

As a consequence of the new coin finds rescue investigations took place during the summer 2010; they revealed that the history of the site was much more complex than hitherto expected. Two distinct burnt layers appeared, one was probably Neolithic, the other was clearly from the Iron Age, and pottery from the latter layer seems to belong in the (Early?) Germanic Iron Age.[455] Although the denarii were picked up from the disturbed layers before archaeologists arrived on the site, there are clear signs they had been associated with a burnt layer. Therefore we assume that the Roman denarii from Lilleborg derived from an Iron Age

---

453 Isler 2004.

454 FP 8493.

455 I thank Finn Ole Nielsen and Michael Thorsen for presenting the ongoing excavation to me and for readily sharing information on the stratigraphy of the site.

occupation period of the castle mound lasting into the Germanic Iron Age. The nearby Viking Age fortification Gamleborg (*Old Castle*) in Almindingen[456] therefore is not only a forerunner of Medieval Lilleborg, but perhaps also a successor of an earlier Iron Age phase at Lilleborg.

Borresø

Lilleborg castle mound is almost surrounded by the lake Borresø *(Fig. 94)*, where a mixed denarius and gold hoard was found in 1832 in connection with draining of the lake. Initially some gold spiral fingerrings were found in the mud. One was recovered, others were lost. Together with the gold rings were several Roman silver coins of which 16 were handed over to the later National Museum. The objects were found close together 'as if packed into something which had now disappeared'.[457] Thus it is clear from the outset that the Borresø Hoard consisted of a mixture of Roman denarii and gold rings, and that it contained more objects than those known today. The known denarii range in time from Trajan to Commodus and must be regarded as typical of denarius finds from Bornholm. In the following years Borresø yielded several other finds from different periods, among them was a Roman (type) bronze statuette.[458]

Ravnebrohus

It is hard to give a proper evaluation of the six solidi found during works at Ravnebrohus in 1889.[459] There is no additional information of the find circumstances and the area has never been subject to re-investigation. The toponym Ravnebro indicates the proximity to a ford/bridge in the wetlands Ravnemyr (myr = moor) and Ravnekær (kær = pond/marsh).

The material from the three sites in Almindingen is important archaeological evidence for Iron Age occupation of the area, which is supported by the presence of Prehistoric field systems at several places in the forest and by pollen analysis of a sample from Græssøen close to Borresø, showing that the area was deforested and taken under cultivation from around 400 BC onwards, thus there was open landscape around Græssøen during the Late Roman and Germanic Iron Ages.[460]

The coastal area

Close to Rønne two large denarius hoards had already been discovered in the 19th century at Robbedale and Udmarken. The area was then marginal soils as indicated by the name 'Udmarken' ('Outlying fields'). There is no modern agriculture in the area, and today it is characterized by plantation and lakes created by modern gravel exploitation. Thus it is an environment which is largely unsuitable for detector surveys. There are, however, remains of prehistoric field systems, but so far no other Iron Age finds have been recorded in the immediate vicinity of these sites.

Udmarken in Knudsker parish has yielded a total of 217 denarii. The finds arrived in the Royal Collection of Coins and Medals on three different occasions. The first 157 denarii (by Breitenstein termed Udmarken 'A', FP 122) were sent to the museum on April 15, 1853, and only one week later another 53 coins followed (Udmarken 'B', FP 123). The find spots of the two consignments were not described as being identical, still, if not identical, they must surely have been found not far from each other. The last seven denarii (Udmarken 'C', FP 169) were sent to Copenhagen on August 25, 1857, and there is little doubt that they derived from the same spot as the Udmarken 'B' coins. Unfortunately all the coins were heavily worn, and it was not considered important preserve them. The majority of the coins were disposed of, only 20 denarii were given to the Museum for Nordiske Oldsager, predecessor of the Collection of Danish Prehistory, where 16 have been identified.

The finds from Udmarken have variously been interpreted as one or two hoards, but it seems impossible to establish this with certainty. In spite of the uncertainty I have decided to treat all these coins as one find. The exact find spot remains unknown, but the site was undoubtedly part of Skovgård (112. Slg.)/Kroggård.[461]

Fig. 95. The Robbedale Hoard. Photo Nationalmuseet.

---

456 Klindt-Jensen 1957, 229-231.
457 Breitenstein 1944, 33-35 find no. 3, with references; Klindt-Jensen 1957, 156 and fig. 128.3-4.
458 Antqvariske Efterretninger, Bornholm, *Nordisk Tidsskrift* 1836, 312-313. Present whereabouts unknown.
459 060305 sb 176. FP 571. Breitenstein 1944, 66-68 no. 26; Horsnæs 2009, 245-6 no. 12.

460 Claus Malmros in Nielsen 2000, 218.
461 Breitenstein 1944, 3-7, find no. 1. Dept. of Danish Prehistory/NM I Inv.no. 13 100. Now registered as

The Robbedale Hoard was sent to the National Museum in 1893. It consisted of 253 denarii found together with the 'bottom and other fragments of an urn', probably a ceramic pot. The find was made while digging up a stone, and a few days later two more denarii were found on the same spot.[462] Robbedale is situated only *c.* 1 km south of the presumed location of the Kgs. Udmark Hoard(s) on the road leading from Rønne to Aakirkeby.

In the zone east of the above-mentioned hoards and south of Smørenge 14 minor sites have been located. Most of them have produced only a couple of Roman coins and rarely any later numismatic material. Three coin finds from this coastal area were known already to Breitenstein, all single finds of solidi. One derived from an unknown site in Nylarsker parish,[463] another allegedly came from Blemmelyng,[464] and the third was found at Kirkebjerget, near Sose in Vestermarie.[465] A dirham was found at Kølleregård in 1923, and recent detector surveys in that area have yielded another dirham, two Danish coins of the 13th century and a single denarius.[466]

The remaining 10 sites were discovered during detector surveys undertaken from the late 1990's onwards. The finds are all situated between the 25 and 50 m con-

Fig. 96. Denarii from Tornegård Syd/Brede and Lillevang Øst. FP 8103.1-2 and FP 8106.1-3.

site 060301 sb 66 (Kroggård).

462 060304 sb 20. KMMS inv.no. FP 636; 238 denarii were handed over to the Prehistoric Department in 1895 and inventorized as C 7776. The find was first published by Chr. Jørgensen 1900, who noted the heavy wear of the coins that made identification of types difficult. For parallels he referred to the catalogue of Ancient coins of the Royal Collection of Coins and Medals (Ramus 1816) and to the type catalogue of Cohen. Breitenstein 1944, 7-33, find no. 2.1-255 and figs. 1-5 listed the coins with reference to Jørgensen, but he added a verbal description of the coins and placed the coins into the *RIC* typology. Unfortunately the pottery(?) fragments of the container were not transferred to the National Museum.

463 060303 sb 256. Breitenstein 1944, no. 40; Horsnæs 2009, no. 14.

464 060303, without sb no. Breitenstein 1944, no. 42; Horsnæs 2009, no. 13.

465 060305 sb 101. Breitenstein 1944, no. 45; Horsnæs 2009, no. 15.

466 060303 sb 209. BMR 2369. FP 1592, 6125 and 7783: Denarius Antoninus Pius (Marcus Aurelius Caesar), unidentified type.

tour lines, slightly pulled back from the sea, but with a good view. Until now most of them have produced only a single or few denarii, but at Vestergård there are five Roman coins from a settlement area,[467] and from the two neighbouring sites Tornegård Syd/Brede and Lillevang Øst (parts of one larger settlement area) there are a total of ten Roman denarii *(Fig. 96)*.[468] The coins from Vestergård are four denarii of very different state of preservation and a small, probably 4th century, bronze coin. The rim of the bronze coin has been cut away, perhaps to allow for a secondary function as a weight *(Fig. 42)*.[469] The denarii from Tornegård Syd/Brede and Lillevang Øst are almost completely covered by corroded material that seems fairly homogeneous, but on both sites denarii have been found more than 100 m apart and probably represent multiple depositions. The sites have also yielded Viking Age material: two dirhams and Baltic Ware from Brede and one dirham from Lillevang Øst.

Lille Myregård has produced more than 200 detector finds, among which are two denarii, six Viking Age coins and six Medieval coins.[470] Fibulas from the site are dated to the Late Germanic Iron Age and the Viking Age, and together with the coin finds they indicate that the settlement was in use for an extended period.

The same longevity into the Medieval Period applies to Tornegård Vest although the overall number of finds seems to be smaller. Coin finds include four Medieval coins, two Viking Age coins, and a single denarius struck by Hadrian.[471]

A number of sites have been located only recently, and they have as yet produced limited numbers of finds: Vellensbygård Syd 2 is an Iron Age settlement with surface finds of pottery and a glass bead; it has produced two denarii of Antoninus Pius.[472]

Lille Strandbygård has yielded an Antoninus Pius denarius of 156-157 AD and pottery finds indicate the presence of a settlement from the Late Roman/Early Germanic Iron Age.[473] Fragments of fibulas from a settlement site at Ankersminde SSV indicate a period of use in the Late Germanic/Viking Age period, but in spite of this of the only numismatic find from the site so far is a small fragment of a Hadrianic denarius.[474]

In Vestermarie parish two sites have been found in topographical positions comparable to the abovementioned sites: Store Dalbygård NØ is a settlement area with several finds from the Germanic Iron Age and the Late Viking Age. An illegible denarius seems to be the oldest find from the site.[475] Two denarii from Bækkegård Vest are the only finds recorded from this site.[476]

A considerable number of localities in Åker parish share topographical characteristics with the previous ones. In the coastal area west of Læså four sites are situated not far from each other. The sites have produced one or two Roman coins each, and in general the number of coin finds from these sites is low. Two sites at Brogård have produced a single denarius, and on one of them (sb 223) there are six Viking Age coins.[477] Stagegård has produced only few finds among which are a denarius and five Viking Age coins,[478] while Lille Munkegård has yielded more finds in general but only two denarii, two Viking Age coins and a single Medieval coin.[479]

Following the Læså inland two important finds of solidi have been made near Kalby. With 36 coins the

---

467 060303 sb 190. BMR 1672. FP 6642, 6695, and 7514.
468 060305 sb 223. BMR 2656. (Tornegård Syd/Brede): von Heijne 2004, no. 5.89; FP 6245-6, 8106, and 8268. To these should be added coins in process of registration. 060305 sb 251. BMR 3495. (Lillevang Øst): FP 8103 and 8474.
469 BMR 1672x13. FP 6995.3. Weight 0.79 g.
470 060303 sb 118. BMR 1233. von Heijne 2004, no. 5.85. 6073,6089, 6824.1-7,7497, 7850, 8267,
471 060303 sb 231 and 435. BMR 2655. FP 6558, 7842, 8356.
472 060303 sb 214. BMR 2630. FP 6260 and 6640.

473 060303 sb 222. BMR 2838. FP 6261.
474 060303 sb 252. BMR 3436. FP 8095.
475 060305 sb 541. BMR 3145. FP 7391.
476 060305 sb 447. BMR 3272. FP 7007, Marcus Aurelius, *RIC* 378 and 688 (the latter struck for Faustina Minor).
477 060205 sb 223. BMR 1732. von Heijne 2004, no. 5.54. FP 5043, 5056 and 6173. The denarius was struck by Antoninus Pius, *RIC* 208. Sb 246. BMR 2148. FP 5252: Marcus Aurelius, *RIC* 123.
478 060205 sb 256. BMR 2367. FP 57 and 7793. The denarius is a subæratus of the Antonine period.
479 060205 sb 273. BMR 2659. FP 6002, 6263, 7006. Both denarii are badly preserved and the types have not been identified.

Soldatergård Hoard is the largest solidus hoard discovered on Bornholm. The first 35 coins were found in 1850 while removing some stones in fields belonging to Soldatergård, and the last coin was added in 1851.[480] There is no information about other finds from the area, nor has the exact find spot been located.

Vasegård is situated in an elevated and easily defendable position next to Læså. The site is probably best known as a Neolithic site with a 'Sarup-type enclosure'.[481] The Vasagård solidus hoard was discovered in 1992, when seven Late Roman solidi appeared within a 15 x 35 m area during detector surveys. Excavations the following year brought to light three more solidi and the remains of at least six Iron Age houses overlying the Sarup enclosure. None of the solidi was preserved *in situ*, but the most likely interpretation of the find is that of a hoard deposited near the houses. During the excavations a denarius was found in a pit with pottery dated to the Early Germanic Iron Age.[482]

South-eastern Bornholm between Åkirkeby and Nexø

Sandegård

Sandegård is the most important site as regards Roman coins from southeastern Bornholm. The first numismatic finds from this settlement site were handed in to the National Museum by Vedel in 1869: Three or four solidi were part of a larger gold hoard, together with among other things a fragment of a bracteate, a spiral finger ring, two twisted gold bars, and an ingot. Two of the three preserved solidi have clear marks indicating an attempt to cut them.[483] The bracteate fragment from Sandegård is part of the largest known bracteate from Bornholm. Other fragments of this specimen had already been discovered in 1829 'while ploughing a field near Rønne'.[484]

The hoard was found on a hillock north of the Sandegård in Åker parish, on a site with a good view over the southern coast of Bornholm. The hoard was found *c.* 30 alen (*c.* 18 m) west of the modern road leading from the farm northwards and *c.* 45 cm below the surface surrounded by 'black soil and burnt bones', but without an urn or a covering stone. The hill was described as covered by fragmented animal bones and pot sherds, comparable to the Sorte Muld area in Ibsker parish. Excavations undertaken by Vedel revealed burnt wood and daub as well as cobbled areas consisting of fist-sized stones and paved areas with slabs of sandstone. In 1952 Klindt-Jensen observed the remains of a building apparently destroyed by fire in the same area.

The gold hoard is in itself remarkable, but Sandegård was also one of the four major Iron Age settlements mentioned by Vedel, and – more recently – it naturally attracted the attention of the amateur archaeologists. It has been surveyed with metal detectors since the 1980s, and in 1990 a small excavation was undertaken because large sandstone slabs (up to 60 x 60 cm) had been ploughed up. In 1999 the site was investigated again as part of the phosphate analysis project. Watt suggested that the site consisted of two contemporary farmsteads with settlement continuity from the Roman Iron Age to the Viking Period, reflected in the two areas with elevated phosphate values on either side of the modern farm road.[485] The cobbled areas or pavements, mentioned by Vedel were

---

480   060205 sb 59. FP 87 and 96. Breitenstein 1944, 46-52 no. 21; Horsnæs 2009, 243-245 no. 10.

481   Kaul *et al.* 2002.

482   060205 sb 203. BMR 1996. FP 5142 and 6037. Horsnæs 2009, 245 no. 11. Here it is stated that no denarius has been found on the site. Finn Ole Nielsen drew my attention to the denarius mentioned in the excavation diary, but not described in the excavation report. Its present whereabouts is unknown.

483   060205 sb 33. *Annaler for Nordisk Oldkyndighed* 1855, 320, 146; quoted by Breitenstein 1944, 69-70 no. 28; Vedel 1886, 400-401 no. 20; Klindt-Jensen 1957, 236 no. 37 and p. 157 fig. 30 (the hoard).

Breitenstein mentioned four solidi (one in the Royal Coll. of Coins and Medals (FP 313), two in the Dept. of Prehistory along with the other finds from the hoard (inv.no. C 336-344), and one lost), which is in accordance with the entry of the handwritten accession list in the Dept. of Prehistory (inv.no. 334-344). Vedel mentioned three solidi and a fourth found and handed in at an earlier time, while Klindt-Jensen described the find as consisting of three solidi.

484   NM I inv.no. MMLIII; *Ikonografischer Katalog* 324. Klindt-Jensen doubted the Rønne provenance; he was convinced that it had in reality been found at Sandegård. This suggestion seems unfounded.

485   This road does not exist on maps from the mid-19th century.

The sites with Roman coin finds

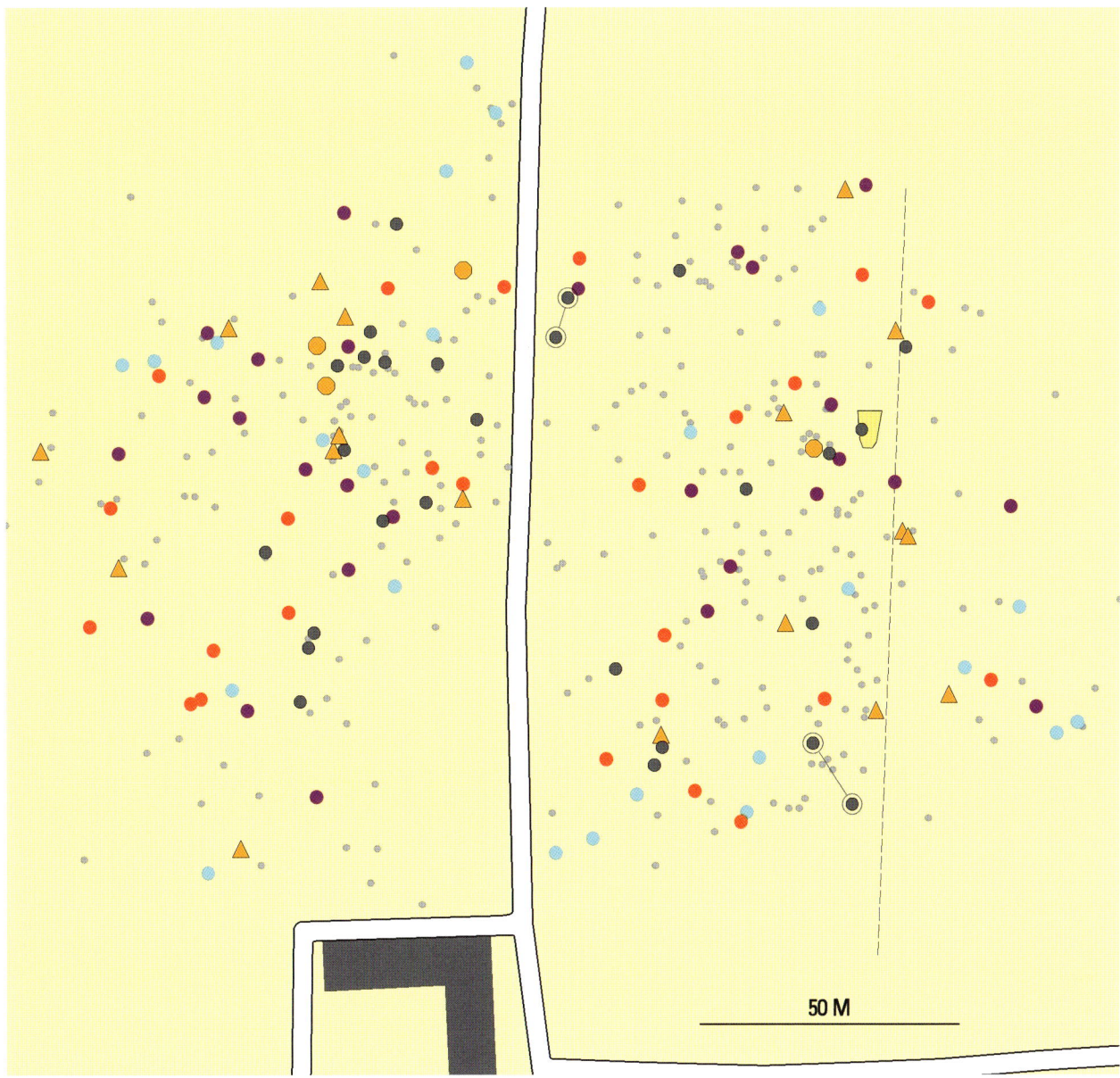

Fig. 97. Distribution of coin finds from Sandegård. The site has been surveyed as three entities. The easternmost field is less intensively surveyed than the two main areas east and west of the modern road. The excavation area from 1990 can only be approximately located, the locations of the two older excavation areas are unknown. Scale 1:1250. Legends as Fig. 55.

dated to the Roman or Germanic Iron Age based on the investigation in 1990.[486] It may be compared to a paving from Agerbygård, dated by pottery to the transition from the Late Roman to the Early Germanic Iron Age. Wet sieved material contained remains of extensive smithing activities (probably from the Roman Iron Age) in the marginal areas of Sandegård.[487]

The finds from Sandegård demonstrate a long continuity in the settlement and a large number of artifacts of high quality and/or precious metal. Detector surveys have resulted in about 1000 finds *(Fig. 97)*,[488] including 121 coins. The majority, 40 coins, are Roman, but the longevity of the site is underlined by the presence of 27 Viking Age coins (i.e. coins struck before 1130), 26 Medieval coins (1130-1536; mainly Danish penninge from the early 14th century), and 28 coins dating after 1536. The denarii have been handed in as part of 11 separate lots of *danefæ*. They present the same degree of wear, but the surface preservation differs somewhat from coin to coin, possibly due to different types of cleaning *(Fig. 98)*.

---

486 Excavation report by Dorte Dam in BMR.
487 Watt 2006, 154-160 and 2009, 95-98.

488 Watt 2006, 154 and 156-160.

Crossing boundaries

Fig. 98. Joining fragments of denarii from Sandegård. FP 5257.2 (two fragments were found c. 10 m apart) and FP 6839.2.

Other sites in southeastern Bornholm

The open, flat-lying landscape of southeastern Bornholm has yielded a considerable number of sites with Roman coins, but apart from the well-known settlement at Sandegård the majority of the settlement sites has been located only recently and consequently they have so far produced only one or a few coins.

Rævekulebakke, Smedegård and Hundshalegård

Just east of the Læså several burial mounds originating from the Late Neolithic Period have been found near Limensgård. At Rævekulebakke secondary burials at the mound include 12 Iron Age graves. Grave E contained the inhumed remains of a male. At his hips a belt with a bronze buckle and four denarii were found. The denarii were blacked from the surrounding organic remains, probably deriving from the belt or a leather purse.[489] The final coin is unusually late. It was struck by Alexander Severus in AD 223, and it provides the numismatic *t.p.q.* for the burial as a whole *(Fig. 34)*.

The Smedegård settlement area was identified by air reconnaissance. Subsequent surveys have produced sherds of Baltic Ware as well as 10 medieval coins.

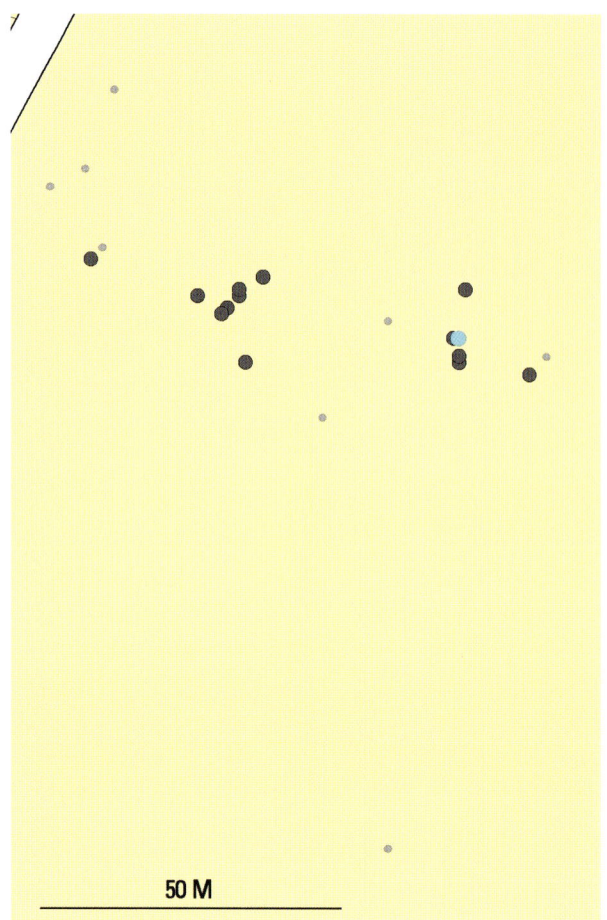

Figure 99. Distribution of coins at Hundshalegård. Scale 1:1250.

The site has produced five denarii and a fragment of a dirham.[490]

Hundshalegård SV is situated c. 400 m west of Smedegård.[491] The first finds from the site were registered in 2001, and the site is known only from the detector finds. It has (until 2010) yielded 29 finds, among which are 17 denarii and a fragment of a dirham *(Fig. 99)*. The denarii are quite worn and the surface of several of them is matt with a violet discolouration suggesting that they have been exposed to either some chemical reaction from the soil or perhaps from heat. There are six fragments, all of which have fresh fractures, which indicate that the coins have become brittle, and indeed, two of these fragments turned out to be of the same coin found several years apart, in 2001 and 2007 *(Fig. 100)*.[492] Several

---

489 060205 sb 198. BMR 1981x34-41. Heidemann Lutz 2010, 329 n. 178 with references.

490 060205 sb 260. BMR 2219. FP 5457, 6067, and 6264.

491 060205 sb 288. BMR 3166. Horsnæs 2002b.

492 Find spot of x28 unfortunately was not recorded.

Fig. 100. Joining fragments of denarius from Hundshalegård, (x11 = FP 6410.11 and x28 = FP 7508.3).

of the denarii were found in stacks. Most of the denarii were found in two small clusters 30-40 m apart in an area north of some building remains visible on air photos. In spite of being found in two clusters, the surface preservation of the denarii indicates that they may derive from a single small hoard. The dirham fragment was found close to one of the joining fragments (with the same GPS values), but its surface preservation differs from that of the denarii. Other finds from the site (two fibulas) are dated to the Early Germanic Iron Age.

Slusegård

At the mouth of the Øle Å the large cemetery of Slusegård has yielded a single denarius. The coin was found in grave 33,[493] a male inhumation burial in a boat grave. The grave goods consisted of a fibula, a bone comb, two knives, a belt buckle and four pots which date the burial to the Late Roman Iron Age. The coin was situated on the pelvis of the deceased. It seems to be quite corroded, but significantly less worn than most of the denarii from Bornholm, and struck by Nerva it is among the earliest denarii from Bornholm.

Shortly inland from the cemetery two small sites at Boesgård have produced one and two denarii respectively.[494]

Between Læså and Øle Å

Several burial grounds have been found at Ndr. Grødbygård, among others a Viking Age cemetery with *c.* 600 burials from the 11th century,[495] and a cemetery with *c.* 235 burials dated to the Roman Iron Age (1-375 AD). Grave 354, a rich male burial, contained a denarius struck by Trajan. The burial furthermore held a full warrior's equipment containing sword, shield, spear, lance, belt, knife and three vessels. According to Lars Jørgensen the warrior was buried in a 'family plot' together with his wife and other family members with less well-equipped graves.[496]

Store Gadegård is one of the major Viking Age sites on Bornholm with traces of several long houses and one (perhaps two) Viking Age *Hacksilber* hoards which also includes coins.[497] In a locality *c.* 100 m west of the main site a denarius and a solidus have been found together with among others Early Iron Age fibulas, the latter probably deriving from cremation burials.[498]

East of Gadegård, Dammegård has produced a large number of Viking Age coins, as part of a *Hacksilver* hoard discovered by metal detector and excavated in 1994. The majority of the coins were Cufic dirhams. The hoard had been buried close to a roof post in a Late Viking Age house (dated by finds of Baltic Ware); remains of at least two other houses were identified. Apart from the dirhams and other Viking Age coins of which the majority most likely derives from the hoard, both Medieval Danish coins and two denarii have been found in the area. The denarii came from an area *c.* 100-200 m from the hoard concentration, so there is no reason to connect the Roman coins with the hoard.[499]

---

493 060203 sb 1. BMR 948. Rasmussen 2010, 435. Heidemann Lutz 2010, 317-318.

494 060203 sb 169. BMR 2337. FP 6069: Marcus Aurelius (Lucius Verus), *RIC* 528 and sb 168. BMR 2336. FP 6068: Antoninus Pius, unidentified type and Marcus Aurelius, *RIC* 378.

495 BMR 1399: Wagnkilde & Pind 1989/90.

496 060205 sb 205. BMR 948x354. Jørgensen 1987, 79-82; for family plots see plan fig. 6B. Cf. also Heidemann Lutz 2010, in part. 337. Denarius: FP 4365.

497 Main site 060203 sb 160. BMR 1978. von Heijne 2004, 312 finds 5.47-48. Coin finds FP 5093, 5238, 5478 and not yet registered coins: Cufic, German and English from late 10th early 11th century, and at least one Danish coin (*t.p.q.* 1060).

498 060203 sb 160/177; BMR 2751; FP 6070.1-2. Horsnæs 2009, 242 no. 8.

499 060203 sb 158. BMR 2000. FP 5092.1-2, 5237.1, 5377.1-116, 5451.1-5, 5452.1-13, 6066.1, 6400.1-21. *AUD* 1994, 138 (excavation); von Heijne 2004, 311 no. 5.43-44 (coin finds). FP 5452.1 Hadrian, unidentified type and FP 6066 Marcus Aurelius AD 161-162 (*RIC* 14, 23, 32, or 51).

Ågård is situated on the east bank of Øle Å, 4 km from the coast and only *c.* 1 km upstream from the Iron Age fortification at Rispebjerg. The relatively few objects found during surveys in 2004/5 include 14 coins: a fragmented denarius, 12 fragmented Viking Age coins and a klipping.[500]

After 2004 a group of sites has been discovered further inland close to the boundary between Åker and Bodilsker parishes. Egebygård SSØ was located in 2009. The site is a large settlement with finds mainly from the Late Iron Age and Viking period, and it has produced a considerable number of finds. Viking Age coins dominate the numismatic finds: there is a considerable number of early dirhams among them, and all coins from the site are cut into small fragments. The presence of *Hacksilber* suggests a possible Viking Age hoard, but the coins are scattered over quite a large area.[501] A gold foil figure is an indication that the site may have had a special status also in the Germanic Iron Age. So far three denarii and three Medieval penninge have turned up, indicating longevity of the site. Two of the denarii are found more than 100 m apart and should be considered single finds.

The settlement sites of Egeby SV[502] and Nygård[503] are situated west of the above-mentioned Egebygård SSØ on either side of the road (Ølenevej) leading from Pedersker to Østermarie. The sites were discovered in 2004 and have yielded two Roman coins each.

Skovgård Syd, situated east of Egebygård SSØ, was located in 2005, but so far only few finds, including a single denarius, have been reported.[504] 500 m to the north, the Skovgård SØ site has produced three de-

Fig. 101. Two denarii from Paradisvej, Nexø. FP 2242.

narii, seven Viking Age coins, and two pre-modern coins.[505] The coins regardless of date are relatively evenly scattered over an area more than 250 x 100 m, and they should probably be interpreted as single finds.

Kastelsgård is situated north of the main road between Åkirkeby and Nexø a bit isolated from other sites with Roman coins. This site was located in 2004 and has so far produced only little material including a single denarius.[506]

In the *hinterland* west of Nexø there is one old single find of a gold coin from Kattesletgård/Faarebro at Øleå below the Døvredal, but no other finds from the immediate vicinity.[507] One of the closest sites is Døvregård SØ *c.* 1 km away, where a single denarius and eight Viking Age coins have been found.[508] The area includes other sites with Viking Age or Early Medieval material (Baltic Ware), among others a Viking Age *Hacksilber* hoard found *in situ* in a small ceramic vessel deposited west of building remains of unknown date.[509]

---

500 060203 sb 196. BMR 2398. FP 8438.1-14.
501 060205 sb 412. BMR 3480. FP 8101 and 8173. Denarii: FP 8101.1: Hadrian for Sabina , *RIC* 390-416 (128-138); FP 8173.1: Antoninus Pius, *RIC* 28 or 45 (139); FP 8101.2: Marcus Aurelius(?), unidentified type (161-180).
502 060205 sb 293. BMR 3332. FP 7270: Denarius, probably Marcus Aurelius, unidentified type and denarius (subæratus) or bronze coin, reworked into weight?
503 060205 sb 427. BMR 3339. FP 7271: Two denarii, struck for Antoninus Pius and Marcus Aurelius, the latter pierced, and two dirhams.
504 060201 sb 323. BMR 3379, FP 7392: Vespasian, *RIC* 108 (77-78 AD), pierced from reverse(?) in front of chin.

505 060201 sb 316. BMR 3435. FP 8113 and 8437. Denarii: two Antoninus Pius, one pierced behind the neck, and on unidentified emperor.
506 060205 sb 426. BMR 3324, FP 7088: Marcus Aurelius for Lucius Verus, *RIC* 515 or 528 (163-165).
507 060201 sb 28. FP 321. Horsnæs 2009, no. 5.
508 060201 sb 148. BMR 2589. FP 6485, 7073, 7639, 8322. Denarius: FP 6485.1 Antoninus Pius for Faustina 1, much corroded, unidentified type.
509 060201 sb 146 Døvregård.

The sites with Roman coin finds

Fig. 102. Roman coins from Duegård VNV.

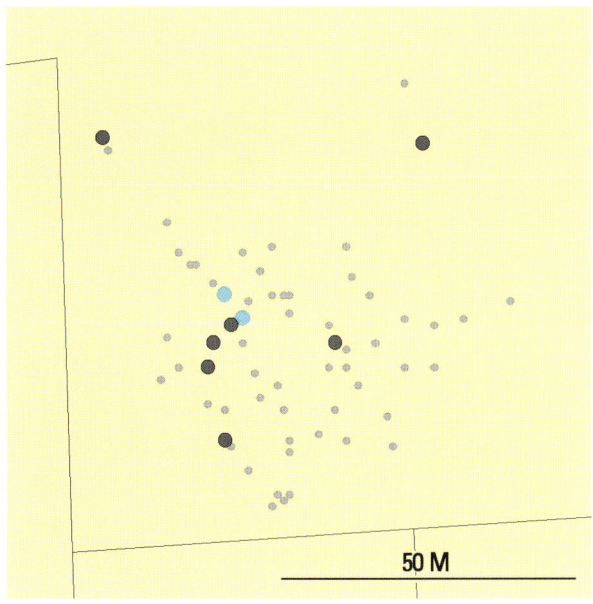

Fig. 103. Distribution of coins from Duegård VNV. Scale 1:1250.

Southwest of Nexø are four sites, each with few denarius finds. A possible settlement area at Soneskoven/Store Kannikegård has produced a single denarius and a dirham.[510] The locality known as Store Kannikegård has produced another denarius.[511] At Langedebygård two denarii and an Otto Adelheid Pfennig from the late 10th century have been found on a site where at least 4 houses are visible as crop marks and where finds from the Late Iron Age to Early Medieval Period (including Baltic Ware) have surfaced.[512] A Viking Age hoard consisting of 65 dirhams (dated 184-341 AH = 800-952 AD) and possibly three German coins (latest coin issued 996-1002) was investigated at Kannikegærdet in 1996. Six dirhams and two denarii were found during later detector surveys of the site.[513]

A hoard consisting of nine solidi was found in 1996 north of the garden of Buddegård in Bodilsker parish, just southwest of modern Nexø.[514] The site is located close to the coastal wetlands, and there is still a small pond on the field. Viking Age settlements have been located south of the site, and along the old coastline north of the solidus hoard there are some Iron Age sites. An excavation following the discovery of the hoard revealed only three undated cooking pits.

West of Nexø, Østre Slamregård has yielded a single find of a denarius,[515] while inside the area of the modern town of Nexø there are two sites with denarius find. At Paradisvej a former gravel pit yielded two denarii in the late 1940's *(Fig. 101)*,[516] and during excavations in 1973 a denarius was found in matr.no. 210d.[517] A bronze coin struck by Maxentius in Rome (307-308

---

510 060201 sb 147. BMR 2686, FP 5989: Hadrian, *RIC* 241A (134-138 AD).

511 060201 sb 136. BMR 1788. Denarius FP 5595: Antoninus Pius for Diva Faustina 1, *RIC* 343-407.

512 060201 sb 132. BMR 1779. FP 6122. The denarii are badly preserved, one is an Antoninus Pius of unidentified type, the other cannot be identified.

513 060201 sb 140. BMR 2292. FP 6083,6927 and 7518. Denarii: Antoninus Pius (unidentified type)

and Vespasian, *RIC* 52, 134 or 362 (72-73 AD). von Heijne 2004, no. 5.35 suggested that the German coins were not part of the hoard, but no arguments for this suggestion were presented.

514 060201 sb 145. BMR 2490. FP 5952. Horsnæs 2009, 241-242 no. 6.

515 060201 sb 152. BMR 2845. FP 6267: Marcus Aurelius for Lucius Verus, *RIC* 86 or 95 (168 AD).

516 060202 sb 13. FP 2242: Antoninus Pius (COS IIII) and Marcus Aurelius for Commodus Caesar (TRP III). Klindt-Jensen 1957, 171 n. 330.

517 060202 sb 15. BMR 45, FP 3278: Commodus, *RIC* 94 (184 AD). Mentioned by Kromann 1983-84, 113 no. 53.

Fig. 104. Two denarii from Munkegård/Standmarksvej. FP 7956.1-2.

AD) was found below a house at Søborgstræde 6, but no details about the context were recorded.[518]

Viking Age coins dominate the finds spectrum in the southern corner of the island. There is, however, also a number of sites with Roman coins and evidence of Roman or Early Germanic contexts. At Duegård VNV seven denarii, and a much worn coin with a high copper content, perhaps an antoninianus, have been found in the same area as a dirham fragment and fragments of a Carolus/Dorestad imitation from Haithabu. The majority of other finds from the site – all retrieved by detector – are dated to the Late Roman and Germanic Iron Ages.[519] The Roman coins were found scattered over most of the area surveyed, and they differ considerably from each other in both wear and corrosion *(Fig. 102-103)*.

Three sites are situated on the edge of the coastal dunes. Duegård N is positioned *c*. 200 m east of Duegård VNV. It is a recently located site that up till now has revealed little material: three Roman denarii and some objects dated to the Late Germanic Iron Age and Viking Age.[520] Further away Munkegård has yielded three denarii *(Fig. 104)*, 12 Viking Age and eight Medieval coins, as well as settlement finds the majority of which is dated to the Late Iron Age/Early Medieval period.[521]

Bedegård appears to be a large settlement area with Iron Age finds including fragments of fibulas and gold as well as four Antonine denarii. However, it seems to have been surveyed only once in, the 1990's.[522] One of the coins is remarkably well preserved (x11), while the remaining ones have been exposed to fire.

The recently located Store Vibegård Ø site has so far produced few finds, among which a single Trajan denarius of unidentified type.[523]

---

518 060202 sb 35. FP 3578. Weight 5.74 g. Kromann 1983-4, no. 55; Horsnæs 2006a, no. 64.
519 060204 sb 94. BMR 3354. FP 7620, 8017, 8475.
520 060204 sb 96. BMR 3370. FP 8016: antonine or severan subæratus, and FP 8479.1-2: Antoninus Pius and Marcus Aurelius, unidentified types.
521 060204 sb 70. BMR 1228. FP 6266, 6345, 6813.3, and 7956.
522 060204 sb 82. BMR 2506, FP 5814.1-4.
523 060204 sb 89. BMR 3318, FP 7954.

Denarii from individual sites
(in numerical order)

060101 sb 217: Denarii from Egesløkkegård, BMR 3140

Emperor	RIC type	w.	From	To	Inv.no.		BMR no.
Antoninus Pius	- Rev.: st.kv.	2.14	138	161	8152		x130
Antoninus Pius ?	-	1.90	138	161	6462	1	x2
Antoninus Pius	-	1.74	138	161	6996	1	x48
Marcus Aurelius	142	2.27	165	165	6924	1	x25
Marcus Aurelius	- IMP II-IIII	2.53	163	168	6462	2	x1
Marcus Aurelius	-	2.49	161	180	6924	2	x27
Marcus Aurelius	-	2.28	161	180	6924	3	x28
Marcus Aurelius	-	2.11	161	180	7237	1	x69
-	-	2.47			6924	5	x26
-	-	2.25			6924	4	x29
-	-	2.35			6996	2	x49

060104 sb 190 and 235: Denarii from Nygård/Skovgård, BMR 1640 and 2001

SB	Emperor	RIC type	w.	From	To	Inv.no.		BMR no.
235	Trajan	119	2.80	103	111	5471	1	BMR2001x42
235	Hadrian	120	2.25	119	122	5605	1	BMR2001x61
190	Hadrian (Sabina)[524]	398a	2.22	128	138	5458	1	BMR1640x46+47
235	Antoninus Pius	48	2.11	139	139	4985	1	BMR2001x2
235	Marcus Aurelius (Faustina 2)	-	2.48	161	176	5605	2	BMR2001x60
235	Barbaric imitation (female portrait?)[525]	Obv and rev barbaric letters	1.72			6082	1	BMR2001x110
235	Barbaric imitation (Aurelius)	- Securitas leaning on column, legs crossed[526]	2.83		300	5810	1	BMR2001x97

---

524 Found in two fragments, c. 1 m apart.
525 Subæratus.
526 Motif more commonly seen in third century coinage.

060104 sb 196: Denarii from Kistehøj/Simblegård, BMR 888

Emperor	RIC type	w.	From	To	Inv.no.		BMR no.
Vespasian	52	2.47	72	73	5228	4	x39
Hadrian (Sabina)	390-416	2.05	128	138	5228	3	x42
Commodus	259a	1.85	191	192	8481	1	x217
-	-	1.24			5228	2	x40

060104 sb 201: Denarii from Rødbjerg, BMR 1611

Emperor	RIC type	w.	From	To	Inv.no.		BMR no.
Hadrian	46, 51, 98 or 137	2.09	118	122	4798	1	x3
Hadrian	94 (?)	2.27	119	122	4798	2	x2
Hadrian	- rev.: restitutor type	2.37	117	138	6081	1	x59
Antoninus Pius	155 or 156	2.60	145	161	7241	1	x90
Antoninus Pius	203, 219, 229a	1.93	151	154	5459	2	x52
Antoninus Pius	-	1.16	138	161	5459	3	x53
Antoninus Pius	- rev.: Fig.st.l.	1.36	138	161	6081	2	x59
Marcus Aurelius	-	1.57	161	180	6081	4	x60
Commodus	273	2.07	180	192	4798	3	x4
Commodus	- rev.: fig.st.l.	2.05	180	192	6081	3	x59
- (pierced)	-	2.16			5459	1	x51

060104 sb 202: Denarii from Møllegård, BMR 1235

Emperor	RIC type	w.	From	To	Inv.no.		BMR no.
Trajan	-	2.44	98	117	5570	1	x153
Hadrian	type not in RIC/RIC 45 var.?[527]	2.58	118	118	4983	1	x40
Antoninus Pius (Faustina 1)?	327-342	1.24	138	141	5137	1	x85
Antoninus Pius	-	257	138	161	4983	2	x39
Marcus Aurelius	306	2.26	174	174	5450	1	x149
Marcus Aurelius(?)	-	1.20	161	180	5570	2	x152
Commodus	60, 62, 73, 74, 83 or 84	2.92	183	184	5253		x103

060104 sb 264: Denarii from Karlshøj/Trommeregård, BMR 2225

Emperor	RIC type	w.	From	To	Inv.no.		BMR no.
Marcus Aurelius	171, 252, 271, 359 or 376	2.43	166	177	5993	3	x7
Marcus Aurelius (Faustina 2)	712	2.21	161	176	5993	1	x8
Marcus Aurelius (Lucilla)	788	1.94	164	169	5993	2	x9
-	-	1.44	79	138	6376	1	x38

060104 sb 351: Denarii from Hebro, BMR 3567

Emperor	RIC type	w.	From	To	Inv.no..		BMR no.
Commodus (Crispina)	288	1.16	180	183	8295	3	x1
Commodus[528]	-	2.14	180	192	8295	2	x3
Septimius Severus (Julia Domna)[529]	559A	2.08	196	211	8295	4	x2
-	rev.: togatus st.l.	1.61			8295	1	x4

527 HADRIANVA AVGVASTVS//...]COS II PIATAS in field. Pietas standing r.(!) at altar in r. field.
528 Small punched hole above portrait.
529 Pierced from obverse behind portrait.

Coin lists

060106 sb 150: Denarii from Bukkegård, BMR 1171

Emperor	RIC type	w.	From	To	Inv. no..		BMR no.
Antoninus Pius	290	2.69	158	159	6463	1	x88
Antoninus Pius	301	1.52	159	160	6463	2	x85
Antoninus Pius	-	2.79	138	161	7238	1	x250
Commodus	71 or 89	2.52	183	184	5230	1	x23
Commodus	136?	1.30	185	185	5230	2	x24
Commodus (Crispina)	288-289	2.10	180	183	6287	1	x40
Marcus Aurelius/Commodus	-	2.13	172	192	7238	2	x251

060204 sb 82: Denarii from Bedegård, BMR 2506

Emperor	RIC type	w.	From	To	Inv.no.		BMR no.
Antoninus Pius (Marcus Aurelius Caesar)	429a	2.69	145	147	5814	1	x11
Marcus Aurelius	-	1.33	161	180	5814	2	x9
Marcus Aurelius/Commodus	-	1.09	172	192	5814	3	x14
-	-	2.13			5814	4	x6

060204 sb 94: Roman coins from Duegård VNV, BMR 3354 (denarii unless otherwise indicated)

Emperor	RIC type	w.	From	To	Inv.no.		BMR no.
Antoninus Pius (Diva Faustina 1)	rev.: fem.st.l.	2.07	141	161	8475	1	x48
Marcus Aurelius	231	2.52	170	171	7620	1	x2
Marcus Aurelius (Commodus Caesar)	613-614	0.72	175	176	8017	3	x34
Marcus Aurelius	-	1.53	161	180	7620	2	x1
Marcus Aurelius?, subæratus?	rev.: CONCORDIA …	3.69	161	180	8475	2	x49
Commodus	139 or 155	1.45	185	187	8017	1	x36
Marcus Aurelius/Commodus	-	2.04	172	192	8017	2	x35
antoninianus(?)	-	3.05	200	300	7620	3	x3

060205 sb 33: Denarii from Sandegård, BMR 1371

Emperor	RIC type	w.	From	To	Inv.no.		BMR no.
Titus (Domitian Caesar)	47, 51	2.31	80	80	5136	2	x148
Trajan	58	1.76	101	102	6839	1	x541
Hadrian	- Class B	2.31	125	128	6059	1	x810
Hadrian	-	2.37	117	138	5257	2	x279 and 280
Antoninus Pius	124, 143, 144, 272, 284 or 305a	2.79	145	161	5257	3	x275
Antoninus Pius	- Pax(?)	2.29	138	161	5136	3	x151
Antoninus Pius	-	1.52	138	161	5058	2	x74
Antoninus Pius	-	1.61	138	161	5446	3	x344
Antoninus Pius	-	2.48	138	161	5257	7	x276
Antoninus Pius?	-	2.25	138	161	6839	3	x540
Antoninus Pius?	-	1.47	138	161	6839	2	x543-544
Antoninus Pius	-	2.59	138	161	4629	2	x9
Antoninus Pius	- Pietas	2.61	138	161	4957	1	x49
Antoninus Pius	-	1.62	138	161	6703	2	x1008
Antoninus Pius	-	2.48	138	161	4957	2	x50
Antoninus Pius	-	1.98	138	161	6703	1	x1009
Antoninus Pius (Diva Faustina 1)	356	2.65	141	161	6265	1	x926

Crossing boundaries

Emperor	RIC type	w.	From	To	Inv.no.		BMR no.
Marcus Aurelius	205	3.17	168	169	5136	5	x149
Marcus Aurelius	261, 276	1.44	171	173	6839	4	x539
Marcus Aurelius	-	2.45	161	180	6265	3	x928
Marcus Aurelius	-	1.56	161	180	6265	2	x927
Marcus Aurelius (Divus Antoninus Pius)	432, 434, 438	3.26	161	180	6557	1	x984
Marcus Aurelius (Diva Faustina 2)	746	2.35	176	180	5136	4	x152
Antoninus Pius/Aurelius/imit??	-	2.39	138	180	5446	2	x343
Commodus	-	2.14	184	189	5257	6	x277
Commodus	-	2.73	180	192	6703	3	x1007
Marcus Aurelius/Commodus (Faustina 2/Lucilla/Crispina)?	-	2.51	161	192	5257	5	x274
Septimius Severus (Julia Domna)	-	2.00	193	211	6839	5	x542
Elagabal	106, 113	1.62	218	222	5058	1	x73
-	-	0.76			5257	4	x284
-	-	2.35			4629	1	x8
-	-	2.24			5257	8	x278

060205 sb 198: Denarii from Rævekulebakke, Grave E, BMR 1081

Emperor	RIC type	w.	From	To	Inv.no.		BMR no.
Antoninus Pius (Diva Faustina 1)	358		141	161	4435	1	
Commodus	71, 89		184	185	4435	2	
Commodus	159		186	187	4435	3	
Severus Alexander	32		223	223	4435	4	

060205 sb 288: Denarii from Hundshalegård, BMR 3166

Emperor	RIC type	w.	From	To	Inv.no.		BMR no.
Hadrian	- Class B	1.99	125	128	6410	1	x3
Hadrian (Sabina)	391 or 399a	2.34	128	138	6643		x20
Antoninus Pius	137	1.87	146	161	7508	1	x26
Antoninus Pius	-	1.51	138	161	7508	2	x27
Antoninus Pius	-	1.80	138	161	6410	3	x4
Antoninus Pius	-	2.59	138	161	6410	2	x7
Antoninus Pius(?)	-	0.58	138	161	6410	11	x11
(same coin as previous)	-	1.45	138	161	7508	3	x28
Antoninus Pius (Diva(?) Faustina 1)	327-407	2.14	138	161	6410	4	x5
Commodus (Divus Marcus Aurelius)	264 or 269	2.18	180	180	6410	9	x1a
Commodus	192	2.59	189	189	6410	5	x1c
Commodus	-	2.14	180	192	6410	6	x2
Commodus	-	1.82	180	192	6410	7	x6
Commodus	-	1.38	180	192	6410	8	x9
Septimius Severus (Julia Domna) Rome/Alexandria	538 or 612	2.32	193	196	6410	10	x1b
-	-	0.34			6410	12	x10
-	-	0.70			7508	4	x29
-	-	0.31			6410	13	x8

060302 sb 124: Denarii from Ndr. Mulebygård, BMR 3227 and 2812

Emperor	RIC type	w.	From	To	Inv.no.		BMR no.
Hadrian	-	2.71	117	138	6411	1	BMR2812x50
Hadrian/Antoninus Pius	-	2.80	138	161	7628	1	BMR2812x143
Antoninus Pius	167	2.10	147	148	6270	1	BMR2812x2
Antoninus Pius (Diva(?) Faustina 1)	327-407	2.08	138	161	6565	1	BMR2812x92
Marcus Aurelius	-	2.42	161	180	7106	1	BMR3227x46
Commodus	212	1.77	190	190	6564	1	BMR3227x6
-	-	1.87			7106	2	BMR3227x47

060303 sb 190: Denarii from Vestergård, BMR 1672

Emperor	RIC type	w.	From	To	Inv.no.		BMR no.
Marcus Aurelius	2	2.23	161	161	6642		x10
Antoninus Pius	-	2.81	138	161	6995	1	x12
-	-	0.88			6995	2	x14
-	-	2.46			7514	1	x30

060305 sb 70: Denarii from Smørengegård, BMR 1469

Emperor	RIC type	w.	From	To	Inv.no.		BMR no.
Vespasian	-	1.84	69	79	7275	1	x510
Trajan	151-228	2.56	103	111	6992	1	x338
Trajan	-; rev.: Mars r.; spear & trophy	2.15	98	117	6693	1	x267
Trajan	-	2.38	98	117	6992	2	x346
Trajan	-[530]	7.02	98	117	6992	19	x333
Trajan	-	2.26	98	117	8492	1	x839
Hadrian	-	2.21	117	138	6271	1	x201
Hadrian?	-	2.23	117	138	7515	1	x600
Hadrian (Sabina)	390-416	1.93	128	138	8492	2	x840
Antoninus Pius	44, 58, 62, 321	2.24	139	143	8154	1	x782
Antoninus Pius	127c	2.27	145	161	6571	1	x251
Antoninus Pius	177	2.34	148	149	8154	2	x781
Antoninus Pius	163, 176, 204, 210, 221, 231, 239 or 244	2.04	147	156	6464	0	x234
Antoninus Pius	274	2.48	157	158	6693	2	x261
Antoninus Pius?	-	0.84	138	161	4999	1	x15
Antoninus Pius	-; rev.: Annona	2.06	145	161	6693	3	x262
Antoninus Pius	-	1.93	138	161	6693	4	x269
Antoninus Pius	-	2.32	138	161	6693	5	x265
Antoninus Pius	-	2.05	138	161	6992	3	x352
Antoninus Pius	-	-[531]	138	161	6992	20	x333
Antoninus Pius	-	1.40	138	161	8154	3	x780
Antoninus Pius?	-	0.62	138	161	8492	3	x838
Antoninus Pius?	-	1.58	138	161	6992	22	x343
Antoninus Pius (Faustina 1)	327-342	2.05	138	141	5449	2	x36
Antoninus Pius (Diva Faustina 1)	343-407	2.59	141	161	6693	6	x264

530   One of three coins in stack.
531   One of three coins in stack.

Antoninus Pius (Diva Faustina 1)	360	1.51	141	161	6992	4	x348
Antoninus Pius (Diva Faustina 1)	362	2.47	141	161	7515	2	x601
Antoninus Pius (Diva Faustina 1)	363	2.25	141	161	6931	1	x307
Antoninus Pius (Diva(?) Faustina 1)	327-407	2.15	138	161	6992	5	x345
Antoninus Pius (Marcus Aurelius Caesar)	424	2.27	140	144	6992	6	x334
Antoninus Pius (Marcus Aurelius Caesar)	438b	2.25	146	147	6072	1	x139
Antoninus Pius (Marcus Aurelius Caesar)	438b	2.14	147	148	6992	7	x347
Antoninus Pius/Marcus Aurelius (Faustina 2)	-	1.89	146	176	6992	8	x342
Marcus Aurelius	33	2.42	161	162	8154	4	x783
Marcus Aurelius	59	1.96	162	163	6693	7	x260
Marcus Aurelius	34; 39; 59; 63	3.04	161	163	6992	9	x337
Marcus Aurelius	164	2.10	166	166	7515	3	x604
Marcus Aurelius	207; 222	2.44	168	170	6072	2	x138
Marcus Aurelius	248	0.90	170	171	6271	2	x202
Marcus Aurelius	-	2.83	161	180	6693	8	x266
Marcus Aurelius	-	2.27	161	180	6693	9	x270
Marcus Aurelius	-	1.41	161	180	6693	10	x271
Marcus Aurelius	-	2.48	161	180	6992	10	x349
Marcus Aurelius	-	1.46	161	180	6992	11	x353
Marcus Aurelius (Divus Antoninus Pius)	441	1.82	161	180	7515	4	x605
Marcus Aurelius (Lucius Verus)	444-567	2.45	161	166	6931	2	x306
Marcus Aurelius (Lucilla)	755-792	2.19	164	169	7515	5	x603
Marcus Aurelius/Commodus	- rev. Fortuna	2.36	172	192	8154	5	x784
Marcus Aurelius/Commodus?	-	1.12	161	192	8154	6	x779
(same coin as previous)	-	0.99	161	192	6992	16	x351
Commodus	47	2.11	183	183	6693	11	x268
Commodus	91(?)	2.51	184	184	6992	12	x336
Commodus	166	1.03	187	188	7515	6	x606
Commodus?	-	2.22	180	192	5449	1	x37
Commodus	-	0.75	180	192	6693	12	x272
Commodus	-	1.94	180	192	6693	13	x263
Commodus	-	2.26	180	192	6992	13	x344
Commodus (?)	-	2.07	180	192	7515	7	x602
Commodus (Crispina)	281	2.23	180	183	6992	14	x350
Clodius Albinus	11b	2.25	193	195	6271	3	x200
Caracalla	166	2.21	206	210	6271	4	x199
Antonine or Severan	-	2.17	138	211	6992	15	x340
-	-	0.41			6931	3	x308
-	-	0.72			6992	17	x339
-	-	0.64			6992	18	x341
-	-	1.02			8154	7	x785
	-	_532			6992	21	x333
"Marcus Aurelius"/imit		2.48			5965		x108

532 One of three coins in stack.

060305 sb 144: Denarii from Smørenge, BMR 766 (735 denarii)

(Inv.no. FP 4218.1-499 was found in 1983: nos. 4, 74, 182, 317, 377, 429, 485, 498 were found during detector surveys before excavation, the remaining coins of inv.no. FP 4218 were found during excavation. FP 6273 was found during excavation in 2000.

RIC type	w.	From	To	Inv.	No.	Ecx.no
Vespasian						
9	2.77	69	71	4218	1	
10	2.96	69	71	4218	2	
76 or 83	2.85	74	74	4218	3	
-	2.58	69	79	4218	4	
Titus						
27	2.47	80	80	8108	3	x1086
Domitian						
60	2.99	85	85	4218	5	
-	1.93	81	96	6646	1	x733
Nerva						
16 or 17	2.98	97	97	4218	6	
36	2.93	97	97	4218	7	
Trajan						
33	2.76	100	100	4218	8	
59	2.52	101	102	4218	9	
61	2.76	101	102	4218	10	
61	2.80	101	102	4218	11	
- (obv. leg. A1)	2.66	98	105	6273	1	x607
-	2.62	98	105	6646	2	x742
59 or 82	2.08	101	111	4218	12	
116	2.88	103	111	4218	13	
129	2.70	103	111	4218	14	
142	2.75	103	111	4218	15	
142	2.87	103	111	4218	16	
147	2.92	103	111	4218	17	
109-148	2.50	103	111	4218	18	
165	2.73	103	111	4218	19	
165	2.93	103	111	4218	20	
165	2.65	103	111	4218	21	
122	2.55	103	111	4218	23	
180 or 275f	2.67	103	114	4218	24	
234 or 286	2.91	111	114	4218	25	
-	1.45	106	114	6273	2	x598
243	2.85	112	117	4218	22	
336 ff	2.83	114	117	4218	26	
357 ff	2.83	114	117	4218	27	
-	1.90	98	117	5249	1	x425
-	1.94	98	117	6646	3	x729
-	1.18	98	117	6646	4	x732
-[533]	4.14	98	117	8491	1	x1297
Hadrian						
13 or 22	2.93	117	138	4218	28	
39?	2.79	118	118	4218	29	
39?	2.35	118	118	4218	30	
47	2.45	118	118	4784	1	x227
50	2.86	118	118	4218	31	
67	3.22	119	122	4218	32	
76	2.57	119	122	4218	33	
78	2.71	119	122	4218	34	
80	2.83	119	122	4218	35	
80	2.85	119	122	4218	36	
83	2.75	119	122	4218	37	
83	2.87	119	122	4218	38	
85	2.59	119	122	4218	39	
90b	1.07	119	122	7057	1	x973
94	2.52	119	122	4218	40	
95	2.99	119	122	4218	41	
98b or 99	2.82	119	122	4784	2	x226
101	2.42	119	122	4218	42	
101	3.19	119	122	4218	43	
110	2.77	119	122	4218	44	
110a	2.34	119	122	4802	1	x272
120	3.23	119	122	4218	45	
137	3.01	119	122	4218	46	
141	2.76	119	122	4218	47	
46; 51; 98 or 137	2.79	118	122	6930	1	x836
137b	2.07	119	122	4698	1	x201A
17-143	2.58	117	122	6273	3	x610
-	2.08	117	122	6646	5	x744
-	2.73	117	122	6930	2	x832
146	2.79	125	128	4218	48	
146	2.66	125	128	5135	1	x386
154	2.5	125	128	6930	3	x846
163	2.93	125	128	4218	49	
175	2.95	125	128	4218	50	
175	2.63	125	128	4218	51	
184	2.95	125	128	4218	52	
-	2.67	125	128	6646	6	x730

---

533 In stack with 8491.2 (cf. Below, unidentified emperor and type).

Crossing boundaries

222	2.63	132	134	4218	53	
233	3.03	134	138	4218	54	
240	2.59	134	138	4218	55	
241a	2.69	134	138	4698	2	x200A
256	2.95	134	138	4218	56	
257	2.84	134	138	4218	57	
261	2.72	134	138	6273	4	x602
261f	2.59	134	138	4218	58	
265(?)	2.73	134	138	6646	7	x725
267	2.84	134	138	4218	59	
267a	2.89	134	138	4698	3	x200B
270	2.7	134	138	4218	60	
282	2.7	134	138	4218	61	
296	2.84	134	138	4218	62	
299	3.21	134	138	4218	63	
299	2.37	134	138	4218	64	
-	2.51	117	138	6273	5	x604
-	1.91	117	138	6930	4	x845
-	2.56	117	138	7057	2	x982
-	2.17	117	138	7057	3	x985
-	2.01	117	138	8491	3	x1295
- rev: Roma seated r.	1.44	117	138	8491	4	x1298
-	1.73	117	138	7057	4	x972
-[534]	5.17	117	138	8108	1	x1085
-	2.38	117	138	8108	4	x1087
Hadrian (Sabina)						
390	2.93	128	138	4218	65	
395	2.32	128	138	4218	66	
Hadrian (L. Aelius Caesar)						
431	3.04	137	138	4218	67	
433	3.25	137	138	4218	68	
434	2.75	137	138	4218	69	
436	2.36	137	138	4218	70	
436	2.50	137	137	8108	10	x1093
Hadrian (Antoninus Pius Caesar)						
445	2.73	138	138	6646	8	x728
Antoninus Pius						
10a	3.06	138	138	4218	169	
25	2.91	139	139	4218	71	
61	3.19	140	143	4218	72	
61	2.65	140	143	4218	73	
61c	2.76	140	143	5088	1	x380
62a	2.55	140	143	5135	5	x385
62	2.11	140	143	4218	74	
64	3.09	140	143	4218	75	
64	2.83	140	143	4218	76	
64	2.94	140	143	4218	77	
69	2.99	140	143	4218	78	
69	2.48	140	143	6273	6	x599
71	3.22	140	143	4218	79	
73	2.80	140	143	4218	80	
73c	2.94	140	143	6273	7	x617
78	2.90	140	143	4218	81	
84	3.14	140	143	4218	82	
85c	2.95	140	143	5135	4	x391
102	2.98	140	143	4218	83	
102	3.19	140	143	4218	84	
112	2.63	143	144	4218	85	
111b	3.1	143	144	4802	4	x266B
111b	3.15	143	144	6930	5	x841
124	3.03	145	161	4218	86	
63 or 126	3.18	140	161	4218	170	
129	2.64	145	161	4218	87	
131	2.79	145	161	4218	88	
136	3	145	161	4218	89	
136	2.69	145	161	5135	2	x384
137	3.15	145	161	4218	90	
137	2.86	145	161	4218	91	
137	2.49	145	161	4218	92	
137	2.72	145	161	7057	5	x987
143	3.28	145	161	4218	93	
154	2.49	145	161	4218	94	
155	3.03	145	161	4802	5	x264
155	2.66	145	161	4218	95	
155	3.1	145	161	4218	96	
162	2.68	147	148	4218	97	
162	3.42	147	148	4218	98	
162	2.92	147	148	4218	99	
162	2.83	147	148	4218	100	
162	2.44	147	148	6930	6	x837
163	0	147	148	8108	6	x1089
163	2.95	147	148	4218	101	
167	2.88	147	148	4218	102	
175	2.71	148	149	4218	103	
175	2.99	148	149	4218	104	
175	3.16	148	149	4218	105	
176	2.97	148	149	4218	106	
176	2.85	148	149	4218	107	
177	3.03	148	149	4218	108	

534 In stack with FP 8108.2.

Coin lists

177	2.67	148	149	4218	109	
167 or 181	2.43	147	149	6930	7	x838
181	2.83	149	150	4218	110	
181	2.99	149	150	4218	111	
181	3.17	149	150	4218	112	
181	2.65	149	150	4218	113	
183	2.93	149	150	4218	114	
186-188	3.29	149	150	6272	1	x717
187-188	2.44	149	150	6272	2	x720
200	2.83	150	151	4218	115	
204	2.99	151	152	4218	116	
204	2.58	151	152	4218	117	
205	2.68	151	152	4218	118	
205	2.9	151	152	4218	119	
205	2.44	151	152	4698	4	x201B
205	2.69	151	152	8491	5	x1296
209	3.08	151	152	6273	8	x609
209	2.03	151	152	4218	120	
210	2.61	151	152	4218	121	
218	2.94	151	152	4218	122	
220	2.73	152	153	4218	123	
220	3.51	152	153	4218	124	
221	2.97	152	153	4218	125	
221	3.08	152	153	4218	126	
221 (TR P XVI?)	2.61	152	153	6273	9	x620
222	2.44	152	153	4218	127	
232	2.90	153	154	4218	128	
238	2.70	154	155	4218	129	
239	3.00	154	155	4218	130	
239	3.50	154	155	4218	131	
239	2.55	154	155	4218	132	
242	2.95	154	155	4218	133	
163; 176; 204; 221; 231; 239 or 244a	2.90	147	156	5601	3	x454
251	2.67	154	155	4218	135	
251	2.71	155	156	4218	134	
252	2.80	155	156	4218	136	
254	2.61	155	156	4218	137	
254	2.59	155	156	4218	138	
272	2.95	157	158	4218	139	
276	2.89	157	158	4218	140	
275	2.94	157	158	5044	1	x348
277	3.41	157	158	4218	141	
179; 188 or 277	2.12	148	158	4698	5	x201C
287 or 288	2.91	158	159	5135	3	x388b
290	3.10	158	159	4218	142	
143; 144; 272a or 290a	3.19	145	161	4218	171	
292	2.88	158	159	4218	144	
292	3.06	159	160	4218	143	
300(?)	-	159	160	3642[535]		
300	3.00	159	160	4218	145	
300	2.88	159	160	4218	146	
301	3.36	159	160	4218	147	
301	2.69	159	160	4218	148	
301	2.87	159	160	4218	149	
303	2.77	159	160	4218	150	
304-305	2.86	159	160	4218	151	
304-305	2.71	159	160	4218	152	
288 or 305	2.80	158	160	6930	8	x835
313	2.78	160	161	4218	153	
313	2.91	160	161	4218	154	
-	1.23	138	161	4698	6	x201D
-	2.68	138	161	4698	7	x200C
-	2.34	138	161	4698	8	x200D
-	2.67	138	161	4698	9	x200E
-	2.81	138	161	4802	3	x268
-	1.54	138	161	5601	1	x457
-	2.73	138	161	5601	2	x442
-	2.35	138	161	6272	3	x718
-	2.69	138	161	6273	10	x605
-	2.38	138	161	6273	11	x611
-	2.87	138	161	6646	9	x741
-	2.38	138	161	6646	10	x737
-	2.27	138	161	6646	11	x738
-	3.11	138	161	7057	7	x988
-	2.73	138	161	7057	8	x981
-	2.68	138	161	7057	9	x991
-	2.26	138	161	7057	10	x969
-	1.88	138	161	7057	11	x976
-	1.60	138	161	7057	12	x977
-	1.05	138	161	7057	13	x968
-	2.30	138	161	8108	7	x1090
-	2.08	138	161	8108	13	x1096
- rev.: Roma seated l.	2.95	138	161	8491	6	x1300
Antoninus Pius (Faustina 1)						
335	3.21	138	141	4218	172	
338	2.96	138	141	4218	173	

---

535 Found "many years" before 1980. Not weighed.

Crossing boundaries

327-342	2.19	138	141	5601	5	x456
327-342	2.45	138	141	8491	7	x1299
Antoninus Pius (Diva Faustina 1)						
343	3.04	141	161	4218	174	
345	2.70	141	161	4218	175	
345	2.97	141	161	4218	176	
345	2.58	141	161	4218	177	
345	3.28	141	161	4218	178	
346	2.85	141	161	4218	179	
347	2.97	141	161	4218	180	
347	3.00	141	161	4218	181	
350	2.80	141	161	4218	182	
350a	2.92	141	161	5601	4	x453
346b; 350a	2.40	141	161	6273	12	x618
351	2.79	141	161	4218	183	
351	2.68	141	161	4218	184	
351	2.88	141	161	4218	185	
351	2.71	141	161	4218	186	
351	3.20	141	161	4218	187	
356	2.60	141	161	4218	188	
358	2.82	141	161	4218	189	
358	2.92	141	161	4218	190	
361	3.10	141	161	4218	191	
361	2.92	141	161	4218	192	
363	3.10	141	161	4218	193	
370	3.23	141	161	4218	194	
378	3.02	141	161	4218	195	
379	2.92	141	161	4218	196	
381a	2.74	141	161	4218	197	
394	2.70	141	161	4218	198	
400	3.00	141	161	4218	199	
400	2.98	141	161	4802	6	x265
400	2.47	141	161	C2852[536]	-	
327-407	1.48	138	161	4802	7	x262
327-407	2.23	138	161	6646	12	x726
343-407	2.41	141	161	6930	9	x840
343-407	1.86	141	161	4802	19	x263B
343-407	2.35	141	161	5135	6	x387
Antoninus Pius (Marcus Aurelius Caesar)						
423	2.29	140	144	4218	200	
424	3.18	140	144	4218	201	
424	3.07	140	144	4218	202	
424	2.64	140	144	4218	203	
424	2.68	140	144	4218	204	
429	2.95	145	147	4218	155	
429	2.90	145	147	5044	2	x351
429 or 432	2.87	145	147	4218	205	
431	3.10	145	147	4218	156	
431	2.63	145	147	4218	157	
433	2.85	145	147	4218	158	
433	2.73	145	147	6273	13	x612
436	3.08	146	147	4218	159	
436	2.89	146	147	4218	160	
436	2.74	146	147	4218	161	
436	2.92	146	147	4218	162	
440a	2.60	147	148	4802	8	x269B
441	3.00	148	149	4218	163	
441	2.94	148	149	4218	164	
442	2.99	148	149	4218	165	
442	2.91	148	149	4218	166	
442	3.20	148	149	4218	167	
450	2.77	149	150	4218	168	
438b, 444 or 450a	2.23	147	150	7057	6	x970
458	2.75	152	153	4218	206	
453, 458 or 461	2.62	151	154	4218	207	
453, 458 or 461	3.19	151	154	4218	208	
461	2.88	153	154	4218	209	
453a; 458; 461	2.87	151	154	4802	9	x270
463	2.88	154	155	4218	210	
459a; 463a	2.72	153	155	4698	14	x200J
472	2.76	155	156	4218	211	
454; 468; 473	3.15	151	157	5448	1	x428
473	3.17	156	157	6273	14	x608
470; 475	2.76	156	157	4218	212	
454; 480	3.12	151	158	4218	213	
483	2.94	151	159	4218	214	
482	2.71	159	160	4218	215	
-	2.79	140	161	6930	10	x833
Antoninus Pius (Faustina 2)						
495	2.61	146	161	4218	338	
495	3.21	146	161	4218	339	
502	3.02	146	161	4218	340	
502	2.86	146	161	4218	341	
Marcus Aurelius						
2	3.07	161	161	4218	216	
3	2.92	161	161	4218	217	
13	1.47	161	161	6272	4	x719
23	2.86	161	161	4218	218	
23	2.73	161	161	4218	219	
33	2.72	161	162	4218	220	

536   Found before 1877.

Coin lists

33	2.34	161	162	4698	13	x200I
35	2.35	161	162	6930	11	x827
51	2.96	161	162	4218	221	
1-57	2.82	161	162	4218	222	
1-57	2.67	161	162	4218	223	
58	2.72	162	163	4698	12	x200H
33; 38; 58	2.49	161	163	6273	15	x619
59	2.64	162	163	4218	224	
59	3.06	162	163	4218	225	
60	2.86	162	163	4218	226	
60	2.67	162	163	4218	227	
60	2.95	162	163	5135	13	x389
59; 64	2.21	162	163	4559		
67	1.70	162	163	6646	13	x745
68	2.83	162	163	4218	228	
70	2.88	162	163	4218	229	
70	2.91	162	163	4218	230	
70	2.43	162	163	5971		x522
81	2.94	163	164	4218	231	
81	2.78	163	164	4218	232	
91	2.72	163	164	4218	233	
91	2.85	163	164	4218	234	
91	2.81	163	164	4218	235	
91	3.07	163	164	4218	236	
91	2.78	163	164	4218	237	
91	2.90	163	164	4218	238	
95	2.85	161	180	4218	318	
102f	2.65	163	164	4218	239	
102	2.91	163	164	4218	240	
102f	2.47	163	164	4218	241	
102f	3.62	163	164	4218	242	
102	2.42	163	164	4218	243	
112	2.78	163	164	6273	16	x616
-	2.80	161	164	6646	14	x735
125	3.04	164	165	4218	244	
132	3.02	164	165	4218	245	
138	2.60	165	165	6273	17	x606
142	3.08	165	165	4218	246	
142	2.88	165	165	4218	247	
142	2.84	165	165	4218	248	
163	2.68	165	166	2364[537]		
145	2.23	165	166	4218	477	
146	2.59	165	166	4218	250	
148	3.15	165	166	4218	251	
159	2.56	166	166	4218	252	

163	3.00	166	166	4218	253	
163	2.71	166	166	6273	18	x613
164	2.85	166	166	4218	254	
185	2.99	168	168	4218	256	
186	3.30	168	168	4218	257	
170,176 or 186	3.02	166	168	4802	13	x271
170,176 or 186	2.89	166	168	4218	258	
191	2.88	168	168	4698	11	x200G
191	3.07	168	168	4802	11	x276
203	2.92	168	169	4218	259	
203	2.14	168	169	4218	260	
205	2.87	168	169	4218	261	
207	2.93	168	169	4218	262	
207	3.13	168	169	4218	263	
207	2.99	168	169	4218	264	
207	3.04	168	169	4218	265	
207	3.18	168	169	4218	266	
207	2.73	168	169	4218	267	
209	2.67	168	169	8491	8	x1291
211	3.25	169	170	4218	268	
212	3.52	169	170	4218	269	
216	2.77	169	170	4218	270	
218f	2.64	169	170	4218	271	
207 or 222	3.11	168	170	4218	272	
207 or 222	2.24	168	170	5088	2	x381
225	3.41	169	170	4218	273	
225	2.98	169	170	4218	274	
225	3.06	169	170	4218	275	
225	3.31	169	170	4218	276	
226	2.51	169	170	4218	277	
227	2.49	170	171	4218	278	
231	3.33	170	171	4218	279	
231	3.00	170	171	4218	280	
216 or 234	2.94	169	171	5135	9	x394
235	2.91	170	171	4218	281	
242	3.18	170	171	4218	282	
242	2.58	170	171	4218	283	
248	1.77	170	171	4218	284	
251	3.06	170	171	4218	285	
251	3.08	170	171	4218	286	
type not in RIC	2.65	170	171	4784	5	x224
251	2.59	171	172	4218	287	
252	2.94	171	172	4218	288	
259	2.96	171	172	4218	289	
261	2.67	172	173	4218	290	

537 Found c. 1951

Crossing boundaries

242, 259 or 275	2.75	170	173	4218	291	
242, 259 or 275	2.59	170	173	4784	4	x223
261 or 276	2.95	171	173	5448	3	x427
282	2.51	172	173	4218	292	
285	2.68	172	173	4218	294	
285	2.97	173	174	4218	293	
289	2.87	173	174	4218	295	
290	2.90	173	174	4218	296	
263, 282 or 296	3.09	171	174	4218	297	
308	2.89	174	174	4218	298	
310	2.33	174	175	4218	299	
325	3.04	175	175	4218	301	
334	2.99	175	175	4218	303	
252, 271, 304 or 314	2.70	171	175	7057	14	x979
325 or 348	2.89	175	176	4218	304	
348	2.80	175	176	4218	305	
329 or 355	[538]	174	176	4218	306	
356	2.79	175	176	4698	10	x200F
369	1.93	176	177	5135	7	x390
373	2.38	176	177	4218	307	
373	2.63	176	177	4802	10	x267
378	2.87	176	177	4218	308	
385	2.69	177	178	4218	309	
385	2.19	177	178	4218	310	
- (III; 238-243)	1.04	175	178	5601	6	x455
406	2.57	179	179	4218	312	
406	2.73	179	179	4218	313	
402	2.66	179	179	4698	20	x200P
404 or 411	2.83	179	180	4218	314	
425a	2.62	176	180	4218	315	
144ff	2.36	165	180	4218	249	
324ff	2.80	175	180	4218	300	
326ff	1.95	175	180	4218	302	
396ff	2.85	178	180	4218	311	
-	2.62	161	180	4218	316	
-	2.08	161	180	4218	317	
-	2.60	161	180	4218	498	
-	2.07	161	180	4784	3	x229
-	1.78	161	180	4802	12	x261
-	2.32	161	180	5044	8	x354b
-	1.62	161	180	5135	8	x383
-	2.46	161	180	5601	7	x456A
-	2.38	161	180	5601	8	x452
-	2.40	161	180	5601	10	x458
384-409	2.48	177	180	6273	19	x603
-	0.92	161	180	6646	16	x743
-	1.66	161	180	6646	17	x724
- imp X (?)	2.09	179	180	6930	12	x824
-	1.82	161	180	6930	14	x842
384; 396; 406 or 417	2.26	177	180	7057	15	x980
-	2.47	161	180	7057	20	x978
-	1.37	161	180	7057	21	x983
-	1.35	161	180	7057	22	x992
-	1.07	161	180	8491	9	x1292
Marcus Aurelius (Lucius Verus)						
463	2.86	161	161	4802	15	x274
463; 482	2.79	161	163	4218	328	
482	2.85	161	162	4218	327	
515	3.04	163	164	4218	329	
516	2.80	163	164	6930	13	x844
546	2.94	165	166	4218	330	
551[539]	2.89	165	166	4218	331	
553	2.56	165	166	4218	332	
555	2.81	165	166	4218	333	
561	2.97	166	166	4802	14	x273
576	2.66	166	167	6273	20	x600
577	3.09	166	168	4218	334	
578	3.01	167	168	4218	335	
586	2.59	168	168	4218	336	
596	1.66	169	169	7057	16	x971
596b	3.05	168	169	4218	337	
- rev.: Fig. St. l.	2.87	161	169	6646	15	x746
Marcus Aurelius (Commodus Caesar)						
606	2.78	175	176	4218	383	
622	2.93	172	175	4218	384	
661	3.18	179	179	4218	385	
666	2.63	179	179	4218	386	
666	2.71	179	179	4218	387	
666	2.78	179	179	4218	388	
666	3.14	179	179	5044	3	x349
-	2.82	172	180	4218	390	
Marcus Aurelius (Faustina 2)						
668	2.65	161	176	4218	342	
668	2.88	161	176	4218	343	
668	2.86	161	176	4218	344	
668	2.58	161	176	4218	345	
669	2.81	161	176	4218	346	
677	2.93	161	176	4218	347	

538 Weight not given.
539 Type only known as aureus according til RIC.

677	2.79	161	176	4218	348	
677	3.00	161	176	4218	349	
677	2.71	161	176	4218	350	
677	2.80	161	176	4698	15	x200K
686	2.83	161	176	4218	351	
686	2.10	161	176	4802	18	x263A
688	2.87	161	176	4218	352	
688	2.87	161	176	4218	353	
688	3.04	161	176	4218	354	
689	2.73	161	176	4218	355	
690	2.89	161	176	4218	356	
694	2.86	161	176	4218	357	
694	2.89	161	176	4698	18	x200N
697	2.53	161	176	5448	2	x429
706	3.41	161	176	4218	358	
706	2.76	161	176	4698	16	x200L
710	2.96	161	176	4218	359	
714	2.72	161	176	4218	360	
715	3.20	161	176	4218	361	
734	2.95	161	176	4218	362	
735	3.02	161	176	4218	363	
-	2.74	161	176	4218	370	
-	2.37	161	176	7057	17	x974
Marcus Aurelius (Diva Faustina 2)						
741?	1.09	176	180	7057	18	x986
743	2.25	176	180	4218	364	
744	3.10	176	180	4218	365	
744	2.50	176	180	4698	17	x200M
744	2.88	176	180	5135	10	x392
745	2.54	176	180	4218	366	
745	2.33	176	180	4218	367	
746	2.28	176	180	7057	19	x989
-	2.4	176	180	6043	1	x520
Marcus Aurelius (Lucilla)						
757	3.17	164	169	4218	371	
758	2.39	164	180	5044	7	x354a
763f	2.97	164	180	4218	372	
763	3.00	164	180	4218	373	
770	2.20	164	180	4218	374	
770	2.97	164	180	4218	375	
772	2.83	164	180	4218	376	
781	2.56	164	180	4218	377	
784	2.92	164	180	4218	378	
786	2.70	164	180	4218	379	
786	2.92	164	169	-[540]		M2?
787-	2.80	164	180	4218	380	
787-	2.66	164	180	4218	381	
788	2.76	164	180	4218	382	
789	2.63	164	180	5601	11	x443
-	2.66	164	180	4218	499	
-	2.45	164	183	6273	21	x615
Antoninus Pius/Marcus Aurelius						
-	0.67	138	180	5601	9	x444
Commodus						
2	2.34	179	180	4218	391	
12	3.45	181	181	4218	392	
12	2.42	181	181	4218	393	
19	2.13	181	181	4218	395	
19	2.58	181	181	4218	396	
22	2.91	181	181	4218	397	
27	2.56	181	182	4218	398	
27	2.64	181	182	4218	399	
14 or 28	2.84	181	182	4218	394	
30	2.30	181	182	4218	400	
30	2.75	181	182	4218	401	
30	2.92	181	182	4218	402	
31	2.30	181	182	6273	22	x597
36	2.28	181	182	4218	403	
45	3.07	182	182	4218	404	
47	2.38	183	183	4218	405	
66	2.70	183	183	4784	7	x225
67	2.58	183	183	4218	410	
67	2.43	183	183	4218	411	
59, 73 or 83	3.16	183	184	4218	406	
74	2.73	183	184	4218	407	
74	2.45	183	184	4218	408	
59 or 83	2.98	183	184	4218	409	
72	3.07	183	184	4218	412	
74	2.80	183	184	4218	413	
76	2.70	183	184	4218	414	
75 or 91	1.56	183	184	4218	415	
- (imp VI cos IIII pp)	2.13	183	184	6043	2	x521
79	2.38	193	184	6646	18	x740
120	2.27	185	185	4218	389	
102	1.88	184	185	4218	416	
102	2.42	184	185	4218	417	
102	2.42	184	185	4218	418	
106	2.63	184	185	4218	419	
98a or 112	2.61	184	185	4218	420	
102	3.15	184	185	4802	17	x275

[540] The coin appears in an early list of finds, but it has not been possible to verify it.

Crossing boundaries

117	2.48	186	186	4218	421	
124	2.63	186	186	4218	422	
124	2.48	186	186	4218	423	
124	2.25	186	186	4218	424	
127	3.24	186	186	4218	425	
131	2.95	186	186	4218	426	
131	2.61	186	186	4218	427	
132	2.06	186	186	4218	428	
132	2.53	186	187	4218	429	
146	2.35	186	187	4218	430	
110-148	2.80	184	187	4218	431	
155?	3.09	186	187	4218	432	
140-161	2.60	186	187	4218	433	
161	2.82	186	187	4218	434	
160	2.45	186	187	4698	19	x2000
150a?	2.64	186	187	5088	4	x379
161	2.86	186	187	6273	23	x621
164	2.97	187	188	4218	435	
164	3.22	187	188	4218	436	
165	2.49	187	188	4218	437	
165?	3.32	187	188	4218	438	
167	2.92	187	188	4218	439	
167	2.95	187	188	4218	440	
167	2.40	187	188	4218	441	
167	2.98	187	188	4218	442	
169	2.58	187	188	4218	443	
169?	2.78	187	188	4218	444	
175	2.92	188	189	4218	445	
175	3.15	188	189	5044	4	x350
176	2.57	188	189	4218	446	
179	2.35	188	189	4218	447	
189	2.28	189	189	4218	448	
191a	2.53	186	189	4218	449	
192	2.47	186	189	5088	5	x377
195	1.98	186	189	6930	15	x829
202a	2.38	189	189	4218	450	
205	2.24	190	190	4218	451	
205	1.78	190	190	4218	476	
208	1.82	190	190	4218	452	
191-209	2.92	186	190	4218	453	
209	2.63	190	190	4218	454	
212	2.78	190	190	4218	455	
206 or 218	2.45	189	190	4218	456	
135, 189, 208 or 219	2.29	186	190	5135	12	x393

219?	2.46	190	191	4218	457	
207 or 220	2.22	190	191	4218	458	
220	2.89	190	191	4218	459	
220?	2.39	190	191	4218	460	
222a	2.87	190	191	4218	461	
222a	2.55	190	191	4218	462	
222a	2.31	190	191	4218	463	
222a	2.22	190	191	4218	464	
227a	2.56	190	191	4218	465	
227	2.15	190	191	4218	466	
227	2.27	190	191	4218	467	
227	2.27	190	191	4218	468	
219	2.37	190	191	5088	3	x378
219 or 220	2.03	190	191	5135	11	x388a
207, 220, 229a	1.98	190	191	6273	24	x623
234	3.14	192	192	4218	469	
235	2.20	192	192	4218	470	
236	2.57	192	192	4218	471	
-	2.59	180	192	4218	472	
-	3.01	180	192	4218	473	
-	2.69	180	192	4218	474	
-	2.84	180	192	4218	475	
-	2.53	180	192	4218	478	
-	2.03	180	192	4698	21	x200Q
237	2.71	192	192	4802	16	x266A
-	2.48	180	192	5044	6	x353
-	2.60	180	192	5249	2	x424
-	2.06	180	192	6646	19	x734
-	1.60	180	192	6646	20	x739
-[541]	-	180	192	8491	2	x1297
-	2.46	180	192	6930	16	x831
-	2.36	180	192	6930	17	x834
-	2.19	180	192	6930	18	x828
-	2.15	180	192	6930	19	x830
-	1.58	180	192	7057	23	x975
Commodus (Divus Marcus Aurelius)						
264	2.73	180	180	4218	319	
264	2.97	180	180	4218	320	
265	2.44	180	180	4218	321	
266	2.33	180	180	4218	322	
266	3.01	180	180	4218	323	
273	2.98	180	180	4218	324	
273	3.13	180	180	4218	325	
275	2.96	180	180	4218	326	
266, 270 or 274	2.45	180	180	4802	2	x269A

541   In stack with FP 8491.1

Commodus (Crispina)						
278?	2.25	180	183	6273	25	x614
279	3.12	180	183	4218	479	
281	2.90	180	183	4218	480	
282	3.11	180	183	4218	481	
283	2.96	180	183	4218	482	
283	3.03	180	183	4218	483	
286	2.83	180	183	4218	484	
286a	3.02	180	183	5135	14	x382
276-290	2.83	180	183	4218	485	
276-290	2.20	180	183	4784	6	x228
276-290	2.49	180	183	6273	26	x622
Late Antonine; unidentified						
-	2.64	161	192	7057	24	x984
-	2.06	161	192	7057	25	x993
Pertinax						
13a (IV.i; 8)	2.67	193	193	4698	22	x200R
Didius Julianus						
1	2.69	193	193	4218	486	
2	2.91	193	193	4218	487	
3	2.77	193	193	4218	488	
Clodius Albinus						
11	2.84	193	195	4218	489	
Septimius Severus						
1-17	3.31	193	194	4218	490	
18	2.78	193	194	4218	491	
22	2.48	193	194	4218	492	
32	2.81	194	194	4218	494	
27-32	2.82	194	195	4218	493	
-	3.38		211	4218	495	
-	3.34		211	4218	496	
-	0.92	193	211	6930	20	x825
Elagabal						
88 (IV.ii; 34)	2.00	218	222	7057	26	x990
Unidentified emperor						
-	2.68			6646	23	x727
-	1.98			6646	24	x723
-	1.73			6646	25	x731
-	1.46			5044	5	x352
-	1.73			5448	4	x430
-	1.52			5601	12	x459
IMP VI	2.10			6273	27	x596
-	0.55			6638		x823
-	1.61			6930	21	x826

-	0.70		6930	22	x843
-	0.46		6930	23	x839
(same coin as previous)	0.48		7057	28	x967
-	2.73		7057	27	x966
-	0.60		7057	29	x995
-	0.46		7057	30	x994
_[542]	-		8108	2	x1085
-	3.47		8108	8	x1091
-	2.71		8108	9	x1092
- (subæratus)	0.98		8108	11	x1094
- (subæratus)	1.27		8108	12	x1095
-	0.50		8108	14	x1097
-	0.44		8108	15	x1098
-	1.88		8491	10	x1294
-	2.19		8491	11	x1293
Denarii in stack	13.37		6646	21	x758
Denarii in stack	9.43		6646	22	x736
AR; coin?[543]	1.55		4641		
Imitations					
"Hadrian"	1.84		8108	5	x1088
"Marcus Aurelius (Faustina 2)"	2.61		4218	368	
"Marcus Aurelius (Faustina 2)"	2.62		4218	369	

---

542 In stack with FP 8108.1
543 Surface find; BMR 1245.

060305 sb 151: Denarii from Lilleborg, BMR 24

Emperor	RIC type	w.	From	To	Inv.no.	BMR no.
Trajan	-	0.98	98	117	2542	
Hadrian	222	2.68	132	134	2542	
Hadrian	-	2.48	117	138	8493.1	x20
Antoninus Pius	238	1.72	154	155	2496	
Antoninus Pius	298	2.05	159	160	2496	
Antoninus Pius	-	2.09	138	161	1674	
Marcus Aurelius	35	2.61	161	162	2496	
Marcus Aurelius?	-	-	161	180	CCCXLII.1	
Marcus Aurelius (Divus Lucius Verus)	596b	1.82	169	169	1674	hist.afd.7318
Marcus Aurelius (Faustina 2)	669	3.39	161	176	3579	
Marcus Aurelius (Lucilla)	781	2.31	164	169	2496	
Marcus Aurelius (Lucilla)	-	2.73	161	180	8493.3	x114
-	-	2.35			8493.2	x113

060305 sb 223 and 251: Denarii from Tornegård Syd/Brede, BMR 2656 and Lillevang Øst, BMR 3495

SB	Emperor	RIC type	w.	From	To	Inv.no.		BMR no
223	Marcus Aurelius (Divus Antoninus Pius)	429	2.81	161	180	6245	1	BMR2656x26
223	Commodus	32	2.92	181	182	6245	2	BMR2656x27
223	Marcus Aurelius	-	1.33	161	180	6246	1	BMR2656x39
223	Hadrian	110?	2.57	119	122	8106	1	BMR2656x83
223	Marcus Aurelius?	-	1.19	161	180	8106	2	BMR2656x85
223	Commodus	-	2.12	180	192	8106	3	BMR2656x84
223	Marcus Aurelius (Faustina 2/Lucilla)	-	2.24	161	180	8268	1	BMR2656x138
251	Antoninus Pius	- rev.: Fem.st.spear/sceptre in l.hand	2.47	138	161	20	1	BMR3495x2
251	Marcus Aurelius (Commodus Caesar)/Commodus	-	2.03	161	192	8103	2	BMR3495x1
251	-	-	0.89			8474	1	BMR3495x20

060305 sb 405: Denarii from St. Smørengegård, BMR 1697 (25 denarii)

Emperor	RIC type	w.	From	To	Inv.no.		BMR no
Vespasian	-	1.86	69	79	6993	1	x165
Hadrian	-	1.40	117	138	6993	2	x166
Hadrian (?)	-	2.07	117	138	6572	1	x4
Antoninus Pius	40, 44, 58, 62 or 321	2.57	139	143	6572	2	x6
Antoninus Pius	162	2.63	147	148	7038	1	x220
Antoninus Pius	-	2.06	138	161	6993	3	x162
Marcus Aurelius	1	2.83	161	161	7038	2	x223
Marcus Aurelius	- TR P XXVII	2.18	172	173	6993	4	x164
Marcus Aurelius	263, 282, 296 or 307	1.43	171	174	6572	3	x8
Marcus Aurelius	-	2.18	161	180	6993	5	x161
Marcus Aurelius	-	2.01	161	180	7038	3	x221
Marcus Aurelius (?)	-	2.08	161	180	6572	6	x7
Marcus Aurelius (Lucius Verus)	540, 548	2.57	165	166	6572	4	x3
Marcus Aurelius (Faustina 2/Lucilla)	-	1.41	161	180	6572	5	x5[544]

544 In two fragments.

Commodus	11a	2.31	181	181	6993	6	x163
Commodus	76 or 92	0.84	183	184	7038	4	x222
-	-	2.33			6993	7	x160
-	-	1.34			7261	1	x236
-	-	0.98			6993	8	x167
-	- FAV..?	0.60			6993	9	x168
5 denarii in stack	-	10.28			6993	10-14	x159

060305 sb 554: Denarii from St. Smørengegård NV, BMR 3550

Emperor	RIC type	w.	From	To	Inv.no.		BMR no
Marcus Aurelius	-	2.03	161	180	8296	1	x21
Marcus Aurelius	-	2.68	161	180	8296	2	x23
Marcus Aurelius (Divus Antoninus Pius)	442	2.63	161	180	8296	3	x20
Marcus Aurelius (Diva Faustina 2)	743	1.76	176	180	8296	4	x22
-	-	1.02			8296	5	x19
-	-	0.95			8296	6	x18
-	-	0.21			8296	7	x17

060403 sb 74: Denarii from Sylten I, BMR 789 (9 coins)

Emperor	RIC type	w.	From	To	Inv.no.		BMR no
Vespasian	103	2.51	77	78	5966	1	x597
Trajan	363	2.04	114	117	5966	2	x596
Antoninus Pius	- Annona cos IIII	2.60	147	156	7029	1	x687
Antoninus Pius	-	1.68	138	161	7029	3	x686
Marcus Aurelius	145, 164, 171, 178, 192	2.39	165	168	5454	8	x209
Marcus Aurelius (Lucius Verus)	540	2.06	161	169	4700		x13
Marcus Aurelius (Lucius Verus)[545]	?	-	161	168	4675		x10
Marcus Aurelius (Lucilla)	782	1.63	164	180	5069	1	x101
Marcus Aurelius (Commodus Caesar) /Commodus	- ...COMMODVSAV	2.02	178	182	5966	3	x595

060403 sb 74: Denarii from Sylten II, BMR 789

Emperor	RIC type	w.	From	To	Inv.no.		BMR no
Tiberius	26 (2nd ed.)	1.59	14	37	6074	1	x606
Nero	53 or 64 (2nd ed.)	2.40	64	68	6549	1	x657
Vespasian	89 or 99	2.65	75	76	5330	1	x173
Nerva	REV.: Fortuna	2.66	96	98	5330	2	x172
Trajan	115-135	2.35	103	111	6045	1	x284
Hadrian	-	2.30	117	138	4782		x32
Hadrian (Sabina)	395?	2.35	128	138	5068	1	x113
Hadrian	- class E	2.33	134	138	5330	3	x174
Antoninus Pius	- TR P XII	2.64	148	149	8099	1	x743
Antoninus Pius	- (III, 56-59; IMP II)	1.93	155	158	5454	2	x192
Antoninus Pius	-	1.62	138	161	5600	1	x218
Antoninus Pius	-	1.29	138	161	6240	1	x632

---

545 Coin not available for consultation.

Antoninus Pius	-	2.17	138	161	7029	2	x688
Antoninus Pius (?)	-	2.00	138	161	5454	1	x191
Antoninus Pius (Diva Faustina 1)	348	2.39	141	161	7435	2	x711
Antoninus Pius (Diva Faustina 1)	362	2.39	141	161	6549	2	x658
Antoninus Pius (Diva Faustina 1)	368	2.44	141	161	7435	1	x709
Antoninus Pius (Diva Faustina 1)	393-4	2.34	141	161	6074	2	x600
Antoninus Pius (Diva Faustina 1)	394a	2.63	141	161	8099	2	x744
Antoninus Pius (Marcus Aurelius Caesar)	429	2.33	145	147	6045	2	x283
Antoninus Pius (Marcus Aurelius Caesar)	433	2.58	145	147	4800	3	x56
Antoninus Pius (Marcus Aurelius Caesar)	446	2.22	148	149	4701		x31
Antoninus Pius (Marcus Aurelius Caesar)	- Minerva	2.73	147	150	4800	2	x54
Antoninus Pius (Marcus Aurelius Caesar)	- COS II	2.09	145	161	5812	2	x484
Antoninus Pius (Marcus Aurelius Caesar)	-	1.81	138	161	7435	3	x712
Antoninus Pius (Faustina 2)	507c	3.00	161	161	5068	4	x112
Marcus Aurelius	3	2.41	161	161	5454	3	x188
Marcus Aurelius	- TR P XVII, close to RIC 102	2.72	162	163	8313		x770
Marcus Aurelius	- TR P XXIX	2.30	174	175	5454	5	x190
Marcus Aurelius	- …COSIII	1.15	161	177	5068	2	x114
Marcus Aurelius?	-	0.82		180	4800	1	x57
(same coin as above)	-	0.66		180	5454	6	x193
(same coin as above)	-	0.58		180	5966	5	x599
Marcus Aurelius	-	2.25	161	180	5068	3	x110
Marcus Aurelius	-	2.06	161	180	5454	4	x189
Marcus Aurelius?	-	0.93	161	180	5600	2	x219
Marcus Aurelius	- fem.st.l.. with ? and cornucopia	1.50	161	180	5812	4	x486
Marcus Aurelius (Divus Antoninus Pius)	442	1.74	161	180	5330	4	x172
Marcus Aurelius (Lucius Verus)	566	2.32	166	166	4800	4	x55
Marcus Aurelius (Commodus)	649, 653 or 657-8	2.35	177	179	5068	5	x111
Marcus Aurelius (Faustina 2)	688	2.33	161	176	5812	3	x483
Marcus Aurelius (Lucilla)	755-792	1.37	164	169	6240	2	x633
(same coin as above)	-	0.57	164	169	6835		x667
Commodus	29	2.26	181	182	8099	3	x745
Commodus	- …LAVG[brit]	2.36	184	191	6240	3	x631
Marcus Aurelius - Septimius Severus	- rev.: fig.seat.	1.64	161	211	5812	1	x485
-	-	0.45			7435	6	x710
-	-	0.42			6074	3	x607
-	-	0.60			7435	4	x713
-	-	0.68			5454	7	x194

060403 sb 93. Denarii from Sorte Muld, BMR 1191 (292 coins)

RIC type	w.	From	To	Inv. No.		Exc.no
Vespasian						
67	2.49	73	73	4673	74	x328RB
-	2.74	69	79	4697	2	x351R
Titus						
24a	2.91	80	80	4955	1	x644RB
Titus (Domitian Caesar)						
50	3.07	80	80	4673	3	x288R
50	2.69	80	80	6201	1	x1017R
Domitian						
16 or 17	2.67	81	81	7253	1	x1926R
rev. as RIC 34	2.85	85	94	6201	2	x1019R
rev. as RIC 34	3.22	85	94	4955	7	x651R
171	3.09	93	94	4673	4	x344RA
Domitian?						
-	1.47	81	96	6688	1	x1513R
Nerva						
41	2.52	97	97	4697	1	x360R
Trajan						
52	2.85	101	102	5251	4	x758Rb
57	2.48	101	102	5251	10	x745Ra
58	2.40	101	102	5464	1	x789R
102	2.93	103	111	5140	4	x672Rc
115	1.93	103	111	5140	34	x715R
119	2.98	103	111	5464	2	x838Ra
120	2.74	103	111	5464	3	x770R
126 (or 120)	2.88	103	111	6688	2	x1515R
166	2.78	103	111	5251	3	x749R
147	2.52	103	111	5140	6	x720R
252	3.26	112	114	5251	2	x745Rc
288	2.85	112	117	4673	16	x305RB
291	2.80	112	114	4673	5	x304R
294	3.02	112	114	4673	6	x338RA
318	2.66	114	117	5464	4	x887R
-	5.38	98	117	8088	1	x2202R[546]
-	2.21	98	117	6453	1	x1379R
-	2.83	98	117	4673	73	x324R
-	2.71	98	117	4673	1	x327RA
-	2.60	98	117	4672	1	x12A
-	1.77	98	117	5140	1	x700R
Trajan?						
-	1.82	98	117	5140	3	x668R
Hadrian						
4c	2.75	117	117	6372	1	x1426R
- Class A	2.62	117	122	5464	5	x863R
55-141 (Class A)	2.73	119	122	6201	3	x1006R
77	2.75	119	122	7253	2	x2029R
114-142	2.97	119	122	4955	4	x643R
127	2.94	119	122	5140	13	x721R
137	2.74	119	122	4673	59	x335RR
139	2.70	119	122	4673	10	x310R
141	2.71	119	122	5140		x705R
146	2.96	125	128	4955	3	x650R
146	2.82	125	128	4673	8	x338RB
154	2.62	125	128	4673	7	x265R
163	2.41	125	128	5140	8	x726R
182c	2.66	125	128	6201	4	x1015R
230d	2.79	134	138	5464	6	x850R
234	2.49	134	138	4673	13	x311RB
234	2.48	117	138	4673	23	x332R
256	2.80	134	138	6453	2	x1380R
257	2.57	134	138	5464	7	x828R
268	2.76	134	138	6038	1	x1188R
269	2.50	134	138	5140	7	x713Ra
274a	2.78	134	138	5464	8	x786R
343	2.69	134	138	4673	9	x341R
-	2.81	117	138	4673	69	x312R
-	2.64	117	138	5464	9	x840Ra
- IMPC…	0.67	117	138	6372	2	x1430R
-	2.51	117	138	4673	60	x251R
-	2.25	117	138	4626	1	x511 AA 19
Hadrian (Sabrina)						
422c	2.79	128	138	4697	3	x499R
Antoninus Pius						
7	2.91	138	138	4673	51	x344RB
3	2.56	138	138	4697	4	x426R
3	2.71	138	138	4673	11	x307RA
26	3.04	139	139	4673	54	x372RB
70	2.85	140	143	5464	10	x795Rb
95	2.19	140	143	4673	65	x306RA
102	2.98	140	143	4626	3	x548 M 21
124	2.79	145	161	4673	2	x346R
127	3.27	145	161	6201	5	x1016R
128, 162 or 175	2.64	145	149	6372	3	x1427R
156	2.60	145	161	8309	1	x2417R
162	2.84	147	148	4673	24	x330R
163	2.47	147	148	4673	22	x340R
165, 177d or 178	3.04	147	149	5464	12	x778Ra

546 In stack with FP 8088.2 (unidentified emperor).

Crossing boundaries

167 or 181	2.27	147	149	6038	3	x1187R
175	2.54	148	149	4673	66	x306RB
175	3.06	148	149	4673	15	x311RA
176	2.76	148	149	4673	39	x270R
179	2.66	145	161	5140	18	x683R
180	3.07	148	149	4673	26	x314R
183	2.98	148	149	4673	27	x308R
200	2.66	150	151	5140	5	x704Ra
200	2.68	150	151	5140	10	x713Rb
54b or 139	2.84	139	161	5251	5	x746Rb
129	2.73	145	161	5464	11	x785R
200	2	150	151	5140	12	x671Ra
210	2.82	151	152	5464	13	x834R
204	2.85	151	152	6453	4	x1376R
222	2.92	152	161	4673	57	x377RA
222	2.78	152	153	8091		x57
231	2.42	153	154	6038	4	x1193R
203, 219 or 229a	2.64	151	154	6453	3	x1382R
248	2.78	155	156	6688	3	x1593R
250 or 262	2.33	155	156	6201	6	x1018R
293a or 294ba	2.95	158	159	5464	15	x778Rc
272a or 305ab	2.61	157	160	5464	14	x778Rb
311	2.41	160	161	5140	9	x684Ra
-	2.72	138	161	4672	2	x12B
-	2.91	138	161	5464	16	x838Rb
-	2.03	138	161	4673	36	x187
-	2.41	138	161	5140	11	x714R
-	2.96	138	161	5251	11	x745Rb
-	2.18	138	161	4673	18	x302R
-	2.60	138	161	6038	2	x1194R
Antoninus Pius ?						
-	1.84	138	161	5464	25	x839Ra
Antoninus Pius						
-	2.37	138	161	6453	5	x1381R
Antoninus Pius (Diva Faustina 1)						
327-342	2.56	138	141	7422	2	x2072R
327-342	2.76	138	141	5464	18	x844R
327-342	2.74	138	141	5464	17	x870Ra
335	2.72	138	141	4673	20	x345R
327-407	2.52	138	161	6201	9	x1021R
- veiled woman	3.16	141	161	5251	6	x758Ra
370	3.23	141	161	4673	37	x262
391	2.81	141	161	4673	25	x318R
369	2.5	141	161	4626	4	x1058 32/79
343-407	2.61	141	161	5464	20	x804R
348	2.70	141	161	4955	2	x622R

384a	2.53	141	161	6201	7	x1010R
394a	3.13	141	161	6201	8	x1022R
393	2.54	141	161	6038	5	x1195R
358(?)	2.64	141	161	5813	1	x1101R
343-407	0.84	141	161	6372	4	x1429R
343-407	2.6	141	161	6453	6	x1378R
360	2.59	141	161	4673	29	x305RA
361	2.77	141	161	5140	33	x671Rb
344	2.6	141	161	5140	14	x723R
350	2.31	141	161	4673	71	x326RB
370	2.58	141	161	4673	49	x334R
343-407	2.29	141	161	5464	19	x797Ra
360(?)	2.89	141	161	5813	2	x1099R
Antoninus Pius (Marcus Aurelius Caesar)						
415a but: CAES	2.82	140	140	5464	21	x867R
424	2.93	140	144	4673	33	x168A
424	2.61	140	144	6038	6	x1189R
427	2.8	144	144	4673	48	x315R
429	2.74	144	144	4673	28	x261R
429	2.8	144	144	4697	5	x297R
442	2.42	161	161	4626	2	x464 DD/7
444	2.1	148	149	6688	4	x1512R
444 or 450	2.91	148	150	4955	5	x635R
455	2.56	150	151	4697	9	x551R
458	2.84	152	153	6201	10	x1008R
459	2.67	153	154	5464	22	x795Ra
479	3.23	158	159	4673	46	x321R
Antoninus Pius (Faustina 2)						
507	2.82	141	161	5140	20	x672Rd
503	2.9	141	161	5140	21	x684Rb
502	2.07	146	161	5464	24	x790R
506	2.96	141	161	5140	29	x672Re
513	2.68	141	161	4697	10	x300R
Antoninus Pius (Marcus Aurelius Caesar/Aurelius)						
-	1.57	138	161	5464	23	x830Rb
Marcus Aurelius						
3	2.36	161	161	5140	23	x671Rc
22 or 24	2.51	161	161	6201	11	x1013R
48	2.63	161	162	6038	7	x1186R
59	2.90	162	163	6372	5	x1428R
Marcus Aurelius						
62	2.90	162	163	4673	63	x301RA
62	2.68	162	163	6201	12	x1007R
91	2.42	163	164	4673		x301RB
92 or 124	2.53	163	165	5813	3	x1102R
109	2.72	163	164	5140	30	x678R
109	2.54	163	164	5140	32	x722R

Coin lists

109	2.73	163	164	5140	2	x717R
109	1.82	163	164	5140	15	x724R
109	2.57	163	164	5140	31	x704Rb
109	2.20	163	164	5140	16	x716R
148	2.95	165	166	4673	32	x282
157	2.90	165	166	4673	78	x303R
163	2.63	166	166	5464	26	x766R
171	2.90	167	168	4673	14	x258R
176	3.04	167	168	7729	1	x2155R
185	2.71	168	168	4697	12	x552R
198 or 211	2.57	168	170	5464	27	x884R
204	2.53	168	169	4673	12	x320R
212 or 232	1.67	169	171	7253	3	x1928R
214 or 233	2.22	169	171	6038	8	x1197R
222	2.22	169	170	4673	72	x326RA
231	2.99	170	171	4673	31	x256R
231	3.10	170	171	4673	58	x377RB
297	2.90	173	174	4673	30	x253R
306	3.03	174	174	6201	13	x1012R
323	2.86	175	175	4673	35	x319RA
325	2.51	175	175	5140	19	x672Rb
333	1.28	175	175	4673	70	x325R
353 (?)	2.68	175	176	6201	14	x1009R
394, 399 or 403	2.01	177	179	5464	28	x888
403	2.59	179	179	5251	7	x760R
404 or 411	2.33	179	180	5464	29	x857Ra
405	2.36	179	179	7448	1	x2117R
412	2.73	176	180	4673	68	x307RC
- Rev.: St. woman	1.88	161	180	6688	5	x1545R
-	2.89	161	180	6201	15	x1014R
-	2.10	161	180	5464	34	x797Rb
Marcus Aurelius?						
-	2.93	161	180	6920	3	x1766R
Marcus Aurelius						
-	2.44	161	180	5464	32	x782R
Marcus Aurelius (Divus Antoninus Pius)						
431	2.80	161	180	4673	53	x347R
438	2.77	161	180	7031	1	x1880R
Marcus Aurelius (Lucius Verus)						
463(?)	2.34	161	161	6688	6	x1485R
482	2.73	161	163	4697	13	x579R
491	2.90	162	163	4673	56	x376R
553	2.15	165	166	6920	2	x1768R
555	2.88	165	166	5140		x704Rc
555	2.70	165	166	4673	34	x331R
555	2.53	165	166	6201	16	x1023R
555	2.85	161	169	5140	22	x725R
561, 576 or 578	3.22	166	168	5251	8	x746Ra
Marcus Aurelius (Divus Lucius Verus)						
596	2.88	169	169	4673	45	x328RA
596b	2.81	169	180	5464	30	x768R
Marcus Aurelius (Commodus)						
653	2.65	177	178	6038	9	x1196R
Marcus Aurelius (Faustina 2)						
676	2.84	161	176	4673	42	x337R
672b? only recorded as AV	2.33	161	176	4673	44	x316R
686	3.36	161	176	6201	17	x1005R
694	2.83	161	176	4673	21	x285R
734	4.44	161	176	6688	7	x1514R
-	2.01	146	176	4785	2	x600R
Antoninus Pius/Marcus Aurelius (Faustina 2)						
-	2.17	161	176	4626	6	x283 T16
Marcus Aurelius (Lucilla)						
759	2.57	164	180	4673	41	x168B
759	2.30	164	180	5464	31	x794Rc
762	2.97	161	180	4673	43	x339R
762	2.98	164	180	6038	10	x1190R
763	2.45	164	180	8088	3	x2203R
770	2.67	161	180	4673	40	x319RB
786	2.11	164	180	6038	12	x1192R
786	2.43	164	180	6038	11	x1191R
-	2.84	164	169	6453	7	x1377R
Antoninus Pius/Marcus Aurelius (Faustina 2/Lucilla)						
-	2.34	161	180	6688	8	x1581R
Commodus						
10	2.41	180	180	5464	35	x858Rb
10 or 36	1.40	180	182	6201	19	x1011R
22	2.49	181	181	4697	8	x354R
24	2.46	181	181	5140	27	x706R
Commodus						
26	2.56	181	182	4697	6	x350R
27	2.24	181	182	4673	55	x375R
33	2.15	181	182	5140	28	x719R
73, 74 or 76-78	2.40	183	184	5251	9	x758Rc
98a or 112	3.23	184	185	5813	4	x1100R
102	2.15	184	185	5464	36	x765R
131	2.86	186	186	5464	38	x839Rc
124	2.66	186	186	5464	37	x794Ra
143	2.73	186	187	4673	47	x313RB
149	2.56	186	187	4673	76	x329R
149	3.11	186	187	4673	77	x313RA
140 or 161	2.43	186	187	5464	39	x839Rb
169	2.43	187	188	4697	11	x523R

150	2.23	187	188	4697	7	x585R
139 or 155	2.46	186	188	6038	13	x1185R
201	1.95	189	189	5140	26	x718R
205	1.94	190	190	4673	67	x07B
209	3.50	190	190	8087	1	x2253R
222a	2.94	190	191	5464	40	x794Rb
227	2.31	190	191	5464	41	x870Rb
?	2.34	191	191	4785	1	x604R
232	1.57	192	192	5140	24	x672Ra
339	2.46	192	192	4673	75	x327RB
-	2.45	180	192	4955	8	x644RA
-	2.52	180	192	4673	52	x344RC
-	2.25	180	192	4673	61	x259R
-	2.29	180	192	4626	7	A 4
-	2.59	180	192	5140	17	x686R
-	1.75	180	192	8088	4	x2204R
-	2.92	180	192	5464	45	x857Rc
-	2.81	180	192	5464	43	x857Rb
-	3.32	180	192	5464	44	x840b
Commodus (Divus Marcus Aurelius)						
266 or 270	2.71	180	180	5464	42	x858Ra
Commodus (Crispina)						
283	2.51	181	183	4673	62	x263R
Septimius Severus						
22	2.96	193	194	4626	9	x71
38a	547	193	194	4673	79	x317R
411	3.91	194	195	4955	6	x623R
?	2.52	193	211	4673	38	x309R
Septimius Severus (Julia Domna)						
574 or 643	2.11	196	211	5464	47	x783R
561 or 641	2.70	196	211	5464	46	x769R
-	1.39	196	211	5464	48	x890R
Elagabal						
Severus Alexander						
35	2.30	224	224	8087	2	x2254R
?	0.76	222	235	4671		x146
Maximus Thrax						
4-6	1.52	236	238	6920	4	x1769R
Unidentified						
-	2.50			6688	9	x1486R
-	2.56			6920	5	x1767R
-	0.84			7031	2	x1810R
-	0.69			7031	3	x1809R

-	2.48			4673	50	x212R
-	2.73			7253	4	x1927R
-	1.32			8309	2	x2418R
-	548			4673	64	x303
-	549			8088	2	x2202R
Imitation						
-	2.38	100	250	6688	10	x1516R
Hybrid or imitation obv: Antoninus/M Aurelius / rev: Trajan						
115-6 / 119	2.42	138	161	6920	1	x1764R
Hybrid: Diva Faustina/M Aurelius						
216 or 234 (Aurelius)	2.18	161	180	7422	1	x2071R
Imitation(?)/Marcus Aurelius (Faustina 2)						
-	2.66	145	250	6201	18	x1020R

---

547 Not weighed.
548 Not weighed.
549 In stack with FP 8088.1 (Trajan).

Coin lists

060403 sb 93: Denarii from Sorte Muld Syd/Paradisgård, BMR 3141

Emperor	RIC type	w.	From	To	Inv.no.		BMR no
Nerva	1, 4, 13 or 16	2.80	96	97	8157	1	x84
Hadrian	Class B	2.12	125	128	7035		x35
Hadrian	-	2.08	117	138	7294	1	x46
Antoninus Pius	-	1.89	138	161	7294	2	x48
Marcus Aurelius	4, 5, 35 or 49	1.96	161	162	6923	1	x21

060403 sb 93: Denarii from Fuglesangsageren, BMR 2649

Emperor	RIC type	w.	From	To	Inv.no.		BMR no
Trajan	169	2.58	103	111	6645	1	x105
Trajan	220-222)	2.55	103	111	5969	1	x15
Hadrian	178	2.59	125	128	6844	1	x213
Hadrian	264	2.34	134	138	5969	2	x14
Antoninus Pius	222 or 232	2.12	152	154	6844	2	x212
Antoninus Pius	257, 271	2.39	156	158	6403	1	x19
Antoninus Pius (Diva Faustina 1)	384	2.32	141	161	8151	1	x230
Marcus Aurelius	12, 22 or 50	2.33	161	162	6844	3	x211
Marcus Aurelius	37	1.95	161	162	7034	1	x226
Marcus Aurelius	138-139	1.11	165	165	6844	4	x214
Marcus Aurelius	-	2.43	161	180	5969	4	x13
Marcus Aurelius	-	0.79	161	180	6403	2	x20
(same coin as previous)	-	1.37	180	192	7034	2	x225
Marcus Aurelius (Commodus Caesar)	662	2.38	179	179	7258	1	x231
Commodus	88	2.20	184	184	6403	3	x25
Commodus	209	2.00	190	190	5969	3	x12

060403 sb 96-97: Denarii from Højemark, BMR 1092, 2510 and 265

Emperor	RIC type	w.	From	To	Inv.no.		BMR no
Vespasian	57, 66	2.29	73	73	6079	1	BMR1092x73
Trajan	91-148	2.25	103	111	6079	2	BMR1092x74
Trajan	139	2.52	103	111	8096	1	BMR2651x107
Hadrian	190	2.77	125	128	6374	1	BMR2510x34
Hadrian	256-7	2.53	134	138	6374	2	BMR2510x30
Hadrian	-	1.15	117	138	7424		BMR2651x44
Hadrian	- rev.: fig. enthroned l.	2.11	117	138	8096	2	BMR2651x108
Hadrian (Sabina)	390-416	1.09	128	138	6244	1	BMR1092x126
Antoninus Pius	137	1.86	145	161	6247	2	BMR2651x24
Antoninus Pius	162	2.52	147	148	8096	3	BMR2651x106
Antoninus Pius	163, 176, 204, 221, 231, 239, 249	2.24	147	156	6090	1	BMR2651x6
Antoninus Pius	200 or 216	0.83	150	152	8314	1	BMR2651x160
Antoninus Pius	211-2(?)	2.50	151	152	8310	1	BMR2755x9
Antoninus Pius	-	1.85	138	161	5248		BMR1092x5
Antoninus Pius	-	2.32	138	161	6079	3	BMR1092x72
Antoninus Pius	-, COS III or IIII	2.44	138	161	5807		BMR1092x63
Antoninus Pius	-	2.31	138	161	6374	3	BMR2510x31

Emperor	RIC type	w.	From	To	Inv.no		BMR no.
Antoninus Pius (Faustina 1)	327-342	2.41	138	141	6374	4	BMR2510x32
Antoninus Pius (Diva(?) Faustina 1)	327-407	2.06	138	161	6247	1	BMR2651x25
Antoninus Pius (Diva Faustina 1)	363	2.45	141	161	6244	2	BMR1092x124
Antoninus Pius (Marcus Aurelius Caesar)	417	2.32	140	140	8310	2	BMR2755x10
Antoninus (Marcus Aurelius Caesar)/ Marcus Aurelius	-	2.39	160	165	6247	3	BMR2651x23
Marcus Aurelius	205	2.80	169	170	5593		BMR1092x16
Marcus Aurelius	207 or 222	2.60	168	170	6244	3	BMR1092x125
Marcus Aurelius	- rev.: Liberalitas	2.45	165	175	6374	5	BMR2510x33
Marcus Aurelius	-	2.09	161	180	8096	4	BMR2651x109
Marcus Aurelius	-	0.65	161	180	6247	4	BMR2651x26
Marcus Aurelius (Lucius Verus)	- , COS II	2.22	161	166	7763	1	BMR2651x98
Marcus Aurelius (Divus Antoninus or Divus Verus)	429-434 or 596	1.00	161	180	7423		BMR2755x5
Marcus Aurelius (Lucilla)	786-787	1.94	164	169	7763	2	BMR2651x97
Commodus	141-161 (TR P XII)	2.25	186	187	4676		BMR1092x2
Commodus	- ..]PFEL[..	1.81	184	192	7763	3	BMR2651x99
Pertinax/Septimius Severus(?)	- , COS II	1.93	193	211	7763	4	BMR2651x100
Caracalla	311b	2.38	213	217	4783		BMR1092x4a
-	-	2.07			6374	6	BMR2510x35
(denarius?)	-	0.19			8096	5	BMR2651x110

060403 sb 107: Coins from Brændesgård, BMR 1653

Emperor	RIC type	w.	From	To	Inv.no		BMR no.
Hadrian	- ..TRAIANHADRIAN…	2.11	117	122	6051		x176
Antoninus Pius	-	2.55	138	161	5236	1	x49
Marcus Aurelius	-	1.93	161	180	5479	1	x69
Commodus	67	2.37	183	184	5479	2	x71
Commodus	-	1.72	184	189	5063		x6
Commodus	- (..AVGBRIT)	2.37	184	189	5479	3	x72
Clodius Albinus	11	2.69	193	194	6124	1	x205
Elagabal	46	2.71	220	222	8158	1	x299
-	-	1.33			5236	2	x50

060403 sb 160: Coins from Engegård, BMR 2280 and 3185

Emperor	RIC type	w.	From	To	Inv.no.		BMR no.
Trajan	212	2.54	103	111	6050		BMR2280x4
Trajan??	-	1.39	98	117	7254	1	BMR3185x35
Hadrian	343	2.68	134	138	6842	1	BMR3185x18
Hadrian	-	2.19	117	138	7449		BMR2280x142
Antoninus Pius	43, 54, 97 or 136	2.62	139	161	6547	0	BMR3185x1
Antoninus Pius	- COS IIII	2.25	145	161	7393		BMR2280x138
Antoninus Pius	-	3.09	138	161	7254	2	BMR3185x34
Antoninus Pius	- rev. Fem.st.l.	2.31	138	161	8148	1	BMR2280x149
Antoninus Pius	- COS IIII	2.39	145	161	8018	1	BMR2280x143
Antoninus Pius (Diva(?) Faustina 1)	327-407	2.30	138	161	6842	2	BMR3185x17
Antoninus Pius (Diva Faustina 1)	343-407	1.01	141	161	8020	1	BMR3185x69
Antoninus Pius (Faustina 2)	502a	1.67	146	161	6559	2	BMR2280x8

Emperor	RIC type	w.	From	To	Inv.no.		BMR no
Antoninus Pius (Faustina 2)	502a	1.98	146	161	6559	1	BMR2280x10
Marcus Aurelius	259	2.12	171	172	6929	1	BMR2280x133
Marcus Aurelius	- Mars st.r.	1.81	161	180	8318	2	BMR2280x179
Marcus Aurelius (Lucius Verus)	463	2.49	161	161	6928	1	BMR2280x110
Marcus Aurelius (Faustina 2)	683	1.75	161	176	6929	2	BMR2280x134
Antoninus Pius/Marcus Aurelius (Faustina 2)	-	2.14	146	176	8318	1	BMR2280x180
Marcus Aurelius?? (Lucilla)	- LV…/person st.l. w. sceptre/lance	0.95	161	180	8318	3	BMR2280x181
Commodus	54	2.08	183	183	8318	4	BMR2280x178
Commodus	56	2.01	183	183	7254	3	BMR3185x38
Commodus	113 or 136	1.89	184	187	6559	3	BMR2280x11
Commodus	-	2.40	180	192	7733	1	BMR3185x60
Commodus (Divus Marcus Aurelius)	264	2.45	180	180	7254	4	BMR3185x36
Commodus (Crispina)	276-290	2.06	180	183	6928	2	BMR2280x109
Pertinax	-	2.07	193	193	6929	3	BMR2280x132
-	-	0.61			7254	5	BMR3185x37
-	-	1.65			6559	4	BMR2280x9

060403 sb 135: Coins from Dalshøj, BMR 1639 (east of Højevej)

Emperor	RIC type	w.	From	To	Inv.no.		BMR no
Vespasian (Domitian Caesar)	242?	1.35	79	79	5462	1	x105
Trajan	292-293 or, 313	2.72	112	117	5250	1	x74
Trajan	-	1.78	98	117	4815	1	x12
Hadrian	2-22, 35-52, portrait class A	2.41	117	119	4815	2	x13
Hadrian	52 or 141	1.16	118	122	6364	1	x302
Hadrian	-	1.76	117	138	4997	1	x32A
Antoninus Pius	128, 162, 175 or 230	2.96	145	161	6551	1	x322
Antoninus Pius	163, 176, 204, 210, 221, 231, 239 or 244	2.63	147	156	6551	2	x321.1
Antoninus Pius	229a	2.49	153	154	4997	3	x36
Antoninus Pius	239	2.87	154	155	4997	2	x33
Antoninus Pius	264	2.25	156	157	4997	5	x3X
Antoninus Pius	300	2.30	159	160	5250	2	x70
Antoninus Pius	- Rev.: fem.st.	2.67	138	161	8153	2	x514
Antoninus Pius	- (rev:.fem.st.,spear in l.hand	1.52	138	161	8092	1	x460
Antoninus Pius	- Rev.: fem.st..	2.04	138	161	8153	3	x515
Antoninus Pius	- Rev.: fem.st.	2.,31	138	161	8153	1	x487
Antoninus Pius	-	2.21	138	161	7256	1	x411
Antoninus Pius	-	2.54	138	161	7256	2	x410
Antoninus Pius	-	1.16	138	161	7433	1	x417
Antoninus Pius	-	2.08	138	161	6551	3	x325
Antoninus Pius	-	2.49	138	161	6243		x280
Antoninus Pius	-	2.61	138	161	4997	4	x30
Antoninus Pius	-	2.80	138	161	5250	3	x73
Antoninus Pius (Diva Faustina 1)	344	2.74	141	161	7256	3	x409
Antoninus Pius (Diva Faustina 1)	378	2.61	141	161	4815	3	x15
Antoninus Pius (Marcus Aurelius Caesar)	424 or 429c	2.36	140	147	4799	1	x7
Antoninus Pius (Marcus Aurelius Caesar)	448, 451, 456	2.27	148	152	6551	4	x326

Emperor	RIC type	w.	From	To	Inv.no.		BMR no.
Antoninus Pius (Marcus Aurelius Caesar)	454, 462, 468, 473	2.55	151	157	4815	4	x16
Antoninus Pius (Faustina 2)	502a	2.60	146	161	4997	7	x38
Antoninus Pius (Faustina 2)	515	2.62	146	161	4799	2	x8
Antoninus Pius/Marcus Aurelius (Faustina 2)	-	2.49	146	176	7727	2	x431
Marcus Aurelius	22 or 54	2.54	161	162	6551	5	x321.2
Marcus Aurelius	23 or 51	2.01	161	162	6551	6	x324
Marcus Aurelius	37	2.88	161	162	6551	7	x323
Marcus Aurelius	66-73	2.23	162	163	5250	4	x72
Marcus Aurelius	92	2.77	163	164	7727	1	x430
Marcus Aurelius	211	2.50	169	170	2273	18	(House A)
Marcus Aurelius	212	2.14	169	170	4997	10	x37
Marcus Aurelius	248		170	171	2302	1	(House A/B)
Marcus Aurelius?	-	1.96	161	180	7727	3	x432
Marcus Aurelius	-	1.80	161	180	7023	1	x382
Marcus Aurelius (?)	-	2.48	161	180	6364	2	x300
Marcus Aurelius (Lucius Verus)	482	2.03	161	162	8153	4	x516
Marcus Aurelius (Faustina 2)	677	2.17	161	176	7023	2	x383
Marcus Aurelius (Lucilla)	758	2.47	164	180	4997	8	x32B
Marcus Aurelius (Lucilla)	781	2.06	164	180	4997	6	x34
Marcus Aurelius/Commodus (Caesar)	-	2.29	172	192	4997	9	x35
Commodus	36	2.78	181	182	6551	8	x321.4
Commodus	36	3.04	181	182	6841		x346
Commodus	- rev.: fem.st., COS III	3.37	181	182	6551	9	x321.3
Commodus	92 or 167	1.24	184	188	5462	2	x104
Commodus	150a	2.00	187	188	4799	3	x5 and x6
Commodus	205	2.97	190	190	6049		x121
Commodus	-	2.29	180	192	7256	4	x408
Commodus	-	2.25	180	192	6364	3	x301
Commodus	-	2.75	180	192	5250	5	x71
Commodus (Crispina)	283	2.51	180	183	4815	5	x14
antonine dynasty ?	-	0.76	138	190	8153	5	x488
Septimius Severus	2-17	2.56	193	194	4815	6	x17
-	-	0.71			7727	4	x433
-	-	1.56			7433	2	x416
-	-	0.36			8153	6	x517
-	-	0.68			7023	4	x384
-	-	0.72			7023	3	x385
-	-	1.71			6551	10	x327

060403 sb 166: Denarii from Biskopenge VI, BMR 790

Emperor	RIC type	w.	From	To	Inv.no.		BMR no.
Antoninus Pius	- rev. Annona	2.58	147	155	5972		x25
Antoninus Pius	-	2.24	138	161	6268		x31
Antoninus Pius	-	2.19	138	161	6840	1	x44
Marcus Aurelius	-	2.08	161	180	8007	1	x48
Marcus Aurelius (Diva Faustina 2)	739	2.27	176	180	6840	2	x45
Commodus	13, 14, 17, or 22?	1.30	181	181	6840	3	x46

060403 sb 168: Denarii from Sylten IV, BMR 1077

Coins marked with an '-' in the column 'fire' have no visible traces of exposure to fire/heat

Emperor/RIC type	From	To	w.	Inv.no.	Exc.no.	fire
Vespasian						
-	69	79	[550]5.17	5594	1	x125
-	69	79	0.72	8315	1	x228
Domitian						
86	86	86	2.39	4674	1	x70
Trajan						
- SPQROPTIMO…	103	111	2.08	4674	3	x54B	-
91-148 COS-VPPSPQR…	103	111	2.15	4699	1	x73	-
266	112	114	2.35	4674	2	x33
-	98	117	2.63	4674	25	x5
-	98	117	2.49	5247	1	x114
-	98	117	2.66	8100	1	x200
Hadrian						
75(?)	117	138	2.06	4674	36	x67
77	119	122	2.26	4674	6	x39	-
133	119	122	2.05	4674	11	x59	-
- IMPCAESAR-TRAIANHADR..	117	122	2.54	4674	8	x47A	-
- IMPCAESAR-TRAIAN…	117	122	2.18	4674	9	x51
-	117	122	1.99	4674	13	x63
- Class B(?)	125	128	2.32	4699	2	x78
220	132	134	2.19	4674	4	x24
241a? Fides Publica	134	138	2.43	4674	5	x32
241A	134	138	2.23	4674	7	x46
299(?) Class D	134	138	3.15	5594	2	x130
321-329 Restitutor type	134	138	2.44	7030	1	x186
-	117	138	2.28	4674	10	x58A	-
-	117	138	2.30	4674	46	x38
-	117	138	2.66	5066	1	x104
- seat fem., altar l.	117	138	2.42	5066	2	x103
- st fem	117	138	2.05	5066	6	x97
-	117	138	2.24	5594	7	x128
-	117	138	[551]5.38	7030	2	x190
-	117	138		7030	3	x190
-	117	138	1.60	8161	1	x212
-	117	138	5.17	8161	2	x214
Hadrian (Sabina)						
391	134	138	2.46	4674	15	x65A
396	134	138	2.76	5247	2	x113A
Hadrian (L. Aelius Caesar)						
438	137	138	2.25	4674	47	x57
Antoninus Pius						
13-40 ..HADRAN-TONIN... st fem. rudder on globe & corn	138	138	2.62	5066	5	x107
169?	147	148	3.20	4699	4	x82B
- TRPXI(I)	146	148	2.51	5066	8	x101	-
162	147	148	2.43	8161	3	x213
176	148	149	2.37	4674	22	x17	-
-	149	150	2.29	5066	4	x99	-
202?	150	151	2.47	4674	24	x21
- Annona	151	156	2.33	5066	7	x102
205, 211 or 251	151	156	2.25	7030	4	x189
288	158	160	2.53	4674	20	x10A	-
137	145	161	2.51	4674	16	x37
127	145	161	2.64	4674	17	x41	-
156	145	161	2.49	4674	21	x16
156	145	161	2.46	4674	23	x20
-	138	161	2.45	4674	44	x25
-	138	161	2.10	4674	55	x23
-	138	161	2.37	4699	3	x80
-	138	161	2.43	4699	6	x81
-	138	161	2.34	5066	11	x96	-
-	138	161	0.57	8315	2	x227
Antoninus Pius (Faustina 1)						
-	138	140	2.13	5594	5	x129
-	138	140		5594	6	x126
Antoninus Pius (Diva Faustina 1)						
361	141	161	2.08	4699	5	x76
370	141	161	3.00	4674	26	x4	-
378	141	161	2.65	4674	28	x15
382b	141	161	2.63	4674	27	x7	-
-	140	161	2.71	5594	4	x123
Antoninus Pius (Marcus Aurelius Caesar)						
423?	140	144	1.94	4674	33	x43
426ff	144	161	2.44	4674	12	x62
441	148	149	2.67	4674	37	x69	-
- …PIIFIL	148	156	2.07	4674	32	x42
Antoninus Pius (Faustina 2)						

---

550 In stack with FP 5594.6.

551 In stack with FP 7030.3.

502	146	161	2.35	4674	41	x55	-
Antoninus Pius/Marcus Aurelius							
-	138	161	2.46	4674	19	x9	
-	144	180	0.78	8161	4	x208	
Marcus Aurelius							
-	138	161	2.47	4674	18	x65B	
- IMPMAVRELAN-TONINVSAVG	161	162	2.58	4699	7	x82A	
- IMPMAVRELAN-TON…	161	162	2.05	5594	9	x122	
-. rev.: Armenia	163	165	2.44	5247	3	x115	
183 or 205 TRPXXII(I)	168	169	1.96	4674	38	x6	
TRPXXIIII	169	170	1.81	4674	31	x36	
-	161	180	2.72	4674	14	x18	
		180	2.58	4674	35	x-	
-	161	180	2.65	8100	2	x201	
-	161	180	1.29	8100	3	x202	
-	161	180	1.78	4674	30	x35	
		180	-	4674	34	x45	
-	161	180	2.31	7030	5	x188	
-	161	180		8161	5	x214	
Marcus Aurelius (Divus Antoninus Pius)							
429-442	161	180	2.43	5594	3	x124	
Marcus Aurelius (Lucius Verus)							
516	163	164	2.29	5066	9	x98	-
540	161	168	2.63	4674	42	x54A	-
Marcus Aurelius (Commodus Caesar)							
-	161	180	2.02	4674	43	x48	
-		180	2.22	4674	56	x10B	
Marcus Aurelius (Faustina 2)							
734	161	176	2.29	4674	39	x52	
712	161	176	1.96	4674	40	x53	
- rev. Juno w. peacock (=BMC 146, p. 404)	161	176	2.05	8161	6	x211	
Antoninus Pius/Marcus Aurelius (Faustina 2)?							
-	138	180	2.55	4674	51	x2	
-	117	180	2.99	4699	8	x74	
-		180	3.94	4699	10	x75	
-	140	180	2.44	5594	8	x127	
Marcus Aurelius/Commodus							
-	161	192	0.95	5066	12	x105	
-	180	192	1.32	8161	7	x210	
Commodus							
- (III, nos. 376ff)	184	191	1.89	4674	50	x47B	-
- MCOMMOD-VSANTONINVS..	180	192	1.94	4674	29	x58B	
- seat fem	180	192	2.21	5066	3	x100	

- st fem	180	192	2.87	5066	10	x106
-	180	192	1.91	5247	4	x113B
-	180	192	1.74	7030	6	x185
Septimius Severus						
-	193	211	2.60	4674	45	x34
Unidentified denarii, fragmented and/or melted						
-			0.24	4699	11	x79
- laureate r.			0.25	8315	3	x225
-			0.41	8161	10	x207
-			0.57	8315	5	x229
- laureate r.			0.58	8315	4	x226
-			0.89	8161	9	x206
-			1.20	7030	7	x187
-			1.40	5066	13	x95
-			1.73	5594	10	x131
-			1.75	4674	54	x13
-			1.91	4674	52	x12A
-			1.94	4699	9	x77
-			2.36	8161	8	x209
-			2.45	5247	5	x113C
-			2.71	4674	53	x12B
			3.77	4699	13	x84
-			5.67	4674	48	x56
-			8.72	4674	49	x61
			23.4	4699	14	x85

Coin lists

060403 sb 169: Denarii from Sønderhøj, BMR 802

Emperor	RIC type	w.	From	To	Inv.no.		BMR no.
Domitian	101, 109	2.65	87	88	6546	1	x176
Trajan	- , COS III, type as RIC 67 (AD 101-102)	2.57	100	100	8162	1	x255
Trajan	37, 49	2.61	100	102	6075	1	x116
Trajan	360	2.10	114	117	6546	2	x167
Hadrian	71	2.16	119	122	6075	2	x117
Hadrian	121	1.68	119	122	6412		x159
Hadrian	245A	2.73	134	138	5229		x14
Antoninus Pius	118	3.01	144	144	8162	2	x254
Antoninus Pius	264	2.09	156	157	8162	3	x256
Antoninus Pius (Diva Faustina 1)	343-407	2.43	141	161	6546	4	x177
Antoninus Pius (Diva Faustina 1)	368	1.55	141	161	6238	1	x141
Antoninus Pius (imit.?)	-	2.29	138	161	6546	3	x178
Marcus Aurelius	78-86 or 121-122	2.08	163	165	6238	4	x140
Marcus Aurelius	148	2.34	165	166	6238	3	x138
Marcus Aurelius	264, 282, 296, 307	2.02	171	174	6075	3	x107
Marcus Aurelius	-	0.94	161	180	7239	1	x238
Marcus Aurelius (Lucilla)	755-792	2.12	164	169	6238	2	x139
Marcus Aurelius (Lucilla)	784-785		164	180	8021	1	x248
Commodus	-	1.88	184	191	6075	4	x108
Commodus	235	1.78	192	192	8162	4	x257
Commodus	-	1.95	180	192	6075	5	x118
Elagabal	153	2.92	218	222	6546	5	x190

060403 sb 175: Denarii from Kanonhøj, BMR 1430 and 2650

Emperor	RIC type	w.	From	To	Inv.no.		BMR no.
Vespasian	10	2.55	69	71	7732	1	BMR2650x37
Vespasian	65	2.44	73	74	5970		BMR2650x2
Vespasian/Titus?	-	1.48	69	81	5329	2	BMR1430x76
Domitian (?)	-	1.91	81	96	5811	1	BMR1430x316
Trajan	128	2.41	103	111	5436		BMR1430x151
Trajan	-]ANOAVGGERDAC[	1.87	106	112	6242	1	BMR1430x461
Trajan	-	2.57	106	114	6044	1	BMR1430x198
Trajan	343	2.48	114	117	6044	2	BMR1430x195
Trajan	-	2.47	98	117	7765	1	BMR1430x574
Hadrian	- Class B	2.40	125	128	6242	2	BMR1430x460
Hadrian	257? - Class D	2.51	134	138	7765	2	BMR1430x576
Hadrian	299	2.55	134	138	5588	1	BMR1430x153
Hadrian?	-	1.41	117	138	8163	1	BMR1430x590a+b
Antoninus Pius	54 or 97	2.49	139	143	6044	3	BMR1430x193
Antoninus Pius	111b	2.34	143	144	6413	1	BMR1430x429
Antoninus Pius	137	2.31	145	161	5968		BMR1430x425
Antoninus Pius	137	1.79	146	161	7259	1	BMR1430x530
Antoninus Pius	273	2.41	157	158	6413	2	BMR1430x428
Antoninus Pius	-	0.54	138	161	7765	3	BMR1430x577
(same coin as previous)	-	0.87	100	250	7020		BMR1430x398

Emperor	RIC type	w.	From	To	Inv.no.		BMR no
Antoninus Pius(?)	-	2.24	138	161	8312	1	BMR1430x607
Antoninus Pius	-	2.58	138	161	6044	5	BMR1430x196
Antoninus Pius	-	1.47	138	161	6413	4	BMR1430x430
Antoninus Pius	-	2.82	138	161	6242	3	BMR1430x459
Antoninus Pius	-	1.44	138	161	6834	1	BMR1430x500
Antoninus Pius	-	1.83	138	161	6044	4	BMR1430x194
Antoninus Pius	- rev. Fig.st.	2.17	138	161	5329	3	BMR1430x71
Antoninus Pius	-	1.14	138	161	6242	4	BMR1430x463
Antoninus Pius	-	2.44	138	161	5329	4	BMR1430x72
Antoninus Pius	-	2.10	138	161	6556	1	BMR1430x489
Antoninus Pius	-	1.87	145	161	7259	2	BMR1430x529
Antoninus Pius (Diva Faustina 1)	343	2.52	141	161	4702	1	BMR1430x9
Antoninus Pius (Marcus Aurelius Caesar)	424a	2.57	140	144	4702	2	BMR1430x10
Antoninus Pius (Marcus Aurelius Caesar)	-	2.35	140	161	4958	2	BMR1430x38
Marcus Aurelius	48	2.38	161	162	8163	2	BMR1430x589
Marcus Aurelius	- TRPXVII...(?)	2.34	162	163	5329	5	BMR1430x73
Marcus Aurelius	- rev. providentia deorum	1.89	161	164	5588	2	BMR1430x152
Marcus Aurelius	124	1.83	164	165	5811	2	BMR1430x315
Marcus Aurelius	306	2.33	174	174	6044	6	BMR1430x192
Marcus Aurelius	413	2.32	176	180	7765	4	BMR1430x575
Marcus Aurelius	-	1.65	161	180	4958	3	BMR1430x39
Marcus Aurelius	-	1.54	161	180	8494	1	BMR1430x608
Marcus Aurelius	-	2.22	161	180	5329	6	BMR1430x74
Marcus Aurelius	-	2.00	161	180	7259	3	BMR1430x528
Marcus Aurelius(?)	-	1.03	161	180	7432		BMR1430x536
Marcus Aurelius	-	1.68	161	180	6242	5	BMR1430x462
Marcus Aurelius/Commodus (Lucilla/Crispina)	-	1.23	164	183	6413	3	BMR1430x431
Commodus	12(?)	2.25	181	181	5811	3	BMR1430x314
Commodus	235	1.87	192	192	8312	2	BMR1430x606
Antonine dynasty?	-	1.74	138	192	6044	7	BMR1430x197
Elagabal	172	1.97	219	219	5329	7	BMR1430x75
-	-	0.47			5329	8	BMR1430x77
-	-	0.69			5811	4	BMR1430x317

060403 sb 182: Denarii from Biskopenge V, BMR 1760

Emperor	RIC type	w.	From	To	Inv.no.		BMR no
Hadrian	17(?)	2.52	117	117	8307		x21
Antoninus Pius	137	2.74	145	161	7049	1	x15
Marcus Aurelius	-	1.45	161	180	7049	2	x14
Marcus Aurelius/Commodus (empress)	-	2.08	161	192	7049	3	x12
-	-	0.88			7049	4	x11

060403 sb 191: Denarii from Nr. Fuglesang, BMR 2353

Emperor	RIC type	w.	From	To	Inv.no.		BMR no
Trajan (?)	-	1.97	98	117	7024	1	x43
Antoninus Pius	-- rev. Pietas or Salus	2.42	138	161	7024	2	x42
Marcus Aurelius (Lucius Verus)	595	2.41	168	168	6798		x31

Emperor	RIC type	w.	From	To	Inv.no.		BMR no
Marcus Aurelius (Lucius Verus)	-	2.51	163	169	7257	1	x107
Marcus Aurelius (Faustina 2)	689 or 697	2.74	161	176	7731	1	x109

060403 sb 195: Denarii from Biskopenge IIIb, BMR 1795

Emperor	RIC type	w.	From	To	Inv.no.		BMR no
Titus	27	1.51	80	80	6415	1	x54
Trajan	-	2.33	98	117	6080	1	x25
Hadrian	71	2.20	119	122	6080	2	x22
Hadrian (Sabina)	398	1.98	128	138	7028	1	x87
Marcus Aurelius	138 or 155	2.74	165	166	7028	2	x81
Marcus Aurelius (Lucilla)	758	2.61	164	169	6080	3	x24
Commodus	11a-45	1.39	181	183	6080	4	x26
Commodus	29 (15?)	2.91	181	182	7730	1	x101
Commodus	72, 82	1.80	183	184	6415	2	x53
Commodus	155	2.03	186	187	6922	1	x66
Caracalla Caesar	26	1.81	198	198	6241		x48
-	-	2.02			6080	5	x23
-	-	2.21			7028	3	x88

060403 sb 263: Denarii from Biskopenge IX, BMR 3314

Emperor	RIC type	w.	From	To	Inv.no.		BMR no
Hadrian	207	2.94	132	134	7429	1	x6
Antoninus Pius	136	2.38	145	161	8089	1	x17
Antoninus Pius	- TR P XIII(?)	2.43	149	150	8089	3	x16
Antoninus Pius	232	2.48	153	154	8089	2	x15
Antoninus Pius	254	2.88	154	155	7429	2	x5
Antoninus Pius	- (rev. Fem.l.,sacrificing over altar	2.71	138	161	8102	1	x9
Antoninus Pius (Faustina 1)	327-342	2.61	138	141	8105		x8
Antoninus Pius (Diva(?) Faustina 1)	327-407	2.92	138	161	7429	3	x4
Marcus Aurelius	34 or 59	2.52	161	163	7429	4	x2
Marcus Aurelius	79, 80 or 121	2.42	163	165	8266	1	x20
Marcus Aurelius	163	2.46	166	166	8266	1	x19
Marcus Aurelius	-	1.67	161	180	7429	6	x7
Marcus Aurelius (Divus Lucius Verus)	596b	2.44	169	169	8266	1	x18
Marcus Aurelius (Lucius Verus)	655	2.66	177	178	8089	4	x13
Marcus Aurelius (Diva Faustina 2)	741	2.77	176	180	7429	5	x3
Commodus	-	1.53	184	192	8089	5	x14

060405 sb 144 and sb 207: Denarii from Krogegård I, BMR 2153 and 2252

Emperor	RIC type	w.	From	To	Inv.no.		BMR no
Sb 144							
Trajan	-	2.39	98	117	6461	1	BMR2153
Sb 207							
Hadrian	182(?)	2.65	125	128	5574	1	BMR2252x67
Hadrian	-	2.35	117	138	5574	2	BMR2252x65
Antoninus Pius	111b	2.22	143	144	5574	3	BMR2252x68
Antoninus Pius	- rev.: Annona(?)	1.32	147	156	5997	1	BMR2252x113

Antoninus Pius (Faustina 1)	327-342	1.99	138	141	5574	4	BMR2252x69
Antoninus Pius/Marcus Aurelius (Faustina 2)	-	2.36	146	176	5574	6	BMR2252x66
Marcus Aurelius (Lucilla)	789	2.56	164	180	5574	5	BMR2252x35
Commodus	218	1.92	190	191	5574	7	BMR2252x28

060405 sb 201: Roman coins from Agerbygård, BMR 1523

Emperor	RIC type	w.	From	To	Inv.no.		BMR no.
Vespasian	90	2.51	75	75	5141	2	x20
Titus (Divus Vespasianus)	63	2.45	80	81	5141	1	x19r
Trajan	243(?)	2.25	112	114	6000	1	x142
Trajan	298	2,55	114	117	6000	2	x375
Hadrian	76	2.36	119	122	5443	1	x126
Hadrian	260	2.57	134	138	6000	3	x232
Antoninus Pius	200c or 216c	2.40	150	152	6078	1	x578
Antoninus Pius	231	3.10	153	154	5443	2	x125
Antoninus Pius (Marcus Aurelius Caesar)	473	2.36	156	157	5443	3	x124
Antoninus Pius	275	2.12	157	158	5243	1	x55
Antoninus Pius	290	2.20	158	159	6000	4	x563
Antoninus Pius (Faustina 2)	516 var.?. type not in RIC, but legend 3 and bust left	2.51	141	161	4954		x4
Antoninus Pius (Diva Faustina 1)	362	2.60	141	161	6239	1	x599
Marcus Aurelius	206	2.58	168	169	5243	2	x56
Marcus Aurelius (Caesar?)	-	1.16	138	180	5443	5	x130
Marcus Aurelius (Divus Antoninus Pius)	430 or 431	2.13	161	180	6000	5	x141
Commodus	192	1.40	186	189	6239	2	x600
Septimius Severus	172 var.	2.42	200	201	5443	4	x123

Possible Subærati

Parish	SB	Site	Emperor	RIC prototype	w.	From	To	Exc.no.	Inv.no.	
060104	202	Møllegård	Marcus Aurelius(?)	-	1.20		180	BMR1235x152	5570	2
060104	235	Skovgård	Imitation[552]	-	1.72		250	BMR2001x110	6082	1
060104	264	Karlshøj	Marcus Aurelius	171, 252, 271, 359, 376 (III, 227-242)	2.43	166	177	BMR2225x7	5993	3
060204	70	Munkegård	Trajan	-	2.38	98	117	BMR1228x29	6266	1
060204	94	Duegård VNV	Marcus Aurelius?	- rev.: CONCORDIA …	3.69	161	180	BMR3354x49	8475	2
060204	96	Duegård N	Antonine/Severan	-		150	211	BMR3370x1	8016	1
060205	33	Sandegård Vest	Antoninus Pius[553]	124, 143, 144, 272, 284, 305a (III, 42-63)	2.79	145	161	BMR1371x275	5257	3
060205	256	Stagegård	Antonine?	-		138	192	BMR2367x4	7793	1
060302	0	Ndr. Mulebygård II Øst	Marcus Aurelius	-	2.42	161	180	BMR3227x46	7106	1
060304	20	Robbedale	Marcus Aurelius[554]	-		161	180		636	176
060305	70	Smørengegård	Marcus Aurelius (Lucius Verus)	444-567	2.45	161	166	BMR1469x306	6931	2

---

552 AUD 1999, 267.
553 AUD 1993, 248.
554 Breitenstein 1944, 7-33, no. 2.176.

Coin lists

Parish	SB	Site		Prototype	Motif / note	w.	From	To	Exc.no.	Inv.no.	
060305	70	Smørengegård		Trajan	151-228	2.56	103	111	BMR1469x338	6992	1
060305	70	Smørengegård		Antoninus Pius, left	St.female	1.58		250	BMR1469x343	6992	22
060305	70	Smørengegård		Commodus (?)	-	2.07	180	192	BMR1469x602	7515	7
060305	70	Smørengegård		Hadrian?	-	2.23	117	138	BMR1469x600	7515	1
060305	144	Smørenge		-	-	0.46		250	BMR766x839	6930	23
060305	144	Smørenge		-	-	1.73	100	250	BMR766x430	5448	4
060305	144	Smørenge		Trajan[555]	-	1.90	98	117	BMR766x425	5249	1
060305	144	Smørenge		Trajan	-	1.94	98	117	BMR766x729	6646	3
060305	144	Smørenge		-	-	1.61		250	BMR766x826	6930	21
060305	144	Smørenge		-	-	0.98		250	BMR766x1094	8108	11
060305	144	Smørenge		-	-	1.27		250	BMR766x1095	8108	12
060305	144	Smørenge		-	-	1.88		250	BMR766x1294	8491	10
060403	74	Sylten II		Tiberius[556]	26	1.59	14	37	BMR789x606	6074	1
060403	74	Sylten II		Marcus Aurelius	-	2.06	161	180	BMR789x189	5454	4
060403	74	Sylten II		Marcus Aurelius	3	2.41	161	161	BMR789x188	5454	3
060403	93	Sorte Muld		Commodus	98a, 112	3.23	184	185	BMR1191x1100R	5813	4
060403	93	Sorte Muld		Severus Alexander[557]	-	0.76	222	235	BMR1191x146	4671	
060403	135	Dalshøj		Marcus Aurelius (Lucius Verus)	482	2.03	161	162	BMR1639x516	8153	4
060403	160	Engegård Syd		Antoninus Pius/Marcus Aurelius (Faustina 2)	-	2.14	146	176	BMR2280x180	8318	1
060403	160	Engegård Syd		Pertinax	-	2.07	193	193	BMR2280x132	6929	3
060403	182	Biskopenge V		_[558]	-	0.88		250	BMR1760x11	7049	4
060403	195	Biskopenge IIIB		Caracalla Caesar[559]	26	1.81	198	198	BMR1795x48	6241	

Denarius imitations

Parish	SB	Site	Prototype	Motif / note	w.	From	To	Exc.no.	Inv.no.	
060104	235	Skovgård		-	2.83			BMR2001x97	5810	1
060104	235	Skovgård.		- subæratus	1.72			BMR2001x110	6082	1
060204	70	Munkegård	Marcus Aurelius	- rev: Mars st.r., spear, l.hand on shield		161	180	BMR1228x151	7956	1
060205	33	Sandegård øst	Antoninus Pius/Aurelius	-	2.39	138	180	BMR1371x343	5446	2
060304	20	Robbedale	Marcus Aurelius	RIC 359		175	180	hoard	636	180
060305	70	Smørengegård	Marcus Aurelius	-	2.48	161	180	BMR1469x108	5965	
060305	70	Smørengegård	Antoninus Pius?	- subæratus	1.58	138	161	BMR1469x343	6992	22
060305	144	Smørengård	Marcus Aurelius (Faustina 2)		2.61	161	180	hoard	4218	368
060305	144	Smørengård	Marcus Aurelius (Faustina 2)		2.62	161	180	hoard	4218	369
060305	144	Smørengård	Hadrian,	-	1.84	117	138	BMR766x1088	8108	5
060403	169	Sønderhøj Syd	Antoninus Pius	-	2.29	138	161	BMR802x178	6546	3
060403	93	Sorte Muld		-	2.38	138	161	BMR1191x1516R	6688	10
060403	93	Sorte Muld	hybrid obv: Antoninus RIC 115-6, rev: Trajan RIC 119		2.42	138	161	BMR1191x1764R	6920	1

---

555 AUD 1993, 249.
556 AUD 1999, 271.
557 AUD 1989, 215.
558 Pierced.
559 AUD 2000, 296.

Pierced denarii

Parish	SB	Site	Emperor	RIC type	w.	From	To	Exc.no.	Inv.no.	
060104	351	Hebro/Tornbygård II	Commodus	-	2.14	180	192	BMR3567x3	8295	2
060104	196	Simblegård	Hadrian (Sabina)	390-416	2.05	128	138	BMR888x42	5228	3
060104	351	Hebro/Tornbygård II	Septimius Severus (Julia Domna)	559A	2.08	196	211	BMR3567x2	8295	4
060104	201	Rødbjerggård/Torneby	-	-	2.16	100	250	BMR1611x51	5459	1
060201	323	Skovgård Syd	Vespasian	108	2.10	77	78	BMR3379x1	7392	
060201	316	Skovgård Øst	Antoninus Pius	26, 37, 43, 54, 97, 136	1.48	139	161	BMR3435x1	8437	1
060205	427	Nygård, Åker	Marcus Aurelius/Lucius Verus	-	1.56	138	180	BMR3339x2	7271	2
060302	124	Ndr. Mulebygård II Øst	-	-	1.87			BMR3227x47	7106	2
060305	70	Smørengegård	Trajan	-, rev.: Mars r., spear & trophy	2.15	98	117	BMR1469x267	6693	1
060305	144	Smørenge	Marcus Aurelius	67	1.70	162	163	BMR766x745	6646	13
060305	144	Smørengegård	Commodus??	-	2.48	180	192	BMR766x353	5044	6
060403	93	Sorte Muld	Severus Alexander	35	2.30	224	224	BMR1191x2254R	8087	2
060403	93	Sorte Muld	hybrid: Diva Faustina/M Aurelius RIC	216 or 234 (Aurelius)	2.18	161	180	BMR1191x2071R	7422	1
060403	96	Højemark 1	Caracalla	311b	2.38	213	217	BMR1092x4a	4783	
060403	135	Dalshøj I	Marcus Aurelius	23, 51	2.01	161	162	BMR1639x324	6551	6
060403	160	Dalshøj Nord omr. III	Commodus	56	2.01	183	183	BMR3185x38	7254	3
060403	170	Brændesgård	Hadrian	- Class B(?)	1.49	125	128	BMR1219x13	7260	1
060403	182	Biskopenge V	-	-	0.88			BMR1760x11	7049	4
060403	194	Ndr. Brændesgård 5.-6. slg. Omr.2	Antoninus Pius	-	2.85	138	161	BMR2155x58	8473	1
060405	376	Glasergård	Antonine period?	-		138	192			
060405	376	Glasergård	Antonine period?	-		138	192			

Roman bronze coins

Parish	SB	Site	Emporer	RIC type	Denom.	Mint	w.	From	To	Exc.no.	Inv.No.	
060405	178	Rytterbakken	Trajan	-	sesterts		22.11	98	117	BMR750x66	4801	
060305	417	Skørrebro øst	Antoninus Pius	-	sesterts			138	161	BMR2079x19	8269	1
060403	135	Dalshøj	Commodus	494, 523 (III, 423, 426)	sesterts		16.22	186	189	BMR1639x299	6364	4
060000		Bornholm	Aurelius /Commodus?	-	sesterts		19.65	161	192	-	5987	
060403	93	Sorte Muld	Maximinus 1 Thrax	64, 66 (IV.ii, 145)	aes		6.44	235	236	BMR1191x829R	5464	49
060403	93	Sorte Muld	-	-	sesterts		9.60	100	250	BM-R1191x1425R	6372	6
060201	322	Mejerivej 22	Galerius Maximianus Caesar	18b (VI, 581)		Cyzicus	3.23	295	296	BMR1073x1	4141	
060305	70	Smørengegård	Antoninus Pius?	-	Æ or denarius?		1.58		300	BMR1469x343	6992	22
060202	35	Søborgstræde 6	Maxentius	202a		Rome	5.74	307	308		3578	
060403	169	Sønderhøj Syd	constantinian period	camp gate		-	1.75	320	330	BMR802x168	6546	6
060403	96	Højemark	-	GLORIA EXERCITVS	-			330	335	BMR2651x161	8314	2
060303	190	Vestergård, omr. A	-	-			0.79	350	400	BMR1672x13	6995	3
060105	220	Bakkegårdsvej 4b	Justin 2	BMC 215	20 nummia	Constantinople	5.99	565	578	BMR2005x1	4952	
060403	160	Engegård NV	-		-					BMR3198x4		
060403	195	Biskopenge IIIB	-	-	Bronze, coin?		1.12			BMR1795x68	6922	3

Indices

174 sites with Roman coins, in geographical numerical order

Site no.	SB	Name	Pages
060101	217	Egesløkkegård	89, 92, 134-135, 161
060102	158	Hasle Byvang	139
060104	60	Bekkegård	64, 93, 139
060104	190	Skovgård	55, 136-139, 149, 156, 161, 192, 193, 194
060104	196	Kistegård / Simblegård	139, 162
060104	200	Hoglebjerg / Gl. Skovgård	139
060104	201	Rødbjerg / Tornbygård	89, 136-137, 162, 194
060104	202	Møllegård	138-139, 162, 192
060104	235	Nygård / Skovgård Syd	55, 136-138, 192, 193
060104	239	Jydegård Nord	-
060104	251	Brogård NØ	138
060104	252	Sigård	138
060104	264	Karlshøj	139, 162, 192
060104	351	Hebro / Tornbygård II	137, 162, 194
060104	357	Klemensker parish	-
060105	55	Vedby SV	49, 137
060105	219	Gl. Skovgård	137
060105	220	Bakkegårdsvej 4b, Allinge	195
060106	37	Kåsbygård	64, 93, 94, 135-136
060106	138	Vang	136
060106	150	Bukkegård	45, 136, 163
060106	167	Tuleborg / Almegård	136-137
060106	168	Dalshøj / Krakken	136-137
060106	215	Bakkegård	136
060107	52	Lindeskov	-
060107	116	Nyvang	135

Site no.	SB	Name	Pages
060201	28	Kattesletgård	156
060201	132	Langedebygård	157
060201	136	St. Kannikegård	157
060201	140	Kannikegærdet	157
060201	145	Buddegård	93, 157
060201	147	Soneskoven	157
060201	148	Døvregård SØ	156
060201	152	Østre Slamregård	157
060201	316	Skovgård SØ and Øst	156, 194
060201	322	Mejerivej 22	195
060201	323	Skovgård Syd	156, 194
060202	13	Paradisvej, Nexø	156-157
060202	15	Nexø parish, matr. 210d	157
060202	35	Søborgstræde 6, Nexø	158, 195
060203	1	Slusegård	24, 155
060203	158	Dammegård	155
060203	168	Boesgård	155
060203	169	Boesgård	155
060203	177	St. Gadegård	155
060203	196	Ågård	156
060203	197	Pedersker parish?	-
060204		Poulsker parish?	68-69
060204	70	Munkegård	158, 192-193
060204	82	Bedegård	158, 163
060204	89	St. Vibegård øst	158
060204	94	Duegård VNV	65, 157-158, 163, 192
060204	96	Duegård Nord	158, 192

197

Crossing boundaries

Site no.	SB	Name	Pages
060204	104	Krogegård	-
060204	199	St. Loftsgård	-
060205	33	Sandegård	22, 26, 65, 89-90, 92-93, 152-154, 163, 192, 193
060205	59	Soldatergård	64, 94, 96, 152
060205	198	Rævekulebakke	60, 154, 164
060205	203	Vasagård	61-62, 90, 92, 94, 152
060205	205	Ndr. Grødbygård	24, 155
060205	206	Smedegård	154
060205	223	Brogård	151
060205	246	Brogård	151
060205	256	Stagegård	151, 192
060205	273	Lille Munkegård	151
060205	288	Hundshalegård SV	52, 92, 154-155, 164
060205	293	Egeby SV	156
060205	412	Egebygård SSØ / St. Egebygård SØ	156
060205	425	St. Myregård	-
060205	426	Kastelsgård	156
060205	427	Nygård	156, 194
060205	428	Åkirkeby, coast south of	-
060301	66	Udmarken "A", "B" and "C".	25, 27, 49, 52, 60, 81, 91, 92, 149
060302	124	Ndr. Mulebygård	57, 60, 137, 139, 165, 192, 194
060303		Blemmelyng	150
060303	118	Lille Myregård	151
060303	190	Vestergård	67, 151, 165, 195
060303	207	Vellensbygård	57
060303	209	Kølleregård	150
060303	214	Vellensbygård Syd 2	52, 151
060303	222	Lille Strandbygård NØ	151
060303	223	Tornegård Syd / Tornegård SØ / Lillevang	150-151, 176
060303	251	Lillevang Øst	150-151, 176
060303	252	Ankersminde SSV	151
060303	256	Nylarsker parish	150
060303	435	Tornegård Vest	151
060304		Rønne	-
060304	20	Robbedale	25, 27, 52, 55-56, 59, 81, 91- 92, 149-150, 192, 193
060305	21	Stensgård	64, 145
060305	50	Kongens Udmark (Pindeløkkegård)	67, 145
060305	70	Smørengegård	28, 65, 92-93, 140-145, 165, 192-195
060305	101	Kirkebjerget, Sose	150

Site no.	SB	Name	Pages
060305	144	Smørengegård	52, 55-57, 140-144, 167-175, 193, 194
060305	151	Lilleborg	25-28, 43, 96-97, 145-147, 176
060305	154	Borresø	25, 27, 52,-53, 59, 92-93, 96-97, 146-147, 149
060305	176	Almindingen / Ravnebro	64, 93-94, 149
060305	405	Store Smørengegård	65, 142, 176
060305	407	Stenshøj / Ringeby	-
060305	412	Ellebygård	145
060305	417	Skørrebro Øst	145, 195
060305	419	Pindeløkkegård	145
060305	429	Smørengegård	140
060305	433	Almegård SØ	145
060305	446	Mellemste Myrebygård	144
060305	447	Bækkegård Vest	151
060305	448	Hullegård	144
060305	539	Hakonsgård / Ringeby	-
060305	541	Store Dalbygård	151
060305	550	Løkkegård	-
060305	554	St. Smørengegård NV	92-93, 140, 144, 177
060305	609	Præstegård NNØ	-
060402	221	Gudhjem	129
060403	58	Hintzegård	108
060403	68	Saltholmgård	64, 93, 94, 108, 128-129
060403	74	Sylten 1 and 2	49, 122-123, 177-178, 193
060403	93	Sorte Muld / Sorte Muld Syd / Fuglesangsageren	22, 26, 37, 41, 44, 555-57, 60, 65, 67, 76, 92-93, 96-97, 102, 105-114, 119, 127-128, 152, 179-182, 193, 194, 195
060403	96	Højemark 1, 2 and Øst / Kølleregård	62, 64, 120-122, 194, 195
060403	107	Ndr. Brændesgård	62, 114, 184
060403	135	Dalshøj	22, 26, 28-29, 57, 59, 61-62, 64-65, 91, 93, 105, 107-108, 115-119, 128, 137, 185-186, 193, 194, 195
060403	138	Biskopengen 1950	127
060403	160	Dalshøj Nord III / Engegård Syd	65, 115, 184
060403	166	Biskopenge VI and VII	125, 186
060403	168	Sylten 4, Kølleregård	35, 91-92, 123-124, 127, 187-189
060403	169	Sønderhøj Syd / Brændesgård	55, 193, 195
060403	170	Sønderhøj Vest	119
060403	175	Kanonhøj I/NØ / Paradisgård / Brændesgård	120, 189-190
060403	179	Rabækkegård	129

Indices

Site no.	SB	Name	Pages
060403	180	Helledsgård / Sejersgård / Sejrshøj	129
060403	181	Biskopenge VII / Frennegård	125
060403	182	Biskopenge V	127, 137, 190, 193, 194
060403	189	Sylten 4/6 / Kølleregård	123
060403	190	Baunehøj / Brændesgård / Sønderhøj Nord	119
060403	191	Frennegård	44, 124
060403	193	Sylten 3	123
060403	194	Brændesgård 5.-6.slg.	115, 194
060403	195	Biskopenge IIB, IIIA and IIIB	125, 191, 193, 195
060403	199	Sønderhøj	119
060403	201	Bækkegård	129
060403	206	Stenskov / Grydehøj	122
060403	207	Kanonhøj Sydøst / Kanonhøj II / Brændesgård	120
060403	214	Frennegård / Hallebrøndshøj	44, 124
060403	215	Biskopenge VIII / Rendestensklippen Øst	-
060403	217	Højemark Nord	120
060403	218	Dalshøj Sydøst, omr. II	119
060403	220	Frennegård / Hallebrøndsgård	124
060403	263	Biskopenge IX / Svanegård	36, 92, 126, 191
060403	264	Biskopenge	125
060403	273	Kanonhøj Syd / Brændesgård	120
060403	274	Ndr. Brændesgård	115

Site no.	SB	Name	Pages
060403	275	Fuglesangsageren NØ	-
060403	276	Engegård SØ	115
060403	277	Sylten	123
060403	278	Svaneke, near the town	64
060404	5	Svaneke Vang	-
060404	27	Svanegård SV	-
060405	144	Krogegård	132-134, 191
060405	146	Spagergård	93-94, 96, 129-130
060405	157	Kirselykkegård / Kysseløkkegård	65
060405	162	Damaskegård	134
060405	178	Rytterbakken	130, 195
060405	199	Nørre Sandegård	68-69, 132
060405	201	Bakkegård / Agerbygård	26, 62, 89-90, 92, 130-131, 153, 192
060405	207	Krogegård I	132-134, 191
060405	218	Agerbygård	130
060405	235	Lensgård Nord	135
060405	337	Bækkegård / Glasergård	131
060405	376	Glasergård	59-60, 131, 194
060406	6	Kløvegård	129-130
060406	134	Østermarie parish	65, 129
060406	198	Maglegård	130
060406	316	Østermarie parish	129
060406	317	Rynsegård	129-130
060406	318	Store Frigård	68-69, 131-132

199

174 sites with Roman coins, in alphabetical order

Site no.	SB	Name	Pages
060405	201	Agerbygård	26, 62, 89-90, 92, 130-131, 153, 192
060405	218	Agerbygård	130
060205	428	Åkirkeby, coast south of	-
060106	167	Almegård	136-137
060305	433	Almegård SØ	145
060305	176	Almindingen	64, 93-94, 149
060303	252	Ankersminde SSV	151
060403	201	Bækkegård	129
060405	337	Bækkegård	131
060305	447	Bækkegård Vest	151
060106	215	Bakkegård	136
060405	201	Bakkegård	26, 62, 89-90, 92, 130-131, 153, 192
060105	220	Bakkegårdsvej 4b, Allinge	195
060403	190	Baunehøj	119
060204	82	Bedegård	158, 163
060104	60	Bekkegård	64, 93, 139
060403	264	Biskopenge	125
060403	195	Biskopenge IIB, IIIA and IIIB	125, 191, 193, 195
060403	263	Biskopenge IX	36, 92, 126, 191
060403	182	Biskopenge V	127, 137, 190, 193, 194
060403	166	Biskopenge VI and VII	125, 186
060403	181	Biskopenge VII	125
060403	215	Biskopenge VIII / Rendestensklippen Øst	-
060403	138	Biskopengen 1950	127
060303		Blemmelyng	150
060203	168	Boesgård	155
060203	169	Boesgård	155
060305	154	Borresø	25, 27, 52,-53, 59, 92-93, 96-97, 146-147, 149
060403	169	Brændesgård	55, 193, 195
060403	175	Brændesgård	120, 189-190
060403	190	Brændesgård	119
060403	207	Brændesgård	120
060403	273	Brændesgård	120
060403	194	Brændesgård 5.-6.slg.	115, 194
060205	223	Brogård	151
060205	246	Brogård	151
060104	251	Brogård NØ	138
060201	145	Buddegård	93, 157
060106	150	Bukkegård	45, 136, 163
060106	168	Dalshøj	136-137

Site no.	SB	Name	Pages
060403	135	Dalshøj	22, 26, 28-29, 57, 59, 61-62, 64-65, 91, 93, 105, 107-108, 115-119, 128, 137, 185-186,193, 194, 195
060403	160	Dalshøj Nord III	65, 115, 184
060403	218	Dalshøj Sydøst, omr. II	119
060405	162	Damaskegård	134
060203	158	Dammegård	155
060201	148	Døvregård SØ	156
060204	96	Duegård Nord	158, 192
060204	94	Duegård VNV	65, 157-158, 163, 192
060205	293	Egeby SV	156
060205	412	Egebygård SSØ	156
060101	217	Egesløkkegård	89, 92, 134-135, 161
060305	412	Ellebygård	145
060403	276	Engegård SØ	115
060403	160	Engegård Syd	65, 115, 184
060403	181	Frennegård	125
060403	191	Frennegård	44, 124
060403	214	Frennegård	44, 124
060403	220	Frennegård	124
060403	93	Fuglesangsageren	109, 113-114, 183
060403	275	Fuglesangsageren NØ	-
060104	200	Gl. Skovgård	139
060105	219	Gl. Skovgård	137
060405	337	Glasergård	131
060405	376	Glasergård	59-60, 131, 194
060403	206	Grydehøj	122
060402	221	Gudhjem	129
060305	539	Hakonsgård / Ringeby	-
060403	220	Hallebrøndsgård	124
060403	214	Hallebrøndshøj	44, 124
060102	158	Hasle Byvang	139
060104	351	Hebro	137, 162, 194
060403	180	Helledsgård	129
060403	58	Hintzegård	108
060104	200	Hoglebjerg	139
060403	96	Højemark 1, 2 and Øst	62, 64, 120-122, 194, 195
060403	217	Højemark Nord	120
060305	448	Hullegård	144
060205	288	Hundshalegård SV	52, 92, 154-155, 164
060104	239	Jydegård Nord	-
060201	140	Kannikegærdet	157
060403	175	Kanonhøj I/NØ	120, 189-190

200

Indices

Site no.	SB	Name	Pages
060403	207	Kanonhøj II	120
060403	273	Kanonhøj Syd	120
060403	207	Kanonhøj Sydøst	120
060104	264	Karlshøj	139, 162, 192
060106	37	Kåsbygård	64, 93, 94, 135-136
060205	426	Kastelsgård	156
060201	28	Kattesletgård	156
060305	101	Kirkebjerget, Sose	150
060405	157	Kirselykkegård (Kysseløkkegård)	65
060104	196	Kistegård	139, 162
060104	357	Klemensker parish	-
060406	6	Kløvegård	129-130
060303	209	Kølleregård	150
060403	96	Kølleregård	62, 64, 120-122, 194, 195
060403	189	Kølleregård	123
060305	50	Kongens Udmark (Pindeløkkegård)	67, 145
060106	168	Krakken	136-137
060204	104	Krogegård	-
060405	144	Krogegård	132-134, 191
060405	207	Krogegård I	132-134, 191
060201	132	Langedebygård	157
060405	235	Lensgård Nord	135
060205	273	Lille Munkegård	151
060303	118	Lille Myregård	151
060303	222	Lille Strandbygård NØ	151
060305	151	Lilleborg	25-28, 43, 96-97, 145-147, 176
060303	223	Lillevang	150-151, 176
060303	251	Lillevang Øst	150-151, 176
060107	52	Lindeskov	-
060305	550	Løkkegård	-
060406	198	Maglegård	130
060201	322	Mejerivej 22	195
060305	446	Mellemste Myrebygård	144
060104	202	Møllegård	138-139, 162, 192
060204	70	Munkegård	158, 192-193
060403	107	Ndr. Brændesgård	62, 114, 184
060403	274	Ndr. Brændesgård	115
060205	205	Ndr. Grødbygård	24, 155
060302	124	Ndr. Mulebygård	57, 60, 137, 139, 165, 192, 194
060202	15	Nexø parish, matr. 210d	157
060405	199	Nørre Sandegård	68-69, 132
060104	235	Nygård	55, 136-138, 192, 193
060205	427	Nygård	156, 194

Site no.	SB	Name	Pages
060303	256	Nylarsker parish	150
060107	116	Nyvang	135
060406	134	Østermarie parish	65, 129
060406	316	Østermarie parish	129
060201	152	Østre Slamregård	157
060403	175	Paradisgård	120, 189-190
060202	13	Paradisvej, Nexø	156-157
060203	197	Pedersker parish?	-
060305	419	Pindeløkkegård	145
060204		Poulsker parish?	68-69
060305	609	Præstegård NNØ	-
060403	179	Rabækkegård	129
060205	198	Rævekulebakke	60, 154, 164
060305	176	Ravnebro	64, 93-94, 149
060304	20	Robbedale	25, 27, 52, 55-56, 59, 81, 91-92, 149-150, 192, 193
060104	201	Rødbjerg	89, 136-137, 162, 194
060304		Rønne	-
060406	317	Rynsegård	129-130
060405	178	Rytterbakken	130, 195
060403	68	Saltholmgård	64, 93, 94, 108, 128-129
060205	33	Sandegård	22, 26, 65, 89-90, 92-93, 152-154, 163, 192, 193
060403	180	Sejersgård	129
060403	180	Sejrshøj	129
060104	252	Sigård	138
060104	196	Simblegård	139, 162
060305	417	Skørrebro Øst	145, 195
060104	190	Skovgård	55, 136-139, 149, 156, 161, 192, 193, 194
060201	316	Skovgård SØ and Øst	156, 194
060104	235	Skovgård Syd	55, 136-138, 192, 193
060201	323	Skovgård Syd	156, 194
060203	1	Slusegård	24, 155
060205	206	Smedegård	154
060305	70	Smørengegård	28, 65, 92-93, 140-145, 165, 192-195
060305	144	Smørengegård	52, 55-57, 140-144, 167-175, 193, 194
060305	429	Smørengegård	140
060202	35	Søborgstræde 6, Nexø	158, 195
060205	59	Soldatergård	64, 94, 96, 152
060403	199	Sønderhøj	119
060403	190	Sønderhøj Nord	119
060403	169	Sønderhøj Syd	55, 193, 195
060403	170	Sønderhøj Vest	119

201

Site no.	SB	Name	Pages
060201	147	Soneskoven	157
060403	93	Sorte Muld	22, 26, 37, 41, 44, 555-57, 60, 65, 67, 76, 92-93, 96-97, 102, 105-114, 119, 127-128, 152, 179-182, 193, 194, 195
060403	93	Sorte Muld Syd	109, 113, 183
060405	146	Spagergård	93-94, 96, 129-130
060205	412	St. Egebygård SØ	156
060203	177	St. Gadegård	155
060201	136	St. Kannikegård	157
060204	199	St. Loftsgård	-
060205	425	St. Myregård	-
060305	554	St. Smørengegård NV	92-93, 140, 144, 177
060204	89	St. Vibegård øst	158
060205	256	Stagegård	151, 192
060305	21	Stensgård	64, 145
060305	407	Stenshøj / Ringeby	-
060403	206	Stenskov	122
060305	541	Store Dalbygård	151
060406	318	Store Frigård	68-69, 131-132
060305	405	Store Smørengegård	65, 142, 176
060403	263	Svanegård	36, 92, 126, 191
060404	27	Svanegård SV	-

Site no.	SB	Name	Pages
060404	5	Svaneke Vang	-
060403	278	Svaneke, near the town	64
060403	277	Sylten	123
060403	74	Sylten 1 and 2	49, 122-123, 177-178, 193
060403	193	Sylten 3	123
060403	168	Sylten 4, Kølleregård	35, 91-92, 123-124, 127, 187-189
060403	189	Sylten 4/6	123
060104	201	Tornbygård	89, 136-137, 162, 194
060104	351	Tornbygård II	137, 162, 194
060303	223	Tornegård SØ	150-151, 176
060303	223	Tornegård Syd	150-151, 176
060303	435	Tornegård Vest	151
060106	167	Tuleborg	136-137
060301	66	Udmarken "A", "B" and "C".	25, 27, 49, 52, 60, 81, 91, 92, 149
060106	138	Vang	136
060205	203	Vasagård	61-62, 90, 92, 94, 152
060105	55	Vedby SV	49, 137
060303	207	Vellensbygård	57
060303	214	Vellensbygård Syd 2	52, 151
060303	190	Vestergård	67, 151, 165, 195
060203	196	Ågård	156

Abbreviations

DMS   Jensen, J.S. *et al.*: *Danmarks Middelalderlige Skattefund*, Nordiske Fortidsminder, ser. B., Bind 12, 1992.
RIC   (Various authors): *Roman Imperial Coinage*, vols. I-X, London 1923-1994. Throughout the work references to Vol. I are to the 2nd edition (London 1984), unless otherwise indicated. References to all other volumes are to the 1st edition, unless otherwise indicated.

Bibliography

Adamsen, Chr. et al. (eds.) 2009: *Sorte Muld. Wealth, Power and Religion at an Iron Age Central Settlement of Bornholm*, Rønne.

Alföldi, A. 1935: Eine spätrömische Helmform und ihre Schicksale im germanisch-romanischen Mittelalter: mit einem Exkurs über den Fund von Brangstrup, Fünen, *Acta Archaeologica* 5, 99-144.

Alföldi, M. & Stribrny, K. (1998): Zu den Münzbeigaben im Childerichgrab, in: M. Müller-Wille: *Zwei religiöse Welten: Bestattungen der fränkischen Könige Childerich und Chlodwig*, Akademie der Wissenschaften und der Literatur Mainz, Abhandlungen der Geistes- und sozialwissenschaftlichen Klasse 1, Stuttgart, 37-43.

Arne, T.J. 1931: Solidusfynden på Öland och Gotland, *Acta Archaeologica* 2, 1-28.

Axboe, M. 2001: Om forholdet mellem medaillonefterligninger og brakteater, eller: Hvad var der i Gudmes guldrum?, in: Magnus, B. *et al.* (eds.): *Vi får tacka Lamm*, Studies in the Museum of National Antiquities 10, Stockholm, 39-46.

Axboe, M. 2002: Sølvkræmmerhuset og Balders død, in: Pind, J. et al. (eds.): *Drik og du vil leve skønt. Festskrift til Ulla Lund Hansen på 60-årsdagen 18. august 2002*, Publications from the National Museum. Studies in Archaeology and History 7, Copenhagen, 295-303.

Axboe, M. 2009: Gold bracteates, in: Adamsen 2009, 34-41.

Axboe, M. 2011: Katalog der Neufunde, in: Heizmann, W. & Axboe, M. (eds.): *Die Goldbrakteaten der Völdkerwanderungszeit – Auswertung und Neufunde, Ergänzungsbände zum Reallexikon der Germanischen Altertumskunde*, Band 40, Berlin, 893-999.

Aarslef, E. 2010: Detector finds from the Viking Age on Bornholm – a new perspective, in: Lund Hansen & Bitner-Wróblewska 2010, 337-350.

Aspeborg, H. 2012: Et sensationellt men svårtolkat myntfund, *Myntstudier* 2012:1, 20-22.

Balling, J. 1966: De romerske møntfund fra Skåne, Halland og Blekinge, *Nordisk Numismatisk Årsskrift*, 5-81.

Becker, C.J. 1958: [Review of] Ole Klindt-Jensen: Bornholm i Folkevandringstiden og forudsætningerne i tidlig jernalder, *Fornvännen* 53, 142-147.

Bitner-Wroblewska 2001: *From Samland to Rogaland. East-West connections in the Baltic basin during the Early Migration Period*. Warszawa.

Bland, R. 1997: The changing patterns of hoards of precious-metal coins in the Late Empire, *Antiquité Tardive* 5, 29-55.

Bodzek, J. 2009: Remarks on the influx of Roman coins into Southern Poland in the second half of the 4th and in the 5th centuries A.D., in: Wołoszyn 2009, 155-204.

Bogucki, M. 2010: The beginning of the dirhamimport to the Baltic Sea zone and the question of the early emporia, in: Lund Hansen & Bitner-Wróblewska 2010, 351-361.

Breitenstein, N. 1944: Romerske møntfund fra Bornholm, *Nordisk Numismatisk Årsskrift* 1944, 1-85.

Bursche, A. 1996: *Later Roman-Barbarian Contacts in Central Europe, numismatic evidence. Spätrömische Münzfunde aus Mitteleuropa. Ein Beitrag zur Geschichte der Beziehungen zwischen Rom und den Barbaricum in 3. und 4. Jh. N. Chr.*, Studien zu Fundmünzen der Antike (SFMA), Band 11, Berlin.

Bursche, A. 1996b: Denarii subaerati from the Jakuszowice settlement in North Małopolska, *Wiadomości Numizmatyczne* XL, 1-2 (155-156)/ Polish Numismatic News VI, 1997, 31-42.

Bursche, A. 1997: Roman coinage from Jakuszowice settlement in north Małopolska, *Notae Numismaticae* II, 119-157.

Bursche, A. 2002: Roman coins in Scandinavia. Some remarks from the Continental perspective, in: Pind 2002, 69-78.

Bursche, A. 2003: Solidi from the Zagórzyn Hoard, *Wiadomości Numizmatyczne* XLVII, 41-60.

Bursche, A. 2008: Function of Roman coins in Barbaricum of Later Antiquity. An Anthropological Essay, in: Bursche, Ciołek & Wolters (eds.), 395-416.

Bursche, A. 2011: *Illerup Ådal 14, Die Münzen*. Jutland Archaeological Society Publications XXV: 14. Aarhus.

Bursche, A., Ciołek, R. & Wolters, R. (eds.). 2008: *Roman coins outside the Empire. Way and Phases, Contexts and Functions. Proceedings of the ESF/SCH Exploratory Workshop Radziwill Palace, Nieborów (Poland) 3-6 September 2005*, Moneta 82, Wetteren.

Bursche, A., Kaczanowski, P. & Rodzińską-Nowak, J. 2000: Monety rzymskie z Jakuszowic, in: R. Madyda-Legutko & Bochnak, T. (eds.): *Svperiores Barbari. Księga ku czci Profesora Kazimierza Godłowskiego*, Kraków, 101-130 [German summary: Römische Münzfunde von Jakuszowice, 127-128].

Butcher, K. & Ponting, M. 2005: The Roman denarius under the Julio-Claudian emperors: mints, metallurgy and technology, *Oxford Journal of Archaeology* 24, 163-197.

Callu, J.-P. 1983: Structure du dépôts d'or au IVe siècle, Frézouls, E. (ed.): *Crise et redressement dans les provinces européennes de l'Empire (milieu du IIIe – milieu du IVe siècle ap. J.-C.)*, Strassbourg, 157-174.

Callmer, J. 1976: Oriental Coins and the Beginning of the Viking Period, *Fornvännen* 71, 175-185.

Chantraine, H. 1982: *Novaesium VIII. Die antiken Fundmünzen von Neuss*. Gesamtkatalog der Ausgrabungen 1955-1978. Berlin.

Ciołek, R. 2001: *Katalog znalezisk monet rzymskich na Pomorzu*, Swiatowit Supplement Series A: Antiquity, vol. VI, Warszawa.

Ciołek, R. 2003: Die römischen Münzfunde in Pommern, *Wiadomości Numizmatyczne* XLVII, 25-39.

Ciołek, R. 2007: *Die Fundmünzen der römischen Zeit in Polen. Pommern*, Moneta 67, Wetteren. [updated and extended version of Ciołek 2001]

Ciołek, R. 2008: Ein Beitrag zur Funktion römischer Münzen in der Wielbark und in der Przworks-Kultur, in: Bursche, Ciołek & Wolters (eds.), 157-170.

Ciołek, R. 2008: *Die Fundmünzen der römischen Zeit in Polen. Schlesien*, Moneta 83, Wetteren.

Ciołek, R. 2009: Znaleski monet rzymskich na Śląsku: wnioski z nowego inwentarza/Roman coin finds from Silesia: conclusions from the new inventory, *Wiadomości Numizmatyczne* LIII, 2, 146-181.

Ciołek, R. 2009b: Der Zufluss von Solidi in die südliche Ostseegebiete, in: Wołoszyn 2009, 217-229.

Ciołek, R. 2010: Goldene Münzen des 4.-5. Jahrhunderts in den südlichen Ostseegebieten, in: Lund Hansen & Bitner-Wróblewska 2010, 377-388.

Depeyrot, G. 2009: *Les trésors et les invasions (Les enfouissements d'or et d'orfèvrerie de 379 à 491)* I-III, Moneta 85-87, Wetteren.

Depeyrot, G. & Moisil, E. 2008: *Les Trésors de deniers de Trajan à Balbin en Roumanie*, Moneta 73, Wetteren.

Dymowski, A. 2007: Skarby monet rzymskich odkryte w ostatnim czasie na terenie Jury Krakowsko-Częstochowskiej [English summary: The hoards of Roman coins found recently in the Cracow-Częstochowa Upland], *Wiadomości Numizmatyczne* LI, 1, 54-78.

Dymowski, A. 2009: Recording recent Roman coin finds from Poland (2004-2007) [Polish summary: Rejestracja znalesk monet rzymskich z terenu Polski (2004-2007)], *Wiadomości Numizmatyczne* LII, 2, 195-207.

Ekengren, F. 2009: *Ritualization–hybridization– fragmentation. The mutability of Roman vessels in Germania Magna AD 1-400*. Acta Archaeologica Lundensia. Series in prima 4o no. 28. Lund.

Ethelberg, P. 2000: *Skovgårde. Ein Bestattungsplatz mit reichen Frauengräber des 3. Jhs.n.Chr. auf Seeland*, Nordiske Fortidsminder, Serie B bd. 19. København.

Fagerlie, J. 1967: *Late Roman and Byzantine solidi found in Sweden and Denmark*, Numismatic Notes and Monographs no. 157, New York.

Farkas, E. & Torbágyi, M. 2008: Sarmatians and the Roman coins, in: Bursche, Ciołek & Wolters 2008, 255-266.

Feveile, C. 2010: Høgsbrogård-skatten – en brudsølvsskat fra ældre germansk jernalder i Sydvestjylland, *Arkæologi i Slesvig - Archäologie in Schleswig* 13, 111-123.

Fischer, S., López Sánchez, F. & Victor, H. 2011: A Preliminary Result from the LEO-project: The 5th Century Hoard of Theodosian solidi from Stora Brunneby, Öland, Sweden, *Fornvännen* 106, 189-204.

Frey-Kupper, S. et al. 1995: *Usure e corrosion / Abnutzung und Korrosion*, Bulletin IFS ITMS IRMS 2, Supplément, Lausanne – Zürich.

Galster, G. 1929: Møntfundet fra Store Frigaard, *Aarbøger for Nordisk Oldkyndighed og Historie*, 283-315.

Galster, G. 1980: Vikingetids møntfund fra Bornholm, *Nordisk Numismatisk Årsskrift*, 5-246.

Grimm, O. & Pesch, A. (eds.) 2011: *The Gudme/ Gudhem phenomenon: papers presented at a workshop organized by the Centre for Baltic and Scandinavian Archaeology (ZBSA) Schleswig, April 26th and 27th*, 2010, Neumünster.

Grinder-Hansen, K. 2000: *Kongemagtens krise. Det danske møntvæsen 1241-1340*. København.

Grinder-Hansen, P. & Märcher, M. 2013: Korsskatten fra Østermarie – Skandinaviens yngste vikingetidsskat, *Nationalmuseets Arbejdsmark 2013 (in press)*

Hauberg, P. 1895: Skandinaviens Fund af romersk Guld- og Sølvmynt før 550, *Aarbøger for nordisk Oldkyndighed og Historie*, 326-377 (offprint pp. 1-52).

Hauberg, P. 1911: Lilleborg, *Bornholmske Samlinger*, 133-149.

Hedeager, L. 1978: A Quantitative Analysis of Roman Imports in Europe North of the Limes (0-400 A.D.), and the Question of Roman-Germanic Exchange, in: K. Kristiansen & C. Paludan-Muller (eds.): *New directions in Scandinavian Archaeology, Studies in Scandinavian Prehistory and Early History* vol. 1, 191- 216.

Heidemann Lutz, L. 2010: *Die Insel in der Mitte: Bornholm im 2.-4. Jahrhundert regionale und vergleichende Untersuchungen der jüngerkaiserzeitlichen Grabfunde*, Berliner Archäologische Forschungen 9.

von Heijne, C. 2004: *Särpräglat. Vikingatida och tidligmedeltida myntfynd från Danmark, Skåne, Blekinge och Halland (ca. 800-1130)*, Stockholm 2004.

von Heijne, C. 2010: Ravlunde – myntfund från romersk järnålder till vikingatid, *Myntstudier* 2010:1, 15-22.

Helgesson, B. 2002: Central places and Regions in Scania during the Iron Age Some Examples, in: Larsson, L. and Hårdh, B. (eds.): *Uppåkrastudier 7. Centrality – Regionality. The Social Structure of Southern Sweden during the Iron Age*, 323-335.

Herschend, F. 1980: Två studier i öländska guldfynd. I. Det myntade guldet, II. Det omyntade guldet, TOR Tidsskrift för nordisk fornkunskap XVIII (1978-1979), 33-294.

Herschend, F. 1983: Solidusvikt, *Numismatiska Meddelanden* XXXIV, 49-74.

Hobbs, R. 2006: *Late Roman Precious Metal Deposits c. AD 200-700. Changes over time and space*, BAR International Series 1504.

Horsnæs, H.W. 2002a: New gold hoards from Bornholm with rare types of Valentinian III solidi, *Revue Numismatique* 158, 131-138.

Horsnæs, H.W. 2002b: Nye romerfund fra Bornholm, *Nordisk Numismatisk Unions Medlemsblad* 1, februar 2002, 6-8.

Horsnæs, H.W. 2003: Fund af romerske mønter i Danmark – nogle tanker i utide, *Meddelelser fra Klassisk Arkæologisk Forening* 54, marts, 21-33.

Horsnæs, H.W. 2006a: Roman bronze coins from Barbaricum – Denmark as a case study, in: Horsnæs & Moesgaard 2006, 63-99.

Horsnæs, H.W. 2006b: Many coins from one site. Towards a method to distinguish between single finds and hoards in detector material, in: Horsnæs & Moesgaard 2006, 100-108.

Horsnæs, H.W. 2008a: Danske fund af romerske bronzemønter – og det der ligner, *Nordisk Numismatisk Unions Medlemsblad* 1, 8-13.

Horsnæs, H.W. 2008b: Roman coins and their contexts in Denmark, in: Bursche, Ciołek & Wolters (eds.), 135-145.

Horsnæs, H.W. 2009: Late Roman and Byzantine coins found in Denmark, in: Wołoszyn 2009, 231-270.

Horsnæs, H.W. 2010a: *Crossing Boundaries. An Analysis of Roman coins in Danish Contexts, Vol. 1: Finds from Sealand, Funen and Jutland*, Publications from the National Museum. Studies in Archaeology and History Vol. 18:1, Copenhagen.

Horsnæs, H.W. 2010b: Roman coins from Bornholm – a preliminary overview, in: Lund Hansen & Bitner-Wróblewska 2010, 433-448.

Horsnæs, H.W. 2012: Kortlægning af detektorfund. Perspektiver for udforskningen af bopladser fra jernalder til middelalder, *Nordisk Numismatisk Unions Medlemsblad* 2, 2012, 49-53.

Horsnæs, H.W. 2013: Gold imitations of Roman coins produced in Outer Barbaricum, in: L. Bjerg, J. Lind & S. Sindbæk: *From Goths to Varangians. Communication and Cultural Exchange between the Baltic and the Black Sea*, Black Sea Studies vol. 20, Århus, 85-128.

Horsnæs, H.W. & Moesgaard, J.C. (eds.) 2006: *6th Nordic Numismatic Symposium, Single Finds: the Nordic Perspective, Nordisk Numismatisk Årsskrift* 2000-2002. København

Høilund-Nielsen, K. 1987: Chronologie der jüngeren germanischen Eisenzeit auf Bornholm, *Acta Archaeologica* 57, 47-86.

Iluk, J. 2007: *Aspects économiques et politiques de la circulation de l'or au Bas-Empire*, Moneta 64, Wetteren.

Ingvardson, G.T. 2010: *Møntbrug – fra vikingetid til vendertogter*, Aarhus.

Ingvardson, G.T. 2012: Nørremølle – The largest Viking Age silver hoard of Bornholm (Denmark), *Journal of Archæological Numismatics* 2, 281-346.

Isler, R. 2004: Genstandene fra Lillebrog, *Bornholmske Samlinger* III, 18, 69-86.

Jonsson, K. 2010: Myntcirkulationen på Gotland i belysning av skattfyndprojektet, *Myntstudier* 1, 10-15.

Jonsson, K. & Östergren, M. 1992: Roman denarii and solidi on Gotland – Break or continuity? in: Nilsson, H. (ed.): *Florilegium Numismaticum, studia in honorem U. Westermark edita*, Numismatiska Meddelanden XXXVIII, Stockholm, 183-188.

Jørgensen, Chr. 1900: Denar-Fundet fra Robbedale, *Aarbøger for Nordisk Oldkyndighed og Historie*, 92-102.

Jørgensen, L. 1987: En bornholmerpige fra 700-årene, *Nationalmuseets Arbejdsmark*, 75-86.

Jørgensen, L. 1988: Family burial practices and inheritance systems. The development of an Iron Age society from 500 BC to AD 1000 on Bornholm, Denmark, *Acta Archaeologica* 58 (1987), 17-53. København.

Jørgensen, L. 1989: En kronologi for yngre romersk og ældre germansk jernalder på Bornholm [German summary: Eine Chronologie der jüngeren Kaiserzeit und älteren germanischen Eisenzeit auf Bornholm], in: Jørgensen, L. (ed.): *Simblegård – Trelleborg. Danske gravfund fra førromersk jernalder til vikingetid*, Arkæologiske Skrifter 3, 168-187.

Jørgensen, L. 1990: *Bækkegård and Glasergård. Two cemeteries from the Late Iron Age on Bornholm*. Arkæologiske Studier 8. København.

Jørgensen, L. 1991a: Schatzfunde und Agrarproduktion – Zentrumsbildung auf Bornholm im 5.-6. Jh. n.Chr., *Studien zur Sachsenforschung* 7, Hildesheim, 153-186.

Jørgensen, L. 1991b: Våbengrave og krigeraristokrati. Etableringen af en centralmagt på Bornholm i 6.-8. århundrede, in: *Fra Stamme til Stat i Danmark 2. Høvdingesamfund og Kongemagt*. Jysk Arkæologisk Selskabs Skrifter XXII/2, 109-125.Århus.

Jørgensen, L. & Nørgård Jørgensen, A. 1997: *Nørre Sandegård Vest: a cemetery from the 6th-8th centuries on Bornholm*, Nordiske fortidsminder, serie B; vol. 14, Copenhagen.

Kaczanowski, P. 2010: Zur Kulturgeschichtlichen Taxonomie des mittel- und nordeuropäischen Barbaricums, in: Lund Hansen & Bitner-Wróblewska 2010, 49-58.

Kaul, Fl., Nielsen, F.O. & Nielsen, P.O. 2002: Vasagård og Rispebjerg. To indhegnede bopladser fra yngre stenalder på Bornholm, *Nationalmuseets Arbejdsmark*, 119-138.

Kemmers, F. 2006: *Coins for a legion. An analysis of the coin finds from the Augustan legionary fortress and Flavian canabae legionis at Nijmegen*. Studien zu Fundmünzen der Antike, 21. Mainz am Rhein.

Kent, J.P.C. 1994: *Roman Imperial Coinage vol. X, The Divided Empire and the Fall of the Western Parts 395-491*, London.

Kjær, H. 1907: Om Bornholm i jernalderen, *Bornholmske Samlinger* I, 111-153.

Kolníková, E. & Pieta, K. 2009: Spätrömische und völkerwanderungszeitliche Münzhorte und andere Münzfunde im nördlichen Karpatenbecken, in: Wołoszyn 2009, 117-154.

Klindt-Jensen, O. 1957: *Bornholm i Folkevandringstiden og forudsætningerne i tidlig jernalder*, Nationalmuseets Skrifter, Større Beretninger II, København.

Kromann, A. 1983-84: Recent Roman coin finds from Denmark. Supplement to Breitenstein and Balling, *Nordisk Numismatisk Årsskrift*, 59-122.

Kromann, A. & Jensen, J.S. 1993: The Hoard of Lillegærde in Bornholm, in: Tony Hackens & Gh. Moucharte (eds.): *Proceedings of the XI*th *International Numismatic Congress Brussels 1991*, vol. 3, Louvain-la-Neuve, 73-80.

Kromann, A. & Watt, M. 1984: Skattefundet fra Smørenge. En nedgravet skat fra folkevandringstid på Bornholm, *Nationalmuseets Arbejdsmark*, 29-41.

Kubiak, S. 1979: *Znaleziska monet rzymskich z Mazowsza i Podlasia*, Wrocław – Warszawa – Kraków – Gdańsk.

Kunisz, A. 1985: *Znaleziska monet rzymskich z Małopolski*. Wrocław – Warszawa – Kraków – Gdańsk – Łódź.

Kyhlberg, O. 1980: *Vikt och värde. Arkeologiske studier i värdemåtning, betalingsmedel och metrologi under yngre järnålder. I Helgö, II Birka*, Stockholm Studies in Archaeology 1, Stockholm.

Kyhlberg, O. 1983: Aureus solidus. Metodologiska studier i 400- och 500-talens myntskatter, *Numismatiska Meddelanden* XXXIV, 5-48.

Kyhlberg, O. 1986: *Late Roman and Byzantine Solidi, An archaeological analysis of coins and hoards*, in: Excavations at Helgö X. Coins, Iron and Gold, Stockholm, 13-126.

Laursen, R. & Watt, M. 2011: Guldhullet, *Skalk* 4, 2011, 3-9.

Lind, B. 1991: *Gravformer og gravskikke, Slusegårdgravpladsen* III, 13-91.

Lind, L. 1981: *Roman denarii found in Sweden 2, catalogue, text*, Acta Universitas Stockholmiensis, Stockholm Studies in Classical Archaeology 11:2, Stockholm.

Lind, L. 1988: *Romerska denarer funna i Sverige*, Stockholm.

Lind, L. 2006: Roman denarii found on Gotland: single finds, in: Horsnæs & Moesgaard 2006, 44-52.

Lind, L. 2006b: Gresham's law and the disappearance of the pre-Severan denarii in the Roman Empire during the third century AD, in: M. Asolati & G. Gorini (eds.): *I ritrovamenti monetali e la legge di Gresham, Atti del III Congresso Internazionale di Numismatica e di Storia Monetaria, Padova, 28-29 ottobre 2005*, 57-68.

Lind, L. 2007: A group of barbarous Roman denarii represented in Sweden and Hungary (and Germany and Britain?), in: Andersen, M. et al. (eds.): *Magister Monetae, Studies in Honour of Jørgen Steen Jensen*, Publications of the National Museum 13, Copenhagen 2007, 53-58.

Lind, L. 2007b: Fynd av romerska sestertier på Gotland, *Myntstudier* 3, 13-16.

Lind, L. 2008: En ny grupp imitationer av romerska denarer representerad på Gotland, Myntstudier 2, 9-13.

Lund Hansen, U. & Bitner-Wróblewska, A. (eds.) 2010: *Worlds Apart? Contacts across the Baltic Sea in the Iron Age. Network Denmark-Poland, 2005-2008*, Nordiske Fortidsminder, Ser. C, vol. 7, København – Warszawa.

Lund Hansen, U. 2010: Iron Age research on Bornholm – an overview, in: Lund Hansen & Bitner-Wróblewska 2010, 29-48.

Lund Hansen et al. 2009: Perspectives, in: Adamsen 2009, 184-187.

Magomedov, B. 2008: Coins as a source of insight on Chernyakhiv tribes, in: Bursche, Ciołek & Wolters 2008, 171-178.

Martin, M. 2004: Childerichs Denare – Zum Rückstrom Römischer Silbermünzen ins Merowingerreich, in: Friesinger, H. & Stuppner, A. (eds.): *Zentrum und Peripherie – Gesellschaftliche Phänomene in der Frühgeschichte, Materialien des 13. Internationalen Symposiums "Grundprobleme der frühgeschichtlichen Entwicklung im mittleren Donauraum", Zwettl, 4.–8. Dezember 2000*, Wien, 241-278.

Matthiesen, H. 2006: The effects of soil type on corrosion of archaeological coins, in: Horsnæs & Moesgaard 2006, 346-356.

Metcalf, D.M. 2005: Viking Age Numismatics 1. Late Roman and Byzantine Gold in the Northern Lands, *Numismatic Chronicle*, 413-441.

Militky, J. 2008: Die römischen Fundmünzen in Böhmen – Kontexte und Funktionen. Notizien zu dem heutigen Stand der Forschung, in: Bursche, Ciołek & Wolters 2008, 231-244.

Militký, J. 2010: *Finds of Greek, Roman and Early Byzantine coins in the territory of the Czech Republic. I. Bohemia vols. I-III*, Moneta 107-109, Wetteren.

Moesgaard, J.C. 2006: The import of English coins to the Northern Lands: Some remarks on coin circulation in the Viking age based on new evidence from Denmark, in: Cook, B. & Williams, G. (eds.): *Coinage and History in the North Sea World c. 500-1250. Essays in honour of Marion Archibald*, Leiden, 2006, p. 389-433.

Montelius, O. 1869: *Från Jernaldern*, Stockholm.

Myrberg, N. 2009: An island in the middle of an island. On cult, laws and authority in Viking Age Gotland, in: Regner, E. *et al.* (eds.): *From Ephesos to Dalecardia. Reflections on body space and time in Medieval and Early Modern Europe*, Stockholm Studies iin Archaeology 48, 101-118.

Myzgin, K. (Мизгін, К.) 2010: Античні Монети На Пам'ятках Черняхівської Культури, unpublished dissertation, Kiev.

Myzgin, K. 2011: Die römischen Fundmünzen im Gebiet der Černjachov-Kultur, Paper presented in Bonn, December 2011.

Mørkholm, O. 1969: De romerske mønter fra Lilleborg, *Nordisk Numismatisk Unions Medlemsblad*, 137-140.

Natuniewicz-Sekuła, M. & Seehusen, C.R. 2010: Baltic Connections. Some remarks about studies of boat-graves from the Roman Iron Age, in: Lund Hansen & Bitner-Wróblewska 2010, 287-314.

Naum, M. 2008: *Homelands lost and gained. Slavic migration and settlement on Bornholm in the early Middle Ages*, Lund Studies in Historical Archaeology 9, Lund.

Nielsen, F.O.S. 1994: *Bebyggelsesarkæologiske undersøgelser på Bornholm: nogle forudsætninger og muligheder*, København.

Nielsen, F.O.S. 1996: *Forhistoriske interesser*, Rønne.

Nielsen, F.O.S. 2004: Bornholms Museums antikvariske arbejde 2002-2003, Bornholms Museum – Bornholms Kunstmuseum 2002-2003, Rønne, 61-84.

Nielsen, F.O.S. 2006: Museumsbestyrer J.A. Jørgensen, 1840-1908, Bornholmske Samlinger, Rk.3, bd. 20, 15-20.

Nielsen, V. 2000: *Oldtidsagre i Danmark, Bornholm*, Jysk Arkæologisk Selskab.

Noll, R. 1974: *Vom Altertum zum Mittelalter: spätantike, altchristliche, völkewanderungszeitliche und frühmittelalterliche Denkmäler* 2nd ed., Wien 1974.

Nørgård Jørgensen, A. 2008: *Porskjær Mosefund*, Jysk Arkæologisk Selskab.

Nørgård Jørgensen, A. 2011: The road to Gudhjem – the 'Via Appia' of Bornholm, in: Grimm, O. & Pesch, A. (eds.): *The Gudme/Gudhem phenomenon: papers presented at a workshop organized by the Centre for Baltic and Scandinavian Archaeology (ZBSA) Schleswig, April 26th and 27th*, 2010, Neumünster 2011, 127-146.

Paulsson, J. 1999: Metalldetektering och Uppåkra. Att förhålla sig till ett detektormaterial, in: Hårdh, B. (ed.): *Fynden i centrum. Keramik, glass och metall från Uppåkra*, Acta Archaeologica Lundensia, series in 8°, no. 30 = Uppåkrastudier 2, Lund, 41-58.

Périn, P. & Kazanski, M. 1996: Das Grab Childerichs I., in: *Die Franken. Wegbereiter Europas. Vor 1500 Jahren: König Chlodwig und seine Erben [Katalog der Ausstellung im Reiss-Museum Mannheim 8. September 1996 bis 6. Januar*

1997], Mainz, 173-182.
Peter, M. 1990: *Eine Werkstätte zur Herstellung von subaeraten Denaren in Augusta Raurica*, Studien zu Fundmünzen der Antike 7, Berlin.
Pochitonov, E. 1955: Nálezy antických mincí, in: Nehojlová-Prátová, E. (ed.): *Nálezy Mincí Čechách na Moravě a ve Slezsku*, Praha, 92-308.
Poulsen, B. 1982: Et bornholmsk vikingetidsmøntfund, "Poulsker 1838", *Nordisk Numismatisk Unions Medlemsblad*, 7-11.
Price, M.J. 1991: *The coinage in the name of Alexander the Great and Philip Arrhidaeus*, Zürich/London.
Poházka, P. 2009: Ost- und weströmische Goldmünzen des 5. Jahrhunderts im Karpatenbeckens, in: Wołoszyn 2009, 83-116.
Ramus, C. 1816: *Catalogus numorum veterum græcorum et latinorum musei regis Daniæ*, Hafnia.
Rasmussen, B.M. 2010: *Slusegårdgravpladsen: Bornholm fra 1. årh. f. til 5. årh. e.v.t, vol. 5: Fundoversigt og genstandstyper*, Århus.
Rasmussen, M. (ed.) 2007: *Iron Age houses in flames. Testing house reconstructions at Lejre*, Studies in Technology and Culture vol. 3.
Romanowski, A. 2007: Znaleziska monet rzymskich z terenów kultury wielbarskiej na Podlasiu, prawobrzeżnym Mazowszu i zachodniej Białorusi [English summary: The finds of Roman coins from the area of the Wielbark Culture in Podlasie, east-of-the-Vistula Mazovia and western Belarus], *Wiadomośći Numizmatyczne* LI, 1, 29-53.
Romanowski, A. 2008: *Die Fundmünzen der römischen Zeit in Polen. Rechtsufriges Masowien und Podlachien*, Wetteren.
Romanowski, A. 2009: Kolejne denary rzymskie z miejscowości Podzamcze, pow. Garwoliński. Rejon ujścia Okrzejki w świetle znalesk monet rzymskich [English summary: More Roman denarii found in the village of Podzamcze, the Garwolin District. Region of confluence of the Okrzejka and Vistula rivers in the light of Roman coin finds], *Wiadomośći Numizmatyczne* LIII, 2, 225-233.
Seehusen, C.R. 2009: Where were the dead buried?, in: Adamsen (ed.) 2009, 124-131.
Skovmand, R. 1942: *De danske Skattefund fra Vikingetiden og den ældste Middelalder indtil omkring 1150*, Aarbøger for nordisk Oldkyndighed og Historie, København.
Stribrny, K. 2003: *Funktionsanalyse barbarisierter, barbarischer Denare mittels numismatischer und metallurgischer Methoden: zur Erforschung der sarmatisch-germanischen Kontakte im 3. Jahrhundert n. Chr.*, Studien zu Fundmünzen der Antike 18, Mainz.
Sørensen, P.Ø. 2009: Excavations at Fuglesangsageren, in: Adamsen 2009, 134-141.
Thomsen, C.J. 1827: Mynter, *Antiqvariske Annaler* 4, 388-399.
Ungaro, L. 1985: Il ripostiglio della casa delle Vestali, Roma 1899, *Bolletino di Numismatica* 1 (5), 47-160.
Vasić, M.R. 2001: Osvrt na nalaz IV veka iz Starčeva, *Zbornik Narodnog Muzeja – serija: Arheologija* 17.1, 175-201 (English summary on pp. 200-201: Review of the fourth-century find from Starčevo).
Vedel, E. 1873: *Undersøgelser angaaende den ældre Jernalder paa Bornholm*, København.
Vedel, E. 1878: *Nyere Undersøgelser angaaende Jernalderen paa Bornholm*, København.
Vedel, E. 1886: *Bornholms Oldtidsminder og Oldsager,* Kjøbenhavn.
Vedel, E. 1890: *Bornholmske Undersøgelser med særligt Hensyn til den senere Jernalder*, Kjøbenhavn.
Vedel, E. 1897: *Efterskrift til Bornholms Oldtidsminder og Oldsager*, Kjøbenhavn.
Vennersdorf, M. 2000: Smørenge 2000. Udgravning af en formodet skat fra yngre jernalder, unpublished BA project, University of Copenhagen.
Vennersdorf, M. et al. 2006: Smykker fra Smørenge – endnu et spændende fund fra Bornholms yngre jernalder [English summary: Jewellery from Smørenge – another fascinating find from the Late Iron Age on Bornholm], *Nationalmuseets Arbejdsmark*, 167-183
Vennersdorf, M. & Watt, M. 2009: Phosphate and Cultural Layers, in: Adamsen et al., 158-161.
Vest, K.B. 2006: Museumsinspektør Peter Christian Hauberg 1844-1928, *Bornholmske Samlinger*, 29-46.
Wagnkilde, H. & Pind, T. 1989/90: En gravplads ved Ndr. Grødbygård i Åker fra tiden omkring kristendommens indførelse, *Fra Bornholms Museum*, 53-66.
Wagnkilde, H. 2000: Gravudstyr og mønter fra

1000-tallets gravpladser på Bornholm, *Hikuin* 27, 91-106.

Watt, M. 1983: Skattefundet fra Smørenge, *Fra Bornholms Museum*, 32-38.

Watt, M. 1991: Sorte Muld. Høvdingesæde og kultcentrum fra Bornholms yngre jernalder [English summary: Sorte Muld. A chieftain's seat and cult site from the Late Iron Age in Bornholm], in: *Fra Stamme til Stat i Danmark 2. Høvdingesamfund og Kongemagt*. Jysk Arkæologisk Selskabs Skrifter XXII/2, 109-125. Århus, 89-107.

Watt, M. 1997: Overfladerecognoscering af jernalderbopladser. Nogle kildekritiske betragtninger over samarbejdet mellem arkæologer og detektoramatører, in: Callmer, J. & Rosengren, E. (red.). »…gick Grendel att söka det höga huset…« *Arkeologiska källor till aristokratiska miljöer i Skandinavien under yngre jänrålder*. Hallands länsmuseum, Halmstad, 131-143.

Watt, M. 1998: Bopladser med bevarede kulturlag og deres betydning for studiet af bosættelsesmønstre og centerdannelser i jernalderen, in: L. Larsen and B. Hårdh (eds.): Centrala platser - centrala frågor. Samhällsstrukturen under järnaldern. Acta Archaeologica Lundensia, Ser. in octavo, nº. 28, p. 205-216.

Watt, M. 2000: Detektorfund fra bornholmske pladser med bevarede kulturlag – Repræsentativitet og metode, in: Henriksen, M.B. (ed.): *Detektorfund – hvad skal vi med dem? Dokumentation og registrering af bopladser med detektorfund fra jernalder og middelalder. Rapport fra et bebyggelseshistorisk seminar på Hollufgård den 26. oktober 1998*, Skrifter fra Odense Bys Museer 5, Odense, 79-97.

Watt, M. 2004: The Gold-Figure Foils (*Guldgubbar*) from Uppåkra, in: L. Larsson (ed.): *Continuity for Centuries: A ceremonial building and its context at Uppåkra, southern Sweden*. Stockholm, 167-221.

Watt, M. 2006: Detector sites and settlement archaeology on Bornholm, *Journal of Danish Archaeology* 14, 139-167.

Watt, M. 2009: *Beretning om og evaluering af resultaterne af sondageundersøgelser på bornholmske jernalder- og vikingetidsbopladser med bevarede kulturlag*, Kulturarvsstyrelsen, København (download from http://www.kulturstyrelsen.dk/fileadmin/user_upload/kulturarv/publikationer/emneopdelt/arkaeologi/sondage_bornholm.pdf)

Watt, M. 2009b: Gold-foil Figures, in: Adamsen 2009, 42-53.

Watt, M. 2010: Settlement sites with cultural layers in Bornholm – field surveys and scientific perspectives in: Lund Hansen & Bitner-Wróblewska 2010, 563-578.

Watt, M. 2011: Sorte Muld, Bornholm, an example of transformation and regional contacts during the 5th to 7th centuries in the Baltic Sea area, in: Babette Ludowici (ed.): *Transformations in North-Western Europe (AD 300-1000)*, Proceedings of the 60th Sachsensymposion19.-23. September 2009 Maastricht, Neue Studien zur Sachsenforschung Band 3, 139-148.

Watt, M. forthcoming: *Sorte Muld. Guldgubberne og Ibskerbygden* [Sorte Muld - the gold foil figures and settlement complex], Nordiske Fortidsminder, Ser. C. In preparation.

Werner, J. 1988: Danceny und Brangstrup, *Bonner Jahrbucher* 188, 241-286 .

Westermark, U. 1980: Fynn av äldre romerska guldmynt i Kungl. Myntkabinettets samling, *Nordisk Numismatisk Unions Medlemsblad*, 99-104.

Westermark, U. 1983: Solidi found in Sweden and Denmark after 1967, *Numismatiska Meddelanden* XXXIII, 29-40.

Wiséhn, E. 1992: *Myntfund från Härjedalen, Jämtland och Medelpad*, Sveriges Mynthistoria Landskapsinventeringen 7, Stockholm.

Wołoszyn, M. 2008: Byzantine coins from the 6th and the 7th c. from Poland and their East-Central European context. Ways and Phases, contexts and functions, in: Bursche, Ciołek & Wolters (eds.), 195-224.

Wołoszyn, M. (ed.) 2009: *Byzantine Coins in Central Europe between the 5th and 10th Century*, Moravia Magna vol. III, Kraków.

Zapolska, A. 2007: Denary rzymskie znajdowane w kontekstach wczesnośredniowiecznych na ziemiach polskich (English summary: Roman denarii found in early medieval contexts in Polish lands), *Wiadomości Numizmatyczne* (Polish Numismatic News) LI, 2, 149-178.

Zapolska, A. 2009: Roman denarii in the Bogaczewo and Sudovian cultures [Polish summary: Denary rzymskie w kulturach bogaczewskiej i sudowskiej], *Wiadomości Numizmatyczne* (Polish Numismatic News VIII) LII, 2, 139-166.

Östergren, M. 1981: *Gotlandska fynd av solidi och denarer. En undersökning af fyndplatserna*, RAGU Arkeologiska skrifter 1, Stockholm.

Östergren, M. 1986: *Silverskatter och boningshus: skattfyndprojektet 1, en studie av gården Gannarve i Hallnas, Gotland*, Stockholm.